WHY ANGELS FALL

WHY ANGELS FALL

A Journey Through Orthodox Europe
from Byzantium to Kosovo

VICTORIA CLARK

St. Martin's Press
New York

ISBN 0-312-23396-5

Engraving of Pasij Velyčkovs'kyj from an 1817 biography printed at
the Monastery at Neamţ. Reprinted from *The Life of Pasij Velyčkovs'kyj*,
trans. J.M.E. Featherstone (Cambridge, MA, 1989), with the permission of
the Ukranian Research Institute, Harvard University.

Library of Congress Cataloging-in-Publication Data available upon
request from the Library of Congress.

First published in hardcover in Great Britain 2000 by
MACMILLAN PRESS LTD

First St. Martin's edition: December 2000
10 9 8 7 6 5 4 3 2 1

CONTENTS

LIST OF ILLUSTRATIONS XI
FOREWORD XV
ACKNOWLEDGEMENTS XVI

MOUNT ATHOS
Byzantium

I

THE SERBS
*Krka Monastery, Bijeljina, Sarajevo, Ravanica Monastery, Kosovo,
The Monastery of Jovandol*

45

MACEDONIA
Skopje, Lake Ohrid, Veljuša Monastery, Kastoria, Thessaloniki

103

GREECE
*St John the Theologian Monastery Patmos Island,
the Peloponnese, Athens*

151

CONTENTS

ROMANIA

Monastery of the Birth of the Mother of God, Transylvania,
Snagov Island, Bistriţa Monastery

201

RUSSIA

Solovetsky Monastery, North Russia, Moscow,
Trinity Sergeyev Monastery, Optina Pustyn Monastery,
Verkhoturye

253

CYPRUS

Nicosia, Kykko Monastery, Troodhos Mountains, Limassol,
Nicosia, Apostolos Andhreas Monastery

345

ISTANBUL

399

GLOSSARY 417
CHRONOLOGY 420
NOTES 426
BIBLIOGRAPHY 438
INDEX 451

For my dear parents,
without whom, etc . . .

Division Line between
Orthodox East and
Catholic/Protestant West

3000 Kilometres

SIBERIA

SIA

MONGOLIA

Vladivostock

GYZSTAN

STAN

NORTH
KOREA

SOUTH
KOREA

N

CHINA

JAPAN

NEPAL

BHU

BANGLA-
DESH

INDIA

BURMA

TAIWAN

THAILAND

LAOS

VIETNAM

CAMBODIA

PHILIPPINES

SRI
LANKA

LIST OF ILLUSTRATIONS

All photographs are copyright of the author unless otherwise stated.

1. Warning signboard, Mount Athos's land border
2. a) Krka monastery, Croatia
   b) Ilija flanked by Serbs in Krka's courtyard
3. a) Archimandrite Benedict in Bijeljina, Bosnian Serb Republic
   b) Bishop Vasilije Čačavenda of Tuzla and Zvornik at the 600th anniversary of the Battle of Kosovo celebrations (Marcus Tanner)
4. Fourteenth-century monastery of Gračanica (Hutchinson Libary)
5. Father Sava of Dečani monastery, Kosovo
6. a) Archbishop Amfilohije Radović of Montenegro anointing the bones of the dead
   b) Archbishop Amfilohije, the author and Goran taking tea at Jovandol monastery
7. a) Nineteenth-century white timbered buildings, the former Yugoslav Republic of Macedonia
   b) Kastoria, northern Greece
8. a) Bishop Naum of Strumica with nuns at Veljuša monastery
   b) Veljuša's thirteenth-century church
9. a) Bust of Bishop Germanos of Kastoria, Thessaloniki
   b) Grand Lavra, the oldest monastery on Mount Athos (Marc Dubin/Travel Ink)
10. a) Sarandi at Easter lunch on Patmos Island
    b) John Kritikos by the church his grandfather built, Patmos Island

11. a) Archimandrite lecturer in Nafplio, the Peloponnese
    b) Count Ioannis Capodistrias, Greece's first president (Hulton)
12. a) Archbishop Serapheim of Athens' state funeral, 1988
    b) Archbishop Serapheim's successor Christodoulos, 'The Thunderbolt' (P A News)
13. a) Road to the Monastery of the Birth of the Mother of God, Transylvania
    b) Monastery of the Birth of the Mother of God, Targu Mureș, Transylvania
14. a) Monks building a monastery near Targu Mureș, Transylvania
    b) Bread rolls and books after Union Day Service, Alba Iulia, Transylvania
15 a) Ion-Innocentie Micu-Klein, the first Uniate bishop of Translyvania (R. W. Seton, *A History of the Roumanians* (plate XI), 1934, Cambridge University Press)
    b) The eighteenth-century Ukranian hesychast, St Paissy Velichovsky (Ukranian Research Institute, Harvard University)
16. a) Nun cleaning the windows of the monastery of Moldovița
    b) Details of the sixteenth-century Petru Rareș and his family, Moldovița monastery (Alcor Edimpex SRL)
17. a) Solovetsky monastery, Solovetsky Island
    b) Sunday church parade around Solovetsky monastery
18. a) Ivan the Terrible (Bridgeman Art Library)
    b) Tsar Nicholas II and Tsarina Alexandra in medieval Muscovite fancy dress (David King)
    c) Rasputin (David King)
19. a) Moscow's new cathedral of Christ the Saviour
    b) Sretensky monastery's rose gardener, Moscow
20. a) Igumen Tikhon of Nikolayevsky monastery, Verkhoturye, Siberia
    b) Verkhoturye's eighteenth-century cathedral
21. a) Archbishop Makarios, President of Cyprus 1960–1974 (Peter Mitchell/Camera Press)
    b) The Archbishop of Cyprus' palace with statue of Makarios in the garden

22. a) Ariko, the 'mukhtaris' of Kambos at Easter lunch
   b) The Russian chapel at Limassol
23. a) Archbishop Chrysostomos of Cyprus
   b) Monastery of Apostolos Andhreas, Kapas peninsula, North Cyprus
24. a) Ecumenical Patriarch Bartholomaios I of Constantinople and Archbishop Christodolous of Athens (P A News)
   b) Father Dorotheos at the theological seminary on Heybeliada Island, Turkey

FOREWORD

For my at best sketchy treatment of Bulgaria, Ukraine, Georgia, Belarus and Moldova in this survey of Eastern Orthodox Europe I offer profuse apologies, and plead lack of space.

My presentation of the former Yugoslav Republic of Macedonia and the northern Greek province of Macedonia in a single chapter makes useful historical rather than contemporary sense. It should not be interpreted as an argument in favour of revising national frontiers.

ACKNOWLEDGMENTS

The writing of this kind of book is entirely dependent on the help and goodwill of others.

My most heartfelt thanks go to the dozens of Orthodox Church people – monks, nuns, priests, bishops, archbishops and the Ecumenical Patriarch – who were generous with their time and hospitality and gracious enough to speak their minds to me.

Without the friends cum fixers cum interpreters cum protectors my travels would not have been nearly as interesting, safe or enjoyable. I dare say Goran Gocić, Bogdan Zlatić, Ljupčo Spasovski, Viorel Hirşan, Dan Ciachir, Vanya Kochkarev and Lena Vozdvizhenskaya did not suspect that agreeing to help me meant inclusion in the story. I am extremely grateful to all of them.

Journalist friends were unfailingly generous with contacts, book loans and accommodation. Particular thanks are due to Marcus Tanner, who first suggested exploring Romania's painted monasteries in 1986 and has shared my interest in Eastern Orthodox Europe ever since. To Bill MacPherson in Washington goes a big thank you for recommending that I abandon my newspaper job in London to write a book. Chris Stephen kindly put me up in Sarajevo, Helena Smith in Athens and Alison Mutler in Bucharest. Tim Judah and Marc Champion lent me books and contacts. Sophie Russell, Andrew Sparke and Elizabeth Randall read work in progress. Bruce Clark helped with foreign spellings. Natasha Fairweather, Richard Beeston, Broo Doherty, Anatol Lieven, Colin Smith, Kate de Pury, Tom de Waal and Justin Huggler all contributed.

Fathers Silhouan and Simeon at the Orthodox Monastery of St John the Baptist in Essex, Graham Speake of the Friends of Mount Athos Society, Greek Orthodox Bishop Kallistos Ware of Oxford, Dr Anthony Bryer of Birmingham University, Bishop Ambrose Baird of Fili near Athens, Father Christopher Hill in Moscow, the staff of the *Cyprus Mail* in Nicosia, John Nassis at the Ecumenical Patriarchate in Istanbul and Malcolm Walker at Keston College in Oxford were all very helpful.

Without the work of dozens of historians I would never have been able to write this book. None of them is responsible for any of the judgements, misjudgements and mistakes I have gone on to make.

Grateful thanks are also due to the *Observer*, the newspaper which sponsored my seven year sojourn in the Balkans and Russia between 1990 and 1996 and so helped prepare the ground for this book. Mark Frankland, Martin Huckerby, Adrian Hamilton and Ann Treneman took a special interest.

To my editors at Macmillan, Tanya Stobbs and Becky Lindsay, goes a big thank you for having the imagination and enthusiasm to back the project. Many thanks also to Nicky Hursell, who chased up photos so diligently. I also owe a huge debt of thanks to my agent, David Godwin, who first challenged me to define precisely what I found so engaging about Eastern Europe and then agreed that I should write about it.

A last but not least thank you goes to my parents and to my sister Nicola, for services ranging from listening to my Orthodox anecdotes, to painting the cover illustration, to correcting grammar and sharing a love of history.

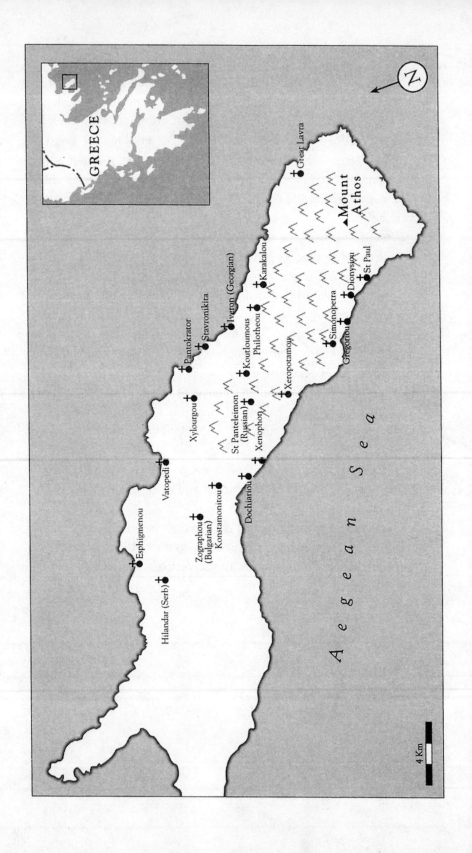

GREECE

N

Great Lavra

Mount
Athos

St Paul
Dionysiou
Karakalou
Simonopetra
Iveron (Georgian)
Gregoriou
Stavronikita
Pantokrator
Philotheou
Koutloumous
Xeropotamou
Xylourgou
St Panteleimon (Russian)
Xenophon
Dochiariou
Konstamonitou
Vatopedi
Zographou (Bulgarian)
Esphigmenou
Hilandar (Serb)

Aegean Sea

4 Km

MOUNT ATHOS

Byzantium

Only an angel could have rejoiced at my first glimpse of the Holy Mountain through a fug of cigarette smoke and a rain-streaked porthole on a squally April morning. Imprisoned on a boat, peering up at the Byzantine monasteries clinging damply to their rocky fastness like outsize birds' nests, I could not begin to appreciate the thousand-year-old stronghold of Eastern Orthodox spirituality in Europe.

A sudden blaze of Greek sunlight to transform the sea from base grey to silver, to glance off the monastery crosses and lift the mist from the summit of Mount Athos itself might have helped, but not much. A closer view would have been nice, but still second best, because access to those forty square kilometres of earthly paradise – one of three crooked fingers of land dangling into the Aegean Sea off the south-eastern edge of Europe – was essential if I was to achieve what I had set out to do.

Once on the Holy Mountain I would wander the ancient paths between those crumbling fortresses of Orthodoxy, breathing the smells of incense, woodsmoke, beeswax and old stone and listening to the monks' voices echoing in the courtyards and churches. I would see how the world's hectic quickstep can stop in a spot where generations of men have observed the same round of liturgies, saints' days and church feasts for a thousand years. I would begin to imagine how Mount Athos' two thousand or so monks have come to believe they are imitating God's angels . . .

But what was the sense in dreaming? I would do none of these things for the simple reason that, for the past nine hundred years, the Holy Mountain has been out of bounds to all women. Any genderless angel, any monk, any male for that matter, could rush in where I was for ever forbidden to tread.

The ban on women setting foot on Athos was some elderly monks' response to an outbreak of fornication on the peninsula at the close of the eleventh century. Saucy women, masquerading as

3

nomad shepherds to lead some of the younger monks astray, had scandalized the old men into forging a patriarchal order outlawing not only women but any female creature. As recently as the 1930s an Athos monk was defending the full provisions of the originally forged document, saying it was in order that the animals' 'mating may not furnish an outlandish spectacle to souls which detest all forms of indecency, and are daily being purified'.[i] The section of the rule relating to female animals has been relaxed, but to this day the monks of the Holy Mountain make one exception only where women are concerned, for the Mother of God. Shipwrecked on the Holy Mountain a few years after the death of her son, the Blessed Virgin Mary is said to have taken a special fancy to the place and claimed it as her own. 'Let this land be for ever mine – given to me by my son and God,' she is said to have said. 'The Garden of the Mother of God' is how the monks still like to refer to their rocky stronghold.

Tradition was all very well and, of course, there was no competing with the Mother of God, but here was I at the start of the twenty-first century, a citizen of a secular European Union guaranteeing freedom of movement for all within its borders* and equality of the sexes. Travelling in Greece, which is a member of that union, earnestly seeking a closer acquaintance with the world of Eastern Orthodox Christianity in Europe, I had found that a mere accident of gender barred me from examining its heart. Surely, I reasoned, it behoved me to storm this last bastion of masculinity in Europe? I would not have been the first to attempt it.

A hundred years after a fourteenth-century Serbian queen found refuge on Mount Athos from the ravages of the plague, the Virgin Mary startled a trespassing Eastern Orthodox sultana who was bound for a monastery bearing gifts of gold and frankincense. She commanded her to 'Come no further, for here is another queen than thou – the Queen of Heaven.'[ii] The Ottoman Turkish governors of Mount Athos politely forbore from parading their harems before the monks

---

* When Greece joined the EEC in 1984 a rare exception to the rules – a 'derogation' – was made regarding freedom of movement on Mount Athos. The exception has been challenged but so far unsuccessfully.

4

for the next four hundred years. However, a crowd of Greek refugees, fleeing the wrath of the Ottomans during the Greek War of Independence in the early nineteenth century, included a few women and thereafter the number of violations and attempted violations increased. An Edwardian adventuress in the company of two men put ashore one summer for a bit of a lark, and was kindly received by the monks. Shortly afterwards a Frenchwoman wrote a highly suspect account of a sojourn among the monks of Athos, made possible, she claimed, after she had sliced off her breasts. In the early 1930s a Swedish woman, dressed as a man and armed with her brother's passport, failed to gain admittance after collapsing in a fit of giveaway giggles as she was about to step ashore. More recently, a few Italian holidaymakers who, ignorant of their whereabouts, weighed anchor off the peninsula to sunbathe on the beach, were the reason for the formulation of a new rule. All boats carrying women must steer a course 500 metres from the shores of the Holy Mountain.

Despondently studying the faces of the Greek, Serbian and Romanian women who made up most of the boat's cargo, however, I saw no signs of resentment at their exclusion. Their shoulders draped in coats, they were sitting drinking coffee from plastic cups, chain-smoking and chattering. Whenever the amplified voice of a tour guide alerted them to the distant view of a monastery by reeling off names and dates in their own language, they crowded around the portholes, silent and rapt. United in their shared heritage of right belief or worship, which is the literal translation of the word ortho-doxy, they seemed to be accepting the 500-metre rule.

A Serbian woman told me she would be quite content to hear what her husband had to say about his stay at the Holy Mountain's Serbian monastery of Hilandar when they were reunited in a day's time. A young Romanian woman, a stockbroker from Bucharest, said she believed that men and women should know their proper places and that a woman's proper place was certainly not on Mount Athos. A young Greek, a native of the area living off the booming tourist trade in this Halkidiki region of northern Greece, sighed impatiently. 'Look,' she said, 'a lot of the monks are sick – sick in mind or in body or both, nothing special at all. But there are some – perhaps just a few – who are doing something so holy there that they are saints. I'm sure of that. They need peace and silence to do this work.'

'Yes, but . . .'

She knew what I was about to say and waved a hand dismissively. 'The European Union will never force Athos to allow women in just because Greece is a member of it. What kind of human rights would that be? Where is the freedom in that?'

Quite so, but what about *my* freedom and the good liberal rule of thumb of striving to attain the maximum good for the majority of people, not just for a handful of 'saints' who happened to believe they were emulating angels? That was the question I wanted to ask but sensed I would be wasting my time and hers if I did so. Our minds were not meeting.

What she was not aware of was that someone like myself could seriously consider sneaking across the monastic republic's land border. The previous evening I had taken a short walk from the last secular village on the Athos peninsula, Ouranopoli, in order to reconnoitre the terrain. I had reached a three-foot-high concrete wall topped with chicken wire and a large signpost crowned with a gilt Byzantine double-headed eagle, reminding me in all the major western European languages that, as a woman, I could go no further. But by turning right along that wall, and following it down to the beach where it tapered off into the sea, I calculated that I could probably clamber over the final obstacle of a few rocks and round to the other side. Once there I would unpack a rucksack, don a long black beard and a black robe, adopt a rolling stride and proceed to wander among the monasteries. As soon as I plucked up the courage to enter one, I would be arrested by the Mount Athos police and incarcerated in a Greek jail for up to a year. But from jail I could fight my case in the European Court of Human Rights and maybe even win it.

In the process, I would stir up a deal of trouble, I calculated, for my brave stunt would be serving a higher purpose. It would highlight a barrier to European unity so high and immovable that at last there would be no evading the truth of a hunch I have had for the best

6

part of a decade spent living and working in Eastern Orthodox countries: that more than half of the continent we call Europe is the heartland of not just another branch of the Christian religion but of another culture entirely. The half of the continent that stretches back east from today's Bosnian Serb Republic in the west, through the eastern Balkans all the way to the Urals in Russia and on across Siberia as far as Vladivostok on the Pacific only superficially resembles the western half of the continent. Eastern Orthodox Europe – the twin that our Catholic and later Protestant western Europe carelessly lost touch with a millennium ago – is an entity whose separate values, traditions and therefore history we have at best denigrated, at worst ignored.

The end of the Cold War might have broken this pattern and inspired a reappraisal of what the continent had been and could become, but somehow it did not. Traditionally Roman Catholic or Protestant Poland, East Germany, Hungary and Czechoslovakia greeted their reopening to the traditionally Roman Catholic or Protestant western Europe with joy, and western Europe soon made plans to include them in Nato and the European Union. But the Eastern Orthodox countries of former Eastern Europe – Serbia and Montenegro, the former Yugoslav Republic of Macedonia, Romania, Bulgaria, Moldavia, Ukraine, Belarus, Russia – were shut out, disqualified on the grounds of being insufficiently democratic and economically non-viable. There is little chance of any of these countries joining either Nato or the EU in the first decades of the new century. This means that both organizations' eastern borders are set to follow almost exactly Europe's oldest political fault-line, which dates back to the second century AD and the division of the Roman empire into two halves – the western ruled from Rome, the eastern from Constantinople. By 1054 the line had gained a religious dimension and marked the schism between the Roman and the Byzantine Christian Churches. West of the line lay Catholic Christendom headed by Rome, east of it Orthodox Christendom headed by Constantinople.

East of that old line people are confronting a double challenge today. Almost all the region is having to deal with the aftermath of

7

Communism, but in addition cope with the influx of a fundamentally alien western culture, and sometimes that of an increasingly muscular Islamic world to the south as well. The combination of these pressures was almost guaranteed to make Eastern Orthodox Europe ineligible for entry to the European Union and Nato. The same pressures have been at the root of most of the turbulence in Europe since the Iron Curtain collapsed. The Serbs' murderous exclusivity in the former Yugoslavia, the resurgence of nationalism and anti-Semitism in Russia, the *enfant terrible* status of Greece in the EU and Nato, violent scuffles over church property between Catholics and Orthodox in the borderlands of Romania and Ukraine, anti-Islamic feeling in Bulgaria, and the slow-burning fuse of a Cyprus (still unresolved a quarter of a century after partition) are all connected. Each is a battle front in the larger defensive war that Eastern Orthodox Europe is waging to hold its own – spiritually and territorially – in an area threatened by godless materialism from the West and a population explosion from Islam to the south. Uncomfortably sandwiched between these two dominant cultures Eastern Orthodox Europe has been shrinking and embattled since the eleventh century. The end of its agony is nowhere in sight.

Mount Athos was not necessarily the best place to explore all this. So no brave stunts, I thought, as the boat chugged on through the choppy sea and the women sipped their coffee. I would not stoop to nocturnal raids or sneaking about in a false beard because, in a sense, Eastern Orthodox Europe was already present in that boat filled with Orthodox women. Not so much the monks on Mount Athos and my wrong gender but my western culture, Catholic upbringing and, most importantly, my lack of religious faith were what would bar me from knowing its finest points. I believed I could penetrate Eastern Orthodox Europe as deeply as any other western European could by unravelling parts of its history, exploring its home territories and seeking out the company and opinions of its chief defenders and custodians – monks and nuns, priests and bishops, archbishops and even a patriarch.

After all, I consoled myself, my entry to Byzantium was as barred as my entry to Athos, and Byzantium was at least as crucial to an understanding of the Orthodox world as Mount Athos. Without Byzantium there would have been neither Mount Athos nor Orthodoxy. And Byzantium itself would never have been without the Roman empire. It is a good story and those hours on the boat, while the rain lashed the portholes and the battleship-grey sea dashed the sides, seemed the ideal moment to begin its telling.

In the Roman empire in which Jesus Christ lived, set up his Church and died, all the Christian denominations – Eastern Orthodoxy and Roman Catholicism with its later offshoots of multiple forms of Protestantism – were undreamed of. The Church, with Christ mysteriously present wherever two or three were gathered in His name, was a single community. As such it was flourishing by the beginning of the fourth century AD. The Roman Emperor Constantine himself had seen the light.

Oddly susceptible to visions and omens, this bull-necked soldier had been marching towards Rome for a final showdown with his chief rival, when he received a direct communication from God. Constantine apparently saw the shape of a cross in front of the sun and heard a voice telling him to go forth and conquer 'in this sign'. The fact that about one in five Romans was already Christian, including his mother, suggests that his conversion was hardly miraculous, but the ensuing victory must have stiffened his resolve.

The old Roman gods were out of favour, their magic faded and out of date. Christianity was fresh, vigorous and its devotees admirably organized. The new religion was just the thing for an empire beginning to feel its age after five hundred years. By AD 323 the Roman empire had a single uncontested emperor again and Constantine was encouraging Christianity with tax breaks for the Church and applications of pressure on the wealthy to build fitting houses of worship for the new God.

Wedging a nail of the True Cross in his bejewelled helmet and another in his horse's bit, Constantine determined to make a fresh start. The sprawling empire urgently needed a second administrative

9

centre in the east. A spot at the mouth of the Bosphorus on the Black Sea, strategically placed at the 'thwarted kiss of two continents,'[iii] a town called Byzantium after an obscure Greek colonizer, seemed the ideal place to realize the project. This creation, soon to become known as the New Rome or Constantinople, was ready for inauguration by AD 330 and Constantine was bullying scores of Roman worthies into abandoning their comfortable old villas in the Old Rome in favour of new ones in his New Rome, with its dank sea mists and winds in winter and its sweltering summer heat.

The new capital of the eastern Roman empire prospered and grew fabulously rich. It could hardly have done otherwise. Surrounded by a set of three impregnable walls at the mouth of the Bosphorus channel which widens out after a few miles into the Black Sea, it was a gigantic bustling fortress controlling all the main trade routes between Europe, Asia and Africa. For the best part of a thousand years, but especially while the old Rome was being sacked by Goths, Visigoths, Slavs and Vandals during western Christendom's chaotic fifth to ninth centuries, the New Rome was the dazzling, busy hub of the known world. Grain from the Nile Delta, slaves, wax, honey and furs from Russia, wine and oil from the Mediterranean, wool and silver from northern Europe, spices from India and silk from China poured into and through the 'City of Cities'. With their bodily needs so richly assured, Constantinople's inhabitants could afford to focus their attention on spiritual needs.

To a much greater extent than western Christendom, the Byzantine empire could afford to make over vast stretches of land to monasteries filled with able-bodied young Christians, men and women, living 'the angelic life'. It is reckoned that by the ninth century the Byzantine empire was supporting a small army of a hundred thousand monks. Constantinople itself was full of monasteries but wilder, more isolated spots – deserts, mountain-tops, islands and hidden valleys – were equally favoured by armies of contemplatives preparing themselves and the world for the supremely important and seemingly imminent occasion of Christ's Second Coming. Contributing nothing more material than prayers to the empire, they were a vivid reminder that the next world, not this one, was what counted.

Whether sternly ascetic or not the monks had at least as vital a role to play in the empire as merchants, married or military men. As one modern Orthodox theologian has put it, 'The spiritual work of a monk living in a community or a hermit withdrawn from the world retains all its worth for the entire universe, even though it remains hidden from the sight of all.'[iv] A fourth-century bishop wrote that the Emperor Constantine sought to arrange 'his earthly government according to the pattern of the divine original'[v] but the hermitages and monasteries acted as a permanent and uncomfortable reminder that the gulf between the empires of Heaven and Earth yawned wide. Blunt criticism of the world, raving prophecies, dreams, half-starved visions, threats and forebodings were the weapons the monks wielded against the State. Emperors, patriarchs and bishops grown too worldly with power, ignored these armies of earthly 'angels' at their peril. Time and time again throughout the Byzantine empire's 1,123-year life-span, the monasteries were able to mobilize city mobs in defence of the True Faith and in opposition to the State.

Monastic influence might be more subtle, but at least as powerful via the relationship that famously spiritual monks could enjoy with any number of 'spiritual children'. Everyone, from an emperor down, sought out a 'spiritual father' to whom he would confide the darkest secrets of his heart and from whom he would solicit advice of a spiritual, but also of a practical, kind. Unquestioning obedience was the proper attitude to a spiritual father. St Symeon the Young has left an account of how to find and then behave towards such a mentor: 'Go and find the man whom God, either mysteriously through Himself, or externally through his servant, shall show you. He is Christ himself. So you must regard him and speak to him; so must you honour him; so must you learn from him that which will be of benefit to you.'[vi]

A spiritual father's advice to an emperor or a general might run as far as encouraging a *coup d'état* or a military campaign. A spiritual father could provide not only direct moral guidance but the basis for a political alliance among a number of his spiritual children. Mount Athos acquired much of its influence as a breeding ground of spiritual fathers to the richest and most powerful Byzantines. St Athanasius, who founded the first monastery on the Holy Mountain in 963 for men to pursue their 'angelic calling' by praising and glorifying God like the angels, was the Emperor Nikephoros Phokas' spiritual father. Ample imperial funding was made available for the construction project.

But who were these people we call Byzantines and generally assume to have been Greeks, but who described themselves as *Romaioi*, the Greek word for Romans? The educated among them spoke Greek, the lingua franca of the eastern Roman empire, but had no sense of nationality as we understand it today. First, their Christian faith and, second, their allegiance to the Byzantine emperor was what united them. Citizens of the Byzantine empire might originally have been what we would now call Greeks, Romanians, Egyptians, Palestinians, Ukrainians, Turks or Serbs, but they regarded themselves as simply Christian Romans whose language was Greek and who lived in the eastern rather than the western half of the Roman empire. Mount Athos is the last surviving witness to this admittedly now shrunken but originally universal Christian ideal. The Holy Mountain is a self-governing monastic republic peopled with Orthodox monks from Greece, Russia, Serbia, the former Yugoslav Republic of Macedonia, Romania, Moldavia, Cyprus, Bulgaria, Ukraine and Belarus, not to mention a sprinkling from all the states of western Europe and beyond.

Those early *Romaioi* believed they were God's chosen people. In much the same way as the golden background of Byzantine icons and mosaics signalled the sacred, timeless context of their subjects, so Christianity was the sacred, timeless context of the Byzantine empire. The True Faith of the Great Church was the *sine qua non* of an empire destined to last until the arrival of the Anti-Christ, the end of the world and Christ's Second Coming. It was the mystical alchemy that turned the empire's already incomparably rich traditions of Greek philosophy and learning, Roman law and Oriental autocracy to pure gold. In the heavenly order of Byzantine things, God arranged the Heavens and the Byzantine emperor ordered the *Oikumene* – the inhabited Earth.

Since their first emperor Constantine had been vouchsafed such a direct sign of heavenly favour, all Byzantine emperors ruled by divine right as God's Vice-Regents on Earth and the equals of the apostles, until they were overthrown by the superior force of a *coup d'état* which placed a rival on the throne. Since nothing could happen without God willing it, the newcomer naturally also ruled by divine right. Such an empire and its faith were too perfect to require further evolution, the Byzantines believed, and that perfection lay in unwavering fidelity to tradition. Its rigid conservatism is one of Orthodoxy's most pronounced and admired characteristics today.

Church and State were conceived as one perfect harmony, or *symphonia*, in the Byzantine empire. No detailed attempt was made to define the spheres of responsibility allotted to each because both emperor and the Ecumenical Patriarch of Constantinople were assumed to be equally engaged in the central task of reproducing Heaven on Earth. Church and State were just as mystically and paradoxically one and yet two, as the Holy Trinity's God the Father, the Son and the Holy Spirit are one but also three. If the harmonious ideal was not always attained that was because practical interests did not always coincide. Sometimes an emperor gained the upper hand, sometimes a patriarch. An eleventh-century patriarch was apparently 'much vexed'[vii] because the empire was being governed by a woman in the shape of the Empress Theodora. He was determined to seize the reins of government but she, at least as capable of ruling as any of her male predecessors, 'abominated' and defeated him.

The average Byzantine could rejoice in the knowledge that fortunately their empire's real ruler was neither an empress, nor an emperor, nor a patriarch but Christ himself. A copy of the four gospels sat on an empty throne in the imperial palace vividly symbolizing his presence among his chosen people. On the other hand the Byzantines saw nothing strange in an emperor preaching a sermon to his court, or in an artist portraying him as a saint, with a golden halo around his head. The word 'saint' was often used in conjunction with the title 'emperor'. Other high officials of state were referred to as 'Your Sincerity' or 'Your Sublime and Wonderful Magnitude' or 'Your Illustrious and Magnificent Highness'. To insult the emperor was blasphemy. Plots against his rule invited excommunication from the Church. Every war – and they were usually defensive rather than aggressive since the Byzantines liked to conquer by force of culture and religion rather than arms – was a holy war waged on God's behalf for the protection of his kingdom on Earth. The Byzantine victory cheer was not 'Byzantium has triumphed!' but 'The Cross has conquered!'

Living and breathing religious fervour, the *Romaioi* brought to their three-personed God and His Mother Mary the all-consuming passion of a besotted lover for his beloved. Heart, soul and mind were fully engaged in disentangling heresies and perceiving the Truth. Gregory of Nyssa who was around for the building of the New Rome famously commented:

> the city is full of workmen and slaves who are all theologians . . . if you ask a man to change money, he will tell you how the Son differs from the Father. If you ask the price of a loaf he will argue that the Son is less than the Father. If you want to know if the bath be ready you are told that the Son was made out of nothing.[viii]

Religion coloured every activity. Political riots erupted over whether 'the Son is less than the Father,' and thousands died in defence of the right to use icons, or alternatively for their belief that those lovely pictures implied sinful worship of graven images. Popular Byzantine literature was not light romantic fiction but the improving lives of saints. The Byzantine equivalent of a football match, an outing to the Hippodrome to see the horse races and support the Blue or Green team, was but another excuse for worship. Cheerleader-like cantors directed the ritualized chants which went:

Cantors: Holy, thrice Holy, victory to the Blue!
People: Yes, Victory to the Blue!
Cantors: Lady, Mother of God!
People: Yes, Mother of God, victory to the Blue!
Cantors: Power of the Cross!
People: Yes, Power of the Cross, victory to the Blue!'[ix]

Byzantinologists have wondered if there has ever been such a long time in the world's history when so many men and women were so sincerely anxious about their relations with their God. The poet W. B. Yeats once wrote that if he had been granted a month of antiquity he would have spent it in early Byzantium: 'I think I could find in some little wine shop some philosophical worker in mosaic who could answer all my questions . . . I think that in early Byzantium, as maybe never before or since in recorded history, religious, aesthetic and practical life were one . . .'[x]

It was not that the *Romaioi* were uncommonly virtuous. They were certainly not, of course, but the perfect immaterial world on which they believed their world to be modelled was uncommonly present to them. Ideally the Byzantines were as Yeats hoped, balanced in mind and heart, a subtle, superbly cultured and devout people. Often, however, they were untethered to any recognizable reality. Bewitched by their 'higher reality', they were mythically drifting in a blind haze of thunderclouds and sunbursts stuffed with miracles, omens, visions and prophecies. In the year 398 a sulphur-scented red cloud was seen approaching Constantinople. It caused a panic-stricken stampede to the churches for baptism in preparation for the end of the world. The Emperor himself led the exodus to a nearby field, leaving the city deserted and silent for a few hours.

As if its thirteen miles of mighty walls and fortified gates were not sufficient protection against invasion, Constantinople boasted a finer collection of prophylactic saints' relics than any other Christian city in the world. Like the monks of Mount Athos, the Byzantines chose the Mother of God as their special protectress. Paraded around the walls of the city in 860 when Constantinople seemed about to fall to Russian invaders, her miraculous robe soon saw off the enemy. 'Truly,' wrote the mightily relieved Patriarch of the day, 'is this most holy garment the robe of God's Mother! It embraced the walls, and the foes inexplicably showed their backs; the city put it around itself and the camp of the enemy was broken up as at a signal . . .'xi

Her belt was similarly miracle-working. A precious icon of her, thought to have been painted by St Luke from life, was ritually paraded around the walls of the city whenever catastrophe threatened, as it did increasingly often after the Russian Vikings' abortive expedition. Byzantium also treasured and venerated the Infant Jesus's swaddling clothes, the blood-spattered cloak Christ had worn en route to the crucifixion, the lance that pierced his side and the Crown of Thorns. Each of these items was honoured with a jewel-studded silver or gold reliquary, within a sanctuary, within a church of its own, as were the head of St John the Baptist, the assorted limbs of the Holy Apostles Luke, Timothy and Andrew, and a host of saintly digits, teeth and so on.

The city, boasting at its zenith some 450 glittering icon-filled churches, amazed all who went there, including a French crusader who stopped off there in the eleventh century, on his way to Jerusalem.

> O, what a splendid city! How stately, how fair, how many monasteries therein, how many palaces raised by sheer labour in its broadways and streets, how many works of art, marvellous to behold; it would be wearisome to tell of the abundance of all good things; of gold and silver, garments of manifold fashion, and such sacred relics!xii

After attending a service in the great Emperor Justinian's Haghia Sophia church, in the centre of the city close to the royal palace and the Hippodrome, some dazzled late tenth century Russian envoys reported back to their sovereign in Kiev from Tsargrad, as they called Constantinople, that 'we knew not whether we were in Heaven or on earth. For on earth there is no such splendour and beauty, and we are at a loss how to describe it. We only know that there God dwells among men.'xiii

One could seek one's fortune in Constantinople and, especially after the Norman invasion of 1066, many Englishmen did just that. It is estimated that in about 1075 at least ten thousandxiv English decided they could not bear to bow their heads under the Norman yoke so set sail for Constantinople, or Micklegarth, as they called it. They expected to find work in the city of cities and a spiritual environment more congenial and free than that being foisted on England by the Normans and the Pope. On arrival, they found Constantinople undergoing one of its periodic sieges by Turks, whom they saw off efficiently enough to win the gratitude of the then Byzantine Emperor. Over four thousand of them settled in Constantinople itself, and many were rewarded with jobs in the imperial army. One of their churches was still standing in the middle of the nineteenth century.

Those Englishmen arrived in Byzantium twenty-one years after the event that marked the splitting of Christendom, and therefore Europe, in two. At the time no one dreamed the Schism of 1054 presaged anything permanent. The Byzantine East did not read its meaning until the fourteenth century, by which time the First Crusaders had deepened the divide by kicking Byzantine hierarchs out of their ancient Orthodox churches of Antioch and Jerusalem and installing Latin ones in their place, and the Fourth Crusaders had sacked and conquered Constantinople. Nevertheless, if the Schism of 1054 hardly merited a mention in the chronicles of the time, its religious, cultural and political consequences reverberate down a millennium to the present day and the dissolution of Yugoslavia. Perhaps the Schism was almost unnoticed by contemporaries because it was part of a continuum, of a gentle downward slide which no one imagined would prove irreversible.

Christian churchmen of East and West were much given to disagreement. Since the earliest days of the Church there had been ferocious theological squabbles between the patriarchs of the different Christian centres because all were passionately concerned to defend the True Faith against a multitude of vile heresies. They convened councils for this purpose. Often they were riotous occasions which one witness likened to 'gatherings of cranes and geese'[xv], but beneath all that squawking and pecking about heresies, it became increasingly clear that the very different historical experiences of east and west Christendom were slowly splitting the Church. Some have located the seeds of trouble in the West's preference for the rigorous logic of Aristotle and the East's for the more essentially mystical and speculative teachings of Plato. Where the Romans of Rome developed their aptitude for law and their love of authority, the *Romaioi* of Byzantium nurtured their taste for speculative philosophy and mysticism. Some have pointed out that they were bound to have different priorities given that they were fighting different heresies at opposite ends of Europe. Some suggest that the language barrier – with one side thinking in Latin and the other in Greek – may have fostered the growing lack of understanding between the two. As the eminent Byzantinologist Sir Steven Runciman has wisely and shortly put it, they 'felt differently about religion; it is difficult to debate about feelings'.[xvi]

East and West had evolved different ways of apprehending Man's relation with his God. Sensible and rational, the Latins believed that Man must wait until after death to know if he was saved or damned. Idealistic and mystical, the Byzantines believed Man could be saved before death. By the grace of God, Man could become God, in the sense of knowing and participating in his divine energy, while still alive. A central tenet of Eastern Orthodox Christianity is that 'God became human so that we might be made God.'[xvii] Deification, *theosis* in Greek, is precisely what the few 'saints' on Mount Athos are striving towards today, as generations of monks have for centuries, becoming 'like a golden chain with each of them a link, bound to all the preceding: saints in faith, love and good works . . . one single chain, in one God'.[xvii]

Eastern Orthodox churchmen and laity today will grant all of the above in discussing their differences with western Christendom, but emphasize that it was the 'egotistical and absolutist aspiration of the

Pope to become leader and despot, judge and sovereign of the whole world'[xlix] that eventually and inevitably led to the Schism. Church historians would put it more mildly, saying that the Roman Church's role as the one beacon of civilizing light during western Europe's early Middle Ages quite naturally caused it to assume a powerful universal role. To support their claim to supremacy over all the other branches of the Church the popes pointed to the fact that it was the Apostle Peter, the first Vicar of *Rome*, who was the 'rock' on which Christ built his Church. From the sixth century onwards the popes never stopped pushing their Roman supremacy line at the councils. Generations of Byzantine patriarchs either did not bother to think through the momentous implications of the claim, or could not believe that the popes were serious about it. Uninterested by and distrustful of western theology's legalistic niceties, they evolved no consistent line with which to oppose Rome's pressure.

But they knew which way the wind was blowing. On Christmas Day 800 the Pope crowned the Frankish chieftain Charlemagne Holy Roman Emperor, a move shortly followed by a serious East versus West contretemps over the insertion of the filioque in the Creed. This was all about whether the third person of the Trinity, the Holy Spirit, 'proceeded from the Father *and* the Son' or just from the Father. It suited Charlemagne and the western religious mind-set to maintain the former, the Byzantines' to uphold the latter. They went their separate ways on the matter, but unhappily. The cracks were showing. A hundred years later the blood of the *Romaioi* boiled when a papal delegation arrived in Constantinople with a letter from the Roman Pope which referred to the German king Otto I as 'the August Emperor of the Romans' and to the Byzantine Emperor as only the 'Emperor of the Greeks'. 'To style a poor barbaric creature "Emperor of the Romans!" O Sky! O Earth! O Sea! What shall we do with these scoundrels and criminals?'[xx] they ranted, according to Luitprand of Cremona, Otto I's ambassador to Constantinople.

By this time the churches of East and West were strenuously and sometimes acrimoniously competing for influence in central Europe and the Balkans, with each side employing missionary churchmen as their shock troops. Although Serbs and Bulgars had wavered for a while between eastern and western Christianity, weighing up the relative advantages to be gained from each, they eventually opted for the East. The Byzantine empire granted them more control over their own affairs and preached the gospel in something closer to their own language than Latin. Furthermore, Constantinople was the richest and most civilized city on earth.

In 1001 a high hope for the happy reunion of Christendom was dashed when the western Emperor Otto III, who had been all set to marry Zoe, a Byzantine princess, died at the tender age of twenty-two. It was only a matter of time, just over fifty years, before the final break came.

Possibly the most catastrophic event ever to have befallen Christendom, the Schism arose out of a sordid personal feud between a narrow-minded bureaucrat of a Patriarch of Constantinople and an arrogant Roman cardinal who led a papal delegation to Byzantium. The fact that the cardinal's master, the Pope, had died by the time he arrived in the city and that the Patriarch's partner in power, the Byzantine Emperor, was inclined to take a conciliatory line did not deter this pair from bringing their political and theological differences to a head. Provocation followed insult and insult followed fresh provocation until three o'clock on the afternoon of 16 July 1054. At that moment the members of the Roman delegation, dressed in their full canonical robes, strode into Constantinople's Haghia Sophia church where a liturgy was about to be performed, marched up to the high altar, plonked down their bull of excommunication and marched out again.

Two days later they headed back to Rome. The Constantinople mob, led by monks, rioted so violently in support of the Patriarch that order was only restored once the entire papal delegation had been anathematized, the Emperor almost unseated, and the offending bull ritually burned. Via their leading church hierarchs, eastern and western Europe were divorcing each other. Although the formal anathemas were eventually cancelled in 1965, the scar remains to this day.

After 1054 the rift between them widened. Henceforward there were two Christendoms, both claiming universality. The fault-line between them ran north to south from the Baltic to the Mediterranean. To the west of it, the Church of Rome went on to become a separate power from the State, thanks in great measure to the influence of St Augustine of Hippo's fifth-century treatise, *De Civitate Dei*. But it was a worldly and blatantly fallible power, which set its sights not on harmonious *symphonia* but on theocracy, and failed in its aim just as soon as the western rulers stopped fearing excommunication. Its sacramental meaning as the sum of its believers was replaced by a new one. The western Church became 'a social and corporational organism'.[xxi] Financially and spiritually it underwrote the flowering of humanism and the Renaissance, which set man instead of God at the centre of the universe and in so doing forfeited real spiritual influence. Next came the backlash of the Reformation and fragmenting Protestantism. The Counter-Reformation was only half successful and was followed by the Age of Reason, with its sneering modern disregard for Byzantine Christianity and for religion in general. This is the climate in which Christianity still finds itself today in western Europe.

To the east were the peoples whom Byzantine missionaries had converted to Christianity. The Byzantine Orthodox Church clung to the definition of the Church as a community of individuals rather than as an institution or state of its own. No Patriarch of Constantinople ever commanded foreign kings and armies. In the East there was no full flowering of a Renaissance, no Reformation, no Age of Reason as the West knew them. Miracles kept their power and monasteries most of their wealth in a world the modern West dismissed as medieval and unenlightened. The Byzantine Orthodox Church remained organically bound to the Byzantine state until the fifteenth century, fuelling the Byzantines' terror of encircling heretical enemies and shrinking territories with gloomy pronouncements about the empire having sinned on a grand enough scale to forfeit divine protection. In 1453 Constantinople fell to the Ottomans.

Under Ottoman rule from the mid-fifteenth to the mid-nineteenth centuries, the Orthodox Church hierarchy in Asia Minor and most of the Balkans became the tolerated, even privileged servant of its Muslim master. A Turkish governor of Mount Athos, at the time of the Greek War of Independence from the Ottomans in the early nineteenth century, was heard to opine that the monks of the Holy Mountain would come to miss the Ottoman yoke they were fighting to be free of:

> Look at these thousands of monks. Of what, in reality, can they complain? Have we touched their rules? Have we violated their property? Have we forbidden their pilgrimages? Have we altered even a little of their secular constitution? What race, I ask you, what conqueror, could have treated these people with greater humanity, greater moderation, greater religious tolerance? . . . They will regret us.[xxii]

Eastern Orthodox churchmen had accepted their good treatment at the hands of the Ottomans but devoted themselves to keeping alive both the hatred of the infidel and an idealized memory of their glorious 1,123-year-old empire on the Bosphorus. These preoccupations easily complemented modern western notions of nationhood in the nineteenth century. Each Orthodox nation began demanding its own state and an autocephalous, or independent, Orthodox Church. The Ecumenical Patriarchate of Constantinople, itself no longer a model of *symphonia* but more like a privileged slave, lacked the power to stop the fragmentation. By the beginning of the twentieth century it was helpless against the rise of religious nationalism, or Phyletism. Events since the end of the Cold War have shown that neither Russia's seventy years nor the Balkans' forty-five of state socialism has succeeded in destroying that ugly legacy.

With the old Rome fallen into heresy and the new to the Ottomans in 1453, Moscow lost little time in styling itself the Third Rome, closely modelled on the last one. Imperial Russia flew the Byzantine double-headed eagle until the murder of the Romanov imperial family in July 1918. After almost a century of state-sponsored atheism, the bird is back as the proud emblem of the new Russia.

So the eastern Roman empire survived, in its vital religious essence, as a civilization uncomfortably sandwiched between the western and Islamic worlds, both of which it had early learnt to fear and mistrust. It survived as another world in its way of ordering Church and State relations, in its mode of thinking about man and God, about history and the non-Orthodox world. The West was not much interested in the fate of its Christian brothers in the East. Roman Catholic and Protestant Europe declared itself the chief inheritor of the only good things the East had ever produced: ancient Greece and Christianity. Even today, we usually understand the history of Europe to comprise only the history of western Europe.

The still unfolding tragedy of the continent is that by the 1054 Schism each side lost something it could not happily do without. One might say that East and West, the one tending too much towards reason and worldliness and the other too much towards spirit and otherworldliness, was sadly deformed for lack of the other. To put it very baldly and at the risk of over-simplifying the case for the sake of clarity, western Christendom can be said to have lost its heart, eastern Christendom its mind.

At around the time of the eleventh-century Schism an Athos monk devoted some years of his life to obeying a verse of Psalm 49, moving about the Holy Mountain on all fours, grazing the grass like a sheep. He may have lost his mind but there can be few more heartless chapters in the West's relations with the East than the sacking of Constantinople by western Crusaders, which happened in 1204, less than two hundred years after the Schism.

Europe's Eastern Orthodox have neither forgotten nor forgiven the episode for it caused them to wonder if the West merited the term 'Christian' at all and to hate their brother Christians in the West more than Islam. It was the reason why, another two hundred years later when Constantinople was falling to the Ottomans, many could honestly review their lack of options and find themselves preferring to submit to the rule of 'a Sultan's turban' rather than to that of 'a cardinal's hat'. The First, Second and Third Crusades had all succeeded in deepening the antipathy felt by West and East for each other but the Fourth Crusade was what sealed Europe's divorce, and the West must bear all the blame for it.

From the outset, the Fourth Crusade to liberate the Holy Land from the Infidel was a bungled business. Proclaimed by Pope Innocent III, it lacked sufficient funding. The Crusaders found themselves short of cash to pay their transport costs to the Venetians, who were the only people capable of laying on 480 ships. Venice's octogenarian Doge might have been stone blind but he could still spot a good business opportunity. He told the Crusaders that he thought he could see his way to giving them a reduction if, in exchange, they would oblige Venice by stopping off for a moment on their way to the Holy Land to grab back the port of Zara from the Hungarians.

Although the Pope – alarmed by the prospect of inter-Roman Catholic strife – protested loudly, the Crusaders were impatient to be off and reckoned they had no option but to agree. The Crusade set sail, Zara was sacked and won back for Venice, and all Venetians duly excommunicated by the Pope. That was a poor enough start to the venture, but it was not long before the Crusaders faced fresh pecuniary temptation.

It appeared in the form of a pretender to the Byzantine throne who solicited the Crusaders' help in deposing his uncle and installing him instead. Young Alexius, Byzantine to the core in his capacity for wishful thinking, was promising a wonderfully attractive package in exchange for this service: unlimited funds for the Crusade, extra forces and, best of all, Byzantium's immediate submission to the Roman Pope and adoption of Catholicism. Next stop for the doughty Crusaders? Not the Holy Land but Constantinople.

This, according to Geoffrey de Villehardouin, a French leader of the Crusade and its best chronicler, was how the first sight of Constantinople struck the assorted west Europeans in June 1203:

> ... when they saw those high ramparts and strong towers with which it was completely encircled, and the splendid palaces and soaring churches – so many that but for the evidence of their

own eyes they would never have believed it – and the length and breadth of that city which of all others is sovereign, they never thought that there could be so rich and powerful a place on earth.[xxiii]

Envy mixed with greed at the sight of all those riches was the final temptation the Crusaders faced and succumbed to less than a year later. They attacked the city of cities.

The horrified Byzantines tried to fight off the invaders but without success. For all the splendour of 'the City', the Byzantine empire was in deep trouble and sinking fast. The last Emperor had so mismanaged the empire's affairs that he had sold the entire Byzantine fleet to the Venetians. Before long, therefore, the Crusaders deposed the reigning Emperor and replaced him with the young pretender. Unsurprisingly, young Alexius found himself unable to keep his lavish promises. No one would co-operate with him, least of all the Constantinople clergy who first balked at his plans to raise funds by melting down their church plate then exploded at the news that he expected them to ditch the True Faith and recognize the supremacy of the heretic Roman Pope. Meanwhile the Catholic Crusaders – impatient to be off about their real business of battling the Infidel – behaved like delinquent louts in a Byzantine basilica. First they indulged in petty vandalism, and then, by setting fire to a church, they burnt down huge areas of the city.

At any moment the Doge could have averted catastrophe by ordering them all to board ship and set sail for the Holy Land, because he had long given up hope of seeing any of the money owed to him. But he seems to have been nursing a special grudge against the city whose Byzantine inhabitants had deprived him of his eyesight during some anti-Latin riots there a couple of decades earlier. His wickedly ambitious new agenda entailed conquering his Christian brothers and their empire, and putting a Venetian yes-man on the Byzantine throne.

On 9 April 1204 the Crusaders relaunched their attack on the city and took it. There followed a three-day-long victorious orgy of rape and pillage, an evil explosion of frustrated energy, a trashing the like of which the medieval world had not seen since the barbarian invasions of the West at the onset of the Middle Ages, and much of the Crusaders' spleen was vented against the Byzantine Church. A grief-stricken Byzantine witness to these events, Nicetas Choniates, did his best to record them:

> I know not how to put any order into my account, how to begin, continue or end. They smashed the holy images and hurled the sacred relics of the Martyrs into places I am ashamed to mention, scattering everywhere the body and blood of the Saviour . . . As for their profanation of the Great Church, [Haghia Sophia Cathedral] it cannot be thought of without horror. They destroyed the high altar, a work of art admired by the whole world . . . And they brought horses and mules into the Church, the better to carry off the holy vessels and the engraved silver and gold that they had torn from the throne, and the pulpit, and the doors, and the furniture . . . and when some of these beasts slipped and fell, they ran through them with their swords, fouling the Church with their blood and ordure.[xxiv]

A nobleman, Choniates fled the city with his family. En route he overtook the Patriarch, almost alone, hardly clothed and riding a donkey. The equal of an emperor almost, the old man had been reduced to a state 'of almost apostolic poverty', as Edward Gibbon notes, with a characteristic jibe at the Eastern Orthodox Church. Gibbon went on to mock-lament that 'Immense was the supply of heads and bones, crosses and images, that were scattered by this revolution over the churches of Europe . . .'[xxv]

Indeed. One Abbot Martin was seen ordering an old Byzantine priest to open up an iron trunk filled with relics, plunging his hands into it then waddling off down towards the harbour with his booty, which included a trace of Christ's blood, a piece of the True Cross, assorted portions of St John, St James's arm, St Cosmas's foot and St Laurence's tooth, all stashed in the folds of his cassock. On the way he greeted fellow Crusaders 'with a smiling face as usual and the merry words "We have done well," to which they replied, "Thanks be to God!" [xxvi] The Venetians were true connoisseurs of the riches they coveted. They carted home the splendid bronze horses that Constantine the Great had placed atop the Hippodrome. They adorned the roof of St Mark's Cathedral until pollution began to destroy them and they were removed inside. But the cathedral's sanctuary remains stuffed with relics pilfered from Constantinople.

Pope Innocent III was dismayed to hear the latest news about his bungled Fourth Crusade. He understood very well that the Crusaders' barbaric conquest of Constantinople was quite the wrong way to set about reuniting Christendom and represented no lasting victory for Rome. He wrote:

> How is the Church of the Greeks, when afflicted with such trials and persecutions, to be brought back into the unity of the Church and devotion to the Apostolic See? It has seen in the Latins nothing but an example of perdition and the works of darkness, so that it now abhors them worse than dogs. For they who are supposed to serve Christ rather than their own interests, who should have used their swords against the pagans, are dripping with the blood of Christians. They have spared neither religion, nor age, nor sex and have committed adultery and fornication in public, exposing matrons and even nuns to the filthy brutality of their troops. For them it was not enough to exhaust the riches of the Empire and to despoil both great men and small; they had to lay their hands on the treasures of the Church . . . seizing silver valuables from the altar, breaking them into pieces to divide amongst themselves, violating the sanctuaries and carrying off crosses and relics. [xxvii]

But Old Rome's remorse was no consolation to the New Rome's shocked and broken-hearted *Romaioi*. The horror of 1204 meant that thereafter not just churchmen but lay people on each side of Europe demonized the other. Soon two inoffensive words that literally denoted the languages spoken rather than nationalities included in the eastern and western halves of Europe were in use as pungent swear-words. 'Latin' in the East and 'Greek' in the West became 'synonymous with evil, heresy and hostility'.[xxviii]

For a miserable fifty-seven years the Latins clumsily lorded it over the Byzantine empire, which was, anyway, but a shrunken shadow of its old glorious self. It had lost Arabia, Jerusalem itself and Egypt including Alexandria and its famous library, to the Muslims as early as the seventh century. For centuries Turkic tribes had been seeping into Asia Minor and battering on the gates of Constantinople. By failing to appreciate the extent to which Church and State were one in Byzantium, the Latins proceeded to make bad matters still worse by importing western churchmen with their heretical rites and by reordering the Orthodox bishoprics. Insecure amid their ill-gotten spoils, they built fortresses. One, whose ruins are still visible today, stands just short of the Holy Mountain's frontier. On Athos they set about torturing the monks and ransacking their monasteries, until the perhaps conscience-stricken Pope intervened to guarantee the monks' protection.

Half a century later Byzantium had a glorious Indian summer of a Second Coming.

By 1261 the Latins were manifestly failing in their efforts to manage the remains of the eastern Roman empire. The Byzantine diaspora, that had taken refuge and regrouped at Nicaea, today the southern Turkish town of Iznik, staged a successful come-back and recapture of Constantinople under Michael Palaeologus, the first of Byzantium's last dynasty of Palaeologan emperors. 'We have undergone so many failures to take Constantinople . . . because God wished us to know that the possession of the city was a grace dependent on his bounty. He has reserved for Our reign this grace . . .'[xxix] he told his subjects, who believed him well enough to embark on their own Byzantine double-barrelled Renaissance. This was a scouring of the Church and a flowering of the arts and scholarship that pre-empted and rivalled the Reformation and Renaissance about to happen in western Europe. The huge difference between the two rebirths of East and West was that while in the West the State triumphed over the

Church, it is possible to say that in the East the Church – with Mount Athos masterminding its campaign – managed a sad sort of triumph over the State.

During the last two centuries of Late Byzantium there was no avoiding the tragic truth that, however much the Byzantines wanted to believe themselves the beneficiaries of divine favour once more, their empire's days were numbered. Most ominously, the Slavs with whom they had kindly shared the gift of Christian civilization in the ninth century were gaining power and land at Byzantium's expense. The Bulgarians had taken northern Thrace and Macedonia, and in the mid-fourteenth century the similarly Orthodox but aggressively expanding Serbian empire was to come close to invading 'the City'. Furthermore, by this time the Italian states together constituted the world's maritime super-power so Constantinople, for all its artistic flowering, was far from the hub of the known world. Vast areas of the city were derelict. In a state of permanent crisis, Byzantium was struggling to keep up an appearance that could match its claim to be the earthly replica of God's heavenly kingdom. One historian has succinctly described that ongoing crisis as brought about by 'the ever-growing gulf separating myth from reality'.[xxx]

True to form, the old *Romaioi* of Byzantium fixed on what, in a crisis, was always their first priority: the safety of their immortal souls. After 1261 a whole third of state revenues was siphoned off to the Church. The licence fees of fishermen and huntsmen, for example, accrued to the Patriarch and were used to buy candles and oil for the Haghia Sophia cathedral while next door, by the end of the fourteenth century, the Emperor's palace was going to rack and ruin. Emperor Andronicus II was in thrall to his Patriarch Athanasius, an angry martinet of a man with a mission to reform the empire along the lines of monastery. It was probably Athanasius who penned the decree which Andronicus signed, saying, 'I declare that I wish to keep the Church not only entirely free, but to have towards it the obedience of a slave and to submit myself to it in all that which is legal and conforms to the will of God . . .'[xxxi] The Byzantine Church gained power in Late Byzantium, fulfilling more diplomatic and administrative duties than ever before. Byzantium was moribund but the Church was digesting its latest territorial acquisitions. From the shores of the Adriatic in present-day Croatia, to Serbia, Macedonia, Bulgaria and most of present-day Romania, from the Black Sea littoral and up to Moscow and even further north to Novgorod, Orthodoxy in Europe had never been livelier.

In Constantinople itself there were three main responses to the imminent demise of the empire. First, there was an enfeebled imperial one, founded in a belief that neither Church nor State could survive without the other. Patriarch Antony IV of Constantinople spelt out this creed in a letter to Grand Prince Basil of Moscow in 1393: 'It is not possible for Christians to have a Church and not have an Emperor. Empire and Church have a great unity and community, nor can they be separated one from another.'[xxxii] Here was a nice philosophical justification for Byzantine nationalism to knock down Moscow's growing presumption. But it was all very well for a patriarch to preach such certainties. The last few emperors of Byzantium knew that the only hope of saving the empire lay with the West. The price of such a western rescue mission was non-negotiable: the recognition of the Pope as supreme chief of the Christian Church and the inclusion of his accursed filioque in the Eastern Orthodox creed.

In 1274 Pope Gregory X, a pragmatic man, did his best to make things easy for the Byzantine Emperor, Michael Palaeologus. He told him that all he required was the submission of the Eastern Orthodox bishops, not of the entire clergy. He must have calculated that since the real opposition to any reunion of the Churches was coming from the monasteries it was best to ignore the monks. Michael agreed and sent the Patriarch and his retinue off to Lyon for a quick ecclesiastical summit to sign the pact. All went according to plan, until the patriarchal delegation arrived home, where news of their dubious achievement caused an eruption of furious anger against the Emperor. The Byzantines felt that they had no sooner stopped rejoicing at their liberation from the boorish misrule of the Latins than their own Emperor was taking it upon himself to sell them straight back into it. No amount of reasoning, never the Byzantines' strongest suit anyway, could assuage the outrage which, as usual when the True Faith was at stake, was being orchestrated from the monasteries. The Emperor felt compelled to crack down hard, not least on the Holy Mountain. Some of the monasteries, which then numbered about forty, were torched. Some monks were banished and a few drowned. Twenty-six monks of Zographou monastery were burnt alive in a tower.

The Union of Lyon was a failure but Pope Gregory's successor, Nicholas III, could not resist pressing home the Catholic advantage. He insisted that 'the clergy of every fortress, village or any other place'[xxxii] must personally put his name to every detail of the union. The Orthodox Church and most of the laity were having less and less of any union. The craze for crusading was waning, so there was no western help forthcoming when Muslim Turks and Orthodox Serbs threatened Constantinople.

In 1369 the Byzantine Emperor made personal obeisance to Rome, although by then there was no question of his people following his lead in this respect. Four years later, he found himself compelled to pay an Ottoman overlord tribute in the form of cash and soldiers. His successor, Emperor Manuel Palaeologus, was crowned on his return from doing military service for the Sultan, with the royal regalia in pawn to the Venetians and the Sultan at the gates of his city. Facing a horrible fate, he tried to forestall it by murmuring the same prayer every morning: 'O Lord Jesus Christ, let it not come about that the great multitude of Christian peoples should hear it said that it was during the days of the Emperor Manuel Palaeologus that the City, with all its holy and venerable monuments of the Faith, was delivered to the Infidel.'[xxxiv] More practically, at the turn of the century, he set off on a three-year tour of western Europe. It was a last-ditch attempt to impress upon the western monarchs that his empire was on the point of falling to the Infidel. Surely they could see that once Constantinople was taken it was only a matter of time before the Turks swarmed their way across into western Europe? They were already in the Balkans so it could not be long.

In late 1400 the glamorously arrayed Emperor Manuel and his white-robed entourage were the talk of London. King Henry IV, himself none too steady on his throne thanks to trouble in Scotland, exerted himself to invite the Emperor to a splendid Christmas lunch at his palace of Eltham, near Greenwich. Manuel seems to have inspired admiration tinged with pity wherever he went. Adam of Usk, a lawyer, mused at 'how grievous it was that this great Christian prince should be driven by the Saracens from the furthest East to these furthest western islands to seek aid against them ... O God, what dost thou now, ancient glory of Rome?'[xxxv] For all that he touched hearts, the Emperor's begging expedition proved futile.

Events were hurtling to their inevitable conclusion. By the early fifteenth century it was time for another great effort to reunite the Churches of East and West to save Christendom from the Infidel. The Emperor John Palaeologus prepared for yet another Church summit by gathering a mighty delegation of seven hundred church-men and intellectuals for use as ammunition against the Latins, and set sail with them for Italy. On departure he lectured them about the importance of keeping up appearances: they were not to 'appear filthy' before their Latin counterparts.

So it was that, on arrival at the papal palace in Ferrara, they acted as proud as ever. The Patriarch refused to kiss the Pope's foot. The Emperor made a fuss about having to approach the throne on horseback in order to avoid the indignity of being seen dismounting. In the end he was carried into the papal palace, his feet never touching the ground. All this was followed by a long, and for the pope, who was paying all the Byzantines' living costs, expensive hiatus while Emperor John waited in vain for the secular rulers of western Christendom to show up.

An outbreak of plague meant the entire affair had to relocate to Florence, where – to the Pope's great relief – the Medicis agreed to foot the bills. In Florence the two teams of churchmen grasped the filioque nettle and managed to agree that the Holy Spirit did indeed proceed from the Father *and* the Son in as much as it proceeded from the Father *through* the Son. First round to the Latins, and soon after, it was over. By July 1438 the Byzantines were too homesick, offended and befuddled by the Latins' ceaseless brainy nit-picking over the

Faith – 'What *about* Aristotle? Aristotle – a fig for your Aristotle!'[xxxvi] – to think about anything but how they were going to afford to get home. Most signed the decree of union on the Latins' terms.

If the Council of Florence represented an abominable disaster for many of the monks back home in Byzantium, it was a chance for scholars on both sides of the divide to meet and appreciate each other. A second response to Byzantium's dramatic decline after 1261 had been given by the empire's intellectual élite, the best of whom attended the council. This response consisted of a reawakened interest in Ancient Greece and a fresh regard for its ancient secular values, to the detriment of Byzantine Christianity. These intellectuals thought that if the universal Christian empire of Byzantium was doomed that was perhaps because it had overreached itself in its lofty Christian mission. It was time to salvage the best of the empire – Ancient Greek secular values, Greek learning and a more exclusive sense of Hellenism – and leave the rest. By the fourteenth century the Byzantine Emperor was styling himself 'Emperor of the Hellenes' and for its last few decades Constantinople was a self-consciously Hellenic city. Here, with hindsight, were the more dangerous seeds of what would become not so much the Byzantine nationalism of the diehard imperialists but the Greek nationalism of today, which rejoices in having produced the glory that was Ancient Greece as well as Byzantium.

The Florentines of 1438 saw nothing of the sort. They were just beginning to appreciate what they regarded as Byzantium's greatest service to the West: its careful preservation of Ancient Greek texts throughout the turmoil of the West's early Middle Ages. While the churchmen wrangled about prepositions and the like, one of the greatest Byzantine intellectuals and new-style 'Hellenes', Gemisthus Plethon, held forth to spellbound Latins about Plato. The intellectual power of Plethon and his sort was what impressed the Latins at the Council of Florence, not the desperately pretentious grandeur of the Emperor or his churchmen.

Most of the Byzantine clergy who accompanied their emperor to Florence had been carefully selected for their biddability so suffered few pangs of conscience about signing the decree of Church union. There was one, however, who did attend, but boldly asserted the Byzantine Church's right to disagree with an emperor by refusing his signature on the decree. He was Metropolitan Mark Eugenicus of Ephesus. On being told that this prelate had not signed up, the prescient Pope replied, 'Well, that means we have achieved nothing,'[xxxvii] and reports of the manner in which the Byzantine delegates had been received back home in Constantinople only confirmed his feeling. 'As the metropolitans [bishops of the Byzantine Church] disembarked from the ships the citizens greeted them as was customary "What of your business? What of the Council? Did we prevail?" And they answered: "We have sold our faith; we have exchanged our true piety for impiety . . ."'[xxxviii]

The monk-led mob rampaged through Constantinople again and the gulf between 'Unionists' and 'Anti-Unionists' widened still further. Most of the Byzantine bishops hurriedly withdrew their support for Church reunion. Mark of Ephesus resigned his see and was later canonized as a martyr of the Byzantine Church. Neither the Russians nor the Serbs were having any union, and the Russian delegate to the council, Metropolitan Isidore of Kiev, was hounded out of his country.

Isidore defected to the Catholic Church and became a cardinal. It was only as the Pope's ambassador that he dared set foot in the capital of the East again, a year before Constantinople finally fell, for a last attempt to bully the Byzantines into doing Rome's will. By this time, an almost contemporary chronicler reports, the Church at least was united in its opposition to reunion with Rome, and the Emperor was only pretending to agree to it. A horde of hard-line Byzantine nuns called in on their Anti-Unionist leader, a former well-known intellectual now renamed Father Gennadius, who had locked himself away in one of the city's monasteries to bemoan the Emperor's insistence on Church reunion. They asked him what was to be done. Refusing to emerge from his cell, Gennadius nailed his answer to the door: 'O miserable Greeks, why have you strayed, removed yourselves from the hope of God? By putting your trust in the strength of the

Franks you have lost your religion, as well as the city, within which
it is about to be destroyed . . .'ᴸᴸᴸᴸ

Gennadius was right about the foolhardiness of putting any trust
in the Franks, who never did mount an effective Crusade to save
Constantinople. What is more, if they had and managed to halt the
Ottoman advance, they would surely have enforced Church reunion
and papal supremacy, and Orthodoxy would have died. But he was
wrong about the impending destruction of the Byzantine faith.
Eastern Orthodoxy would be saved, thanks to the respect and tolerance Muslims have always had for any faith that preaches, as theirs
does, that there is only one God.

By choosing the lesser of two evils, Islamic over Roman Catholic
rule, Orthodox churchmen could come to view the fall of Constantinople as a bitter little victory for the True Faith. For its holiest
people, men like Gennadius and Mark Eugenicus of Ephesus, there
had never been any question of compromising the central premise on
which the empire had been built and preserved for so long. Their
position had received a huge boost in the thirteenth and fourteenth
centuries from the monasteries', and in particular Mount Athos',
response to the decline of the empire. The third of the three responses
to the threat, Hesychasm, from the Greek word *hesychia* meaning
inner silence, was a form of spiritual practice that flourished on the
Holy Mountain in the steamily doom-laden atmosphere of Late
Byzantium and developed into a political outlook.

Since the eleventh century the monks of Mount Athos had been
devoting themselves to becoming saints, according to the prescriptions of St Symeon, known as the New Theologian, and of St John
Climacus of the Byzantine monastery on Mount Sinai. St Symeon
enjoined true believers to struggle to experience the energies of God
by seeing the Light, 'the splendour and glory of everlasting happiness,
the Light that transforms into light those whom it illumines, the
Light that is uncreated and unseen, without beginning and without
matter, but is the quality of grace by which God makes himself
known'.ˣˡ St John Climacus, no doubt influenced by the neighbouring

Muslims and their practices, explained how to go about seeing that Light by a form of meditation with breathing exercises.

It was an Athos monk who refined this mystic tradition by writing about the right way to pray. The monk, he wrote, should sit down in a corner of his cell and bend forward until his forehead almost touched his navel, in search of his heart from whence his prayers should flow, rather than from his mind. This means of knowing and participating in God by seeing the same light that Christ's apostles saw at Christ's Transfiguration on Mount Tabor near Jerusalem, became the hallmark of Hesychasm. The Prayer of the Heart, or the Jesus Prayer, the constant repetition of the words 'Lord, Son of God, have mercy upon us', in time to regular breathing to a point at which the words became as natural as breathing and so internalized, was another identifying mark of the true Hesychast. A thirteenth century Italian monk of the Holy Mountain has left the following clear instructions and, more importantly, a helpful rationale:

> You know that we breathe our breath in and out only because of our heart . . . so, as I have said, sit down, recollect your mind, draw it – I am speaking of your mind – in your nostrils; that is the path the breath takes to reach the heart. Drive it, force it to go down to your heart with the air you are breathing in. When it is there, you will see the joy that follows: you will have nothing to regret. As a man who has been away from home for a long time cannot restrain his joy at seeing his wife and children again, so the spirit overflows with joy and unspeakable delights when it is united again to the soul . . .[xli]

Six hundred years later a nineteenth-century Russian monk of the Holy Mountain was clearly experiencing the same thing:

> At present your thoughts of God are in your head. And God Himself is, as it were, outside you, and so your prayer and other spiritual exercises remain exterior. While you are still in your head, thoughts will . . . always be whirling about like snow in winter, or clouds or mosquitoes in summer . . . All our inner

disorder is due to the dislocation of our powers, the mind and heart each going their own way.'[lii]

In mid-1998, Father Symeon, the Holy Mountain's only Peruvian monk, who embraced Orthodoxy after meeting a monk who reminded him that 'God became man so that man might become God', called himself 'a very weak half-Hesychast'. A hermit for the past eleven years, he falteringly describes his solitary quest in the following terms:

This heart can be felt in a very special way when you begin to enter it. You are initiated into realities you weren't aware of before. You find joy, you find comfort . . . You feel it when you feel that you love and are loved. Divine Light appears . . . If God can be defined as something he can be defined as Love and as Joy.[xliii]

By the fourteenth century this spiritually back-to-basics way of practising Eastern Orthodoxy was spearheading Byzantine Church reform and not only Byzantine. It was spreading to the Balkans and Russia. Hesychasts were keen travellers. A fifteenth-century Hesychast named Gregory spent several years on Mount Athos, before becoming abbot of a Serbian monastery in Kosovo. He then moved to Moldavia, and on to Lithuania, Moscow and Constantinople, before being made Metropolitan of Kiev in 1415. Everywhere influential Hesychasts firmly opposed the beleaguered nationalism of the Greeks in their dying empire and stood up for the old cosmopolitan Christian ideal of Byzantium, for the Romaioi.

But their spiritual exercises were controversial. Depending on one's point of view, they were either engaged in the most hopeful, glorious and necessary journey of contemplation and inner cleansing in preparation for deification, or they were self-indulgently contemplating their navels while the New Rome burned. The 'Hellene' intellectual élite of Byzantium ridiculed their passive navel-gazing, but the majority of Byzantines respected this exceptionally ascetic road to the Light and salvation. The controversy blew up into a storm when a brilliantly intellectual layman, Barlaam, exposed some of the daftest excesses Hesychasm had led to, which included monks insisting that their hearts were to be found in their navels. It fell to the eminent churchman and former Athonite monk Gregory Palamas to ride to the Hesychasts' rescue with a massive work entitled *Triads for the Defence of the Holy Hesychasts*, a summary of which was signed by most of the abbots of the Mount Athos monasteries. Such a rare sign of near unanimity emanating from the Holy Mountain made a strong and favourable impression on the Emperor of the day and Palamas was quite intellectual enough to deal with Barlaam's criticisms. By 1430, Palamas and mystical Hesychasm, with its insistence on a higher way of knowing than the mind alone is capable of, had triumphed over Barlaam and his brain-bound methods of reasoning and analysing.

It was the Hesychast spirit that inspired a belated reform of the Church, tightening discipline at the monasteries and curbing their fabulous wealth. But those other-worldly Hesychasts were the men who propagated and reinforced the Late Byzantine perception that Byzantium had sinned too grievously to merit further divine protection. The end of the empire was going to be a fitting, divinely administered punishment.

Would the Byzantines have fought harder for their city without Hesychasm? Without this heavy counterweight to Rome's influence might the schism have been healed? Robert Curzon, an Englishman who travelled to Mount Athos at the beginning of the twentieth century, thought so. Curzon was sure that if Barlaam had prevailed over Palamas and the Hesychasts in 1432, Europe would be a very different place:

> What a difference it would have made to the affairs of Europe if the embassy of Barlaam had succeeded! The Turks would not have been now in possession of Constantinople; and in many points of difference having been mutually conceded by the two great divisions of the Church, perhaps the Reformation never would have taken place.[xliv]

The next few hundred years were to prove not only the Greeks but also the Russians, Ukrainians and Romanians worthy guardians of this mystical treasure of Orthodoxy. Its home was the Holy Mountain where it made an English diplomat who visited Mount Athos in the mid-seventeenth century suspect that its practitioners, the monks, would be carried 'farther in their way to Heaven' than westerners would, armed only with their 'Wisdom of the most profound Philosophers or the Wisest Clerks.'[xlv] In 1782 an Athos monk collected the sayings of eastern and western holy men and the sum of their mystical experience into a work called *The Philokalia* – The Love of the Good – which remains the Hesychasts' main instruction manual. Hesychasm is what the young, well-educated and energetic new recruits to the Holy Mountain have been working at reinvigorating since Athos' low point in 1970, when the number of monks dropped below a thousand.

Today this tradition is enormously respected in the East and winning growing numbers of converts to Eastern Orthodoxy in the West.[xlvi] Hesychasm presumably contributed hugely to making Thessaloniki's 'Treasure of Mount Athos' exhibition in 1997 – the first showing of some of the monasteries' most precious icons and artefacts – the most popular exhibition in Europe in 1997. *Hesychia*, that mystical inner stillness, is what westerners are rediscovering, like a part of themselves they never knew they had. With its mystical insistence on that higher way of knowing and relating to God, Hesychasm is one of Orthodoxy's greatest strengths. It acts as a powerful antidote to the infection of Phyletism, religious nationalism.

Twenty-one years after the Hesychasts' triumph, Constantinople fell to the Ottoman Turks. May 29, 1453, was a Tuesday, a day still regarded as ill-fated by many Orthodox, but especially by the Greeks who mark its anniversary. The week preceding the fall of the city had been filled with ghastly omens: a red glow creeping from bottom to top of the Haghia Sophia, the icon of the Mother of God slipping off its stand during a last airing for her intercession, a terrible thunderstorm, an unseasonal fog. At dusk on the eve of the Turks' final assault on the city, its inhabitants found themselves making for the

Haghia Sophia for a last melancholy liturgy in honour of the God who had seen fit to desert his chosen people. At this final hour, in their finest Great Church, the warring 'anti-Unionists' and 'Unionists' buried their hatchets, lit their candles and prayed together, in Greek and Latin. At one thirty the next morning, when the attack began and the church bells tolled the alarm, they fought together to save a single Christendom.

Although thousands of monks took up arms for their empire by manning the battlements, the Byzantines were outnumbered by about two to one in the ensuing hellish mayhem. The most precious miracle-working icon of the Mother of God painted by St Luke was hacked to pieces, and matins at the cathedral was invaded by Turks who massacred the priests at the high altar. Younger nuns threw themselves down wells to escape rape. The last Byzantine Emperor, Constantine XI, fell fighting but his corpse was later identified by the pair of purple buskins embroidered with gold Byzantine eagles on its feet. By early the next morning the Ottomans had taken the Queen of Cities.

'What a city we have given over to plunder and destruction!' wept young Sultan Mehmet II, as he wandered through the ruins of his latest conquest in a pair of sky-blue leather boots, stopping to prevent one of his soldiers hacking at the marble on the Haghia Sophia. The Great Church was to lose most of its shimmering mosaics and acquire the Muslim inscriptions it keeps to this day. The best amends the Sultan could make for all the desecration was to track down old Gennadius, the intellectual and fervently anti-Unionist monk, who was living incognito as a slave in the house of a wealthy Turk, and make him Patriarch. Mehmet allotted him a patriarchate church and granted him not only tax privileges for his clergy but also authority over all the Orthodox Christians in the Ottoman empire.

This might have been some consolation, were it not that Gennadius must have been dazed and beyond feeling at the time. He had lost not just his homeland but a world, a whole universe that had lasted longer than any other empire before or since. Gennadius hardly knew who he was any more: 'I do not call myself a Hellene because I do not believe as the Hellenes believed. I might call myself a

Byzantine because I was born at Byzantium. But I prefer simply to call myself a Christian.'ˣˡᵛⁱⁱ Neither a Greek nationalist nor a Byzantine imperialist, he was a Hesychast, asserting his enduring membership of the only club left worth belonging to: the Church of Christ.

But most Byzantines were Byzantine imperialists at heart who could not distinguish their heavenly faith from their earthly empire. Church and State had always ruled in *symphonia*, the one unthinkable without the other unless you happened to be a hesychast or a Hellene intellectual. Laments composed after the fall of Constantinople were filled with myth-mongering yearning for its return.

> God rings the bells, the earth rings the bells,
> and St Sophia, the Great Church, rings the bells:
> a priest for each bell and a deacon for each priest.
> To the left the Emperor was chanting, to the right the Patriarch,
> and from the volume of the chant the pillars were shaking.
> When they were about to sing the hymn of the cherubim,
> they heard a voice from Heaven and from the mouth of the Archangel:
> 'Stop the cherubic hymn, and let the holy elements bow in mourning.
> You, the priests, take the holy vessels and your candles must be extinguished,
> for it is the will of God that the City fall to the Turks.
> But send a message to the West asking for three ships to come;
> one to take the Cross away, another the Holy Bible,
> the third, the best of them, our Holy Altar,
> lest the dogs seize it from us and defile it.'
> The Virgin was distressed, and the holy icons wept.
> 'Hush, Lady – do not weep so profusely,
> after years and centuries, they will be yours again.'ˣˡᵛⁱⁱⁱ

All the lands of Eastern Orthodoxy mourned a tragedy as earth-quaking as the sack of Jerusalem by the Romans or the end of the world itself. The whole world of the *Romaioi*, their Romania, was lost.

> Romania is dead, Romania is taken:
> If Romania has died it will blossom and bear again.ˣˡⁱᵛ

*

The boat had reached the monastery of St Paul at the far end of the Holy Mountain and turned back. Most of the Serb, Greek and Romanian women were huddled in their coats, snoozing quietly. Rain still spattered the windows.

Restless, I wandered into the captain's cabin. He was watching his radar screen, careful as ever not to stray inside the invisible 500 metre cordon. A snapshot of a bright-eyed Athos monk was stuck prominently but crookedly behind one of his dials. On the wall behind him hung a cheap paper icon. I listened to him snap at a Serbian woman who had dared to ask the whereabouts of the Serbian monastery that there was no such thing, that 'all the monasteries are Greek. And all the monks – even if they are from Russia, Serbia, Romania, Bulgaria, wherever – they are all Greek citizens.'

Yes . . . but emphatically no, I thought.

This latter-day Hellene of a captain was technically right. The treaty of Lausanne in 1923 made the 'self-governing monastic republic of Mount Athos' with all its monasteries an integral part of sovereign Greek territory. All Athos monks do indeed receive Greek citizenship, whatever their original nationality. But he was also wrong because he was missing the universal Christian *raison d'être* of Mount Athos. It struck me that, to avoid sounding like a Late Byzantine Greek nationalist with a haughty mistrust of foreigners, he would need to know how simply *Christian* Patriarch Gennadius had felt back in 1453. To avoid succumbing to that disease of Europe's Eastern Orthodox Churches, religious nationalism, the heresy of Phyletism, he might have to rediscover Mount Athos' Hesychast spiritual tradition.

The wider story of Eastern Orthodoxy in Europe is the story of these two unfamiliar-sounding phenomena – Phyletism and Hesychasm – the one hellish in its practical consequences, the other heavenly in its ideal. The short answer to the question why angels fall, why Eastern Orthodoxy is able to reach for the angelic heights then plunge to hellish depths, is Phyletism. But I was off in search of some longer answers. My excursion into Byzantine history had already furnished me with some, the most important being the shameful part western Christendom had played in the early history of Orthodoxy.

My search would take me through the lands and pasts of those peoples best represented in the 'angelic' population of Mount Athos today – Serb areas of former Yugoslavia, the former Yugoslav Republic of Macedonia and its Greek counterpart, Greece, Romania, Russia and Cyprus. Bulgaria, Belarus, Georgia, Ukraine and Moldavia, which are also majority Orthodox countries, would be bit-players at best because it seemed to me that a closer acquaintance with the others would tell the essential story. Voyaging west as far as Croatia, east as far as Siberia, north as far as the Russian Arctic Circle and south as far as Cyprus, I would be seeking out whatever places and times have proved vital in making Orthodox Europe what it is today.

The boat had reached Ouranopoli. We disembarked. A huddle of Serbian women opened their umbrellas to dash off in the direction of the harbour gift shops. Their country, I thought, is the Eastern Orthodox world's front-line in the war against the West and Islam today. In former Yugoslavia, where fighting has raged for most of this last decade of the twentieth century, I would start, at a recently abandoned Serbian Orthodox monastery in a part of Croatia the Serbs have had to flee.

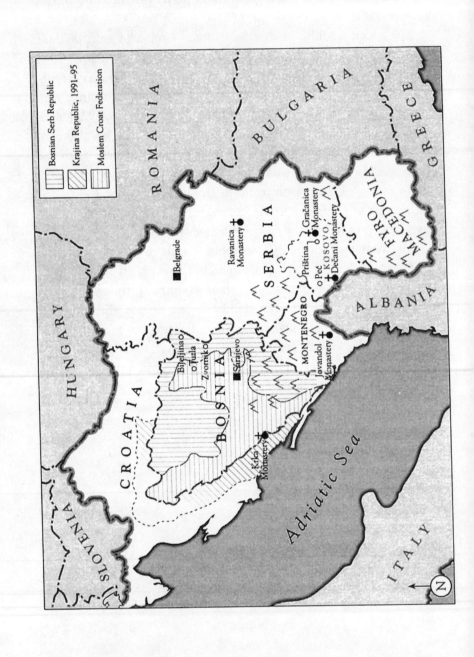

THE SERBS

KRKA MONASTERY
CROATIA

A slow revelation. First the iron cross on the bell-tower, then a cluster of red roofs, last the white buildings and the river winding away out of the narrow valley between high, greenish hills. From a series of hairpin bends descending into the valley, Krka monastery looked as old and emblematic as a scene from a medieval calendar. Ideal, I thought, until my taxi reached the bottom of the hill and drew up in front of the monastery at the spot where I was to meet a Serb priest.

A sleek cleric wearing a long black soutane and a gold-toothed smile of welcome, Father Ilija was flanked by two grim-looking Serbs whose presence he did not explain. Behind them were three Croat policemen, two on guard duty at the monastery and one to check my passport. While the six men attended to the formalities, I surveyed the padlocked monastery gate with its bullet-pocked no-parking sign, and abandoned all hope of communing with the place at leisure, alone. Instead I was going to have to concentrate on walking a tightrope middle course between these Serbs and Croats, tailoring everything I said to suit their still raw sensibilities. They were too present, in both senses of the word, because I was at least as much interested in the distant past here.

For the last thousand years these scrubby green and misty hills of southern Croatia, about fifty miles inland from the brilliantly sunlit Adriatic coast, have been a no-man's or an everyman's land, where the worlds of eastern and western Christianity have overlapped and collided. Lying low here in its river valley for six hundred years, Krka monastery has served not only as tangible proof of the Serbs' long habitation of this predominantly Croat region of the old Yugoslavia but also as the westernmost outpost of Eastern Orthodox Europe. Until 1995 Eastern Christendom in Europe extended back east from this point, for thousands and thousands of miles, all the way to Russia and on across Siberia, as far as the Sea of Japan.

When Yugoslavia began to fall apart at the start of 1990, the Serbs living in these parts, made drunk on vicious anti-Croat propaganda from Belgrade, panicked at the prospect of being reduced to the status of a minority in an independent Croatia. Declaring their own Serbian 'Krajina Republic', they expelled any Croats from it and so lit the fuse for four years of the worst fighting Europe had seen since 1945. The tiny republic lasted until August 1995, when a well-equipped and -trained Croat army wrought a terrible revenge by storming back into the region and kicking the Serbs out. Pushing back the borders of Eastern Orthodoxy, the Catholic Croats brought a millennium of Orthodox Serb habitation here to an abrupt and squalid end. The monks of Krka monastery were among the tens of thousands of Serbs who fled east towards Serbia. The monastery was abandoned.

Small wonder that two years later the three Orthodox Serbs were looking grim and the three Catholic Croat policemen acting pedantically. The Serbs felt ill at ease here on territory reclaimed by the enemy, and the Croat policemen were at pains to show the Serbs how neutrally official they could be.

The detritus left by that last blast of war lay strewn around the monastery courtyard in the shape of a pile of sodden pink mattresses, odd green ammunition boxes, tangles of mud-spattered clothing and empty cans. The seminary's dreary modern buildings and a cloister spattered with bird droppings seemed dismal. With its scanty frescoes the church was barely big enough for the seven of us to shelter inside. Father Ilija handed me a crooked beeswax taper. As I lit it and stuck it in the sand box marked 'LIVING' instead of the one marked 'DEAD', it occurred to me that if the same six men had happened to meet like this two years before they would have felt obliged to butcher each other.

What is it that has been exercising the power of life or violent death over southern Slavs for the best part of the last decade? These people share the same race, language, colour and education. If you take away the manipulations of politicians, only religion – with all its historical, cultural and psychological baggage – divides an

Orthodox Serb from a Catholic Croat, a Muslim Bosnian. Any time-travelling citizen of Late Byzantium who found himself among Serbs in 1990s former Yugoslavia would immediately have recognized his world. It would seem to him that nothing but the scale of operations and the *dramatis personae* had changed in the past four or five centuries. Instead of Orthodox Byzantines fending off the Catholic Pope to the west and Muslim Ottomans to the south, he would find Orthodox Serbs battling Catholic Croats to the west and the Muslims – Bosnians or Kosovar Albanians – to the south. Those Orthodox Serbs would be feeling as fearful and threatened as he felt. Some might even recall his great empire's plight and compare it to their own, but the stark truth that no one had physically threatened Serbia would be hidden from him. He would never hear how the Serbs – equipped with the ex-Yugoslav army's entire stock of weaponry – had themselves initiated the decade's worth of savage warring . . .

The six men were expecting me to say something.

'I hope that Serbs will soon be able to return to this monastery and live peacefully here in Croatia,' I hazarded.

Father Ilija smiled at my courtesy or, rather, a gold tooth glinted in the damp dark. Behind us the Croat policemen, a little the worse for plum brandy, coughing and bored after months of round-the-clock guard duty here, shuffled their feet in irritation and embarrassment. I could almost hear their silent protests that it was not their fault that the Serbs had been chased out of one of their oldest and dearest spiritual homes, that they hadn't started the war by throwing up barricades and declaring a Krajina Republic, that having grabbed back this part of their country now they just wanted to get on with their lives in a civilized fashion. Victorious, it seemed after all that they could afford to be a little generous.

'Any chance of your lot coming back here soon? This guard duty's getting boring for us, you know,' joked one of the Croat policemen with one of the Serbs.

'Maybe – maybe,' replied the grim-faced Serb.

It is hard to imagine quite when. The two hundred staff and

pupils of Krka's seminary have been relocated to a town in eastern Bosnia. Serbs do not feel welcome in these parts and Father Ilija himself was not assisting any healing process. A couple of months before, he had been shown on Croat television news outside a church in a nearby town, brazenly reminding a forlorn remnant of elderly Serbs that this was and always would be Serb land. His little old Peugeot still bore the dents from the battering it had received at the hands of infuriated Croats. Serbs are in no great hurry to forgive and forget the hammering war wounds they received here in 1995. The tiny town nearest the monastery is still a blasted ruin in which a sad remnant of elderly Serbs eke out a miserable existence against what could serve as scenery for a Second World War movie. They have something to mourn but little to fear. It is the young Serbs who will never dare to return to this land their forefathers defended. That is why Krka monastery, so handsomely endowed in the fourteenth century by the great Serbian Tsar Dušan's 'very merciful and charitable' sister Jelena, is likely to remain padlocked and deserted.

Byzantium was shrinking and dying but Serbia's medieval kingdom was at its glorious zenith in the fourteenth century and its Tsar Dušan the most powerful monarch in Europe. In less than twenty years he had hacked his sprawling empire out of conquered Byzantine lands, until it stretched from Krka monastery in the west to the Danube in the north to mainland Greece in the south. It took in Albania, most of Macedonia, including Mount Athos, and a part of Bulgaria. Vaultingly ambitious enough to assume the Byzantine Roman title of Caesar, which translates as 'tsar' in the Slav languages, Dušan had committed the Phyletist sin of setting up an independent patriarchate in 1346 and been punished with excommunication by the Patriarch of Constantinople. But, nothing daunted, he was eyeing those tatters of ancient imperial Rome on the Bosphorus with a view to conquest and boldly styling himself, 'King of the *Romaioi* and Serbs' and 'Lord of almost the whole Roman Empire'.[i] In Constantinople Tsar Dušan was more feared and hated than the Ottoman Turks.

The bad feeling was not reciprocated. Byzantium was the epitome

of civilization at the time and Tsar Dušan loved and revered everything it represented. Portraits of him gracing the walls of Serbian
monasteries show him bearded, eyes cast piously heavenward in the
approved Byzantine style and arrayed in the bejewelled finery of
Byzantine rulers. Every iota of his court ceremonial was modelled
after the Byzantine version. He strove to emulate Justinian, the great
sixth-century law-maker emperor, by producing a comprehensive legal
codex of his own. He copied Byzantium's double-headed eagle
emblem, signed his chrysobulls in red ink like the emperors, and gave
his court officials Byzantine Greek titles – *sebastokrator, despot* and
logofet.

Life at court had come on by leaps and bounds since his father's
time when a visiting Byzantine diplomat had thanked God for not
making him a Serb because he felt as if he 'had come across insects
adorned with necklaces and bracelets'.[ii] Under Tsar Dušan, Serbia
waxed rich as well as large. His army was full of well-paid mercenaries.
In Kosovo and neighbouring Macedonia richly endowed monasteries
multiplied. The Abbot of the Hilandar, the Serbian monastery on
Mount Athos, was Tsar Dušan's spiritual father as well as his chief
ambassador to Byzantium, helping him further his claim to occupy
the throne of the emperors and wooing Byzantine abbots into the
new Serbian Church with guarantees of safety for their monasteries'
land-holdings. In a chrysobull to one Byzantine monastery, Tsar
Dušan brazenly declared himself the 'successor with God's grace of
the great and holy Greek emperors',[iii] and he added a second element
to his charm offensive against the Byzantine Church by attempting
to present the Hesychasts' doughtiest defender, George Palamas, with
a whole town. Palamas declined the gift. For all his Hesychast
universalism he must have been enough of a Byzantine imperialist to
balk at the fact that Dušan's armies were threatening Constantinople
at the time.

Quite clearly Tsar Dušan did not hate Byzantium. The reason for
his unhelpful hastening of the empire's end must be sought elsewhere.
Probably he coveted the throne of Byzantium because it represented
the proper culmination of his life's work as an empire-builder and,

strictly speaking, there was no reason on earth why he should not dare reach for it. The Byzantine Church could not have viewed him as a blaspheming barbarian usurper because, traditionally, the seal of divine approval lay with whoever sat on the Byzantine throne, whatever his means of getting there. But it should also be remembered that the Byzantine ideal of a universal Christian empire, such as the Hesychasts had striven to maintain, was crumbling. The Fourth Crusaders of 1204 had dealt Byzantium a blow from which it was never to recover. In the embattled late empire, Greek nationalism was a powerful counterweight to the old expansive inclusivity. It seems more than likely that, like his royal Nemanja forebears, Tsar Dušan simply copied that nationalism along with everything else about Byzantium. The Serbian Orthodox Church, meanwhile, was too young to remember Byzantium's inclusive heyday. From 1219, when Dušan's great-great-uncle Sava took advantage of Byzantium's parlous state after the Fourth Crusade by wheedling an independent Serbian Church out of the exiled Patriarch of Constantinople, the Serbian Church was a national Church. St Sava was its first head and he remains Serbia's favourite saint.

The Almighty perhaps balked at the prospect of Dušan becoming his Vice-Regent on Earth because the chronicles have it that in 1355, when Dušan was within sight of the walls of Constantinople, he suddenly died of a fever. He was only forty-eight and his demise marked the start of his empire's rapid disintegration. Only ten years after his death a Russian historian noted that already 'the grandeur of the Serbian empire seemed to belong to a remote past'.[iv] Twenty-four years later, in 1389, its last tatters were ground into the mud and blood of the battle fought against the Ottoman Turks on Kosovo Polje, the Field of Blackbirds.

The Battle of Kosovo's interruption of Serbia's golden greatness has become a cataclysm to rival man's expulsion from the Garden of Eden in the minds of Serbs. Almost seven hundred years have passed but no Serb has forgotten how the great Tsar Dušan dressed like a Byzantine emperor, dined off silver plate and wrote codified laws. Nor has the Serbian Church ever forgotten the marvellous extent of the lands it had under its jurisdiction in that golden epoch. All Serbs remember the ensuing four centuries of Turkish rule as a dark night of ceaseless suffering. It was, they say, one long collective martyrdom.

During this unending Calvary, Krka monastery's fortunes waxed and waned. Today is by no means the first time that 'the shelter for the suffering and the fortification of our holy religion'[v] has stood empty and cold. At the end of the sixteenth century, clashes between Turks and Venetians resulted in another exodus. The chronicles say seven Krka monks were among those who fled, carrying with them 'valuable liturgical books and vessels'.[vi] Twenty years later they were back and resisting conversion to Islam by bribing the Turks with 'several bags full of riches'.[vii] Too much tactical plotting with the Venetians against the Turks cost the Krka monks a couple of plunderings and evictions during the seventeenth century. Three centuries later, during the Second World War, Mussolini's troops invaded. Krka's abbot was taken prisoner-of-war. Croat Ustashe fascists court-martialled him and set him to a month's hard labour. Later, Tito's atheist Communist Yugoslavia decorated the poor man for bravery then left him destitute without a pension. 'I am alone, exhausted and I feel quite sick,' wrote Archimandrite Nikodim from Krka towards the end of his life. 'I care about our monastery more than I do about my own life . . .'[viii]

Perhaps it was with all this miserable history in mind that, in August 1995, the local Serb bishop panicked and decamped to Australia some twenty days before the avenging Croats recovered their land and ransacked this monastery. But two years on Father Ilija saw nothing amiss in the flight of his bishop. Indeed, he presented me with a mud-spattered photograph of the man as a souvenir. He was also only too happy to show me the extent of the damage the Croats had wrought, which turned out to be more dramatic than structural, I noted. As we picked our way down a corridor strewn with clothes, among them a besmirched but still gorgeous priest's stole, sky-blue and threaded with gold, Father Ilija grumbled, 'We had fifteen people here to clean up for ten days in the summer. But, of course, it is not necessary to clean everything because people should see all this, shouldn't they?'

A row of portraits of illustrious former archimandrites had been slashed. One gaudily daubed prelate had had his eyes gouged out. The long bare refectory was strewn with plates, its parquet flooring sodden. Father Ilija tut-tutted over a crumpled picture of the head of the Serbian Orthodox Church, Patriarch Pavle, mumbling that if someone had done the same to a photograph of the Pope there would have been no end of a hullabaloo. I was noticing that even the electric light switches had been looted and the ceiling in the Archimandrite's parlour was leaking rainwater. After an hour or so the priest seemed satisfied with my repeated expressions of pity and disgust, and I had seen enough of that devastation.

Back in the taxi, climbing the hairpin bends out of the valley, I found that the sight of the Archimandrite's parlour was jogging memories of an earlier visit to Krka monastery, back at the start of 1992 – which was probably the high noon of the Serbs' little Krajina Republic. I had arrived there, one frosty February morning, in the hope of discovering what the Archimandrite of the region's most famous monastery thought of a United Nations peace plan that entailed international troops moving into the area and disarming the Serbs.

The monastery was on the Serbs' front line of defence at the time so there were at least as many heavily armed camouflage-clad Serb soldiers as black-robed clerics pacing its cloisters that day. Archimandrite Benedict, a fine figure of a prelate sweeping along a cloister in his long black robe, with twin black veils flying from his stovepipe hat, had graciously ushered me into that now derelict parlour and set my heart jumping with nips of brandy and Turkish coffee. He had proceeded to drop grudging hints that he understood the game was up for the Serbs in this part of Croatia. 'The Serbian Orthodox Church knows what the peace plan consists of. We have privileged information. Behind it is something not good for this area, its return to Croatia,' he told me. 'But the people here will fight for their historic land . . .'

Although he appeared to be contemplating war again, he knew that Serbia, under pressure of international sanctions, was abandoning the Krajina Serbs to whatever fate the UN saw fit to fix up for them. He had also understood that the Serbs were not strong enough to stand alone against the world. In fact, as far back as the beginning of 1991, when trouble had started but all-out war was still just a bad dream for most people, he had been sufficiently in the know to take the extraordinary precaution of loading all the monastery's treasures, including the priceless stole of St Sava and a wealth of medieval manuscripts, onto a juggernaut removal van. The entire haul had been sent under police escort to Serbia for safekeeping.

Archimandrite Benedict had not really wanted to go to war again. Indeed, he had been so frightened of living on the front line 'with the Croats looking down on us in our valley, as if we were in a bowl' that he had got himself transferred from Krka in 1994, a whole year before the Croat counter-attack.

BIJELJINA
BOSNIAN SERB REPUBLIC

By the time the Krajina Serbs were fleeing in terror ahead of the advancing Croats, Archimandrite Benedict was safely resettled a couple of hundred miles north-east, in the Bosnian town of Bijeljina, cosily close to the Serbian border.

Bijeljina was strategically vital to the Serb dream of gathering all Serbs into a Greater Serbia. In the spring of 1992, therefore, it had had to be 'ethnically cleansed' of its mostly Muslim inhabitants. Željko Ražnatović, alias Arkan, an indicted war criminal who commanded a freelancing army of paramilitary thugs when there was any ethnic cleansing to be done, set about the grisly task with his bands of 'Tigers', explaining that he was 'fighting for our faith, the Serbian

Orthodox Church'. The television footage of the results of Arkan's springtime rampage though Bijeljina gave Bosnia's Muslim President Alija Izetbegović, a hundred or so miles away in Sarajevo, a first ghastly foretaste of what lay in store for his fellow Bosnian Muslims: 'It was unbelievable almost. The civilians being killed, pictures showed dead bodies of the women in the streets. I thought it was a photomontage, I couldn't believe my eyes. I couldn't believe it was possible,'[ix] he said. War raged for three years, until the Dayton Peace Accord of 1995 made good Arkan's victory by placing Bijeljina within the Bosnian Serb Republic. Ex-Archimandrite Benedict of Krka had moved into a plain one-storey house in the town's freshly renamed Serbian Army Street. It had been forcibly vacated by a Bosnian Muslim woman and her daughter.

Somewhat diminished, of course, without his parlour and his black veils, I found him still stout, and fresh from a morning's religious instruction at one of the town's secondary schools. He was chuffed that the Orthodox Church in the Bosnian Serb Republic had stolen a march on its counterpart in Serbia by introducing compulsory religious education until the age of fifteen. Owing to a natural dearth of people qualified to teach the subject, after almost half a century of official atheism, Archimandrite Benedict was in great demand in Bijeljina in the autumn of 1997.

His front room was gloomy, the bright morning sunshine shut out of it by thick net curtains. Instead it was brimming with icons, doilies and pictures of the exiled Serbian royal family. He bustled about, fussing with coasters and teaspoons, producing coffee, Romanian bilberry juice and brandy, and putting off the distasteful business of reliving his war-time experiences back at Krka.

'When I think of it now I can't imagine how we dared to be there – we were frightened. I was afraid to go to bed. I slept in my clothes. There were times when the Croats seemed to be shelling us but now I don't know if they were deliberately avoiding the monastery or if God was preserving us – all those grenades flew straight over us . . .'

With another tot of brandy he was warming to his theme and divulging that three times while at Krka he had seen fit to call on the services of Arkan's Tigers. 'I'll be honest,' said Archimandrite Benedict, 'we had Arkan's men there for two or three weeks at a time when the situation was really bad and it was the only time I slept well. I'm thankful to him and to God for that, although I have to admit I was afraid of those guys. They only showed themselves at night. God forbid one should ever meet someone like that!' he added, with a nervous giggle.

'I've heard that Arkan* is wanted for war crimes now...' I ventured.

'Oh, I haven't got a clue what else he was doing, I only know he helped us,' was the Archimandrite's swift reply.

Of course, he had no interest whatsoever in the judgements of the UN Hague tribunal. Archimandrite Benedict supported the most wanted war criminal of all at the time, the one man brave and holy enough to lead the Bosnian Serbs along their Calvary to independence – Dr Radovan Karadžić. In the eyes of many Bosnian Serbs and a good proportion of the Serbian Church hierarchy, it was Karadžić – not President Milošević in Belgrade – who was cast in the holy mould of a medieval Serb warrior king.

A few weeks before my visit, when a Nato plan to raid Karadžić's Pale stronghold outside Sarajevo by helicopter and pluck him out of his eyrie was first being mooted, *The Times* had quoted one of his supporters as saying that every man, woman and child would stand up to defend him, every helicopter would be shot down and there would be hundreds, nay thousands left dead, because Karadžić was 'a legend and a poet ... he will walk to heaven with steps seven miles long'.* Karadžić understood his image and was making every effort to sound like a warrior saint when he granted a rare interview to an obscure church weekly in the last months of the war in Bosnia. Modestly denying any leading role in the rebirth of the Bosnian Serb nation, he claimed he had just removed the barriers so that 'the people's spirituality started to flow quite naturally, like a river that

* Arkan was assasinated in the lobby of Belgrade's Intercontinental Hotel in January 2000.

can't be stopped by anyone except God'. He cast himself instead in the role of chief defender of 'our tribe and our Church, hoping to God that we used only as much force as was necessary'.[xi] And he credited the Holy Spirit with inspiring his off-the-cuff speeches to gatherings of the faithful, in the same way as the Holy Spirit guided the Apostles at Pentecost. In all his nefarious works, he claimed, he had not made a single important decision without prior consultation with the Church.

So Archimandrite Benedict would not hear a word against Karadžić, whom he believed President Slobodan Milošević viewed as a dangerous rival. To his way of thinking the Americans, thinly disguised as a Nato force, were only intent on arresting Karadžić because they did not want him ousting their man Milošević. And they did not want Milošević ousted because he had been their man all along, smashing up Yugoslavia with his bungling war-mongering, and thereby giving America the perfect excuse to intervene in Bosnia. And why should America want anything to do with Bosnia? Because a foothold in the Balkans took the Americans, the West, another big step along the way to their ultimate goal of world-domination and, by the way, the extermination of Orthodoxy.

Archimandrite Benedict was in no doubt that the Bosnian Serb Republic would one day be grafted on to Serbia proper and he strongly believed that the Krajina and with it Krka monastery, of course, would be Serb land once more. Helping himself to more brandy he mused aloud: 'Everyone blames the Serbs, but we would never be the first to do evil. You have to remember that there are more Muslims and that they have more children, so they're bound to have more victims . . .'

I was imagining him addressing a classroom full of impressionable young Bosnian Serbs, fascinated by the fluent ease with which he could adapt his priestly authority to a persuasive semblance of political authority. He went on: 'And you know how the Muslims fought in Sarajevo, how they were making themselves victims, shouting "Allah!" – what is it? – yes, that's it, "Allah u Akhbar!" and running headlong into the machine-guns . . .'

It was time to go. He saw me to the door, scowling and squinting heavenward at a Nato helicopter circling threateningly low overhead.

At the nearby Café Byzantium with its bright yellow awning I rejoined my trusty travelling companions, Goran and Bogdan, a couple of freelance journalists from Belgrade. Forgetting for a moment that the Bosnian Serbs were striving to erase any traces of Muslim culture in Bijeljina in as thorough a way as Arkan and his cohorts had supervised the ethnic cleansing of the town, I ordered myself a *turkska* instead of a *srpska kafa*. Goran and Bogdan wriggled uncomfortably in their seats. The waiter frowned.

While drinking my coffee I pondered what a Serb newsman, who runs his own successful press agency in Belgrade, had told me of his experience of Krka sometime in the late seventies. He had recalled with passion how, on a walking holiday with his wife, they had unexpectedly discovered Krka, secreted away in its valley. Going down the hill they had approached the seminary and peeped in through one of its windows. Feeling as if they had 'walked straight out of the twentieth century into the sixteenth or seventeenth', they had been transfixed by the sight of rows of simple peasant boys, Serbs from Bosnia and the Krajina, being yelled at and abused by a foul-tempered monk. As head of the seminary, Archimandrite Benedict, I thought, had had a hand in educating an entire generation of churchmen. That made him a man of influence because, as the newsman had gone on to explain, although the Serbian Church could hardly be said to be an organized force, it did maintain a presence in every village in the shape of the parish priest. They had been the only authority left when Tito's Communist order collapsed. He was convinced that the wars in Croatia and Bosnia would not have happened without the Church and that it was partly because of the Church that nothing could be said to be over. 'Just remember that the Orthodox Church loses by every inch of western progress – telephones, roads, the Internet, whatever,' had been his parting words of advice to me.

As he spoke I had remembered the summer the war erupted, 1991. I had marvelled that Yugoslavia, so much more prosperous than

Romania where I was living at the time, should have been the one to explode into war. It was the first inkling I had had that the new gods of consumerism and democracy – the West's cure-alls for post-Communist ills – could cause a violent allergic reaction in Orthodox Europe.

A column of young soldiers marched past the Café Byzantium. A policeman, sitting at the table beside us, was uncomfortably curious about what I was writing so I put away my notebook. The Bosnian Serb Republic was not a relaxing place to be and Bijeljina was a notoriously crime-infested town. But seediness was one thing, eerie emptiness quite another. The Café Byzantium should have been full that bright, warm lunchtime. The absence of the town's Muslims was painfully obvious. It was as if the place were missing a limb.

Serbia's status as an international pariah was not bringing out the best in its people. Goran, who speaks excellent English and loves backpacking in India, began to tell me that he – just like Archimandrite Benedict – was convinced that America had arrived in the Balkans disguised as Nato in a bid for world-domination. What non-religious Serbs derisively term a *novo pecheni* – a born-again but, literally, newly baked Christian – Goran was one of a breed of post-Communist Belgrade intellectuals that had begun to take an interest in Orthodoxy. He had visited the Serbian monastery of Hilandar on Mount Athos. He had also worked out his own quasi-religious theory about the meaning of Serbia's wars and was confident he had hit on the nub of the matter: 'In places where you have atrocities, places where people stoop very low in the moral sense,' he began slowly, giving me plenty of time to take out my notebook again and write down his every word, 'you also have people who rise very high, unlike in the West where differences are not so great thanks to the legacy of the French Revolution and democratic regimes. In Orthodox countries you have much wider differences between the highest and the lowest, and these are exaggerated even more in time of war. So, I would expect that if Serbia has war criminals and obviously she has, then she has got some real saints as well.'

'But, Goran,' I remonstrated, 'that's a very high price to pay!

How can it be worth tolerating war criminals with the blood of thousands of non-Orthodox on their hands on the off-chance of hatching a few Orthodox saints?'

'Because you can't attain sainthood without this pitch of suffering. The height you can rise to depends on how deeply you can suffer.'

My throat constricted in panic suddenly at the unbridgeable gulf that yawned between us. I was remembering the eerily similar words of the Serbian Patriarch Gavriil, who had died in 1950: '... the entire ascent of the Serbian people in history was won only and exclusively by the sword, in a sea of spilled blood and countless victims, which means that without all this there is no victory, as there is no resurrection without death.'[xii]

Goran drained the dregs of his coffee and grumbled, 'We need someone like a patriarch – like a saint – to get us out of all this shit!'

I had planned to voyage around Orthodox Europe on my own but decided against it on the grounds of safety. Now I was glad that I had opted for company. Goran and his friend Bogdan, who was driving us from place to place in his stately milk chocolate brown 1970s Citroën, were proving invaluable. If Goran's insights about what we were seeing and hearing were useful, Bogdan, a devout Orthodox Christian, was well enough 'in' with his country's churchmen to smooth our path in all directions. In the years I had spent as a foreign correspondent trying to penetrate Romanian, former Yugoslav and Russian politics, I had learnt that such personal contacts are to be prized above rubies. Those countries' style of politicking, often pejoratively branded 'Byzantine', is characterized by an exasperating lack of transparency in the higher echelons of power and the unnerving sensation that all vital decisions are made over a few plum brandies, in a Russian sauna, or on a Greek yacht. On the one hand such informality is irritatingly conducive to paranoia and conspiracy-mongering, but on the other, I had found that the right personal contact could sometimes result in semi-miraculous revelations of the sort a journalist working in the West could scarcely dream of. I was wondering if this lack of what we might call 'responsible transparency' could be traced all the way back to that invisible network of close and important relationships that Byzantine 'spiritual fathers' used to enjoy with their 'spiritual children' . . .

We paid for our coffee and got up to leave because we had an appointment to keep. Across the road a cinema poster advertising an American erotic movie bizarrely titled *A Sense of Sin* caught Goran's eye and restored his good humour. The three of us wandered off down a back street in search of Bishop Vasilije Kačavenda of Tuzla and Zvornik, curious to know why he was not in either of those two towns and instead residing here in Bijeljina.

Bishop Vasilije formed the centrepiece of another emblematically medieval tableau. He was standing in the middle of the street in his long black cassock, surrounded by cement-spattered builders and pointing a finger up at the neo-classical façade of a brand new monastery in the making. His heavy, bearded face was deeply lined and stern, in the style of some of the more frightening depictions of Christ the Pantocrator in the frescoes that adorn the central domes of some Orthodox churches. Behind him I spotted the foundations of a new church, laid in the traditional form of a Greek cross with a short nave. Just to the left stood his brand new palace, with its twin flights of white marble steps leading up to the front door and a porch supported by a couple of fancy Ionic columns. 'I'm not feeling too well – just getting over the flu. You're lucky to find me at home,' he told us.

As we settled down to talk in his comfortable parlour with its twin glass-fronted wardrobes crammed full of gorgeous vestments, I replied that, indeed, I knew I was lucky to find him here in Bijeljina, but also surprised. Before long he was scowling and complaining that I seemed awfully interested in politics for someone writing a book about Orthodoxy. Was I a journalist or a spy? It transpired that he had not set foot in his diocesan capital of Tuzla since the start of the war in Bosnia. Some sixty miles away, inside Bosnia's Muslim-Croat Federation now, the town is lost to what Serbs call *Srpstvo* – Serbdom. He did his best to explain why it was so impossible for him even to show his face in Tuzla that he had had to build himself a palace here in Bijeljina.

'There is a problem with the government there. They say I'm a war criminal.'

'Oh?'

'I'm accused of stealing the treasures of the Serbian Church and people during the war, and of taking the Serb side.'

I later learnt that Bishop Vasilije, although not on the Hague tribunal's wanted list, had been branded a wolf in shepherd's clothing, a prelate so up to his neck in preaching hatred from the pulpit, on the television and radio, and at Serb religious cum political rallies in the months before the war in Bosnia, that even the few Serbs left in Tuzla had decided they never wanted to see him again. When he expressed a wish to spend Easter 1997 in Tuzla, the town authorities fired off a letter to the top international peace envoy warning that they could not accept responsibility for his safety if he came.

A few days earlier I had spoken to a man from Tuzla who had told me that 'Bishop Kačavenda was probably one of the pillars of whatever it was that the Serbs did around here. We have a good Serb priest now in Tuzla, one who is not burdened with the historical past, but Kačavenda is very different.'

He described for me how churchmen like Bishop Vasilije were devilishly skilled at disseminating their messages of hate and fear, without directly incriminating themselves. 'They don't have to use very direct language. But people can read between their lines and everyone here knows exactly what they mean. They know how to stoke up emotions.' He was at least as sure as the Belgrade newsman had been, that 'without the Church we might have had a war here but never the bloody one we had'.

As soon as I asked the Bishop if he thought the war was ended, I saw precisely what that man in Tuzla had meant by churchmen skilled in speaking indirectly while making their meaning quite plain. 'Whether the war is or is not definitely ended,' he began carefully, sitting forward again in his chair, his eyes boring into mine in the charismatic manner in which Rasputin's eyes were said to have bored into those of the susceptible noblewomen of the last Imperial Russian court, 'doesn't depend on the people from here, but on those who started the war. I'm no good at politics but not one of these people here wanted war.'

'You mean America started the war?'

He sat back again and shrugged, as if to say, 'Isn't it obvious? Need I say more?'

I sensed I would do well to keep my cool and ask whatever questions I liked. My first question was, how many Muslim mosques were there in Bijeljina before the war and how many now remained? He fielded those adroitly enough with straight answers and a claim that his protest about the razing of the first four mosques had secured the safety of the fifth. 'You're lucky, I just happen to be in a good mood today,' he observed testily.

'Your Grace, can you tell me why one of your clergymen, Archimandrite Benedict, is living in the house of an evicted Muslim woman?'

His Pantocrator face suddenly clouded over with thunderous anger. 'You English, especially you English!' and he stabbed the air above the doily-draped coffee-table between us with his finger. 'You shouldn't be presuming to teach us about morality and democracy. You'll be paying dearly for it. We're not afraid of Islam. The Bosnian Muslims are only Serbs who converted to Islam, but there are other nations, of different colours. What will happen to the English nation?'

The English, he was implying, would wake up too late to find with horror that their land had been overrun by Asian Muslims and they would have only themselves to blame for not having embarked a little sooner on their own orgy of ethnic cleansing. His anger subsided into some gripes against the Catholic Church, and I made ready to leave. But he was having none of it and embarked on a heavy-handed attempt to win my soul for 'sweet Orthodoxy', as he called it. 'Get to know our Orthodoxy,' he crooned at me, 'go to a little convent where you have candlelight in the church and try to pray to God. There's a special kind of warmth there. The doors are open to everyone who behaves decently. Our nuns are simple and good. They do not paint their nails or pluck their eyebrows . . .'

'That reminds me,' I said, interrupting his lullaby after the storm. 'Why are there so many more nuns than monks in the Serbian Church?'

'Serbs are a rather rough people,' he said, suddenly back in roguish mode. 'It's hard for them to do without women. Maybe in the West you have more monks . . .?'

I couldn't help laughing. This sly impugning of western man's virility was the cleverest thing he had said. Goran and Bogdan enjoyed the joke too. Somehow we moved on from there to Anglican women priests, whom he described as a 'very disgusting phenomenon' and for the second time I tried to make my adieux. For the second time he denied me my exit.

'I think I have tickled your soul, haven't I? If the eyes are the mirror of the soul, I think I have tickled yours a little, no?' he murmured softly, gentle as a lover.

I could feel myself blushing. 'Well, you may have tickled my soul, of course, but there's a problem, you see . . .'

'A problem?' He leant forward in his armchair solicitously.

I confessed that while I wholeheartedly believed in God, I found it hard to believe in the divinity of Christ. Immediately the storm blew up again. His eyes were twin points of furious will, boring into my mirrors, making for my soul. Stern as a patriarch, he warned me against the cardinal sin of pride and talked about the Holy Trinity, on and on, until he could see nothing for it but to ram the point home by punching the air with the three-fingered salute used by Serb royalist *Chetniks* in the Second World War and by Serb fighters in the 1990s. '*Three* persons in *one* God!' he roared.

I retaliated with my own sign for '*One* God' – a single thumb in the air.

He seemed to realize that this kind of rhythm was bringing him nowhere near his goal and abruptly switched back to his softly stroking style. 'I can see in your eyes you're a contemplative type, so I don't believe you think you have your own, personal God. You have to be able to explain what you believe, you know.'

This was strange because if Orthodoxy has one inestimably huge advantage over Catholicism or Protestantism, it is that it has never set much store by explaining or intellectualizing its Christianity.

Bishop Vasilije was still furious. 'I suppose you don't believe in the Last Judgement either! Well, let me tell you something, there are angels and there are *fallen* angels! . . .'

I stood up to leave. The Bishop did, too, at last, and walked us across the marble-paved hallway to the door where he squeezed my hand in his.

Sarajevo
Muslim-Croat Federation, Bosnia

Sweet Orthodoxy, sweet Orthodoxy . . .

Bogdan and Goran had had to go home to Belgrade. I was alone, journeying south by bus down the beautiful winding river Drina, through small ruined towns pacified by Nato tanks. Headed for the heart of the old Bosnia, I was hoping to find 'sweet Orthodoxy'.

I chanced upon it one rainy Sunday morning at the little low Orthodox church in the oldest part of Sarajevo, where the streets are narrow and the buildings low and higgledy-piggledy Ottoman Turkish, rather than pompously central European and built after Austria annexed Bosnia in 1908. This picturesque old part of town was badly war-damaged but had come alive again. On that rainy Sunday it was thronging with German and French Nato soldiers at leisure. Cars with the number-plates of foreign humanitarian aid and political organizations hogged the narrow roads. The marketplace, scene of one of the worst war-time atrocities, was vivid with flower-sellers and their outrageously colourful blooms. Filled with foreigners, the cafés were as busy as they had been back in March 1992, when I first arrived here with a pack of other journalists to witness Bosnia's horrifying descent into war.

One hot Sunday afternoon that spring a wedding took place at this very church. At its doors someone opened fire and someone returned fire. The Serb father of the groom was killed and an Orthodox priest wounded. The Serbs said the incident was 'a great injustice aimed at the Serbian people'.[xiii] The Muslims said the Serbs were asking for trouble, brandishing their national banners in the old Muslim part of town. A provocation or a nervy bungling trigger-happiness, there it was – the spark that ignited the following three years' of carnage. The incident had all the queasy inevitability of the assassination of the Austrian Grand Duke Franz Ferdinand and his wife in Sarajevo, in June 1914.

You have to go down a steep step or two when you enter the little sixteenth-century church because the Ottomans allowed it to be built only on condition that it was hidden behind a stone wall and equipped with a bell-tower that did not rival the height of their soaring minarets. Cosy was the word for its interior, low-ceilinged, but freshly repainted and well lit with its dark wood furniture gleaming and polished, and bright icons. The congregation, scanty and very elderly, could not sing together or in tune, but the church was a very pleasant place to be and the priest, swinging his censer in a cloud of perfumed smoke, had a kind face.

He was a small man who, once out of his vestments, looked oddly like a healthily aged Lenin. Bright eyes, an alert posture and a sharp beard lent him an air of excited energy. Although already retired by the time war broke out Father Krstan was one of only two Serbian churchmen who dared to stay in Sarajevo. Under the hellish assault of his fellow Serbs, settled up above in the hills with their guns and their brain-inflaming brandy, he braved the suspicion and resentment of the city's Muslims and Croats. Trotting back and forth along the treacherous 'Sniper Alley' he conducted services in both Sarajevo's main Orthodox churches.

'It was hard. In those days people used to ask me why I didn't leave the town and go and tell the truth to the world about what was happening here. But I'm just a priest, here to serve God and the Serbs who remained here.'

The old man was no Holy Joe or Serb hero-martyr. He confessed that one good reason for not escaping from Sarajevo to nearby Pale with most of the city's Serbs was his fear of being homeless again. He had spent five years as a refugee after the Second World War. During that war he had served as a young priest in Tito's Partisan Army and worn a Partisan uniform with the bizarre symbol of a cross superimposed on the red star. The nationalist tendencies of the Serbian Orthodox Church had not suited him then and those tendencies, so much in the ascendant again since Tito's death in 1980, did not suit him now, but they had not succeeded in puncturing his Yugoslav patriotism.

'These days many Orthodox churchmen speak very critically of Tito's Yugoslavia but no one has mentioned how many churches were built during the socialist period and,' he added bitterly, 'no one is saying exactly how many churches and mosques have been destroyed in this war.'

I didn't want to contradict him by pointing out that Tito kept the Orthodox Church on a very tight leash, starving it of funds and confiscating most of its property, presumably in a bid to break the mainspring of the spirit of Serbian nationalism. Of all Europe's Orthodox Churches, the Serbian was the most enfeebled by the time Tito died in 1980. I didn't want to put it to him that Tito's treatment of the Church might have been partially responsible for that institution's willingness to co-operate with Slobodan Milošević when he seemed to find a use for it in the late 1980s, and for its present dominant shade of nationalism.

Father Krstan seemed refreshingly sane and involved with the present and short-term future in a way that so many Serbian churchmen were not. He riffled though a copy of that day's newspaper, delightedly pointing out Sarajevo's new climate of hope and optimism as evinced by a good few pages of job advertisements. He could also list the donors to the fund for rebuilding the church roof: Lawrence Eagleburger, the Bavarian Church, the German government, an Italian Catholic charity . . . What an extraordinary line-up and not one of them a brother Orthodox donor!

'Aren't you surprised that it is Catholics and Americans who are donating to your church?' I could not resist asking him, because as far as I had been made aware these were Orthodoxy's archest enemies. It was then that Father Kristan began to speak in a way that set him quite apart from the likes of Bishop Vasilije and reassured me that indeed Orthodoxy could be sweet.

'No, not really. You see, I don't confuse the politics of Nazi Germany with now. In this war Germany took in three hundred thousand refugees and has been feeding them for five years. All our traditional allies did not do as much. As far as America and Nato go, we may grouse and try and find scapegoats, but at some point we have to say thank you because they have stopped the war here. They may not have stopped the economic or political or verbal war but at least they've stopped the killing.'

'Father why is it that you are the only Serb churchman I've met who sees things this way?' I wanted to say, but knew the question would embarrass him. It was enough that I had found one like him. There were not likely to be many more where I was heading next.

Goran and Bogdan would be rejoining me for a foray into Serbia proper and its southern province of Kosovo. I was beginning to suspect that Orthodoxy, and its peculiar apprehension of the circular passage of time, had had a vital part to play in casting the collective Serb psyche back to 1389, when Tsar Dušan's powerful empire met its end at the battle of Kosovo.

RAVANICA MONASTERY
SERBIA

Ravanica, at that time of night, was a little black monastery set in a black valley, among black trees. The nuns there were unpleasantly surprised by an evening visitation from an Englishwoman in the company of two male Serbs from the capital. It was mid-week and the tourist season was over. Bright days were giving way to chilly nights and the twenty-five members of the community were about to perform their evening devotions, before having supper and retiring to bed.

'God help us!' was our traditional and fervent greeting.

'God help you!' came the muttered traditional reply from a black figure framed in a dimly lit doorway.

But a homely nun, almost as wide as she was tall in her black dress, home-knitted black waistcoat and black headscarf, showed us into a visitors' parlour illuminated by an ugly strip-light and furnished with a large framed montage of all Serbia's kings in chronological order until the Second World War. She then left, to return bearing a tin tray loaded with the customary cups of Turkish coffee, glasses of water, a bowl of apricot preserve and three teaspoons. Setting it down on the table, she disappeared again.

We waited, and waited. Goran was bored and Bogdan weary with driving all day through some of Serbia's least inspiring countryside. He drummed his fingers on the table and murmured impatiently, 'Oh, Serbia, dear mother – I'll always call you that!' It was the rousing first line of a Serbian First World War battle-hymn, he explained, before jumping to his feet and going in search of the Abbess of Ravanica.

Our purpose here was not quite innocent. We had not come to imbibe the atmosphere of the candle-lit church, as recommended by Bishop Vasilije in Bijeljina, but rather in the high hope of glimpsing Serbia's holiest relics. Well aware that Sunday, not Thursday, was the day for opening up the coffin containing the fourteenth-century mummified remains of Prince Lazar, we were praying that the Abbess would make an exception.

Prince Lazar is a crucial piece in the jigsaw of the Serbian national psyche, but not so much because of anything he achieved in his lifetime. Although he founded this monastery, gave the monks of Mount Athos a precious camel-hair scrap of the Virgin's girdle and mended a badly broken fence with the Patriarch in Constantinople by promising him that Serbia would not try to invade Byzantium again, Lazar was nothing like as gloriously effective a ruler as Tsar Dušan. He is only important because the myths about him after his death were what turned the Serbs' crushing defeat by the Ottomans at the Battle of Kosovo in 1389 into a glorious spiritual victory. Prince Lazar is the key to understanding the Serbs' deep conviction that, however many wars they initiate, they remain a nation of victims and martyrs.

On the eve of the great battle Prince Lazar is supposed to have received a message from an angel disguised as an eagle, which swooped down from Heaven with a speaking book in its claws. The book's message, as handed down the centuries via the Church-compiled chronicles, but transmitted here in the words of a famous nineteenth-century Serbian nationalist, was as follows:

> Lazar, glorious emperor,
> Which is the empire of your choice?
> Is it the empire of heaven?
> Is it the empire of the earth?
> If it is the empire of the earth,
> saddle horses and tighten girth-straps,
> and, fighting men, buckle on swords,
> attack the Turks,
> and all the Turkish army shall die.
> But if the empire of Heaven
> weave a church on Kosovo,
> build its foundation not with marble stones,
> build it with pure silk and with crimson cloth,
> take the sacrament, marshal the men,
> they all shall die,
> and you shall die among them as they die.[xiv]

Just as Jesus Christ chose a humiliating death on the cross to win eternal life for man, so Prince Lazar chose defeat at the hands of the Turks to win a sort of eternal Most Chosen Nation status for his people. Thereafter, through centuries of wars and humiliations, 'Heavenly Serbia' could perceive itself as living with the consequences of Prince Lazar's agonizing decision. Betrayal, suffering and death were to be the Serbs' lot on Earth, but also righteousness and resurrection. The country's best-loved modern theologian, and spiritual father to four of its most politically active bishops until his death in 1979, reaffirmed the country's Christ-like self-image: 'Our national history is an eloquent proof of Christ's resurrection and power,'[xv] wrote Archimandrite Justin Popović, noting elsewhere that Serbs 'have in all fateful moments of their history always preferred the heavenly to the earthly, the immortal to the mortal, the eternal to the transitory'.[xvi]

The old legends say that on the night before the fated Kosovo defeat Prince Lazar gathered twelve bishops and the Serbian Patriarch for a last holy communion in a tent church. A Last Supper with his knights, including one who would betray him to the Turks, completed his identification with Jesus Christ, and the following morning he spurred his men to their doom with a stirring speech, about how 'sufferings give birth to glory and toils lead to repose'.

Detailed reports of the battle of Kosovo, one of the Ottoman Turks' deepest stabs at the quaking heart of Europe, took time to reach the West. A Russian monk was the first with the story, but he failed to discover where the cataclysm had taken place. Thereafter most reports led with the news that the Ottoman Sultan had died in the battle, and barely mentioned Prince Lazar. Six centuries later it is still not clear whether he fell on the battlefield or was captured and beheaded by the Turks. Nor do we know whether he was officially canonized or not. In Serbia at the time, the lines between saint and ruler, State and Church, were as blurred as they were in Byzantium. Almost every ruler of the Nemanja dynasty, the illustrious and 'holy root' from which Tsar Dušan among others had sprung, was proclaimed a saint.

Within a couple of years of Prince Lazar's death, the Serbian Patriarch, Danilo III, was writing the first 'Narration about Prince Lazar', complete with its pious conceit about forfeiting an earthly kingdom for a heavenly one. In 1391, Lazar's widow Milica brought her husband's bones home to rest here at Ravanica, the monastery he had founded. During more than three hundred years of Ottoman rule a 15 June 'Service to Holy Prince Lazar' was held annually in Serbian Orthodox churches. It referred to Turks as the 'infernal dragon', 'godless people' or 'children of beast and dragon', but the Prince Lazar cult was otherwise wisely muted. Tsar Ivan the Terrible of Russia honoured Lazar more publicly than the Serbs dared to under their

Ottoman overlords. He had Prince Lazar's picture painted on a wall of the Kremlin church of the Holy Archangels in the mid-sixteenth century.

In the late seventeenth century the Serbs' Great Migration north out of Kosovo, their forced abandonment of what they had come to think of as their ancient southern heartland, was what assured the Prince Lazar myth a new lease of life. Some 40,000 Serb families fled the Turk by migrating to what is now Hungary in 1690. There they threw themselves on the mercy of the Austrian Emperor. The monks of Ravanica gathered up the treasured remains of their founder and joined the flood of refugees, led by Patriarch Arsenije III. One of them recalled how they journeyed north 'for forty days and arrived in a place beyond Buda called Saint Andrew's. The Patriarch settled there. We too, the residents of Ravanica, built houses in that place and erected a church, which we made of wood, near the bank of the Danube and laid therein the relics of Saint Lazar.'[xvii]

Seven years later those monks returned to what is now northern Serbia and found a tumbledown monastery in which to lay Prince Lazar's coffin. There his cult flourished, probably in direct proportion to how badly the Serbs were feeling about their Turkish rulers at any given time. Most of the time, for the peasants at least, that was very badly. Lady Mary Wortley Montagu, an English aristocrat touring Serbia in the early eighteenth century, was shocked by the wanton cruelty of the Turkish janizaries, the worst and most visible aspect of Ottoman rule in the Balkans.

> The oppression of the peasants is so great they are forc'd to abandonn their Tillage, all they have being prey to the Janizarys whenever they please to seize upon it. We had a guard of 500 of them, and I was allmost in tears every day to see their insolencies in the poor villages through which we pass'd.[xviii]

By the beginning of the nineteenth century the Serbs were feeling inspired by the doctrines of national liberation that had fuelled the French Revolution and bad enough about the Turks to begin to take active steps to hound them, or at least the janizaries, out of Serbia. It was at this stage that the new Serb nationalists and the clergy, who had devoted the past four centuries under the Ottomans to preserving the memory of the Serbs' medieval empire, made common cause to exploit the old Prince Lazar myths.

The Serbian Church's sermons and chronicles contained the bulk of the subsequent spin-doctoring around Prince Lazar, but one nine-teenth-century oil painting depicts him, Christ-like, at his Last Supper before the battle of Kosovo. A holy shaft of light illumines his face and he is surrounded by the cream of the Serbian nobility, all twelve of them bearded and solemn as Christ's Apostles. In the foreground is another Serb warrior saint waving a dagger and vowing to kill the Sultan. Today, the nuns at Ravanica monastery have a lucrative sideline reproducing the painting in poster form, for sale at monasteries and churches all over Serbia. Imprinted on the Serb mind, the emotive work has doubtless played a little part in turning Prince Lazar into a second Christ, and the Turks and, by extension, all Muslims into hated Christ-killers.

The tale of Lazar's sublime sacrifice continued to inspire some of the modern Serbian kings. King Petar Karadjordjević, took the throne in 1903 and led his people into the First World War and the disastrous retreat before the Germans and Austrians. His son later remembered how he 'got it into his head to die and become a saint, like Lazar at Kosovo. He put on the soldiers' cap, took up a rifle, and joined the men in the trenches.'[xix]

Prince Lazar did not rest long in his north Serbian monastery. During the Second World War a band of Croat fascists opened his coffin and stole his golden rings. Embarrassed by their allies' barbarity, German Nazis helped the Serbs find a new safe-house for him in Belgrade, his home until 1988. The following year, as part of the run-up to the giant state-sponsored celebrations to commemorate the six hundredth anniversary of the battle of Kosovo, he went on tour again as the main attraction in a travelling circus of incense-swinging priests and dazzling ceremonial going from monastery to monastery, all over Serbia and Bosnia, as far as Krka. Little thought was given to the sensitivities of non-Serbs living in the path of the glittering caravan but it drew vast crowds of Serbs, all fired up with the sort of heady old religious nationalism that had inspired the builders of Serbia's medieval empire. Finally, in September 1989, the remains of Lazar were brought home to rest here at Ravanica, in a last glorious blaze of publicity.

'It was magnificent! I'll never forget the day,' enthused the old nun, as we sat side by side in that strip-lit monastery parlour, flicking through a dog-eared album filled with black and white photographs of Ravanica's finest hour.

The pictures looked strangely dated and it was not hard to see why. That had been a grand state occasion being milked for all its political worth. There were shoals of journalists in the sea of Byzantine-robed churchmen. During those early days before the wars, President Milošević had needed the Orthodox Church and its pageantry to help prepare the future battlefields by reminding Serbs who they were after almost half a century of Yugoslav homogenization. And the Church had been delighted to discover that all those centuries spent preserving and propagating the myths about Serbia's medieval greatness and eternal glorious martyrdom were not going to go to waste. The clergy in those photographs looked sternly serene, calm in the knowledge that their hour had come again.

Orthodox time has its own dynamic. Its motion is spiral, not linear, which means that Orthodox history moves in divinely ordained circles, as pleasingly repetitive as the patterns on church vestments. Empires and lands are lost and regained, lost and regained again, lost and regained, until the end of the world. The past is never forgotten because it comes around again, and the future is never new. In an effort to describe another aspect of Orthodox history, a Greek historian says it involves, 'the removal of all those features which bind the historical truth, of necessity, to the terms of common logic. In this way the truth is created which does not belong to sober reality but to the sphere where the present meets the beyond and where God acts within historical time . . .'[xx] We are dealing with myth-history whose perfect patterns must not be spoiled by clashing truths.

75

Serbs do not learn that for most of that medieval heyday the cradle of their medieval empire and nation was not Kosovo at all, but an area slightly to the north and west. Serbs do not like to be reminded that it was Tsar Dušan who caused the Ottomans to gain their first toehold in Europe by attacking Byzantium and forcing the Emperor to accept help from the Ottomans. Serbs do not learn how their forefathers further hastened Byzantium's demise by fighting on the Turks' side in battles fought in 1396, 1444 and 1448. Their myth-history is simpler. Tsar Dušan's great empire, which was destroyed by the Turks at the battle of Kosovo, will one day rise again like Jesus Christ.

Bogdan, as good as his name, which means 'God's Gift', returned with the glad tidings that we could venerate Prince Lazar's corpse in its open coffin, but on condition that we attend the evening church service.

The pitch darkness outside was blinding and a cold wind was blowing hard through the tops of the cypress trees. Stumbling across a stone-paved courtyard down some steps towards the church, we entered it by a low wooden door. Inside there was light and warmth. A cosy golden glow shed by candles and dim electric lights illumined the blue-green frescoes on the walls and the low ceiling. The church smelt of incense and, earthily, of old damp stone. While outside lurked the old dark night of the Turkish oppression or miserable modern Serbia, here inside was the hope and comfort of a bigger and better reality: a heavenly kingdom reproduced on every inch of wall-space in crowds of big-eyed, sword-wielding saints and their faded gold dinner-plate haloes, scenes from the life of Christ and above those, high in his central dome, Christ the Pantocrator, overseeing all.

Over to the right of the iconostasis was Ravanica's 600-year-old treasure. Lying about four and half feet long in a coffin with a glass top, Prince Lazar was wearing a red and gold brocade shroud and matching pointed slippers, but his head was missing. Only his clasped hands, like a huge ball of dark brown earwax, were visible. Bogdan approached the coffin first and piously set about kissing the glass cover, the rim of the box and even the velvet cloth under it. Goran made do with a single kiss planted nowhere in particular. I stood as close as possible and stared, while four nuns to the right of me sang the service.

We three, plus the nuns, two teenage girls in tracksuit tops, long skirts, headscarves and trainers, and a single old man standing well back in the shadows, were a tiny congregation and far outnumbered by the hosts of saints on the walls. But the scene was intimate, and somehow poignant. It was as if all of us, the crowds of saints and Prince Lazar too, had gathered there together for comfort and refuge. The darkness of the present was the darkness of six hundred years ago. The centuries vanished and time telescoped.

Bogdan must have felt it, too, because back in the car he began musing aloud about the meaning of the Prince Lazar myth: 'Lazar chose a heavenly kingdom which is a reality here and now, as we drive ...' he murmured in the dark. In the next village down the road, Goran spotted a restaurant with its name picked out in pink fluorescent lights: 'Lazar's Last Supper'.

KOSOVO

The Serbs' old patriarchate stands just outside the pretty, mostly Muslim Albanian town of Peć, hugging the high mountain wall boundary between Serbia and Montenegro.

The town was lively that golden autumn day, bustling with signs of Albanian commercial activity. On the backs of horse-drawn carts were sacks of bright red peppers, and a flock of sheep was trotting down the main road. Shop mannequins, gaudily got up in Albanian wedding dresses, graced the pavements. On one street corner in the town centre stood a pair of rosy-cheeked Serb policemen. But in the early 1980s it was from here, and the other large towns of Serbia's Kosovo, that the bad news about how the Albanian Muslims' soaring birth-rate was making the Kosovo Serbs feel like a threatened minority in their own Jerusalem started filtering back to Belgrade. A

miserable chorus of wails from the dwindling Serb population was led
by Kosovo's Orthodox churchmen. Before long the Serbs at Hilandar
monastery on Mount Athos were trumpeting their support. '"If we
have lost our kingdom, we have not lost our souls," said the monks of
Hilandar after the battle of Kosovo in 1389. We say the same to all
Serbs in Kosovo and elsewhere. St Sava, the holy patron of Serbia,
has protected us across the centuries; he will continue to protect us
today.'[xxi]

A substantial part of the Serbs' medieval spiritual inheritance was
concentrated in the churches and monasteries of Kosovo. What was
to become of those priceless treasures – the patriarchate churches at
Peć, the jewel of a fourteenth-century church at Gračanica and
the heritage of Prizren – if the Muslim Albanians overran the region?
By 1988 the Serb bishops were *en masse* and officially lapsing into
language more suited to sounding the alarm through Christendom
about the imminent demise of Byzantium than to fair-minded
appraisal of a delicate problem of demographics. They issued a
statement entitled 'The Declaration by the Bishops of the Serbian
Orthodox Church against the Genocide inflicted by the Albanians
on the indigenous Serbian Population, together with the Sacrilege of
their cultural Monuments in their own Country'.

Already, a year before, President Slobodan Milošević had doffed
his Communist apparatchik's sober suit and donned the garments of
a Serb warrior saint by addressing a rowdy rally of Kosovo Serbs with
the words 'No one should dare to beat you.' In 1989 he was back
here again for the climax of the six-hundredth anniversary of the
battle of Kosovo celebrations. Prince Lazar, nearing the end of his
year-long tour, lay ignored at the nearby church of Gračanica while
Milošević stood on a podium at one end of the fourteenth-century
battlefield to address a mighty crowd of Serbs. He was surrounded by
Orthodox bishops, among them the hot-tempered Bishop Vasilije of
Tuzla and Zvornik. Milošević told the crowd, 'The Kosovo heroism
does not allow us to forget that, at one time, we were brave and
dignified . . . Six centuries later, again we are in battles and quarrels.
They are not armed battles – though such things should not be

excluded yet . . .'[xxii] The crowd bellowed its approval. Milošević, the Orthodox Church and millions of Serbs were synchronizing their wrist-watches to run on circular Orthodox time, making their medieval past present again. Battle would have to be joined with Kosovo's Albanians and won by the Serbs, of course. Then there would be Heaven on Earth, not just Lazar's mystical realm but a Greater Serbia here on Earth.

By 1990 there were tanks, extra police and a nightly curfew sowing terror among the Kosovo Albanians. Milošević had revoked the region's autonomous status within Serbia and pressed home Serbia's claim to the province by renaming it Kosovo-Metohija, the latter half of the name deriving from the Greek word for Orthodox monastery estates. Most Yugoslavia watchers, including the American CIA, expected that if there was war, it would start here in Kosovo.

By the autumn of 1997, with two ruinous wars to their discredit, the Kosovo Serbs' confident euphoria was all gone. The Kosovo Albanians had peacefully cut themselves off from Serbia by setting up their own apartheid system with parallel structures of government. More recently, the less patient among them had created a Kosovo Liberation Army and resorted to a campaign of political terror. Kosovo's Serbs were angry and scared. They still feared the Albanians' soaring birth-rate and envied their growing prosperity, but their watches were running to conventional time again and they were bitterly disenchanted with Milošević.

Bogdan slid the Citroën into some shade by the patriarchate gates. Behind its usefully thick and high stone walls there was a hint of the defiantly non-Albanian, more of the pristine Alpine about the white monastery buildings with their dark wood balconies decorated with bursts of geraniums. The flower-beds were cheerily bright and well kept. A bowed old nun in a faded blue apron swept the paths with long slow strokes.

The patriarchate proper consists of a row of no less than three variously frescoed churches furnished with the stone tombs of former Serb patriarchs. They reflect the differing times in which they were built but share walls like London terraced houses, and a connecting hall, a narthex, by which they can each be reached. Gorgeously frescoed, this narthex was the inspired addition of a sixteenth century Serbian patriarch called Makarije, who owed his elevated post entirely to the patronage of his brother Mehmet Sokolović. Like thousands of the best-looking and most intelligent young Christians in the Ottoman Balkans, Mehmet Sokolović had been seized by Turks as a child, taken to Constantinople, converted to Islam, brought up at court and finally promoted to the eminence of Second Vizier. The title, Patriarch of Serbia, had been abolished when the Turks overran the Balkans but in the mid-fifteenth century Second Vizier Sokolović was in a position to bend the rules and do his brother a big favour. It was entirely thanks to him that Serbia had her own patriarch again, until the eighteenth century.

The Edwardian travel writer Edith Durham passed a night at Peć in the early 1900s. Marvelling at its terrace of churches, she waxed nostalgic and elegiac for a time before most of the Balkans was conquered by the Ottomans and known as 'Turkey in Europe': '... this curious, primitive art which now looks exotic, Eastern, foreign, once swayed the art of all Europe. We find its traces in our own Norman architecture; we find them in the early churches of Italy. It reached its highest stage of development in St Sophia and St Mark's, Venice ...'[xxiii] Durham was welcomed with open arms at Peć and treated to a 'tumbler full of boiled milk and sugar for breakfast'.

Our reception, almost a hundred years later, was quite different. The Abbess was guarded, addressing us only from the height of her balcony, from behind a net curtain. She demanded to know our business before reluctantly instructing one of her nuns, who was busily sweeping an adjacent balcony, to descend and see to us. 'You idle people, you come and hang around here while we've got work to do!' was her parting shot. We were shown inside a stuffily furnished building where more nuns were hard at work scrubbing and polishing reception rooms. The obedient nun sat down with a grudging sigh. The expression on her lined face was closed and her body-language hostile. I asked her if there were many visitors to the monastery these days.

'No. Most of the Serbs have moved away out of fear,' she said shortly, and then sighed again. "This year almost no one came – buses and cars have been stoned . . .'

'Really? How terrible! Was that recently?'

No. As I suspected, her Orthodox sense of time meant that she was talking about the 1980s.

'I think America wants to rule the world,' she suddenly burst out. 'They want to direct the whole show. It's a satanic country.'

We seemed to have chanced upon a highly politicized nun, so I asked her to tell me how they felt here in Kosovo, adrift in an ever-growing sea of Albanian Muslims. But no. If she was happy to sound off against a distant land of which she had no direct experience, any mention of the 'Kosovo question', about which she presumably had first-hand knowledge, was strictly taboo.

'You know all about the situation here. I thought you wanted to talk about Orthodoxy. This conversation is falling into politics,' she said furiously, getting up and heading for the door. 'I'm going to get you some coffee and then that's it. I'm not talking any more. We've been betrayed by enough journalists in the past.'

Perhaps, I thought, Serbian journalists had horribly hyped and distorted stories about the Albanians mistreating Serbs. It might easily have happened when President Milošević was working the bellows hard to fan the flames of Serbian nationalism in the late 1980s. On the other hand, there could no doubt that nuns in Kosovo had been prey to some vicious thoughts about the Albanians in those years. Robert D. Kaplan, an American journalist working in the region, met one who warned him, '"I am a Christian but I'll not turn the other cheek if some Albanian plucks out the eyes of a fellow Serb, or rapes a little girl, or castrates a twelve-year-old Serbian boy." She knifed the air over her thighs with her hand.'[xxiv]

All Bogdan's assurances that I was not an American or a journalist, and that we had received the blessings of countless churchmen for our journey could not mollify this nun. 'It sounds like you've got quite enough blessings to be going on with.' She sniffed, slammed down the tray of coffee and watched us while we drank. 'You can leave now.'

Banished from the ancient seat of their church, Goran and Bogdan turned on me angrily. 'Why did you have to ask her that kind of question? You never ask them about politics. They know about things like how to cure a cold. Now you've really spoiled things!'

I apologized but said I thought I might be forgiven for having mistaken her for a political animal.

As Bogdan started the Citroën, another nun poked her head through his car window. News of our disgrace had travelled fast on the monastery grapevine.

'What's she writing a book about?'

'About Eastern Orthodoxy in Europe,' mumbled Bogdan.

'Is she a believer?'

'She's a Roman Catholic,' said Bogdan, letting out the clutch and driving away.

We turned round and headed back east, towards Kosovo's capital city, Priština. As the Citroën purred across the Kosovo plain, I forced myself to view the passing scene through late fourteenth-century-cum-late-twentieth-century Serb eyes. By creeping stealth instead of honest battle the Serbs' Jerusalem had become the land of the Infidel. I counted the grey concrete minarets of dozens of new mosques and the high-walled citadel houses where wealthy Albanians lived with their extended families.

In the middle of Kosovo's capital, Priština, the concrete shell of a large new Orthodox cathedral graced a long-abandoned building site, but up a narrow back street we found the little white Orthodox church of St Nikolaj. We asked to speak to its priest, were told his name was Father Milorad and directed on to his home. It was in a modern block at the top of a long, winding street, lined with pretty mosques, square old wooden houses of Ottoman design whose minarets looked like extra high chimneys.

A burly man in his forties with a dramatic scar running from under his nose to the side of his lip, Father Milorad warned us he had nothing to say about local politics. But his distrustful frown vanished the instant he learnt I was English. After all, he would be delighted to offer us coffee, cigarettes and brandy because he needed me to know his thoughts about the death of Princess Diana. We followed him into his kitchen where his wife, dressed in a tracksuit, was scrubbing at the inside of the oven and his son was lounging in an armchair, smoking.

'We've got satellite television so I watched six hours of coverage of the funeral – CNN, Euronews, Sky. I have no words to describe how impressive I found that church service,' Father Milorad enthused, before asking me what I had made of her death.

'It was a tragic accident...'

'An accident? Pshaw!' he spluttered into his thimble glass of *slivovic*. 'She was killed on the orders of your Queen. Those were not paparazzi, they were commandos hired to kill her. That was her punishment for fucking a Muslim. What did she want to do that for? Haven't we got enough Muslims in this world already? I suppose that Fayed wanted something white and blonde, not dark like him, and only the daughter-in-law of the Queen of England was good enough. Naturally, the Queen could not tolerate a Muslim stepfather for her grandsons – for the heir to the throne? *Impossible!* That was it, wasn't it? It would never have happened if Diana had not left her husband and her home in the first place. Just you tell me why she did that.'

'Prince Charles had been unfaithful to her, I think...'

'Pshaw!' he exclaimed, after taking a quick parish call on his mobile phone. 'Diana should have stayed with her man. Just remember that Eve was produced out of Adam's rib, not the other way around. A woman is the body, a man is the head.'

At this point his hard-working wife chimed in with the unwelcome tidings that a new generation of young women were not obeying their husbands and she, for her part, wished them good luck. She wanted me to corroborate her findings. Her son laughed and helped himself to another of his father's Lucky Strikes. Father Milorad was heartily enjoying himself. His stare was not as bullying as Bishop Vasilije's. A generous host, he produced for my perusal a vast tome, which he claimed weighed four kilos. It was called *The Kosovo Heritage*. Flicking through it, in search of an entry about his own little church, he let slip that the day he was forced to leave Kosovo he would be sure to be carrying that book with him.

I had not expected him to have leaving on his mind. Had he declared that the Serbs' Kosovo heritage was the reason why he would *never* leave his home, I would not have been in the least surprised. But here was a sign that Kosovo's Serbs feared Milošević was capable of abandoning even the cradle of Serbdom, even the very people he had to thank for his rise to power in the late 1980s. They had already watched him betray the Krajina Serbs, then force the Bosnian Serbs to make peace.

'Everything is in here,' Father Milorad was saying, cradling the book in his arms, 'everything that we have had here in Kosovo, all that we have built. No one can tell me afterwards that it was never true, because all the documents are here. And we had so much! In the fourteenth century, when London was nothing, our kings were dining off silver plates with golden cutlery . . .'

I interrupted his reverie to ask him if he thought the good times would come round again, if he believed in Serbia's resurrection.

'Only God knows, but we do know that America wants to take this land as they have taken Bosnia. They're supporting the Albanians against us. But the Albanians have everything they could want here. Not England, not France, not Germany could do more for them.'

His son nodded agreement.

I strongly suspected that were I to return to this house in five years' time, I would be lucky to find Father Milorad here. Like the rest of Kosovo's few remaining Serbs he would have peacefully – or otherwise – admitted defeat and migrated north, with his weighty tome and his nice wife. It seemed sad, and sadder still once we had driven a little way out of town to visit the fourteenth-century church of Gračanica, the most precious product of Serbia's golden age. Without seeing Gračanica, I could not have felt the impending tragedy 'on my own skin', as the Serb expression goes, and I could not have begun to imagine why Serbs cannot openly and frankly admit that Kosovo is as good as lost to them. Without recalling Late Byzantium's gaping gulf between myth and reality I could not have understood how reality does not get a look in when sacred lands are at stake.

Gračanica, with its herringbone-patterned russet brick, its chubbily bubbling domes and little bubble-glass windows, is the most lovable church I have ever seen. Sir Steven Runciman, a historian of Byzantium and the Eastern Orthodox Church, likes it too. He once compared Salisbury cathedral to Gračanica: 'The former may soar gracefully heavenward; the latter with the simplicity of its design, the comprehensive economy of its balance and its stresses and the rich restrained decoration of its interior, is the work of a people no less spiritual but far more sophisticated and cultured.'[xxv]

If any of us in the West possessed such a jewel the full weight of our tourist industry would have been brought to bear on it by now. There would be a tea room and a gift shop, a large car park, audio guides and leaflets. The frescoed interior would have been roped off, perhaps even preserved behind glass. But there is none of that at Gračanica: the past is as tangible here as the present, and that makes the fact of the church's continued existence, in a down-at-heel village on the flat and fertile Kosovo plain, all the more touchingly remarkable. Instead of tourist facilities there are graffiti from the fifteeenth, seventeenth and nineteenth centuries in Russian, Bulgarian, Turkish and Albanian, scratched all over the narthex frescoes, recalling the times when the place was deserted or used as a cattle-shed or a barracks. Inside, candle-wax and paraffin from the lamps, but also chewing-gum and even melted plastic, have stained some of the frescoes a greasy black at around chest level. It was dark. We could hardly make out the crowds of saints, martyrs, angels and kings on every wall, only sense their patient presences.

Tsar Dušan's grandfather, King Milutin, built Gračanica in 1321. It was just one among dozens of churches he erected, perhaps in penance for his lusty taking and discarding of wives. His fourth and last, a Byzantine princess called Simonida, was only six when she journeyed forlornly from golden Byzantium to this darkly forested and comparatively barbarous land to marry a man forty years older than her. Her father had loved his youngest daughter but even then, two and a half centuries before Constantinople fell, Byzantium had needed allies to help save it from the encroaching Infidel. Simonida was simply the high price he had had to pay for King Milutin's help. She features in two of the frescoes. In the first she stands beside her husband, both of them richly arrayed in Byzantine royal dress and caps dripping with pearls. Both are also wearing Serbian crowns and about to receive two Byzantine crowns from the hands of angels, but both have had their eyes gouged out by peasants with a superstitious belief in their miraculous powers of healing. In the second, she is wearing a huge pair of dangling earrings and occupies alongside her husband one branch of the Serbian royal family tree whose 'holy root' sprang from Serbia's first twelfth-century ruler, Stefan Nemanja. Baptized a Catholic for tactical reasons, Stefan Nemanja had converted to Orthodoxy and died a simple monk, setting up a tradition for Serbian kings to end their lives as monks at the Serbs' Hilandar monastery on Mount Athos. Simonida's old rogue of a husband followed the pattern but bent the rule. He became a monk, but only posthumously.

Our guide around the church was the caretaker, a sturdy Serb girl called Snežana, which means Snow White. Because she bore a strong resemblance to Father Milorad I asked her if she knew him. She did, and did not think much of him.

'We have a joke about priests: one of them is drowning in a lake and a fisherman calls out to him from his boat, "Here, give me your hand," but the priest will not, so he drowns. You see, our priests like to take, not to give. We don't respect them too much.'

'What about monks?' I asked her.

'Quite, quite different. They are very holy,' she said.

Father Sava, who lived about fifty miles back west of Priština and not far from Peć, at Dečani monastery, might have been holy but he was certainly as tolerant a churchman as any in Serbia in late 1997.

Another of Kosovo's jewels, Dečani monastery was founded by

King Stefan Dečanski who was unlucky enough to be blinded by his father, lusty King Milutin, then murdered by his son, Tsar Dušan. Stefan Dečanski's chief joy in life seems to have been this monastery, whose name he adopted. A chronicler recorded that 'once he had pitched his tents he stayed there, delighting in such a beautiful abode, for it was set very high and cleared of all kinds of trees, the region being very branchy and very fertile, at once level and grassy.'[xxvi] It was Tsar Dušan who finished building Dečani in 1350, the same year Krka monastery was completed, and richly endowed it with *metohija*, monastery estates, extending way down south into today's Albania. Repenting of his father's murder, he also laid Stefan Dečanski's body to rest in the monastery church, where it made a name for itself by causing a liar's tongue to rot and fall out and a wicked Ottoman pasha to die of spontaneous combustion. Childless local Albanian women, just as much as their Serbian counterparts, took to scuttling under the slightly raised tomb, in the hope that the thirteenth-century saint-king would bless them with babies.

Those were happier times than today for religious tolerance. Before the fault-lines set hard in this unquiet land, Muslim Albanians felt free to partake of the Orthodox magic and the Serbs of the Muslims'. Nor was there anything strange about a Catholic Croat being appointed chief builder of Dečani's church, which is why it looks nothing like Gračanica or any of the other monasteries I saw in Kosovo. Romanesque, not domed and sparingly embellished on the outside, it is white and clean. And the western character of Dečani does not stop there. A very un-Balkan green lawn surrounds the church and, in an office on the second floor of one of the wooden-verandahed monastery buildings, we found Father Sava. He was putting finishing touches to the monastery's new website and inspecting Internet pictures of Serbian police beating up Albanian students.

A big soft man in his early thirties, with pale blue eyes and wispy golden hair escaping from its bun, Father Sava wore a home-knitted black cardigan over his long cassock and looked a little like an overgrown maiden aunt. An excellent English-speaker and a wizard with information technology, he was proving indispensable to his bishop on numerous trips abroad aimed at canvassing international support for a negotiated solution to the Kosovo question. They had jetted in from Chicago the day before.

Turning aside from his computer screen, he rummaged among a pile of books and found a box. Inside was a small airtight plastic bag containing a swab of cotton wool on which was a smear of something greasy and slightly perfumed. He said it was *mira* – myrrh – exuded before his very eyes by an icon of St Nicholas belonging to a Russian Orthodox church in Indiana.

'Here,' he said, holding it under my nose. 'Its smell is sweeter than roses. It is *so* beautiful that God should perform such miracles in America. You know what? I have a feeling that the future of Orthodoxy lies with the West. Here in eastern Europe most people are still too enchanted by the glitter and glamour of the West. The West itself is now ready for the spiritual food we can offer.'

Orthodoxy, he thought, could do with a new image and a fresh marketing strategy. There were western souls out there, he told me, hungering for real spiritual nourishment, gagging on the secularized religions they knew.

'People think of Orthodoxy as one of the branches of Roman Catholicism, but with nationalism and folklore added on, don't they? That tells us we should be doing more about making Orthodoxy more approachable. After all, it is the foundation of European culture,' he said.

I pointed out to him that young Serbs seemed to be finding Orthodoxy perfectly approachable. Dečani was no longer the almost abandoned outpost of Serbian Orthodoxy it had been when Father Sava arrived in 1992. Five years on there were twenty monks. Most were young, middle class and well educated, and the community was still growing. Only a couple of months before our visit the Belgrade newspapers had splashed the news that one of the capital's best-loved young actors had abandoned his hectic lifestyle to become a monk at Dečani. More recently, a young photographer who had visited the monastery mailed Father Sava an album filled with black and white masterpieces of Dečani monks at work and play.

THE SERBS

'Look, this is his entrance ticket to Dečani. He'll be joining us any day now,' said Father Sava, flicking through the album's pages. 'Aren't these wonderful? I think I'll scan some onto our website . . .'

With Father Sava I could raise any of my questions about Orthodoxy without fear of his taking offence. Although Orthodoxy does not lend itself to intellectual debate he patiently answered my every query and left me with the impression that he was wholeheartedly searching for a way to bring his Church out of its medieval impasse without jeopardizing its special grip on the Truth or forfeiting its continued presence in Kosovo. He was in favour of the Church taking an active interest in politics, but deeply regretted its having become enmeshed in what he called the state's 'atheist nationalism'. Serbian elections were due the next day, a Sunday, and he was frankly terrified by the choice of candidates on offer.

'Serbs are now being forced to choose between atheism and open fascism. Both will lead us to the point where we'll have to flee from here, just as the Krajina Serbs fled the Krajina. To be honest, what really scares me is that we Serbs will provoke the Albanians. That's the real danger, when there is so much we could learn from them. They've created a real economic boom here in Kosovo in the past ten years, so I don't wish them any ill. Although, I should add that they don't have a single precious monument or building here. All the oldest mosques were built by the Turks.'

That doughty Edwardian, Edith Durham, had found her way to Dečani too. In those days the monastery was a few miles from the Ottoman empire's fraying northern border so she described it as situated 'precariously, on the bloody edge of things'.[xxvii] Less than a century later, adrift in a sea of Kosovo Albanians desperate to win back the self-rule of which Milošević had robbed them, it seemed about to find itself in the bloody middle of things. I felt for Father Sava and his brother monks.

It was getting late, the bells were clanging, as urgently as a fire alarm, for the evening service, but Father Sava and I continued to talk. Question followed question. I asked him why Orthodox countries had accepted Communism more easily than Catholic or Protestant ones.

'In Yugoslavia Communism found its deepest roots among Serbs,' he agreed, 'and I think that was because Communism was a religion, not just an ideology. It was the same in Russia, of course. We Orthodox people have religion rooted deep in our minds and hearts. I remember once as a child, asking my father, "What will happen when Tito dies?" "Hush, hush," said my father. "He can't die." When he died in 1980 I cried my eyes out . . . You don't approach things in this religious way in the West. You approach things with your mind, with rationalism, rather than with your heart. I fear that England especially has chosen too rational a path and got lost. I was terribly distressed to hear about women priests in the Anglican Church . . .'

Standing in the candle-lit church while the evening service washed over me in a cloud of incense and chanting I found my thoughts straying back to what another young Dečani monk with glowing brown eyes had told us earlier while giving us a quick guided tour of the church. 'Imagine a big sturdy tree and how, suddenly, one of its thick branches decides that it wants to be a tree too so it falls to the ground,' was how he had begun. 'Well, what happens to this branch? It doesn't necessarily rot because it can grow a few twigs there on the ground – but it can never be a tree and nor can it make any fruit. The sturdy old tree, of course, has a hard time without its big branch but it still lives and, what is more important, it can bear fruit . . .'

The tree is Orthodoxy, the errant branch is Roman Catholicism, the twigs are the puny Protestant religions. Europe's Eastern Orthodox Churches are expecting that the branch will come back and join the tree, not that the tree will have to fall down to join the branch. Not for them the search for common denominators and ecumenical consensus. Not for them the dilution of their Right Belief. What would be the point in having that Right Belief if any other was equally valid? If Orthodox belief was 'right', any other kind of belief must be 'wrong'. Religious pluralism and freedom of conscience do not make much sense to most Eastern Orthodox.

Back in the monastery, in the convivial warmth of the white-washed refectory with its dark wood beams, we sat on wooden benches while young monks in aprons bustled around, loading the table with Hungarian smoked cheese, white sheep's cheese, two sorts of puréed ratatouille (one with egg, one without), home-made bread, thick dark wine, stuffed peppers, gooey chocolate cake and apples. I was just helping myself to some bread when Bogdan said, 'Shouldn't we say grace?'

'Of course, if you'd like to – I didn't like to impose,' said Father Sava as I leapt to my feet.

He tucked in with us, chatting about his trip to America, buzzing with ideas he needed to test: 'The flight was only 450 dollars, via Budapest, where we picked up the Air France connection – pretty cheap, really. I was interested to see that the Air France crew were mostly Muslim or black. I suppose that it is inevitable, this mix of races and religions . . . Try this really excellent cheese, pass the wine, please. After all, that is how the Roman and early Byzantine empires were, weren't they? Everyone could be a Roman citizen, couldn't they? On the other hand I do feel that Serbia must retain its particular traditions in order to be able to attain a higher spirituality . . .'

Immediately after supper Goran and Bogdan were led off to a cell for the night, while I was shown up to the monastery's library. Under a window with a view of the ghostly white church and a night sky brilliant with stars, a mattress bed was laid for me on the floor. I slept surrounded by paintings, soft-focus photographs of former abbots and bishops, and books – including the same huge tome on Kosovo's heritage that Father Milorad had shown me back in Priština. At five o'clock I was woken. The sky was only just beginning to lighten as an eerie black figure of a monk, in his long, hooded robe, strode around the church beating the *semantron* – a four-foot-long wooden plank – with a mallet. The noise he made was hollow and scary, like gunshot. Time concertinaed again to a single moment, then assumed its circular pattern. A monk would have performed this ritual on the morning of the day Tsar Dušan had had his father murdered, on the day Prince Lazar had lost Serbia to the Turks, on the day Edith

Durham had paid a visit, on the day Dečani's doughty Russian abbot had ordered a posse of Nazis to leave their guns at the gate, on the day Father Sava had arrived to revive the community . . .

The *semantron* sounded every half-hour until eight, but by then I was modestly attired in headscarf and skirt and on my way down to church. Father Sava was officiating in a white and gold robe over a white surplice. When he opened the little saloon-bar-style gates in the middle of the *iconostasis* and walked through them to the holy altar behind, the pale morning sun shining through the flaps of his robe made them look like angel wings and lit the wisps of his hair to a halo. An ancient powerful magic was being worked in a cloud of incense, a shaft of sunlight, a tinkle of bells and a choir of young monks' voices repeating over and over, '*Gospodi pomiluj*! Lord have mercy!'

It seemed sad that, just as in Edith Durham's time, less than a dozen of us were gathered there – the women standing on the left, the men on the right – to witness this holy ritual. But Serbs are not great churchgoers. Their Orthodox feelings are paradoxically fervent and casual. At the beginning of the twentieth century an eminent Serbian historian and diplomat explained, 'They do not allow anyone to attack her [the Church] nor to compromise her, although, when she is not attacked, they neglect her.'[xxviii]

Proud that Serbia had produced a monk of Father Sava's calibre, Goran and Bogdan agreed that he must be destined for the episcopal, if not the patriarchal, heights. One way or another, I calculated, I was unlikely to find him here at Dečani in five years' time. But we had exchanged e-mail addresses so there was no reason to lose contact.*

---

* Father Sava ran his own e-mail news service when Milošević cracked down on Kosovo in 1998. Dečani sheltered Albanians from the Serb paramilitaries. In March 1999, at the start of the Nato bombing campaign and Milošević's brutal ethnic cleansing, Father Sava left for Montenegro telling the *Evening Standard* on 29 March 1999 that 'I do not want to return to Kosovo again . . . If that is the Kosovo they want, then I hope Nato bombs it to pieces.' He was out of e-mail contact until May 1999. When Nato troops took over Kosovo in June, Father Sava was back in Kosovo, based with Bishop Artemije at Gračanica monastery, and furious that Nato troops

THE MONASTERY OF JOVANDOL
MONTENEGRO

'Oh dazzling May dawn,
Mother, mother – Our Montenegro! . . .'

Goran was in fine voice and high spirits as the trusty Citroën wound its way out of Kosovo, through forests of russet and golden beech trees, up and then down the mountain, into his ancestors' homeland of Montenegro, the tiny Serb mountain stronghold the Turks never managed – some say could never be bothered – to conquer. By 1997 Montenegro, the republic which, at Belgrade's behest, sent its men down from the mountains to shell Dubrovnik in 1991, was disenchanted with big brother Serbia. Which country wants to be hitched up to an international pariah in what western news agencies were referring to as 'rump Yugoslavia'?

Montenegro was in the grip of an identity crisis. On the one hand it had traditionally enjoyed its connection with Serbia and an image of itself as the breeding ground for true, God-fearing, freedom-fighting Serbs like Serbia's first post-Ottoman era king, Karadjordje. On the other hand it was still hankering after the pseudo-independence it enjoyed as an unofficial Russian protectorate during the nineteenth century. Russia had paid Montenegro's minimal expenses in exchange for access to a useful toehold on the Adriatic. Montenegro gained credibility. Her last king, Nikola, was known as 'the father-in-law of Europe' on account of the seven daughters he married off into most of Europe's royal families. Two found themselves at the Russian court of Tsar Nicholas II and his wife Alexandra, and won renown for having introduced the imperial couple to Rasputin.

---

were not preventing the Albanians' revenge attacks against Serbs and the flight of Serbs from Kosovo. By January 2000 his e-mails were reporting the destruction of seventy-six Serbian Orthodox churches and monasteries and 10,000 icons and religious objects had been looted or destroyed.

If Montenegro was split along pro- and anti-independence lines, so was its Church. The Archbishop we were on our way to meet represented the pro-Serbia tendency. His rival, a mere archimandrite, was all for Montenegro's ecclesiastical and political independence from Serbia.*

Bogdan was in a hurry as usual because we needed to be at the top of a certain mountain in Montenegro at nine o'clock the next morning, if we wanted to find the Archbishop and attend his consecration of a new monastery. We certainly did, of course, but it seemed a pity to hurry because the view was dazzling, both my companions were in excellent spirits and the autumn sun was warm through the windscreen.

At nine o'clock the following morning bells clanged out the welcoming alarm, assuring us that we had come to the right mountain. Abandoning the car we climbed the last half-mile to the top, pausing sometimes to allow a stream of Ladas and latest model Land Rovers – the former filled with old women dressed in black, the latter with bearded prelates in their ceremonial best – to rev their way up the track, spraying mud like rally-racing cars. In a crowd of excited locals we passed under the swinging bell through the new wooden gates of St John the Baptist monastery, into a flat, grassy area the size of a football pitch and a half. On the far side of it was the concrete foundation of a new church and around its edge were grouped the new monastery buildings. Cement mixers and building materials lay strewn about the place still, impeding the orderly progress of the crowd. A bottleneck had already formed on a narrow muddy path leading round one of the buildings to the entrance of the new chapel where the dedication of the monastery to John the Baptist, on this the anniversary of his conception, was to be held. Bogdan ran across a friend who had journeyed all the way from Belgrade for the occasion.

Inside the tiny chapel the heat and crowd were stifling. Montenegrin men, as tall and bearded as Goran, their heads piously bowed

* In January 2000 a breakaway Montenegrin Orthodox Church was declared.

and hands folded, were spilling out down the brand-new white marble steps. Out of earshot of the incessant repetition of 'Lord have mercy!' children in their Sunday best scrambled around the cement mixers and sawdust. An army of nuns strode back and forth across the football pitch ferrying trays of food and cutlery, laying the long trestle tables for the coming feast.

Three hours later a river of churchmen, their gold-threaded crimson robes glittering in the noon sun, poured out of the chapel, cascaded down the muddy track and made for the site of the new church, pursued by a swarm of black-robed nuns and laity. At its head was Montenegro's Archbishop Amfilohije, wearing a golden robe and mitre studded with jewels and encrusted with miniature icons, and a pair of reading spectacles.

Amfilohije is an Orthodox prelate like none other in the former Yugoslavia. As head of the Montenegrin Church, he has a particularly august tradition to uphold. Between 1516 and 1830 Montenegro was ruled by several generations of native prince-bishops, called *Vladika*. The Church was the only institution that could bring even a semblance of order to mountain clans too much in thrall to their lawless blood feuds. A *Vladika* was always succeeded by his nephew, since bishops had to be celibate. There being no call for the banal trappings of a modern state, Montenegro's old capital, at Cetinje, consisted of just one large monastery and a handful of stone houses until late in the nineteenth century. Another Englishwoman passed through the tiny republic in the middle of the last century and noted that '. . . the parish priests or popes of Montenegro wear the national dress and carry arms, which they only lay aside while reading the service. They are generally "good heroes", the first at a gathering, the leaders of their flocks in war.'[xxix] In the early nineteenth century a prince-bishop called Petar Petrović-Njegoš II wrote poetry inspired by his Orthodox faith and his loathing of the Turks. His 'Mountain Wreath' ballad which stars a seventeenth-century prince-bishop who incites Montenegrins to murder local Muslims one Christmas Eve, amounts to what one historian has called 'a hymn to genocide'.[xxx] But the Serbs loved it so much that it ran to twenty editions between

1847 and 1913. The following excerpts seem to have lost their poetry, although not their meaning in translation:

> . . . *The blasphemers of Christ's name*
> *We will baptize with water or with blood!*
> . . . *Let the song of horror ring forth*
> *A true altar on a bloodstained rock.*
> . . . *So tear down the minarets and mosques,*
> *Also kindle the Serb Yule logs*
> *And paint our Easter eggs,*
> *The two fasts observe honestly;*
> *As for the rest, do as you will.*[xxxi]

Archbishop Amfilohije was cast in the mould of these *Vladika* prince-bishops. He took his international and local politics seriously and long before the war began had won a reputation for himself as something of a spokesperson for Serbian nationalist laity and clergy alike. Just as the Bosnian war was heating up in 1992, he was asserting boldly that Orthodox Europe was 'the last island of holiness, of untroubled and unpolluted truth' against which 'all the demonic forces are directed'. So adamantly Serb was he that he once declared the term 'Montenegrin' to be an invention of the Vatican. No baby born in Montenegro may have his nationality registered in the parish as anything but Serb. During the war Amfilohije shocked even his flock by consorting with Arkan. He also busied himself with mediating between Milošević in Belgrade and Karadžić in Bosnia. In April 1995, just a month before a peace was signed, he and Patriarch Pavle celebrated Easter together at the church in Karadžić's stronghold at Pale, just outside Sarajevo.

The consecration of the new monastery church was teetering on the edge of chaos. Amfilohije was having to chivvy his priests into doing the dirty job of shovelling sand over the buried foundation stone. One of the churchmen started singing from the wrong page of the service. A bossy young nun struck up a chant that Amfilohije should have sung alone. It was hot out there in the middle of the day and especially hot under those Byzantine robes, I imagined. Tempers were fraying, until the moment when all the clergy and laymen clustered around a makeshift wooden cross on the concrete raft in the middle of the football pitch and spontaneously engaged in an ancient, probably pagan and peculiarly Serb, tribal ritual. It seemed to be a form of physical as well as spiritual communion. Every man held his right arm out straight and placed his right hand on the right shoulder of the man in front for a moment's silence.

By one o'clock stomachs were rumbling but there was still more ritual blessing and chanting of 'Lord have mercy' to be done. The glittering crimson, gold and white river set off again to the far edge of the football pitch with everyone following in its slipstream. In all his gorgeous finery Archbishop Amfilohije scrambled up the steep, muddy incline to a wide ledge in the mountain where a new white marble gravestone had been placed behind an open grave. This was to be the family grave of the Nikčević family which, at the behest of one of its monkish members, had donated this land to the Monte-negrin Church. I was so intent on watching what Amfilohije was up to, in a cloud of incense, with some oil, a cake and some wine laid out on a little table by the graveside, that I did not at first notice two good-sized wooden boxes filled with yellowing human bones, baking in the sun.

'That's five generations of Nikčevićes,' whispered Goran, pointing to the dates on the gravestone 1912 to 1977 and the list of names. 'They've been brought here from all over the world probably. We did the same thing with the bones of my ancestors a couple of years ago – unfortunately I was travelling in India so I missed it.'

Even in death, it struck me, the Serbs go about gathering their people up: one State, one family, one grave, one box. Just then Amfilohije seized what, to judge by its gaudy yellow label, looked like a bottle of table wine but might have been a consecrated vintage wine. He bent low over the boxes, like a cook over an oven when basting a Sunday joint, and poured the contents all over the bones, then vigorously rubbed it into the skulls and anointed every femur. 'The wine is the blood of Christ,' whispered Goran. A strong, sour smell of cooking wine and bones wafted up our nostrils, setting our stomachs rumbling again. The lids were replaced on the boxes and they were lowered into the grave.

That was another magic, not as subtly enchanting as Father Sava's perhaps, but probably at least as potent.

At last it was time for lunch. About a hundred guests settled down at the long trestle table in the middle of the football pitch. As Archbishop Amfilohije's guests we were bidden to the high table, inside a breeze-block garage of a building near the monastery gates. Two long tables were set for another hundred guests inside. There was everything a Balkan stomach could crave in the way of solid Balkan food and drink, even more various and plentiful than our feast at Dečani: roast lamb, stuffed cabbage, Coke, pickled peppers, soup, brandy, Balkan-style samosas, boiled potatoes, beer, salad, fish in breadcrumbs and cakes. Changed out of his finery into a casual black cassock, Amfilohije sat at the head of the table, keeping a tight grip on his episcopal staff and a bright, beady eye on the assembled company.

While Bogdan was bringing his considerable ecclesiastical influence to bear on the matter of arranging for me to speak with Amfilohije, Goran and I fell into conversation with the man who had made the iron cross that topped the chapel. He was a jovial, scruffy-looking Bosnian Serb from just over the border, who described himself as a 'Serbian nationalist and Serbian Orthodox, which comes first – of course'. He boasted that he had spent fifty-two months as a volunteer, fighting in the war in Bosnia, and had made a name for himself as 'Evil Mirko'.

'I was the kind of fighter who put his head where most people wouldn't dare to put their feet! And, I can tell you one thing, I would fight again. I reckon I'm good for another ten years and I would really earn my nickname next time because I'm angry, I'm angry with everyone, the English included – because God is on our side. I'm angry with these Satanists, with that Satan with a baby face . . .'

I was not sure if he was referring to Bill Clinton or President Slobodan Milošević, but was relieved to find Bogdan at my elbow, telling me he had achieved his goal. The Archbishop would see us.

Nuns brought chairs and a table loaded with coffee, lemonade and dainty plates of baklava to a point somewhere on the far side of the football pitch and there we sat for an hour or so as the sun slid down towards the Nikčević mass grave and the guests began to leave.

Amfilohije, a spry fifty-nine-year-old whose long wispy beard made him look much older, seemed none the worse for having spent a total of five hours on his feet, chanting and pouring wine and directing operations. 'Sin tires you, evil tires you – not good,' he proclaimed. The news that I was half Irish delighted him. 'Irish Catholics smell good to the Orthodox,' he said, tweaking the end of his nose. 'They have the spiritual seed of St Patrick in their genes.'

Like Father Sava, he had just returned from foreign parts and had plenty to say about what he had seen there.

'Jerusalem! That is an eternal drama they have there and history is what is produced out of this drama, by God and his people. This battle between all the religions to be the closest to God will last until the end of the world. But you know what delights me most? That Orthodoxy has remained the closest to God. Eighty per cent of the holiest places in the city are held by the Orthodox. The Greek priest who guards Christ's tomb, he's not going to give it up to anyone. Oh, no, not he! It's on this fire of faith that Christ's Church is built. Here, have this photograph of me holding a service in Jerusalem. Take it as a souvenir,' the Archbishop was saying, with a twinkle in his eye.

He has that Serb charm, I thought, remembering someone telling me that in the early 1980s he had been lionized by Belgrade society women engaged in rediscovering the faith of their forefathers after almost fifty years of state atheism. Someone had told me that 'they went to him, their spiritual father, to get infected with his ideas'. Bishop Amfilohije has as little time for ecumenism as all Serb churchmen, these days.

'There is so much disappointment with the West. When the Communists ruled us we looked upon western democracy as some sort of salvation but the West has appeared in quite another form. It has been introducing a new brand of totalitarian rule by means of economic exploitation. It can buy up our newspapers, use our poverty, bribe our consciences and make us more confused than we ever were before. To this we say, "I'll find my own way. Thanks but no thanks for this kind of help . . ."'

He was enjoying his portion of baklava as he spoke. I asked him if he thought the warring was over.

'No, of course not,' he answered unhesitatingly. 'How can we avoid more war when day and night the Americans and Europeans are giving more and more weapons to the Muslims and the Croats? They have peace on their tongues but war in their hearts. Next time around our enemies will be helped by Clinton, Kinkel and John Major – no, it's Blair, isn't it?'

He admitted he was still puzzling over the reasons why Orthodox peoples of eastern Europe had played leading roles in whatever unrest and bloodshed Europe has seen since the collapse of Communism. Was it not strange, I said, that Czechoslovakia had managed to split in half without a drop of blood being spilt?

He paused before answering. 'The hermit St Makarios the Egyptian said that wherever the Holy Spirit is there is great suffering and persecution . . . You should remember that they didn't crucify Herod . . . No, they crucified *Christ*, and they mocked him too . . .'

Suddenly seized by a panicky fear, I wondered where the intoxicating battle of Kosovo spirit would lead Serbia. Had no one sobered up after the dismally fruitless wars against the Catholic Croats and the Bosnian Muslims? How did one deal with an entire nation in the grip of a Christ-the-victim-cum-heavenly-conqueror complex? When and where was this going to end? By the cyclical rules of Orthodox time it would doubtless return to the battlefield of Kosovo and a war with the Kosovar Albanians before the millennium was over.*

Amfilohije was trying to tell me about two conversations he had had, one with the American ambassador to Belgrade, one with Pope John Paul II in the Vatican.

* War broke out eighteen months later. Nato forces intervened to prevent a third campaign of 'ethnic cleansing' by the Serbs – this time against Kosovo's Albanians. By June 1999 Kosovo was under Nato control.

'The American ambassador asked me if I thought Radovan Karadžić was a war criminal. I told him straight, "If you're talking about the justice of God, then I think Hans Dietrich Genscher, Pope John Paul II, Franjo Tudjman, Alija Izetbegović, Archbishop Amfilohije Radović and then Radovan Karadžić should be tried – in that order."'

He had asked the Pope why the Vatican had been so quick to recognize the independence of Croatia in 1991. 'Do you know what the Pope said? He said, "The Vatican is not a political force." "How come?" I said. "You're the state of the Vatican. How do you explain that Germany was allowed to reunite as quick as lightning and then went straight on to break up another country?"' He meant Yugoslavia. It was becoming abundantly clear that the Archbishop reserves his main distrust and dislike for the Catholic Croats, then for the Catholic West, and lastly for the West.

'You know what? You say Karadžić is a war criminal but he did not let Serbs be slaughtered as they were between 1941 and 1945. The [Croat] Ustashes were the main instigators of this war, the same ones who set up concentration camps in the last war. And the Muslims had their own division in the Croat army, you know . . .'

We were back on Orthodox time: 1204 when the Catholic Crusaders sacked Constantinople . . . 1914 to 1918 when Serbia lost a third of her menfolk fighting the Germans, Austro-Hungarians and Croats . . . 1941 when the Croat fascists slaughtered Serbs as well as Jews and gypsies . . . 1991 when the war with Croatia broke out . . . Round and round and round.

It was turning cold on that mountain-top. The sun had gone down.

Macedonia

SKOPJE
THE FORMER YUGOSLAV REPUBLIC OF MACEDONIA

The Citroën's headlight beams paled to a ghostly glow. Illuminating next to nothing, they were abbreviating the Former Yugoslav Republic of Macedonia – known by the acronym, the FYROM – to just a few feet of the road ahead. In the dark patch of the year between Christmas and New Year, the long night drive from the Serbian border to the FYROM's capital seemed interminable and foolhardy, given the fog. Any consolation lay in the thought that it was a fitting entrée to a state whose future was so precariously unclear.

An obscure Balkan fragment in the world view of the average westerner and famously dismissed by the *Encyclopedia Britannica* as 'a political problem rather than a geographical entity', Macedonia lies at the foot of the Balkans, where the European land mass reaches the Aegean Sea. An area too strategic to ignore but too heterogeneous to define, and home to an explosive mixture of every race and religion in the Balkans, its fate has been to be coveted by every one of its neighbours, regularly swept by war and too often drenched in blood. One after another, starting with the Romans, the Bulgars, the Byzantines, the Serbs and the Ottoman Turks, fought and ruled over this region. By the late seventeenth century travellers were penetrating the Ottoman province at their peril, surrounded by armed guards and further hampered by a lack of reliable maps. '. . . to confess the Truth,' wrote a nonplussed Englishman in the area at that time, 'he that travels into Macedonia, will never be able to square the situations of Towns and Rivers to their Positions and Descriptions in Maps'.[i]

By the nineteenth century the long Pax Ottomana had reduced most of Macedonia's countryside to murderous bandit fiefdoms, which merchants traversed at their peril and where browbeaten peasants struggled for the freedom to scrape the barest living. The Ottoman empire was rotting fast and shedding its territories in Europe. The Serbs won their independence, so did the Greeks, Bulgars and

Romanians, but the strategic concerns of a Britain intent on counter-acting Russian influence in the area meant that the various peoples of Macedonia had to suffer longer than most by Turkey's decline – until 1913. And it was not only the Turks in adversity who were corrupt and beastly. The neighbouring new nation states of Greece, Serbia and Bulgaria all played their poisonous part in martyring Macedonia. Under the flimsiest pretext of fishing for souls, each country's new national church pelted Macedonia with its conflicting religious nationalist propaganda. The province's Orthodox Christians were forced to choose a nationality. He or she was a Greek if he or she worshipped in a Greek church, a Bulgarian if their parish had a Bulgarian Exarchate priest, or a Serb if the local Orthodox church came under the Serbian Patriarchate's jurisdiction. Such a crude method of partitioning a region, whose population had always been so mixed that it had given its name to a mixed vegetable or fruit salad often found on French restaurant menus, inevitably led to horrible abuses. The priest of one church might be slaughtered by another and his entire village then made to change its religious and national allegiance at the point of a gun-barrel. Bishops funded political terrorists of whichever persuasion suited their purposes. Assassination became Macedonia's acknowledged forte.

One concerned English journalist's verdict on the province in 1906 was that it seemed to be 'a land where the peasant ploughs with a rifle on his back, where his rulers govern by virtue of their ability to massacre upon occasion, where Christian bishops are commonly supposed to organize political murders'.[ii] A French anthropologist investigating Macedonia's Christian customs in the early years of the twentieth century wrote, 'Death is never a surprise for the Macedonians: some signs, which he takes for fact, herald its arrival. Has one of his hens started singing like a cockerel, or is she singing in her hut? A member of the family will soon die if that hen is not donated to the nearest monastery.'[iii]

The grisly story of Macedonia's relations with her neighbours this century reads like a cautionary tale aimed at illustrating how national pride always comes before a terrible fall. In 1912 the Serbian, Greek and Bulgarian armies arrived in the region to take over from the clerics and terrorists. Co-operating just long enough to kick the Turks out of the province and off the continent, they fell out immediately over the division of the spoils. An American-sponsored inquiry into the causes and conduct of the two Balkan wars of 1912 to 1914 recited a litany of blood-lettings, wanton destruction and the various Orthodox Churches' active involvement in the terror. It concluded almost despairingly,

> The burning of villages and the exodus of the defeated population is a normal and traditional incident of all Balkan wars and insurrections. It is the habit of all these peoples. What they have suffered themselves, they inflict in turn upon others. It could have been avoided only by imperative orders from Athens, Belgrade and Sofia, and only then if the Church and the insurgent organizations had seconded the resolve of the governments.[iv]

Macedonia was deluged in blood again and yet again in each of the world wars. By 1945 it was split between Greece, Yugoslavia, Bulgaria and Albania, the first two countries doing much the best in the share-out. While Greece resettled thousands of Greeks, primarily refugees from Turkey, in her southern share of Macedonia, Tito tactfully forbore from reincorporating his slice into Serbia where it had been between the world wars. Instead, he created the Yugoslav Republic of Macedonia, which gained a 'former' in front of its name in 1991, after it was permitted to withdraw from Milošević's Yugoslavia without a fight.

Today, the fragile new state's Orthodox Slavs think of themselves as Macedonians who speak a language close to, but different from, Bulgarian and perceive themselves as having been crucified by their noisier, greedier neighbours. Those Orthodox brothers, they say bitterly, have worked hard over the centuries to convince the rest of the world that there has never been such a thing as a Macedonian yearning for an independent homeland. Even today the Serbs claim them as southern Serbs, the Bulgarians would have them Bulgarians, and the Greeks maintain they are Bulgarians except in the northern Greek province of Macedonia where they have had to become pure Greek or leave the country. Whether one accepts the Macedonians' claim that they are none of these things seems to depend on whether one agrees with them that a certain eleventh-century tsar was Macedonian, rather than the Bulgarian most history books would have him.

Tsar Samuil might well have been Macedonian, but he thought of himself as a Bulgar because, at the time, the Bulgars were the only people who had managed to build an empire to rival Byzantium, and Samuil needed that precedent to lend weight to his own plans for expansion. The Byzantines certainly knew him as Bulgarian. It was the Byzantine Emperor Basil the Bulgar-Slayer – *not* Basil the Macedon-Slayer – who famously took on the invading Tsar Samuil's army in 1014. In one of the earliest instances of inter-Orthodox warring, Emperor Basil captured some fourteen thousand prisoners, and ordered that all but one in every hundred be blinded. The fortunate few, equipped with one eye apiece, led the mutilated army stumbling home. So shocking was the sight that Tsar Samuil had an apoplectic fit, sank into a coma and died.

Mindful of this appalling history, Macedonians still refer to their immediate neighbours – Serbia, Greece, Bulgaria and Albania – as 'the four wolves'. Since the end of the Cold War and the demise of Yugoslavia they have had to relearn the old reflex of watching for which ravening beast is the most dangerous. While Serbs pursued their plans for Greater Serbia in the early 1990s, Serbia looked like the hungriest wolf. The FYROM watched and trembled at the dismemberment of Croatia and the likely fate of Bosnia. No sooner had she escaped those jaws and gained international recognition of her independence in 1991, than the Greek wolf appeared to prevent her calling herself Macedonia. The Greeks protested that the use of the name Macedonia, the Macedonians' choice of a flag featuring the Vergina star of Alexander the Great and the depiction of the famous White Tower of Thessaloniki on one of her new banknotes, implied that the little republic was not only claiming the exclusively Greek heritage of Hellenized Alexander the Great, but also hatching long-term plans to annex the Greeks' slice of Macedonia. The Greeks calculated that the upstart FYROM-ians, as they called them, would be mad *not* to be dreaming along these lines because they would win three valuable prizes by such an expansion: the rich port city of Thessaloniki, an opening to the sea, and Mount Athos. To the furious and shocked embarrassment of her EU partners, Greece decided in 1994 to punish her little northern neighbour's presumed presumption by vetoing her taking the name Macedonia and saddling her with a crippling trade embargo. Barred from the Greek Macedonian port of Thessaloniki to the south, trying to observe UN sanctions against Serbia to the north, the FYROM was miserably and dangerously isolated for a year. The Greeks lifted the embargo when the Macedonians agreed to swap the Vergina star on their flag for a somewhat similar-looking sun emblem.

But the greediest and most threatening wolf, especially as far as Eastern Orthodoxy is concerned, is already within the FYROM, in the shape of a minority of Muslim Albanians which is growing as threateningly fast as that of neighbouring Kosovo across the border in Serbia. Accounting for around a quarter of Macedonia's population, they do not think of themselves as Macedonians and they can be guaranteed – just like their brothers in Serbia's neighbouring region of Kosovo – to want to hack off a piece of the FYROM and join it to a Greater Albania at some point in the future. As early as 1992 the FYROM's Albanians held a referendum and voted in favour of political and territorial autonomy. In early 1998, American and Scandinavian United Nations peace-keepers were patrolling the mountain roads in their white vehicles. The UN's first ever 'preventive' force, its aim was to stop the Albanian factor making the FYROM another Balkan battlefield and drawing Greece and Turkey – Nato allies – into the fray.*

Meanwhile, the Serbian wolf has not disappeared, just assumed

* At the start of Nato's campaign to prevent the Serbs' 'ethnic cleansing' of Kosovo Albanians in March 1999, over 10,000 Kosovo Albanian refugees crossed the border into Macedonia – tipping the already precarious ethnic balance.

ecclesiastical shepherd's clothing. For the past thirty-five years the FYROM's independent Orthodox Church has been struggling to get free of the Serbian Church's smothering big brotherly hug. The final break came in 1967 but the Serbian Church has never accepted it and continues to view the separation as a disgustingly schismatic ecclesiastical coup and a tragic loss to Serbia. National borders have always been easier to alter than ancient Orthodox ones. The Macedonian Orthodox Church remains a pariah, outside the Orthodox fold, unrecognized by all Europe's other Orthodox Churches, ignored or resented by most.

But the Macedonians have persevered in their ecclesiastical secessionism because, even today, there is a real fear that a small, landlocked Balkan country with hungry wolves for neighbours and a church that has not been recognized by its brother Orthodox Churches, stands precious little chance of prospering. The US State Department understands this too. In January 1996 the American and FYROM ambassadors to Turkey teamed up for a trip to Istanbul's Phanar district, to call on the Ecumenical Patriarch of Constantinople and lodge a joint appeal for the speedy recognition of the Macedonian Orthodox Church. They found Patriarch Bartholomaios sympathetic but unable to help. Canonically speaking, the fate of the Macedonian Church remains in the hands of the Serbian Church.

Was ever a place so unlucky, and what was the betting that the Macedonians were a thoroughly decent, hospitable, peaceful people in spite of all this?

'You know, they were always the nicest people in the old Yugoslavia,' mused Bogdan, relaxed now that we were at last nearing Skopje and the fog was lifting.

'Oh, yes? And who were the worst?'

'The Serbs.' He chuckled.

Had I been wise to invite Bogdan the Serb to join me on this leg of the journey? I wondered. The Macedonians have good reasons to fear and loathe the Serbs. Perhaps we would be refused accommodation, or petrol for the Citroën with its Belgrade number-plates, or an audience with the Archbishop of the self-proclaimed Macedonian

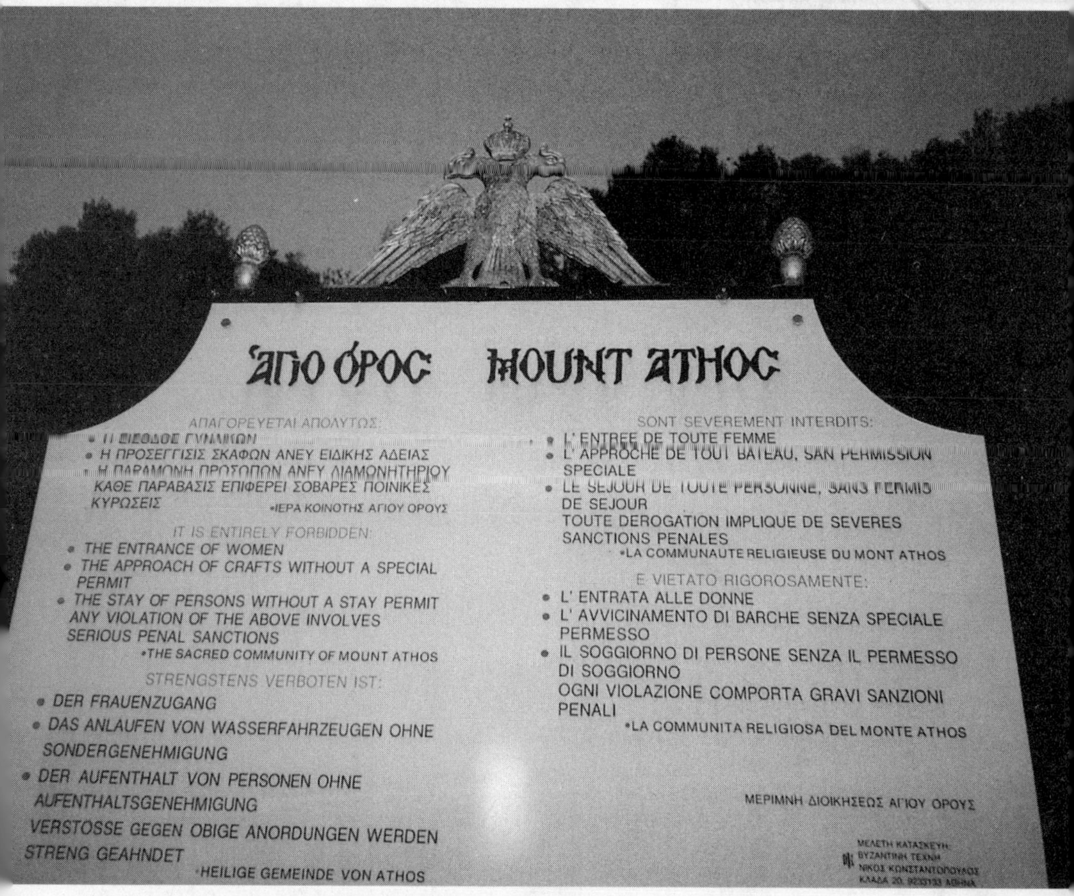

1 Warning signboard at Mount Athos's land border

2A Krka monastery, Croatia
lying low in its valley,
October 1997

2B Father Ilija flanked by two
Serbs in Krka's courtyard,
October 1997

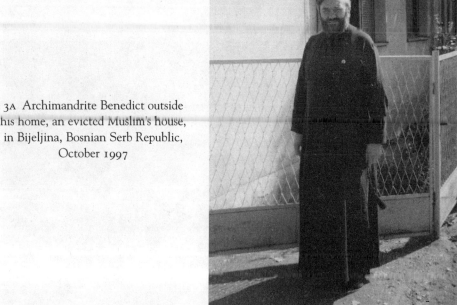

3A Archimandrite Benedict outside his home, an evicted Muslim's house, in Bijeljina, Bosnian Serb Republic, October 1997

3B Bishop Vasilije Cačavenda of Tuzla and Zvornik at the 600th anniversary of the Battle of Kosovo celebrations in Kosovo, June 1989

4 Fourteenth-century monastery of Gračanica, Kosovo

5 Father Sava (left) of Dečani monastery, Kosovo, protesting against the treatment of Serbs and their churches after Nato's offensive in Kosovo, *Guardian*, July 17, 1999

6A Archbishop Amfilohije Radović of Montenegro anointing the bones of generations of dead Nikčevićs at Jovandol monastery, Montenegro, October 1997

6B Archbishop Amfilohije, the author and Goran taking tea at Jovandol monastery, Montenegro, October 1997

7A Nineteenth-century white timbered buildings of Ohrid, the former Yugoslav Republic of Macedonia

7B Kastoria, northern Greece

8A Bishop Naum of Strumica
with nuns at Veljuša monastery,
the former Yugoslav Republic of
Macedonia, December 1997

8B Veljuša's thirteenth-
century church

Orthodox Church. But it was far too late to reconsider. There was some consolation in the thought that fortunately Bogdan was not a monk as well as a Serb.

A fortnight after our meeting at Kosovo's Dečani monastery Father Sava had e-mailed me an account of the frightful indignities awaiting any Serbian churchman trying to cross the FYROM. He had been en route to Mount Athos for some sunny spiritual refreshment before winter when he had fallen foul of the Macedonian border police. Father Sava wrote,

> ... Our southern neighbours [FYROM Macedonians] would not let us pass through their country, as usual. Because we had our monastic robes on, it was only after a very hot discussion that they let us go, but with no right to stop anywhere on the road ... Such behaviour is unfortunately greatly due to the irregular canonic status of the Macedonian church which has not yet been granted independence from the Serbian church after 30 years of schism. I guess that St Sava in the 12th century travelled around the Balkans much more easily than we do at the beginning of the 21st century! ... I bet these Balkan adventures sound very unusual to you in England but this is the reality in which we live ...

I had e-mailed him back immediately, begging for clarification and further details about the contretemps. Was he suggesting that the schismatic Macedonian Church had teamed up with the country's border police to harass and offend their Serb brothers in Christ? Could this petty harassment be the Macedonian Church's revenge for decades of suffering under the yoke of the Serbian Church?

Back came Father Sava's affirming reply, detailing how their passage through to Athos had finally been secured when one of the Serb surgeons he had been travelling with threatened to telephone a complaint to his most illustrious patient – the FYROM's President Gligorov. Otherwise, Father Sava wrote, he would have been forced to disrobe and don civvies for as long as it took to drive to the Greek border. I resolved to raise the matter with the head of the schismatic

Macedonian Church, Archbishop Mihail, just as soon as I could arrange to see him in the FYROM's capital, Skopje.

At two o'clock in the morning the city was quiet and dark, and poorly signposted. The high minarets of Skopje's mosques, lit up near their tops with rows of green, pink or white fluorescent strip-lights, were its most striking landmarks. If I hadn't known better I could have sworn we had arrived in the capital of a Muslim state rather than the city that had served as the capital of Tsar Dušan's great Serbian empire.

But by morning it looked very different.

Elegantly situated beside the sluggish Vardar river, close by the ruin of one of Tsar Dušan's castles, the archiepiscopal palace was a plain white two-storey villa with a large satellite dish on its roof and a heavy black gate. We had been warned that His Beatitude Archbishop Mihail of Ohrid and Macedonia was a stickler for punctuality, and were a full twenty minutes early for our audience.

Graciously accepting that his Serb presence at my meeting might prove obnoxious to the prelate, Bogdan had disappeared in search of petrol. Instead I was accompanied by a young Macedonian named Ljupčo Spasovski, a professor of English philology at Skopje University and a colleague of Archbishop Mihail's daughter, who had facilitated this meeting. I was confident that I had the best of introductions. A smiling middle-aged woman in a pink velour dressing-gown opened the door and ushered us straight into a large reception room, where the Archbishop rose from his plush armchair to welcome us. A handsome old man, he wore his thin white locks combed back off his forehead in the shoulder-length style of England's King Charles I, and his long, white beard was neatly trimmed to mid-chest length, out of the way of the heavy archiepiscopal medallion dangling from its chain. We sat down to take coffee.

'So tell me, what will be the title of your book?' the Archbishop began.

I told him, rather hoping he would fail to catch its meaning, but he immediately saw the point.

'Good, good! Angels fall because they are too proud. We Macedonians are too proud of our past . . .' he murmured, then discarded that uncomfortable thought and continued more confidently, 'We are a people mentioned many times in the Bible: "A vision appeared to Paul in the night; a man of Macedonia was standing beseeching him and saying, 'Come over to Macedonia and help us,'"'v he quoted.

His style of delivery was astonishing. The filthy and famished Desert Fathers could have sounded like him when recounting their visions. Or, if Christ the Pantocrator in those church domes could speak, he might express himself in this sonorous way, with dramatic pauses for enhanced effect and special savouring of a word here and there. With his head slightly tilted towards the ceiling, eyes closed and cassock sleeves falling back to reveal white arms raised in a gesture of perpetual worship, the Archbishop recited an abridged and highly debatable version of Macedonia's history in the two millennia since Christ. Naturally enough, in his version, there was no question that the crucial Tsar Samuil was Macedonian, not Bulgarian.

He was proud that the emphatically Macedonian (rather than arguably Greek or Bulgarian) saints Cyril and Methodius from the suburbs of ninth-century Thessaloniki had been responsible for bringing Orthodoxy to the Slavs in a language they could understand. Those two 'Apostles of the Slavs' – one a professor diplomat, the other a senior civil servant turned monk – had invented first the Glagolithic and then the Cyrillic script, which was a mix of Greek, Latin and Hebrew letters. He explained how they had then translated the old Greek texts into their new language which later became known as Church Slavonic, a tool perfectly suited to the peacefully expansionist purposes of the mightiest Christian power on Earth. The Schism was more than a century away so both the Pope in Rome and the Ecumenical Patriarch in Constantinople were able to bless the Macedonian brothers on their first mission to central Europe to evangelize the kingdom of Moravia. In a letter to the King of that distant province, the Byzantine Emperor had emphasized the worth of his envoys and their books. 'Accept a gift greater and more precious than any gold or silver, than any precious stones or treasure – so that you can be counted among the great peoples who glorify God in their own language,'[vi] he had told him. But Cyril and Methodius found that blessings from on high counted for little on the ground. Moravia's Roman Catholic clergy quickly surmised that these refined Byzantine siblings and their teachings in a language close to the local Slav vernacular spelt ruin for their own Latin business. The brothers were hounded out of Moravia and died considering their mission a tragic failure. But it was thanks to them and their disciples St Kliment and St Naum that Church Slavonic eventually spread as far as Bulgaria, Macedonia, Serbia and today's Ukraine, to become medieval Europe's third lingua franca after Greek and Latin. The fact that even today Serbs, Bulgarians and Russians are still using a basically Macedonian invention to write their Slav languages was a source of gigantic pride to the Archbishop. 'Christianity did not get to the bottom of the Slav *soul* until we heard the gospel in Slavonic . . .' he intoned.

He was equally proud that the first Slav university, founded by St Kliment on the banks of the FYROM's Lake Ohrid, educated 3,500 Slav Orthodox missionaries, each one proficient in 'theology, philosophy, rhetoric, astronomy, mathematics, Greek and even agriculture'. This ninth-century university, he pointed out, later gave birth not just to the first Slav literature but also to the first stirrings of what became the western Renaissance. Similarly proud that all the Balkans and even distant Kiev looked to Ohrid for supplies of Slavonic church texts, he was equally delighted to be able to inform me that Macedonia's first patriarchate there at Ohrid – which most historians would classify as Bulgarian – was established at the end of the ninth century. Over two hundred years older than Peć, it was proving useful ammunition against the Serbian Church.

'The Serbs have always come to Macedonia with their armies. They did not come to enlighten the people. They only used the Church to make people Serbs,' pronounced the Archbishop.

Of that he bears the scars of personal experience. Towards the end of the 1930s, when Yugoslavia was a kingdom ruled by a Serbian royal dynasty and what is now the FYROM was unhappily subsumed into southern Serbia, Archbishop Mihail was a young and excellent graduate of theological school. Returning to his native town of Štip to take up his first post, he presented himself to the local bishop to be assigned his duties. '"Thank God you're ready at last! You're welcome. We've been waiting for you. Now, what work would you like to do?"' he asked me.

'"I'd like to be a religion teacher in a high school."

'"Bright young man, but *fool*! Do you know how much you'll earn for this?"

'"It is enough for me."

'"Look here, you can be so and so's personal secretary and double your salary."

'"But what do I have to do for this?"

'"Nothing much. You just have to tell these people of Štip that they are Serbs."

'"I am not educated for this kind of thing. I've been trained to teach the holy evangelists."

'"You can tie your holy evangelists around the tom cat's tail!" he shouted at me.'

Archbishop Mihail was relishing the old drama. 'I began to sweat. I could not understand how a bishop could use such words. I pinched my hand to see if I was dreaming. I was thinking *Shame* on you! Then I reached to take my handkerchief out of my pocket, because I was sweating. But he thought I was reaching for a gun and he bolted upstairs quickly to make a call to the police. I could hear him shouting into the telephone, "Come quick, there is a young man, a *comitadji*. He's trying to kill me!" The police came immediately and searched me.'

Archbishop Mihail was in his dramatic stride, invoking divine inspiration with his closed eyes and raised arms. As a punishment for that *faux pas* and a host of other insufficiently patriotic activities, he had gone on to serve a prison term in Serbia.

At last he paused long enough for me to broach the delicate matter of Father Sava's humiliating treatment at the hands of the FYROM border police. Ljupčo, who had scarcely believed me when I had related the story to him in the car on our way to the palace, sat alertly forward in his chair. I began explaining the problem to the Archbishop in as tactful a way as I could manage. Although he looked discomfited, he did not deny that it had happened, indeed that it happened regularly. 'It is not our power which forces monks to take off their frocks,' he began rather engagingly, 'it is the law.' But it is a law he does not dispute, apparently, 'because the Serbian Church likes to have its priests and bishops in Macedonia and we cannot let them now. One priest came to stir up trouble in the Crna Gora region north of Skopje. We don't have our priests in Serbia. Everything must be carried out on a *quid pro quo* basis these days.'

The Archbishop could not help betraying his loathing of his neighbouring 'chauvinist Churches', who will not do him the kindness of recognizing his Church. The Greek Church had been consistently hostile towards the Macedonian one, and doubly so since learning that the Archbishop enjoys cordial relations with Pope John Paul II. The Archbishop chuckled proudly over the memory of being obliged to make a television address to the nation on his return from Rome in 1995. His faithful flock had needed ample reassurance that he had not succumbed to any papal blandishments and abandoned Eastern Orthodoxy. But he was happiest on the subject of when his Church would cease to be the pariah of the Eastern Orthodox communion. The millennium was the focus of all his hopes.

'I think that by the jubilee of the Third Millennium there will be a great activity in this sphere,' he said, 'I should be the happiest person in the *world* to one day participate at a gathering of the heads of all the Orthodox Churches!' In an excited aside to his fellow Macedonian, Ljupčo, he said, 'With her book she can help our cause!' and turning back to me he asked, 'When will your book be published?'

Surely, I thought, the other Eastern Orthodox Churches could not be so hard-hearted as to deny this old man his heart's last pious desire. The Serbs, Greeks and Bulgarians must understand the peculiarly strong urge to link ecclesiastical independence from Constantinople to political independence. After all, at one time or another they had all trodden the same rocky separatist road. The question of the status of the Macedonian Church looked to me like an open and shut case, its independence entirely reasonable. But reason is neither here nor there, of course. The ideal of a universal Christian commonwealth ruled from Constantinople is worlds away from the reality of fragmented Orthodox Europe, but disappointing reality has never been any reason to abandon the mythic ideal, to recognize yet another narrowly national Church in violation of the Church canons.

The Archbishop disappeared into his adjoining office.

Narrowly national, even dangerously nationalistic, this Church might well prove to be I thought, as I got up to inspect his wall clock. It was set in a chunk of unvarnished wood, roughly carved in the instantly recognizable shape of a Greater Macedonia, comprising the FYROM, a slice of Bulgaria, another of Albania and, of course, the northern Greek province of Macedonia. Any Greek, noting its extension to the shores of the Aegean and the three crooked fingers, with Mount Athos on the easternmost, would have blanched at the sight and found confirmation of his worst nightmare. 'That was probably just a gift,' said Ljupčo hurriedly, gently taking my elbow and steering me away from the wall.

His Beatitude reappeared, shuffling across the shiny parquet floor in his slippers, to thrust no fewer than four little gilt crosses into my hand as a parting gift. I moved to shake his hand. 'Kiss it!' he commanded.

Back in the car Ljupčo cleared his throat and said, 'Actually, he was being too political for my taste, but right now I think Macedonia needs someone like that.'*

I said nothing. That clock had been a shock. I had cast the Macedonians as blameless victims, especially cruelly set upon by Serbs and Greeks, but I was going to have to reconsider that position in the light of that timepiece. Why should I have thought, even for a moment, that the Macedonians could be immune to the Phyletist plague? It was just that the day before my meeting with the Archbishop I had seen something that suggested they were.

* Archbishop Mihail died in July 1999. The Macedonian Eastern Orthodox Church remains unrecognized.

Bogdan and I had been exploring the centre of smoggy Skopje with its ugly modern buildings and the unmistakable marks of a long, slow economic depression in every boarded-up shop-front and abandoned building-site. The air reeked of diesel fumes, laced with the warm stink of kebab and the more pleasing aroma of strong Turkish coffee. In the winding narrow streets of the old Albanian quarter were rows of little shops displaying dark gold jewellery, probably imported from Turkey. The FYROM, it had seemed to me, was the sort of desperate, barely viable country whose people bought gold with whatever little extra money they had because the metal keeps its value and travels well. In the city's main square we had laughed at a posse of entrepreneurial Father Christmases busily inveigling parents of toddlers into allowing their offspring to hop aboard a fancy makeshift sleigh with them to have their expensive Polaroid photographs taken. Business was not bad for them, but the odd street-seller with only a couple of a lighters or a box of batteries to flog was a better measure of how much poorer the FYROM had become even than Serbia by December 1997.

There was no one hawking the patriotic T-shirts I had been unable to resist on a visit here back in the summer of 1989, jolly articles emblazoned with maps of Greater Macedonia divided into its three (ideally) constituent parts – Eger (Greece's slice), Pirin (Bulgaria's) and Vardar (Yugoslavia's). Macedonians had been dreaming the Greater Macedonia dream in the late eighties, when the euphoria brought on by collapsing Communism had made anything seem possible. No longer, it seemed. Instead of that T-shirt shop Bogdan and I chanced upon a dusty stall selling a battered-looking selection of car stickers and key-rings reading 'MK' for Macedonia. A thick stack of another sort of sticker caught my eye. It was that very same outline map of Greater Macedonia, this time embellished with the distinctive Vergina star emblem of Alexander the Great, a white banner reading 'Death or Freedom' and a fat red heart for 'I love Macedonia'. The thickness of the stack and the layer of dust covering it strongly suggested that the Greater Macedonia dream was either safely dead or dying. I assumed that the bloodbath in Bosnia had convinced the Macedonians that dreaming of territorial expansion could only end in more blood-letting. Joking with the stall-keeper, I had bought a sticker and slapped it straight on the back cover of my notebook.

Now the Archbishop's clock was forcing me to think again. If a Macedonian as influential as Archbishop Mihail himself seemed to be dreaming of reconstituting an entity as vast as the Ottoman province of Macedonia, there were bound to be thousands more like him.

That evening Bogdan and I dined with Ljupčo and his elegant girlfriend Anna, in a chic little private restaurant way out in one of the city's suburbs. Over brandy, pickled vegetables and heavy meat dishes doused in sour cream, the talk turned to assessing the precise degree of humiliation that Ljupčo the Macedonian and Bogdan the Serb had suffered at the hands of the Greeks. Ljupčo was easily winning the contest.

'You know, we have to wait hours to get a Greek visa at the consulate, they keep us guessing until the last moment, and let me tell you why no one was buying those MK car stickers you saw yesterday. You know most of us want to be able to go to Greece to shop but put one of those on your car and you'd only have to scratch it off before you got to the border. What's the point? They're bastards, those Greeks!'

'With us they—' started Bogdan, but Ljupčo had not finished.

'It's a bit too bloody much,' he railed on in his impeccable Oxford English, 'the indignity of being called a *malaka* – that means something like mother-fucker or wanker – by some fat Greek border guard who probably only has primary-school education, – just because I'm a Macedonian!'

So much for the old Byzantine *symphonia* ideal. I was glimpsing the centuries-old source of much of the discord between the Balkan Orthodox nations. Orthodox Slavs in the region strongly suspect that modern Greeks still regard them in the same way as their Ancient and Byzantine Greek forebears did in the sixth and seventh centuries, as uncivilized and uncouth, as barbarians.

The Greeks who ran the patriarchate of Constantinople through-out the Ottoman era busily propagated an ideology based on Greek superiority, which the Ottomans fully endorsed. When Sultan Meh-met had appointed old Gennadius Patriarch of Constantinople in 1453 he had also decided that the old Byzantine Orthodox Church structures would do very well as the bones of a ready-made civil service to run the educational, legal and tax affairs of the entire *Rum-millet* – literally, the nation of *Romaioi*, or all the empire's Orthodox Christians. The independent patriarchates at Ohrid and Peć were abolished. No longer the spiritual half in the Byzantine *symphonia* partnership, Patriarch Gennadius and his Constantinople Greek suc-cessors were the Sultan's privileged vassals, free to lord it over the *Rum-millet* until the second half of the nineteenth century. Theirs was an empire within an empire, and only Russian Orthodox escaped their jurisdiction.

After 1453 the Constantinople patriarchate replaced all non-Greek church leaders in the *Rum-millet* with Greeks. The faith remained, a holy comfort with its promise of a better life to come, but those Greek clergy were distrusted and feared. The cause was simple. Generations of Constantinople patriarchs felt obliged to express their hearty thanks to the Sultan for his endorsement of their appointments by showering him with lavish gifts. The custom soon deteriorated into outright bribery and ever larger sums of cash became the only means of gaining Orthodoxy's highest office. Naturally these crippling costs were passed on to the appointed Greek bishops, who in turn passed them to the lowly parish priests, who had no choice but to squeeze the luckless peasants dry.

Long before the fall of Constantinople the Byzantines had been prone to heavy-handedness in their dealings with the Slavic tribes they pacified and converted to Christianity. When the Byzantines moved into Macedonia after Tsar Samuil's defeat in the eleventh century they 'started suppressing Slavonic written documents, Slav hagiographies etc'.[vii] In Ottoman times the Danubian principalities of Wallachia and Moldavia, today's Romania, bore the brunt of it. By the eighteenth century both their clergy *and* their rulers were Greek.

The principalities, which were known as another 'Garden of the Mother of God' on account of their natural bounty, were raped of their wealth by Greeks who had purchased their posts from the Sultan. Half-way through the same century the Patriarch of Constantinople compounded the Church's errors by prevailing upon the Sultan to close down the briefly regained Macedonian (or Bulgarian) and Serbian patriarchates at Ohrid and Peć because he feared they might become centres of national resistance to challenge his own Greek hegemony. The Bulgarians grew so heartily sick of the Constantinople patriarchate meddling in their affairs that they toyed with the notion of jettisoning Orthodoxy altogether and converting to Roman Catholicism. Instead they won the Ottoman Porte's backing to send their Greek bishops packing and, in 1870, established their own Exarchate Church. Irritated at such a flagrant flouting of the Church canons, the Patriarch of Constantinople coined a brand new heresy to condemn the Bulgarians' schismatic move: 'Phyletism'.

But, of course, there was nothing new about Phyletism. The Greeks, grown fearfully nationalist in their doomed Byzantine Empire after 1204, had been the first to fall into that heresy. They had shown the Balkan Orthodox peoples how to mix their ethnic politics with religion in that lethal way. But then the Greeks might never have grown so defensively exclusive had the Fourth Crusaders never paid their capital a visit.

On the other hand, the self-love of the Greeks might have grown out of their natural pride that Byzantine culture was based on Ancient Greek culture and that Greek was the language of the empire. The Greek clergy monopolized education throughout 'Turkey in Europe'. Even in the nineteenth century they were using religion and language as a means of control and expansion, where Byzantine missionary-diplomats like Cyril and Methodius had tactfully used only the religion.

> *Albanians, Wallachians, Bulgarians,*
> *speakers of other tongues, rejoice!*
> *And ready yourselves all to become Greeks*

Abandoning your barbaric tongue, speech and customs
So that to your descendants they may appear as myths.[viii]

A bright Macedonian, a Wallachian or Moldavian from the Danubian principalities, a Serb or a Bulgarian studied in Greek or not at all. There is the sad tale of a nineteenth-century Macedonian schoolboy who was utterly Hellenized in this way, at a Greek school in the lakeside town of Ohrid. In 1860 he won first prize in a Greek poetry competition and was loudly hailed as a 'second Homer', until the Greek judges discovered his lowly Slavic origins. Mortified, he resolved never to write in Greek again. On his return home he immersed himself in his mother tongue then sat down to write in it. The results were disappointing. 'In Greek I sang like a swan; now in Slavic I cannot even sing like a donkey,'[ix] he mourned.

To be a Slav or a Bulgar meant to be a yokel barbarian. At the feet of Greek clergy, generations of bright young Balkan Slavs imbibed a sense of their racial inferiority and set about Hellenizing themselves. They could not have failed to pick up on the Constantinople Greeks' confidence that their Byzantine empire would be reconstituted, with the Greeks in charge, of course, the moment the Turks were driven back whence they had come. By the mid-nineteenth century, however, those Greek schools, ablaze with western notions about the desirability of nation states, were spawning Slavic freedom-fighters fired with a holy double mission: to throw off the Greek as well as the Ottoman yoke.

The division between Greek and barbarian was as pronounced as ever in the Second Balkan War of 1913, when the Greek press and government whipped up a frenzy of hatred against the enemy Bulgarians. One Greek army commander was heard to opine, 'When you have to deal with barbarians you must behave like a barbarian yourself. It is the only thing they understand.'[x] A popular Greek poster of the time, entitled 'The Bulgar-Eater', shows a boggle-eyed Greek fighter biting a chunk from the cheek of a Bulgarian.

The way Greece's Slav neighbours see it, Greece has managed to blind the West to her true character. How otherwise, they reason, could she have won admittance to the EU as well as Nato? The way they look at it, the naive and gullible West has willfully ignored the fact that there is no connection between the democrats and philosophers of Ancient Greece and the mongrel mix of modern Greeks today. The Greeks, they mutter, are the ones who tortured Macedonia with their trade embargo in 1992, while almost openly championing Serbia's vainglorious and doomed rebellion against the rest of the world. They have a point, I thought. In 1994, it was the Greek Church that saw fit to decorate Radovan Karadžić with the 900-year-old order of St Dionysius of Xanthe and hail him as 'one of the most prominent sons of our Lord Jesus Christ working for peace'. I also remembered Bogdan once telling me that, while holidaying in Greece during the war in Bosnia, he had often been approached by Greeks who slapped him on the back and congratulated him, saying something along the lines of 'You Serbs are doing a great job! Keep at it. I wish our lot had enough guts to take on our Turks like you're taking on yours!' presumably meaning the Turks in northern Cyprus . . .

The Macedonian brandy was doing its devilish work. The conversation had moved on and the bill had arrived. Outside, the quiet of the suburban back-street was shattered by sounds of gunshot. No, just a fire-cracker or two in the hands of delinquent teenagers celebrating the passing of 1997, or auguring the dangers of 1998.

LAKE OHRID

Midwinter, off-season Lake Ohrid and its town looked enchanting.

A setting sun between high black hills was turning the lake a coppery pink and the clouds all the colours of a rainbow trout. The windows of Ohrid's tall white houses, stacked anyhow on the hillside as if jostling for the best view of that water, reflected the same steadily deepening light. Here and there a round street-lamp glowed pearl-white against the jet-black outlines of the trees. Restaurateurs in their shirt-sleeves were out, lacing their lakeside establishments with fairy-lights, in anticipation of new year festivities. A scattering of locals strolled along, silhouetted against the glowing lake.

We parked the Citroën on the stone harbour, facing out across the water. The air was mild, a tonic after Skopje's smog. Climbing a narrow cobbled street, we passed the shadowy church of St Sophia built by the Byzantines as a mini reminder of the great cathedral back home, after they had blinded Tsar Samuil's soldiers and occupied the area. A savour of baking fish wafted out of a nearby restaurant. Bogdan announced that he felt like staying put for a week or two. The place was wonderfully relaxing, but I was remembering something I had read about a Byzantine prelate, posted here from Constantinople a thousand years ago. Even the superior flavour of Ohrid's trout had not compensated Archbishop Theophylactus for his exile from the most civilized city on Earth. He likened the air off Lake Ohrid to 'a deadly breath from Hades'. The smell of the town's inhabitants had reminded him of 'the hide of some ill-scented beast', and the way they had listened to him speaking Greek, of 'donkeys listening to a lyre's notes'.[xi]

It was getting too dark to see much but everywhere there were the rounded outlines of Byzantine church roofs like the ones I had seen in Serbia's Kosovo region, less than a hundred miles away across a national border. Set on stubby round towers, their shallow red-tiled roofs were fetching. Workaday structures, those low stone churches were as solid and serviceable as English country pubs, and they seemed almost as plentiful as houses in that oldest part of the town. Such a thing was not impossible. Between the ninth and eleventh centuries Saints Cyril and Methodius, Kliment, Naum and their disciples had raised this lakeside settlement, the capital of Tsar Samuil's short-lived empire, to the vital spiritual-cum-academic centre Archbishop Mihail had boasted about. Its holy learned lights had shone bright enough to be seen as far away as Kiev. Ohrid had been the Slavic world's Oxbridge, at a time when Oxford was a bustling trading post without even a church spire to speak of.

Thereafter, the place declined for a good nine centuries – at least as the cradle of an independent Macedonia – until, in 1958, the see of Ohrid was elevated to an archbishopric. For Yugoslav Macedonians this was a first step towards the re-establishment of their national Church. The Serbian Orthodox Church meanwhile was dead set against the move. But the Macedonians had atheist Communist Tito's blessing, which then counted for everything. Tito had owed them a favour because thousands of them, churchmen included, had swelled the ranks of his Communist partisans in the Second World War. Delighted by the great leader's clemency, Macedonians had tactfully stopped short of declaring an outright schism with the Serbian Church, and instead confirmed the Serbian Patriarch as their highest authority. It was a compromise, they said, 'made for the sake of the interest of the brotherly peoples with whom the Macedonians were allied in one community'[xii] – Tito's officially atheist Communist Yugoslavia.

There was wild rejoicing. The bells rang out all over Ohrid and Macedonia as the new Archbishop Dositej of Ohrid and Macedonia, seated on a sixteenth-century throne inlaid with mother-of-pearl, clutching the crozier of the medieval archbishops of Ohrid in one hand and a holy icon of St Kliment in the other, addressed his flock. 'Great acts,' he told them, 'are not performed by great nations but by nations which have great souls, nations which are ready and willing to make great sacrifices for their liberty and will never submit to foreign rule.'[xiii] Such fighting talk cannot have gone down well back in Belgrade. Nevertheless, nine years later when the final schism between the Serbian and Macedonian Churches took place, it also had Tito's blessing. The Serbian Church could only grumble about a canonical coup and fume in private.

At the top of the town, with the best view of the lake, was the old but much renovated church of St Kliment, closed up and dark, and surrounded by unswept leaves, discarded plastic bags and Coca-Cola cans. Bogdan remembered it well from a school trip here a quarter of a century before. Best of all he recalled the church's elderly caretaker swearing to him that if he was to go inside and lay his ear against the tomb of St Kliment he would surely hear the holy man's heart still beating. Somehow neither of us was overly surprised when our host that night turned out to be that old man's son. In an overheated main room, our host and his womenfolk plied us with syrupy coffee and brandy. Inevitably they asked what we were up to, a Serb and an Englishwoman, in Ohrid, in late December. When I told them the proposed title of my book, the man gave me a hard, suspicious stare and said, 'But angels *don't* fall. Stars fall but angels live for eternity.' I asked them if they were believers. His wife began slowly, 'Yes . . . we need Christianity like flowers need nourishment . . .' until her husband interrupted her with a firm, 'It is our custom, and our tradition. You know,' he boasted, 'there used to be so many churches in Ohrid that now you can't dig anywhere without finding church foundations. There's one under this very house.'

The following morning we met an old man who was buttoned up tight in a worn overcoat as protection against the stiff breeze and sporadic rain blowing off the lake. He was overseeing the gutting of his home, one of the tall white houses in the old quarter, and had paused to help us find the caretaker in charge of the two little churches opposite.

'Once there were 365 churches in Ohrid – one for every day of the year – until the Turks came. Now there are only forty-eight. They destroyed so many of them and for five hundred years St Sophia was a mosque,' he informed us.

On discovering our nationalities he determined to give his cosmopolitan credentials a good airing. His wife was a Serb from Belgrade, so perhaps Bogdan knew her family. He had once visited England and seen the Barbican Centre and Shakespeare's birthplace at Stratford-upon-Avon.

'The inside of Shakespeare's house was *exactly* like the interiors of our houses here – you go into any one of these houses,' he said, pointing up the cobbled street, 'they're all the same. We could be making a fortune if we opened them all up to the tourists!'

We were starting to wander off towards the little churches with the diminutive old caretaker – who had appeared holding a couple of huge, rusting iron keys – when he called after us, 'Barbican . . . Stratford-upon-Avon . . . Oxford!'

The caretaker led us through a gate into a small courtyard to the 'his' of the 'his 'n' hers' churches facing each other across a cobbled road too narrow for a car to drive down. These were not Macedonian churches but Serbian, built in the fourteenth century, shortly after Tsar Dušan had moved his court to Skopje and had himself crowned 'King of the *Romaioi* and Serbs'. The guide explained that they had been quarantine churches. Visitors to the town in the fourteenth century would have been corralled into them for about ten days, the men into this one, called St Nikolaj the Hospitallers', the women into the Church of the Mother of God. They would have undergone a cursory medical examination and prayed and slept in the enlarged church porches, with frescoes of the saints – including a sprinkling of Serbian Nemanja kings and the Byzantines' Constantine the Great and his mother Helena – on the walls to prepare them for the world to come. My eye was caught by one, a not very old but marvellously vivid fresco depicting a giant wearing curling black moustachoes, fancy fish-net leggings and a pistachio green tunic. He was struggling, legs kicking the air like a can-can dancer's, to free himself from the clutches of a tiny youth who was seated astride his chest, holding a long dagger to his throat. Could this, I wondered, be tiny Macedonia taking on the mighty Turk? The caretaker was unable to enlighten me.

At the 'hers' of the two churches the guide showed us a photo-graph of a mass grave unearthed some time in the 1970s, here at the back of the church. They would have been cholera victims, he said. The original iconostasis was gone. 'I don't know who took it,' he grumbled, 'probably the Greeks, or the Serbs or the Bulgarians – maybe even the British.'

'Do you feel like a real Macedonian, then?' I asked him.

'How could I be anything else?' he grunted.

'Why are there so many churches in Ohrid?' I persisted, as he wielded one of the giant keys to close the gate behind us.

He clicked his one or two remaining teeth in irritation and frowned at my ignorance. 'Because Orthodoxy was born in Ohrid, that's why! The first university in the world was here in Ohrid, that's why!'

'I thought Orthodoxy was born in Byzantium.'

'Byzantium – pah!' he replied.

Bogdan and I strolled on up the town then turned off left, through a small park, and came at last to the site of that first university and the oldest monastery in the Balkans, which is known as the church of either St Kliment or St Panteleimon. Today there is nothing much to see, just a white stone tracing of the outline of the original church in the shape of a Greek cross. The main building is now a square stone mosque built by the Turks from the stones of the old church, stripped and empty save for a handful of workmen engaged in shoring up its roof. From his scaffolding perch one shouted down to us, above the racket of the radio, that it would soon be a church again – Ohrid's forty-ninth.

Thirty kilometres down the right side of the lake, overlooking it and bang on the FYROM's border with Albania, is the monastery of St Naum. We drove down there through brilliant watery sunshine, past steep hillsides pocked with long-empty hermits' caves, and villages named after saints but ruined by off-season package-tour hotels called Hotel Granite and Hotel Concrete. Turning off the road towards the monastery, we passed a large signpost saying in English, 'BORDER ZONE! ONLY PERSONS WITH PERMISSION ALLOWED!' A downpour started.

'St Naum is baptizing us with holy water,' wisecracked Bogdan, as we made a dash from the car to the monastery gates.

Inside the cobbled courtyard, with its little 1,500-year-old stone church in the centre, we were met by a deafening noise, a warlike clattering and drumming of rain-water coursing down the monastery buildings' new tin drainpipes. Seven bedraggled peacocks further enlivened the scene, but I was more interested in the scale of those monastery buildings. Brand new, not quite finished and three storeys high, they dwarfed the pretty church, whose treasure includes a three-hundred-year-old wooden iconostasis with an icon of a redheaded St Naum bearing in his hands a miniature replica of the church. It seemed to me that such a lapse of architectural taste could never have been committed without a very pressing ulterior motive and I was wondering what it might be when there was a *Bang!* . . . BANG! Automatically, I ducked for cover inside the church porch where a jolly monk selling souvenirs laughed and said, 'Take no notice. That's just the Albanians blowing up the mines in their border area. They're at it night and day.'

Whether because of the warrior tattoo of water running down drainpipes, or the shock of the Albanians de-mining their border, it was hard to say, but by the time we left St Naum I was convinced that those buildings, far from housing monks' cells, could not be anything but a barracks, reserved for military use on the day the currently most threatening Albanian 'wolf' turned hungry enough to attack. It seemed to me that only a motive as pressing as national security could have induced the Macedonians to sacrifice the loveliness of one of their favourite churches.

BANG! *Bang!* . . . *Bang!* rang out across the lake.

VELJUŠA MONASTERY

We were heading east under a wide pale sky, along a straight, clear tree-lined road, through bare fields dotted with giant Marlboro cowboy billboards, on the trail of the charismatic young Bishop of Strumica.

Thirty-six-year-old Bishop Naum had been hard at work resuscitating the FYROM's moribund monastic life by calling young Macedonians to leave their families and follow him into God's service. Only two years before the republic had boasted a grand total of five monks and nuns. The fact that by early 1998 she had more than fifty was yet another source of pride to Archbishop Mihail, who had told me that his youngest bishop had been working miracles since arriving home from an eight-year sojourn on Mount Athos. 'Every day there are more monks and nuns – so many now that Bishop Naum has nowhere to put them!' he had joked.

Late December sunshine warmed us through the Citroën's windscreen. Up ahead in the distance were mountains hazy enough to be mistaken for storm-clouds. One would never have guessed we were so near Greece. The light was not that clear white Greek light, but a hazy, dark gold glow. This was old land, scarred as Kosovo or Bosnia. We wound our way up one of the mountains, past horses and carts, through a village and on to the top where we found the monastery of Veljuša with its jewel of a tiny thirteenth-century church whose foundations were seven centuries older. It stood, remarkable and unlikely as a Tardis, between a dark-furrowed vegetable patch and some recently refurbished but already tatty monastery buildings.

I leant over a wall at the far end of the vegetable patch to listen to the oddly amplified sounds of the village below: the clunk of an axe on wood, a tinny radio, a dog barking, a cock crowing, a couple of villagers talking and water flowing. A nun bustled out of one of the monastery buildings to show us around the church and bring us the excellent news that Bishop Naum was expected at Veljuša that very morning.

The church interior was small and cosily warmed by an electric bar heater. I noticed a shaggy sheepskin rug slung over the single chair. Most of the frescoes, while old, were too blackened by smoke to make out. The nun explained that after the First Balkan War of 1912, in which Greece, Bulgaria and Serbia had banded together to push the Turks out of Macedonia and Europe, Veljuša had been in Greek hands. When the three countries had subsequently fallen out over the division of the spoils and embarked on the Second Balkan War of 1912 to 1913, the Serbs had advanced this far east and forced the Greeks to retreat south. Greek soldiers, she said, set fire to their church here before they left, boasting that they would build another the moment they returned.

The Balkan wars were not too hard to picture, largely thanks to H. N. Brailsford, an English journalist who having spent years monitoring the ravages caused by the Turks' retreat from Macedonia and the neighbouring countries' acrimonious partitioning of the province then sat down to write a vivid account of his experiences. Brailsford was mightily struck by the profound faith of the Slav

Macedonian peasant. When he once advised some peasants to flee the hell of their homeland by walking to Bulgaria or catching a train to Serbia, they refused out of love for the local Orthodox monastery. Brailsford wrote, 'This passion for the church represented the ideal element in the life of the village, its sole care that went beyond food and raiment, and it was strong enough to outweigh all the allurements of freedom and ease ... It reminds him of his greater past. It unites him to his fellow Christians throughout the Empire.'[xiv]

The contrasting venality of the Orthodox bishops he had encountered in the Ottoman empire had appalled Brailsford. He described them as bearing themselves 'with a dignity which is partly aristocratic and partly sacerdotal'. They led, he says, a mostly 'sedentary life, rarely venturing beyond their palaces', and he noticed that 'their preoccupation is the incessant round of intrigue and violence by which each church in Macedonia retains its place against its rivals. Their trade is intolerance and their business propaganda.'[xv]

Judging by the flock of black-robed young nuns suddenly crowding the porch of the monastery building, Bishop Naum had arrived.

Tall and fair with large, luminous grey eyes, he had the casual shambolic elegance of an Eton schoolboy, and a slow but ready smile. I had not met a monk quite like him. Even Father Sava at Dečani lacked this languidly understated star quality. Small wonder his Pied Piper recruitment campaign was working so well, I thought, as we settled down to talk at a low table in a sparsely furnished reception room. He removed his dusty velvet cap to reveal untidy, slightly greasy fair hair pinned up in a little bun at the back, and placed his mobile phone on the table in front of him. 'It's very annoying,' he drawled with a gentle wave of his hand and a smile, 'I can't get a signal up here . . .'

Bishop Naum told me that since starting work here two years ago he had resurrected two monasteries. There were two more due for opening shortly and he could think of ten more women just waiting for his go-ahead to devote their lives to God. However, he was not boasting because the truth of the matter was, 'These two years as a bishop seem to me like twenty years – there have been so many problems,' he admitted, suddenly looking not so much languid, as dreadfully tired.

Hardly surprisingly in a region where, over the centuries, the Orthodox clergy have earned themselves such a bad name, Macedonian public opinion has not altogether approved Bishop Naum's mission to reactivate the monasteries. If having an independent Macedonian Church is a *sine qua non* of nationhood, sacrificing one's only child to a life of celibate self-denial is quite another matter. His project had been viewed as a dangerously retrograde development, coming just at a moment when the FYROM needed to look west not east, and focus all her efforts on the uphill struggle to qualify for entry to the European Union. Sacrificing the flower of Macedonian youth to the monasteries seemed to many a criminal waste of resources when the FYROM needed to concentrate all its energies on becoming economically viable.

'I have suffered two years of attacks on me from people who do not understand what being a monk or nun means after decades of Communism. They have tried to put me out of the game by claiming that I'm not patriotic, that I am too close to the Greek and Serbian churches, and that the nation's spiritual life is sick.' Absentmindedly, he picked up his mobile phone again, to fiddle with its buttons and test the signal, but continued, 'The parents of new monks and nuns have accused me of hypnotizing their children and said we are like a sect, and then worse. There were rumours that we were selling drugs and taking drugs and so on. I suppose it's natural that people hate us and try to make problems for us. Our great challenge is to feel love for these people. But there is no other way . . .'

Right on cue, we were interrupted by a curly-haired priest, in a lather about an unholy fracas in a nearby village. An embezzling church council had refused to hand over the keys to the church when its term of service had ended and instead barricaded itself inside the building. The priest had come to seek the Bishop's advice about what measures to take. Should he call in the police? Bishop Naum told him that he had already spoken to them on the subject and had been advised to leave it with them because they had their 'methods' to deal with such situations. But this response had struck him as ominous, so he told the young priest to try not to involve the police. The priest rushed out again and a nun entered, bearing a tin tray loaded with jam-filled pancakes and sweet black coffee. The Bishop tucked into a pancake, explaining that because he was slightly poorly and on a course of antibiotics, he was not able to observe the Christmas fast, which forbade the consumption of sweets, meat and dairy foods.

I asked him if he felt as confident as Archbishop Mihail that the Macedonian Orthodox Church would be recognized by Constantinople and the other Orthodox Churches at the turn of the century. He thought for a moment. 'In the 1970s Patriarch Atenagoras of Constantinople gave us hope, perhaps because he was a Macedonian himself. He said, "If you live the Orthodox way, you will be recognized one day." So we are trying to do just that. The renaissance of the monasteries is a very important part of living in the Orthodox way.'

Unlike his archbishop, he was visibly distressed to hear that Serbian monks were being harassed by border police and forced to change out of their robes. 'This isn't very good, is it? I will certainly speak to someone in the government when I'm next in Skopje,' he said.

That led us smoothly on to an appraisal of the Macedonian Church's relations with its neighbouring Churches. 'There is no communication with the Bulgarian Church,' he said. 'You know they have a war between two rival patriarchs at the moment. But the Romanian Church hierarchy allows me to celebrate the liturgy when I visit, unlike the Greeks or the Serbs. There are two Serbian bishops – Amfilohije and Artemije – who will not even give me holy communion!'

This was not too surprising. I could easily imagine what Archbishop Amfilohije of Montenegro's pungent views on the schismatic

Macedonian Orthodox Church might be. Bishop Artemije was Father Sava's bishop. Father Sava's e-mail had hinted at his opposition to the Macedonian Church's independence.

It was the evident happiness of the nuns at Veljuša monastery that convinced me public opinion had maligned Bishop Naum. Where the Serbian nuns I had met looked in ill-health and even worse temper, the sixteen women here radiated physical and spiritual well-being. I asked the Bishop for his blessing to speak to two who knew some English. One was a qualified dentist, the other something of a poet. They told me that their mothers were gradually accepting the loss of their daughters to the Church, but still wept whenever they visited. The dentist did any sewing that needed doing in the monastery. The poet helped in the kitchen.

'Everything is so simple in our life here,' said the first.

'Because we can give all our time to God,' said the second.

That was all there was to say about it. It was that simple.

Emerging into golden afternoon sunlight, which was glorifying the already glorious little church, I wanted to take a picture of the two nuns there, by the church, laughing and larking around with Bishop Naum, as I had first seen them. The Bishop had no objection to joining them in the picture.

'Natural, please!' I commanded, aiming the camera at them. To no avail: all three had turned as stiff and po-faced as saints in Byzantine frescoes.

'Please come again,' said the nuns. 'Any time – just come . . .'

I said I would love to, and meant it.

KASTORIA
GREEK MACEDONIA

The Greek border crossing was a blaze of white and yellow light and as brilliantly welcome as a heavenly vision that night. Everywhere, the blue EU flag with its yellow stars shone brightly and the smart new chrome fixtures of the barriers and guards' cabins gleamed. Safely behind us lay the FYROM's dark border crossing with its mile-long queue of fume-belching lorries, drunken guards demanding bottles of whisky and surly uniformed women, who had inspected every inch of the Citroën. Bogdan the Serb was welcome in Greece and my red EU passport would hardly need presenting. According to a blue and yellow signpost just the other side of the barrier, Greece's northern province of Macedonia – her rich share of the spoils in the 1913 share-out of Ottoman Macedonia – was welcoming us.

About a hundred miles into Greek Macedonia is the lakeside town of Kastoria, or Kostur, as the Slav Macedonians have always called it. Here, if anywhere, is tangible proof that Macedonia was once a single entity, however heterogeneous and ill-defined, serving as the busy crossroads of south-east Europe and the colourful stamping ground of Greeks, Slavs, Albanians, Turks and Jews.

Like Ohrid, Kastoria is built around a lake and blessed with plenty of those homely little Byzantine churches, most of them founded by disgraced Byzantine nobles exiled here from Constantinople. Some are still in use but hidden now behind tall modern apartment blocks and children's playgrounds. Kastoria's finest buildings, the solid old dwellings of the town's fur merchants, are simply more dilapidated versions of Ohrid's tall white houses. Kastoria has always been a town of furriers. These days, they advertise their wares on garish signboards, in Russian and Serbian as well as Greek.

It seemed a peaceful, drowsy sort of place but it cannot have been so when H. N. Brailsford visited in the early 1900s. Competition over the corpse of Ottoman Macedonia was heating up. The Ottoman Turks had been hanging on grimly and a certain Greek Bishop called Germanos had held sway in Kastoria. His situation had suited him perfectly until the creation of the new Bulgarian Exarchate Church, which first sought to cater for the Slav Macedonians in their own language and then to help wrest Bulgaria's share of Macedonia from the Greeks. By 1903 the prelate was penning a letter of complaint to the Patriarch of Constantinople: 'Is not this situation, most Holy Patriarch, a real persecution? Our faith and our language never have suffered more terribly; we have for so many centuries lived happily under the sway of the Sultan, who always held in respect our religion and our schools and bestowed on us many privileges.'xᵛⁱ

Brailsford noticed that a command of Turkish was more prized in a Greek archbishop than any acquaintance with the New Testament. Firmly convinced that the Greeks had been responsible for corrupting the Turks, not – as received wisdom had it – the other way around, Brailsford described Archbishop Germanos: 'You may see him any day towards noon – a handsome figure with black robe, black beard, flowing locks and chiselled features, prancing up the main street on his white horse from the [Ottoman] prefecture to his own palace on the hill.' Once, Brailsford had called on the Archbishop in his palace and found him disconcertingly Byzantine in his disdain for the facts of any matter. 'His mind moves among abstractions. He talks not of Greeks but of Hellenism, not of fact but of right,' wrote Brailsford. Even then, Alexander the Great and his Greek origins had been trotted out as justification for the Greeks' claim to Macedonia. The two men were plunged deep in an argument about German moral philosophy before Brailsford noticed that 'There above my head, on the wall, in a conspicuous place, hung the photograph of a ghastly head, severed at the neck, with a bullet through the jaw, dripping blood.'xᵛⁱⁱ The head had belonged to a Bulgarian chief whom the Bishop had had murdered by 'a band of bravoes' in his pay.

Brailsford was as shocked and disgusted by the cruelty of Macedonia's Greek bishops as by their high-handed assumption that most of old 'Turkey in Europe' should be subordinated to Greek rule in a new Byzantium, just as soon as the Ottomans had cleared out. 'It is much as though the Roman Catholic Church should claim the greater part of Europe as the inheritance of Italy,' he wrote, begging his readers to imagine how it would be 'if every bishop in France and Germany were an Italian, if the official language of the church were not Latin but Italian, if the church were not Latin but Italian and if every priest were a political agent working for the annexation of France and Germany to Italy'.xᵛⁱⁱ

THESSALONIKI

Bishop Germanos of Kastoria will live for ever in the shape of a white bust on a white pedestal, in one of the public gardens in the capital of Greek Macedonia, Thessaloniki.

Mid-winter sunshine glanced off the roofs of the cars honking through that city's busy streets and danced on the sea, which was just visible at the far end of its long avenues. The FYROM has nothing so grand to show in the way of a metropolis. Is it any wonder, I thought, as the Citroën's engine idled in a lunchtime traffic jam, that some Macedonians have been dreaming of a Greater Macedonia?

Thessaloniki's proximity to Mount Athos and its history as the second capital of Byzantium have made it Greece's spiritual capital. Hidden amongst a forest of modern apartment blocks and often set a little below street level, squat and homely, are dozens of Byzantine churches with their multiple frilly tiled domes and intricate brick patterns. All fly the Byzantine black double-headed eagle on a yellow background twinned with Greece's blue and white national flag. The city's main thoroughfare is lined with shops a-glitter with icons, crosses, and church furniture for sale. Escaping from the din of traffic, people were dropping in and out of tiny pavement chapels, as utilitarian-looking as public lavatories, to light candles and say a prayer. A giant religious bookshop, stocked with brightly covered paperbacks of the sayings of the wise and holy *gerontes* of Mount Athos past and present, occupied the ground floor of an entire downtown block.

The city's St Dimitri's Orthodox Cathedral, the biggest in the Balkans until Slobodan Milošević promoted the construction of Belgrade's St Sava's in 1989, seemed to be on fire that evening but it was just the effect on its glass windows of the hundreds of candles burning inside. The golden backgrounds of Byzantine mosaics glinted, catching light from the enormous chandelier that hung over the nave. Business was brisk at a stall near the door selling icons, crosses and religious literature. A clutch of older women were parked in pews

– the first I had ever seen in an Orthodox church – chatting and chuckling as happily, presumably, as their husbands drinking coffee and playing backgammon in the *kafeneion*. A young mother lifted her toddler son to kiss an icon. A young man sat alone reading while an older man venerated St Dimitri's relics in their pearl-encrusted and gold-engraved casket.

St Dimitri is Thessaloniki's patron saint, the city's defender and help throughout almost two millennia of its often threatened existence. During the sixth- and seventh-century invasions by the barbarian Slavic hordes it was St Dimitri who appeared over and over again, dressed in white and striking terror into the hearts of those hordes by knocking assailants off their scaling ladders with his spear, strolling about on the sea or appearing on horseback to guard the city's gates.

Tales of his fantastic exploits must have played a part in inclining the Serbs and the Bulgarians or Macedonians, or both, towards Orthodoxy. St Kliment of nearby Ohrid was to describe St Dimitri as 'the most glorious martyr' and 'the firm foundation of his fatherland'.[xix] His fame spread to Kosovo where he features in the church frescoes at both Dečani and Peć. The Viking Russians had also heard of him by the time they were besieging Constantinople in the ninth century. According to a chronicler, their still pagan chieftain took two captured Greek maidens for interrogation about the Byzantines' deadliest weapon. 'I hear that you have a great god called Demetrius who works many miracles,' he said to them. 'Embroider me his likeness as an image so that I might venerate him and defeat my enemies while I carry his image in front of my army.' The women at first refused, but then gave in. Having miserably stitched the artefact, they fell asleep crying. That night, the chronicle says, the image was 'miraculously transported by St Demetrius, to his church in Thessaloniki'.[xx] The disappointed Russians honoured this demonstrably powerful saint by dedicating a magnificent new church to him in Vladimir. While Byzantium lasted, there was always stiff competition among the Orthodox peoples of Europe for St Dimitri's favour and military assistance.

Thessaloniki was confusingly busy the next morning but

'Treasures of Mount Athos Exhibition', said a clear signpost, so we drove the Citroën straight to a new red-brick exhibition hall to see what Bogdan had already seen in the course of his many visits to the Holy Mountain but what I, along with millions of other women, was being given a once-in-a-millennium chance to enjoy.

My scribbled notes remind me that I did not much enjoy the exhibition. 'Mother-of-pearl inlaid crozier . . . 18-ton oak wine barrel with ladder up side . . . 18th century flower-painted travelling pharmacy chest of abbot of Vatopedi monastery . . . mid-14th century suit of chain mail . . . "lazy stick" – like upturned T-bar of a ski lift (used by old monks incapable of standing unaided through all-night vigils) . . . Calendar icon, present from Tsar Nicholas II of Russia – saint for every day, 70 images of Virgin and Child . . . early photo of priest flanked by two soldiers against artificial background of flowers . . .' These are some of the random jottings I made, too irritated that my sex was offered these crumbs in lieu of admittance to Mount Athos even to write straight.

Bogdan was equally peevish but for quite another reason. 'They are showing things which should not be shown like this,' he grumbled, barely glancing at the exhibits, 'as if they were only important as art. Everything must have changed on the Holy Mountain since I was there.'

Much *has* changed in the past two decades. Six hundred new monks have joined the community in the last ten years alone, steadily reversing the decline that reached a nadir in 1970, when there were only just over a thousand. Most are Greeks who have been drawn there, as young Orthodox men have always been drawn to join Eastern Orthodox monasteries, by an especially charismatic generation of spiritual fathers. Some would also say that the inevitable backlash resulting from the too speedy westernization of Greece in the past two decades has also played a part in the renewal. By the 1980s the hermitages of Athos were being recolonized by devoted Hesychasts whose ascetic way of prayer has been spreading back to the monasteries ever since. Most of the new recruits are not only spiritually motivated but highly educated and committed to tightening up monastic discipline. This has meant re-imposing the Cenobitic Rule, whereby all monks worship, live, eat and own property in common. The Idiorrhythmic Rule, which allowed the monks of some of the monasteries to make their own money, live separately and only come together to worship, had been phased out by 1992.

This is probably all to the good. The Idiorrhythmic Rule was a legacy of the Holy Mountain's hardest times, when monks who could not fend for themselves by working like peasants or living off private means were not welcome. It was also conducive to the grossest licentiousness. In 1933 a Greek journalist published a damning exposé of the seamy underbelly of life on the Holy Mountain. Themistocles Kornaros managed to penetrate behind the 'smiles, prostrations, praying monks and holy relics' to a cesspit of vice too vile to be ignored. 'Within the twenty monasteries of Athos,' he wrote, 'one finds sellers of narcotics, sellers and buyers of "masculine flesh", schools of alcoholism and systematic training centres of misanthropy and internecine strife.'[xxi] It got worse: 'There one also meets the father who drags his twelve- or thirteen-year-old child from cell to cell to rent it to the monks.'[xxii] Two years after Kornaros' exposé, little had changed. An Englishman, Ralph Brewster, visited Mount Athos in the company of a young Greek friend who was not averse to making a little extra pocket money. Every night of their visit the Greek pussy-footed about between the monks' cells, pleasuring their inmates. Brewster had been warned by a peasant boy living on the Holy Mountain not to go there clean-shaven because there was hardly a monk who wasn't 'like that'.[xxiii] Asked how he himself managed to live there year in and year out without the solace of female company, the peasant boy had nonchalantly replied, 'Oh, there are four or five fairly young monks – regular clients – who are always at my disposal. As a matter of fact, I have lost interest in women, these days.'[xxiv] Kornaros' comprehensive exposé and history of Mount Athos sadly concluded that the next generation of monks could 'be predestined by human providence to put the final stamp of failure upon the material remnants of this greatest of all human experiments of our millennium.'[xxv] It was mistaken.

However, the last twenty years have not only brought rebirth and revival. Many, monks and laity alike, regret the multiple concessions to modernity. Monks in dark glasses revving their four-wheel-drive vehicles up new roads between monasteries are now a common sight, while the old mule tracks are overgrown. Telephones and electricity are the norm where once there were only candles. Mount Athos even boasts its own website. EU subsidies, filtered through the Greek government to assuage the monks' uneasy consciences about taking money from the West, are funding extensive repair and building works at many of the monasteries. In most cases this is the first major refit since the end of the nineteenth century so there is much to be done. The peace and quiet so vital for the *hesychia* of the Holy Mountain is threatened not only by the din of sawing, cement mixers and imported builders, but also by every summer's shoals of tourist boats skirting around the peninsula, and flocks of sightseeing helicopters hovering above it. The number of male visitors to the Holy Mountain increases with every year, but the monks' monastic rule requires them to give shelter and hospitality to all who come there seeking it.

In May 1998, Father Symeon, the Holy Mountain's only Peruvian monk, was regretting the rarity of finding old monks in the grip of *paratesis*, free from the logic and mentality of the world. Kallistos Ware, the Greek Orthodox Bishop of Oxford, who has been visiting Mount Athos since the 1960s, likewise misses the 'spontaneous unselfconscious simplicity and holiness of the older monks'.

The past two decades have also introduced a more insidious disquiet to the Holy Mountain, which threatens to transform the sublime 'Garden of the Mother of God' into a banal fortress of Greek nationalism. The Greek foreign ministry has been striving to ensure that a revival of the Serb, Russian, Bulgarian and Romanian monasteries does not begin to rival that of the Greek monasteries. Requests for monks' and visitors' visas for citizens of these countries have simply been ignored. Letters from the abbots of the foreign monasteries protesting this treatment have gone unanswered. The demise of Communism in eastern Europe in 1989 followed by the bloody

dissolution of former Yugoslavia has only fuelled the Greek authorities' terror of Mount Athos being invaded by thousands of Romanian,
Serb and Russian economic refugees all masquerading as novice
monks, all planning to gain Greek citizenship before disrobing and
quitting the Holy Mountain to seek their worldly fortunes in Greece.

On the other hand, there have been instances of Athos being
forced by the Greek government to receive visitors. A couple of
months before the outbreak of war in Yugoslavia, in April 1991,
Serbia's President Milošević landed his helicopter in the vegetable
garden of the Serbian Hilandar monastery, and was incensed to find
no one there to receive him. The possibly apocryphal story goes that
on learning of Milošević's impending arrival Hilandar's Abbot had
dashed off to oversee some forestry work, hoping to avoid shaking the
hand of a 'Communist'. So, having deposited Milošević, the helicopter went off in search of the luckless Abbot, found him, winched him
up and flew him back to Hilandar to do his duty. Although Milošević
lingered less than an hour at Hilandar, the monks have yet to forgive
him for landing in their vegetable patch.

There have been persistent rumours that the Bosnian Serb leader,
Radovan Karadžić, has sought and found refuge at Hilandar from
capture by Nato troops and judgement at the war crimes tribunal in
The Hague. Karadžić, at least, could never be described as a 'Communist', so it is not outside the bounds of possibility. Oddly enough,
the monks of Mount Athos have long had a reputation for harbouring
criminals. A mid-nineteenth century Ottoman police chief reckoned
there were up to sixty criminals on Mount Athos whom he was
powerless to do anything about because of the monks' attitude 'that
one of the functions of a Christian monastery is to give an opportunity to a sinner to repent, and their expectation that some of these
criminals will ultimately join a monastery'.[xxvi]

In 1994 the governing monasteries of Athos officially complained
to the Greek government about the growing number of infringements
of the monasteries' right to welcome whoever they like, and not
welcome whoever they dislike, to their self-governing monastic republic. The communiqué said: 'In this way the ancient self-governing

status of the Holy Mountain is circumvented, its religious and spiritual mission is hindered, its universality and international repute are undermined, and Greece is discredited as an Orthodox and democratic country abroad.'[xxvii]

But the Greek government could justify its tight controls over the number of foreign monks taking up residence on Mount Athos by pointing to a sobering historical precedent. In the late nineteenth century, imperial Russia could not resist a heaven-sent opportunity to expand her influence a little southwards. Some bribes to the Patriarch of Constantinople and a broken-down old Russian monastery on a rocky spot in the Aegean, which happened to have been freed from Ottoman rule by the treaty of Berlin in 1878, were the magic keys that would unlock the warm southern seas to her. Russia started rebuilding and expanding her run-down Panteleimon monastery on the Holy Mountain and buying up *sketes*, the smaller monasteries attached to each of Mount Athos' main twenty monasteries. She then worked to have the *sketes* upgraded to monasteries with a say in the government of the Holy Mountain. In 1898 Russian monks mounted a campaign to overturn the monastic state's constitution and replace it with a one-man one-vote system. The then Patriarch of Constantinople, Joachim the Magnificent, foiled both Russian attempts to break Greek domination of the community.

Nevertheless, by 1912 Russia boasted one monastery, four *sketes*, thirty-four smaller *sketes* called *kellia*, 187 hermitages and an absolute majority of monks – four thousand or so out of just over six thousand. The Greeks as well as the other nationalities represented on Mount Athos viewed this as an invasion. By the time Russia's Grigory Rasputin arrived on Athos in the early 1900s – he was too shocked by scenes of rampant homosexuality among the Greek monks to linger long – there was talk of the Holy Mountain having become a 'Russian Gibraltar'.

Shiploads of thousands of Russian pilgrims stopping off at the Holy Mountain on their way to Jerusalem were strictly regimented and put up in purpose-built barrack-like tenements. The military atmosphere might have fed persistent rumours that the Russians were

143

simply troops masquerading as monks. It might also have fostered an atmosphere conducive to the unseemly outbreak of internecine strife amongst them in the late nineteenth century. A Russian monk, a former hussars officer attached to one of the *sketes*, lit the fuse by announcing that the name of God, as much as God himself, was divine. When the Holy Synod back in Moscow branded this a vile heresy, the Russian monks formed two opposing camps. Heretics and non-heretics fell to clobbering each other with hatchets and stones. Eventually, the disturbance was halted by the arrival of a Russian battle-cruiser full of troops. But the heretics retreated into the woods like guerrillas, to stone the troops, and the troops opened fire in reply. Over six hundred Russian monks had to be deported back to Russia. Forty who were discovered to have 'criminal pasts' were imprisoned.

Sydney Loch, an English habitué of Mount Athos in the 1950s, found an old Greek monk harbouring bitter memories of the Russian ascendancy but also a grudging respect for the Russian national character: 'A people of rich nature, earthly angels, with one wing-tip sometimes in Heaven and the other occasionally in Hell,' Father Pankratios told Loch. 'There was a time when the sea off Panteleimon was thick with ships. You could have walked ashore on them. And the pilgrims numbered the hairs on my legs. The Russians tried climbing too high . . .'[xxviii] Presumably he meant that in 1917 the Russians had finally got their comeuppance in the shape of a godless Bolshevik state. By the time Robert Byron, the traveller and connoisseur of all things Byzantine, visited Athos in the late 1920s the number of monks at the Russian monastery had fallen by two-thirds. This remnant was almost destitute because the flow of handsome donations from the homeland had been cut off. Today there are not even a hundred Russian monks on Mount Athos.

The Greek authorities and Mount Athos had also been at loggerheads over another, potentially more serious, matter. In the summer of 1997 the Greek government was due to ratify the EU's Schengen Agreement, which envisages the removal of border controls between EU countries. Mount Athos was worried that the directive would directly threaten its ability to enforce the no-women rule. But it was still more publicly exercised by another clause in the agreement, one providing for closer co-operation between EU member states on crime control. The monks were harrowed by an apocalyptic vision of a vast Brussels-run computer database containing information on every single EU citizen, on every individual soul. They foresaw its evil tentacles spreading outside the EU to embrace the whole world and were convinced the information it contained could be misused by 'current and future members of the EU who are friendly or hostile to our country'.[xxix] Presumably they had in mind Muslim Turkey, Greece's enemy in Cyprus. That June there was a sprinkling of Athos monks in the rowdy crowd protesting outside the Greek Parliament in Athens in a last-ditch effort to stop the government ratifying the agreement. Tear gas had to be used but the protestors scored a minor victory when one policeman suddenly threw down his riot shield, slung a cross around his neck and announced that the protesters were right, that their cause was his. But still the Greek government turned its back on the Byzantine legacy of ingrained mistrust of the West, and signed the Schengen Agreement.

When Thessaloniki's Treasures of Mount Athos exhibition opened at the beginning of 1997, four Athos monasteries signalled their disapproval of Greece's plans to sign the Schengen Agreement by refusing to contribute any of their treasures to it. The monasteries sent only junior delegates to the official opening festivities.

The overcrowded exhibition did not hold our attention for long. We left to explore the city and, just round the corner from the Bishop of Thessaloniki's operational headquarters, happened across a beautifully renovated nineteenth-century building of Ottoman inspiration. It contained the Museum of the Macedonian Struggle.

The place preached the gospel of Macedonian history according to the Greeks, an elegant but strident riposte to the gospel according to the FYROM's Macedonians. This is where one learns how dividing up the corpse of Turkey in Europe in the second half of the nineteenth century started out as a struggle between the Greek Orthodox Church, whose mission was to conserve the old ideal of a universal Byzantine Christendom, the Serbian Orthodox Church, which was trying to conserve the unity of Tsar Dušan's patrimony, and the newly independent Bulgarian Orthodox Church, which owed its existence to Russia's determination to oppose the domination of Constantinople. One learns how the battle for Macedonia soon developed into the two shamelessly brutal Balkan wars of 1912 and 1913, with all neighbouring nation states hell-bent on expansion at each other's expense. One also learns how those wars influenced which side Greece and Bulgaria took in the ensuing two world wars. One learns how, during the Greek civil war of 1945-9, fending off Bulgaria's claims to Macedonia became identified for the Greeks with fending off advancing Communism. One sees how the remnant of Slav-speakers in the Greek province of Macedonia were regarded as a dangerous fifth column of Bulgarian or Yugoslav Communists intent on importing the bacillus of godless Bolshevism into Greece. One learns how Church and State banded together to fight against and Hellenize this remnant, outlawing the use of their Slav language and setting obstacles in the way of their continued existence in the province. One is left in little doubt that Greece's northernmost province of Macedonia, only joined to independent Greece in 1913, remains the front line of defence against the invasion of barbarian Slav hordes from the north.

In early 1992 the churchmen of Thessaloniki were in the vanguard of resistance to the FYROM's plans to call itself simply Macedonia. Just as the war in Bosnia was igniting, hundreds of thousands of demonstrators, led by clergy, took to the streets of the city to protest that the name Macedonia was exclusively Greek, and had been Greek for the three thousand years since Alexander the Great. In Athens, the eminent Macedonian Greek historian Dr Evangelos Kofos, at that time attached to the Greek Foreign Ministry, was in the forefront of the propaganda war Greece was waging against Skopje and her own partners in the EU. The latter were furiously angry that the Greeks seemed to be going out of their way to add to tensions in the Balkans, just when the EU needed a common foreign policy with which to confront the waxing Bosnian inferno. Dr Kofos was arguing with members of the western press, who could not understand why Greece was overreacting so wildly to a poor and unarmed apology for a country's attempt to give itself a semblance of an identity. He insisted that by commandeering the name of Macedonia for their newly independent country, the FYROM-ians, as he called them, were signalling 'a double thrust and claim against Greece. One is territorial; the other is our cultural and historical identity. By appropriating the name, it conveys the impression that the republic has control over all things Macedonian.'xxx

Six years later, Dr Kofos – a dapper and charming man speaking excellent English, polished by a couple of years spent as a visiting fellow of Oxford's Brasenose College – happened to drop by the Museum of the Macedonian Struggle on the same day I did. He was more than willing to talk to me, not least because he felt I might be labouring under a dangerous delusion of which he took it upon himself to disabuse me. He needed me to know that I was badly mistaken in viewing Orthodox Europe as a single coherent entity. According to him, the Church of Greece was far in advance of and not to be compared with its sister Churches in Russia, Serbia, Romania and Bulgaria, simply because Greece had not suffered at least forty years of Communism.

'You see,' he explained gently, 'since the end of Communism the other Orthodox countries have had to fight all over again the struggle which had elements of emancipation and national unification. They have all emerged out of Communism with a vision of their Greater whatever it is – Macedonia, Serbia, Romania, Russia. Of course, the Churches were playing their role in this.' (Why 'of course'? I wondered, as he went on.) 'Although it would like to have one, the Greek Church doesn't have a national cause to fight today. From time to time you can see the Bishop here shouting from his balcony – but this is just, how can I put it?'

'Kitsch?'

'Yes, kitsch, precisely the word I would use.'

I was far from convinced by this underplaying of the enduring power and influence of the Greek Church. Only minutes before our chat, I had learnt that the present socialist Greek government's grip

on power was wholly dependent on its slim majority of twelve
fervently Orthodox Macedonian MPs, who peppered their speeches
with religious references and were still insisting that the name
Macedonia pertains exclusively to an area of northern Greece.

Byzantium and Orthodoxy are back in style after a long spell
when this half of the dual Greek heritage – Ancient Greek and
Byzantine – was undervalued. Abused by the military junta of the
Greek colonels with their slogan 'Greece for Greek Christians' from
1968 until 1974, Orthodoxy had become an ugly adjunct to the
colonels' conservatism by the time the socialists came to power. In
the early 1990s, however, Greece's socialist president Andreas Papandreou was visiting monasteries, and his wife, the ex-Olympic
Airways stewardess Mimi, was at least as public about her Orthodox
faith as she was about her penchant for mediums, witches and the
like. It had seemed to me that Kofos was not moving with these neo-
Byzantine times, until he confided to me how extraordinarily touched
he had felt the previous Easter when he had happened to pick up a
copy of the gospels and read a few lines. 'You know, it took me
straight back to when I was a schoolboy and going to Sunday school
and how we went with the priest to bring the Easter liturgy to the
Greek refugees who had arrived in the Macedonian countryside from
Asia Minor. I can see them now, so poor they were paying for their
church candles with eggs. But they were so strong in the faith. I
realized then how it is our Orthodox faith which makes one people
of us Greeks, not our language, because many of those refugees spoke
Turkish.'

Dr Kofos, I concluded, knew exactly how important Greek
Orthodoxy was now and always had been, how it could probe beyond
a fine, western-educated Greek mind to stir an old Byzantine Greek
heart.

Emboldened by its success in masterminding the anti-FYROM
protests, the Church in Thessaloniki was busily stirring more hearts
in battles with the secular Greek state. There had been unholy scenes
of violence outside one of the chief tourist sites of the city, a large
round construction called the Rotonda. The Church wanted the

Rotonda to become once again the functioning house of worship it had been in Byzantine times. The Ministry of Culture, pointing out that it was a pagan Roman emperor's mausoleum temple long before it was ever a church and used as a mosque for long after it was a church, wanted to turn it into a museum bearing witness to all three eras. By 1996 the argument had spilled out of the law courts and into the building itself. When permission was granted to the Church to hold an all-night vigil in January that year, local clergy seized the opportunity to construct a marble altar in the Rotonda, slab by slab. Guards had noticed a large number of clerics scurrying in and out of the place all night, with apparently extraordinarily heavy packages draped in red velvet, but had not imagined they might be stooping to break the law. Matters reached a climax in the autumn of that year when a classical music recital and another all-night vigil were somehow scheduled to take place in the building on the same evening. A crowd of pro-Church laity gathered outside shouting, 'Anti-Greeks, anti-Christians, God will burn you!' Minutes later that crowd was inside, smashing up a piano. A monk was threatening physical violence.[xxxi]

'The situation is still not resolved,' said the nervous-looking young woman, who appeared to prevent me entering the Rotonda one sunny morning in spring 1998. 'The Church will probably win the argument because it is so powerful here. But, if you ask me, I think it should be a cultural place.'

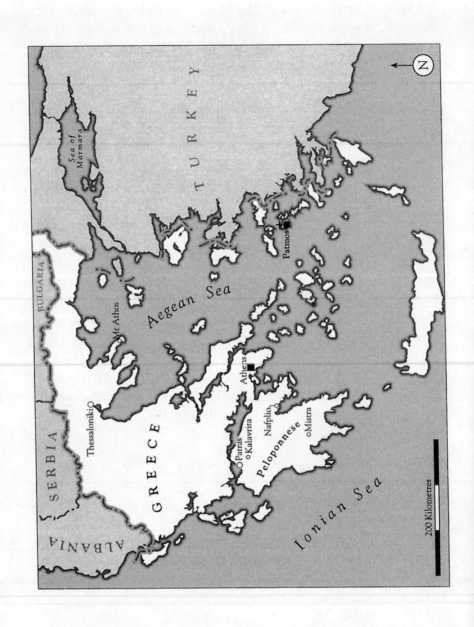

GREECE

'Christos Anesti!' . . . Boom! Bang, bang, bang! 'Halithos Anesti!' . . . Boom! Bang! Christ is risen! . . . Indeed he is risen!

All Easter night long the island rocked to the good news of Jesus Christ's victory over Death, to the nervy crackle of fireworks and thudding dynamite blasts so mighty they shook the foundations of the old buildings and shattered the glass in the windows of a church or two. All of Patmos was out celebrating in this ambiguous fashion. The Turks, only forty-three kilometres away across the dark sea, must have been turning in their beds.

I had lingered long enough up at the monastery church to see its mournfully expectant gloom dispelled by a priest emerging from behind the iconostasis with a single winking taper. That light had been taken from a flame miraculously produced every year in Jerusalem's Church of the Holy Sepulchre. It had travelled from there to Athens by aeroplane, from Athens to Patmos army camp by helicopter, and thence up the hill by flashing police car to arrive at the monastery just in time for that death-defying midnight moment. I had watched the priest solemnly pass on his gift of light to the candles of the faithful, who had passed it to others, and on and on, until everyone in the church, then all the teenage boys huddled on the covered balcony above the monastery gate – from which monks had once tipped boiling oil on marauding pirates – all the children crowding the entrance to the monastery clutching candles almost as tall as themselves, all the well-heeled Athenian holidaymakers chatting on the stone steps outside and all the elderly locals sitting patiently on the stone battlements had received and given the light. A sea of bright faces glowed golden, transfigured.

Without a candle, let alone the 'True Faith' to explain my presence there, I felt ill at ease. Furthermore the fireworks and bigger blasts, like an unrelenting and perfect imitation of combined light and heavy artillery fire, were reminding me of the Bosnian Serbs' siege of Sarajevo. Easter night on the island of Patmos was supposed to have been the high point of my stay in Greece, but I went to bed early with cotton wool in my ears and was woken, soon after dawn, by an especially thunderous dynamite blast somewhere just behind the hotel.

Patmos' yearly virtual bombardment is some measure of the giant fortress monastery's shrinking authority over the island. The monks abominate the custom, fearing not only damage to their property but also that older people will be too terrified to leave their homes to attend the Easter liturgy. The Abbot has complained to the island police, but they claim they are powerless to stop it. Time was, and not so long ago, when the Abbot of the monastery's merest wish was everyone else's command because the monastery owned most of the island. Time was, until the eighteenth century in fact, when the monastery owned *all* of the island.

The monks had the eleventh century St Christodoulos to thank for that. He was a Byzantine monk searching for *hesychia*, in a world in which it was increasingly hard to find. Although flourishing, the Byzantium of his times was also fraught with distractions and dangers. No sooner had Christodoulos spotted somewhere quiet to set up a community of monks than the place was overrun by Saracens or Seljuk Turks, or plundered by pirates, and he had to be on the move again. He was already an old man by the time his eye alighted on an island in the Aegean that was 'utterly desolate and parched, overgrown with thistles and briars, pathless and completely dried up from lack of water.'[i] But he set his heart on having it. 'My ardent desire was to possess this island at the edge of the world, for there were no people, all was tranquillity, no boats dropped anchor here,'[ii] he later wrote. He travelled to Constantinople to lobby the Byzantine Emperor's mother about it, who in turn badgered her son on the old monk's behalf.

Christodoulos was adamant that the island should be a second Mount Athos, without a single lay-person, let alone a woman, to disturb his *hesychia*. The Emperor was not averse to storing up riches for himself in Heaven by giving the old monk the island, but imagined that Christodoulos and his little band of brothers would need a helping hand from some professional builders if they were to erect a stone fortress monastery. Christodoulos firmly declined the offer. He must have played the 'with God's help, everything is possible' trump card because he won the argument and his island. An imperial chrysobull dated 1088 says, 'From today and for centuries to come, Patmos will be entirely separated from the lands over which Our imperial power has rights. Only monks will live there. They will allow no lay people to settle there, engage in trade or any other kind of business. Patmos in its entirety will belong to them ... They will render no account to anyone.'iii

Armed with this document, the delighted saint-to-be went to call on the Patriarch of Constantinople to secure his protection too. Then, having acquired a good boat, he set sail with his monks for Patmos.

Legend has it that no sooner had he stepped ashore than he discovered an elegant relic of pagan Greek times, a marble statue of a goddess. Without further ado he smashed the pre-Christian abomination to the ground and buried its shards. Another legend has it that he pioneered a similarly destructive technique for scaring pirates away. As soon as he saw an approaching pirate ship he would grab the precious icon of St John the Theologian and, standing on the hilltop monastery building-site, flash it at the offending barque until it turned turtle, or to stone.

Of course, the Emperor was soon proved right. Not long after their arrival most of Christodoulos' brothers in Christ fomented a rebellion against the old man. Despairing of ever fulfilling the inhumanly arduous task he had set them of building a fortress monastery, they refused to obey him or to work and finally left the island. Christodoulos and his remnant of monks imported some builders from Constantinople who in turn revolted because they missed their womenfolk. The old monk had to give in again because his first care was for the safety of his 'workshop of virtue', as he called it, which above all needed sturdy walls and mighty ramparts to protect it from all comers, namely pirates. A handful of the workmen's women were settled as far away as possible from the monastery site, at the northern tip of the island.

About four years into Christodoulos' holy project, a Turkish raiding party must have proved immune to the power of the icon. The pirates anchored off Patmos and came ashore. Christodoulos fled with most of his brothers and died in exile a year later, begging to be buried back home on Patmos. This was done and, in spite of the almost sixty-year-old Schism, the miracle-working corpse of the martinet saint was soon renowned throughout the Mediterranean, among Christians of East and West. Once the Turkish pirates had sailed away, work on the monastery continued, assisted by the revenues flowing in from imperial endowments of church estates, metochia, on Crete, and other Aegean islands. Less than ten years after the death of St Christodoulos a hundred monks were at the monastery.

Normans, Arabs, Turks and Venetians also harassed the place, usually with the intention of carrying off Christodoulos' miraculous carcass. In 1204 Patmos was part of the spoils of the shameful Fourth Crusade and occupied by Venetians. Nevertheless, the island's lay community grew, and moved up the hill to the safest spot, just under the monastery's stout walls. The settlement was further swelled by the arrival of Byzantine refugees fleeing the fall-out from the Ottomans' capture of Constantinople in 1453. A poignant note in the margin of one of the monastery's precious manuscripts reads faintly now: 'Today the ship came with the Genoese from the City.'iv Patmos itself fell to the Ottomans a year later.

But the Turkish yoke rested lightly on the island. The fifteenth to the nineteenth centuries were Patmos' heyday. The monastery kept its privileges and acquired a fleet of forty ships, respected everywhere it sailed. More than one abbot pretended that he and his monks had abandoned Orthodoxy and converted to Catholicism in exchange for a pope's protection. Some played a risky game, acknowledging their Ottoman overlords with lavish expressions of loyalty while spying on their movements for whichever western power seemed to guarantee their protection. Diverse popes, Italian dukes,

French kings, grand masters of the Hospitaller Knights of St John, princes of the Danubian principalities (today's Romania) and, finally, the Russian tsars took an interest in Patmos throughout the Ottoman period. The last two, showing particular Orthodox brotherly love, allowed bands of Patmos monks to roam around their countries on begging expeditions, with a few choice relics in their bags and their palms outstretched for alms.

The only big disturbance to the pleasant tenor of the Patmiots' lives occurred in the mid-seventeenth century when the island became caught up in the war between the Turks and the Venetians. An anonymous Patmiot, describing those dire times, has inadvertently left us a useful measure of how startlingly rich the island had become, despite the heavy taxes demanded by both the warring parties. He recounts how the Venetians stole their boats and how they ran out of coins in which to collect the tribute so paid instead 'in silver, in gold and in pearls which were loaded on to galleys in sacks'. Next, 'as if this wretchedness were not enough, there came sixty Turkish galleys and took our folk in bondage, twice, thrice and four times, and all were ransomed with their own possessions . . .' Finally, the Venetians returned, 'and we counted that they took half a million and more in silver and gold and other valuables'.[v]

On the whole Patmos prospered, thanks to brisk business in shipbuilding, cotton-stocking-making, trading and – as likely as not – piracy. The Constantinople refugees lent tone to the place with their sophisticated urban ways. In the town of large white merchants' mansions, which was spreading like a pristine lace altar cloth under the monastery's grey stone battlements, the islanders waxed rich and civilized. While the monastery ensured that they never lost touch with their Byzantine heritage, their constant sea-going made them familiar with the West and they took from her the best she had to offer – luxury furnishings, gorgeous 'Frankish' clothes and, apparently, Venetian mirrors. Their delightful-sounding lives revolved around long sea-trips for trade, interspersed with acquiring property on the island for use as dowries for their daughters, and making generous donations to the monastery, to which at least one member of their families usually belonged. And they built churches. Today the island boasts over four hundred. Most are small and as homely as those of Ohrid or Kastoria, but white and shaped like Hovis loaves instead of domed. They gleam like outsize mushrooms on the spring green hillsides, at roadsides and in fields.

By the eighteenth century Christodoulos would hardly have recognized his monastery. It had become a whole complex of buildings, a labyrinth of stone corridors and wooden stairways, opening off a central courtyard spanned by a skeleton of arches. His successors had abandoned the strict Cenobitic Rule in favour of the more relaxed Idiorrythmic one. The monks had well-developed business interests. At any one time half of them might be off the island, managing the *metochia*. When at home most lived with members of their extended families, and only worshipped in common at the monastery. The monastery's major concession to the more secular times was to make over half the island to the laity in 1720. Aaron Hill, an English poet who visited the monastery in the mid-eighteenth century, seems to have been pleasantly reminded of an English country house. He wrote that he was received there 'as civilly as I could possibly have found an Entertainment in the House of an Acquaintance or Relation, everything was Neat, and Plentiful without Extravagance, becoming the Decorum of religious Livers, yet not devoid of Relish, Form and Delicacy'.[vi]

But the impression of conservative solidity was deceptive. Enlightenment ideas and notions of nationhood were disturbing even Patmos. The islanders were trading with Russia, and that mighty independent Orthodox power had become so much the focus of all their hopes for national liberation that they had taken to shipping home icons of the Russian tsars to hang on their walls. Philanthropist merchant seamen and the monastery teamed up to found a school on the island and supplied it with books brought back from the West as well as the ancient classics. Renowned through all the Orthodox Balkans, the Patmos school was soon turning out generations of budding patriarchs, teachers and, by the end of the eighteenth century, keen Greek freedom-fighters.

Those western books, pouring into centres of excellence like the Patmos school, were helping to precipitate a Greek identity crisis. On the one hand people were starting to value themselves as the heirs of the Ancient Greeks whose civilization was so well known and admired in the West. On the other hand they were still closely bound to Byzantium, a second great Greek civilization, but one which the West had neither interest in nor liking for. The Greeks' fond Byzantine hope that Orthodox Russia would ride to their rescue and kick out the Ottomans was to be disappointed soon after their War of Independence broke out in 1820. The West, in the shape of warships and funds, but also moral and physical support from romantic philhellenes like Lord Byron, who were fired up with the glory of Ancient Greece, proved much more practically helpful. And this was why, when Greece's eight-year liberation struggle was over and an independent new country had been created in 1828, Greeks had determined to face west, and made their new capital in a dusty village called Athens, full of splendid classical ruins. They signalled their rejection of the Byzantine past by declaring ecclesiastical indepen-dence from Constantinople, a schism that dealt the old universal Byzantine ideal a body blow as violent as it had received in 1054 or 1204. Phyletism was back in force and a plethora of national Ortho-dox churches – rather than one inclusive and universal one – the order of the new day.

One of the three men who founded the secret society that planned the overthrow of Ottoman rule and laid the ground work for the Greek War of Independence was a product of the Patmos school. A merchant's clerk called Emmanuel Xanthos, he was the cause of my happy meeting with another Patmiot *émigré*.

I had been lazing awhile on a doorstep in one of the small white stone squares of the old town – quaffing a Coke, enjoying the cool breeze and dark blue late afternoon sky – when an elderly man in a navy blazer with a red silk handkerchief blooming in its top pocket had strolled into the square and greeted a friend who was making his entrance from the opposite side.

'How ya' doin'?' said the first man.

'Fine, just fine – you back for long?' said his friend. 'Business good? Kids?'

Why were these two elderly Greeks conversing in slightly accented American English? I imagined that they must be old schoolfriends who had both emigrated to America in the 1960s when Patmos was an impoverished backwater, long before the island's fortunes had changed for the better when people like the Aga Khan started buying up the old town's white mansions. They had probably returned for Easter at home, and I supposed that to converse in English was to congratulate each other on having made good in the West. Those merchant seamen of the sixteenth, seventeenth and eighteenth centuries, resting at home between voyages, had probably hailed each other in Italian or French for exactly the same reason.

'Could either of you tell me where I can find Emmanuel Xanthos' grave?' I ventured.

It was just round the corner and not particularly impressive, but the man in the blazer and I fell into conversation. He was John Kritikos, a prosperous businessman from Houston who had come home to visit his sister in the old-town white mansion their family had owned for generations. Quite how many generations, he could not say, but he led me on a tour of that old town, greeting everyone as we went, pointing out all the other mansions occupied by cousins and aunts. Up a narrow cobbled lane, round corners, up and down steep stone steps, he walked me. We passed dozens of little white Hovis churches with only a bell or a cross to signify their purpose. I soon lost any sense of direction.

'We had to build these streets narrow like this so we could lurk in the corners to attack pirates,' he explained. 'You know why there are so many churches? If a guy got scurvy or there was a storm at sea and they survived, they'd come back and build a church in thanksgiving.'

We paused to admire the hilltop view over the island, with its spring green hillsides tinted golden by the sunset, a scattering of white dwellings and toy-sized boats down in the harbour all flying the yellow and black double-headed Byzantine eagle flag. Around us the sea glowed lilac tinged with orange. At this time of year, I imagined, old Christodoulos must have felt extra close to his God and blessed in his lunatic, holy endeavour.

'That over there, that's family land, and there, as far as that house with the stable attached at one end and the church at the other,' John was saying. 'We owned most of Patmos at the turn of the century. We've still got five churches. You know what? I guess you're gonna like this. One night my grandfather had a vision of a bush somewhere on his land with an icon hanging from it. What did he do? He found that bush and built a church right next to it. It's still there ... But it's a lotta work all this church stuff. You gotta think about maintenance and getting a priest to say a liturgy on the right saint's day in the right church. That doesn't come cheap, you know, and don't forget the candles and oil for the lamp ...'

I was idly wondering if this friendly Houston businessman had sackloads of pearls, gold and silver stashed away in his mansion. 'John, why do all the boats here fly the Byzantine flag instead of the Greek one?'

He explained that Patmos' monastery was 'stavropegic', which means that it is under the spiritual jurisdiction of a patriarch, in this case the Patriarch of Constantinople, rather than that of the Archbishop of Greece in Athens. 'That's why they fly the double-headed eagle. As a matter of fact, my sister's first husband, who was a Eurocommunist but also very cultured, was the first man to explain to the monastery here that they had the right to fly that flag. Now every church in Greece flies it, all thanks to him! By the way, you doing anything for Easter? My sister'd welcome you to our place for lunch ... I don't know how you're fixed ...'

That was how I was admitted to one of the most sumptuous of the white merchants' mansions up there on the hill, in the shadow of the great monastery.

The festive meal was served in a high-ceilinged dining room hung with sepia-tinted Kritikos family photographs, icons and a crystal chandelier. The latter had to be lit since the thick net curtains were drawn to shut out any sunlight. A table was spread with crisp white linen, silver and crystal glassware, and John had cooked a stew. 'The lamb is ours, from one of my sharecroppers,' he told me. Through the open doorway into the drawing room, I glimpsed gilt-backed chairs, a gilt-edged Venetian mirror and a wall crowded with gilded icons and paintings in gilt frames, all gleaming in the shadows. But for the green velvet-covered armchairs with their lace antimacassars and a couple of Ottoman duelling pistols, I might have been peering into a Byzantine church interior and said as much to John. 'That's the Byzantine in Greece. Gold is wealth,' he said, adding that the house had twenty-five rooms.

There were five of us around that table – myself, John, an old man who was silent throughout the meal, John's lusciously well-preserved sister Elvira with her head of tumbling auburn curls, and her young boyfriend Sarandi, which means 'forty' in Greek. Named after the Forty Blessed Martyrs of Asia Minor, he was a bearded, beefy fellow, wearing a shirt unbuttoned to the waist, jeans, one gold chain round his neck and another round his thick wrist. The old man, who seemed ill at ease amidst all that grandeur, turned out to be Sarandi's father and a devoted Kritikos family retainer.

From time to time, Sarandi grinned and absented himself from the table but it was a while before I realized that his disappearances coincided with the deafening crack of a firework outside in the lane. He showed me an example of his loathsome craft. It was the size and shape of a pear, made of *papier-mâché* wrapped in string, with a fuse for a stalk. During one of Sarandi's absences John grumbled to me, 'I was doing that when I was twelve. This guy's forty! And another thing, he's a Commie!'

While the wine and vodka flowed, Sarandi explained that he was a Communist because Communism somehow stood for 'the right way of life'. I thought I caught an echo of Orthodoxy as the 'right way of worship'.

John chimed in with, 'How could the Russians call themselves Communists? Didn't they love all that gold, just like we do?'

It so happened that one of John's forebears had emigrated to St

Petersburg where he had had a hand in rescuing either Tsar Alexander III or Tsar Nicholas II (John couldn't remember which) from death by drowning and had been rewarded with a lucrative post as a tax collector. When that doughty ancestor had had to flee Russia (John couldn't remember if the year was 1917), he had reached Patmos with 'seven – and I mean *seven* – gallon cans of gold'. Elvira pointed to the cloth of gold covering the *chaise-longue* behind me as further proof of the family's Russian connection and the Russians' love of gold. Then she disappeared but was back a moment later with an ornate silver receptacle, which she shook in my direction, drenching me in a shower of her home-made rose-water. 'Constantinople silver,' she said, 'for church feast days. When they walk in town with icons, I go like so.' She giggled, with another vigorous shake of her weapon.

By the time Sarandi had fixed me another vodka I was hardly surprised when he drew his own weapon from its hiding place beside the dresser. It was a machine-gun, which he hoisted on to his beefy shoulder. Squinting through its sights, he proceeded to mock-fire it. '*Bang! Bang!*' he roared. The Turks, he reminded me, were only forty-three kilometres away so it paid to be vigilant. Then, as if anxious to correct any falsely unfavourable impression I might have formed of him, he produced a sheaf of palm fronds he had woven into the crosses Patmiots wave on Palm Sunday. I asked him his opinion of the monastery, trusting that such a Communist would not shrink from frank criticism of the Church, but he was tight-lipped on the subject. The Abbot of the monastery, he explained, was his cousin.

Neighbours, homing *émigrés* like John, dropped in with shouts of '*Christos Anesti!*' and helped themselves to a succession of stiff Johnnie Walkers. John had not seen one of them for thirty-five years and delighted in recounting how he had once fired his pea-shooter at this old friend's eye and received a sharp rebuke from the boy's uncle, then the Abbot of the monastery. Lacing their Greek with Americanisms, these *émigrés* fell to admiring each other's designer-label ties and boasting about how well their children were doing at college. I did not want to outstay my welcome. Elvira fetched a plastic bag and, stuffing it with three of Sarandi's palm crosses, an Easter cheese pie called a *flaunas* and a bottle of her rose-water, she presented it to me with tears in her eyes.

Patmos is the friendliest place I have ever been. Within a day of arriving there alone by the night boat from Athens, I had made enough acquaintances to ensure that I was never lonely. On my first bright morning, I had walked through the harbour town filled with the smell of fresh bread and coffee, people whitewashing and scrub-bing before Easter and on, half-way up the hill towards the monastery, to the cave where St John the Theologian wrote his nightmare-inducing Book of Revelation.

In AD 95, long before Christodoulos set eyes on Patmos, long before even Emperor Constantine had espoused Christianity and just when the persecution of Christians was in full swing, John was arrested and banished to Patmos. His Book of Revelation opens with an account of how he came to experience a vision of the Apocalypse there.

> I, John, who am also your brother, and companion in tribulation, and in the kingdom and patient endurance of Jesus Christ, was in that isle that is called Patmos, for the word of God and for the testimony of Jesus Christ. I was in the spirit of the Lord's day, and heard behind me a great voice, as of a trumpet, saying, 'I am Alpha and Omega, the first and the last; and, what thou seest, write in a book . . .'[vii]

What John saw and duly described has been striking the fear of God into the hearts of Orthodox Christians ever since. His glimpse of the future amounts to a harrowing alarm-call to humankind to repent of its evil, pagan, fornicating and murdering ways, and believe in Christ or else . . . seas will turn to blood, lands will burn up, dragons will belch pestilence, stars will fall and poison waters and fire and brimstone will cover the earth. Just before the end of the world and Christ's Second Coming, a Beast will rule the Earth, he warns. We will all be able to recognize it by its number, 666, which might appear on a person's hand or forehead and there will come a dreadful time when buying and selling will be impossible without that number. The book ends with a final crescendo of a promise that the Second Coming and the Day of Judgement are imminent when the unrepentant will be slung into 'a lake of fire' while the righteous will join Christ in the New Jerusalem, a heavenly city built of gorgeous stones and gold.

For the Eastern Orthodox, St John's apocalyptic vision of the last days of the world has always been a statement of literal truth. An eighteenth-century Greek's diary has been found with the prophecies of a monk called Dionysus appended to its back cover.

1765 A fearful war throughout all the world
1766 The laying waste of Constantinople
1767 The sinking into the sea of England
1768 All nations will know Christ
1769 A man will appear who can work great miracles, and monsters and terrible things
1770 A world-wide earthquake will take place
1771 The sun, the moon and the stars will fall
1772 The entire world will be annihilated through fire
1773 The fearful Day of Judgement of the Second Coming of Christ.[viii]

I hoped the diarist had treated this dire list as sceptically as most of us treat horoscopes today, but I doubted it because it would appear that even these days Greeks are enormously susceptible to the power of prophecies. A few months before coming to Greece I had been travelling into London by train when I happened to fall in with two Greek trainee nurses from the Peloponnesian port of Patras. One of the young men turned out to be well-versed in prophecies old and new, and informed me that very soon Greece would find herself at war with Turkey for a period of three months, three days or three hours. At first the war would go badly for the Greeks, he said, but a last-minute intervention from Orthodox Russia would finally enable them to recapture Constantinople. A new Emperor Constantine –

one with six toes on one of his feet – would be set on the throne of a New Byzantium.

'You can check,' the earnest young man had urged me. 'You will find that our king, Constantine, who is in exile here in London has six toes on one foot.' I promised to look into the matter and the youth continued, 'People say that with Russia selling those S-300 ground-to-air missile systems to Cyprus now and with Turkey threatening war if they are installed, the situation is preparing itself . . .'

Stranger still, as soon as I had arrived in Greece I had noticed that St John's prophetic Apocalypse was still in vogue: 'NO TO 666!' screamed giant blue graffiti from railway bridges, motorway railings and walls. It would take me some time to fathom the contemporary relevance of the mark of the Beast.

There, in St John's cave on Patmos, Nikos, a sad-eyed theology student from Athens of about the same age as those trainee nurses, kindly set about showing me the saint's workroom. 'Here is a hand-hold, worn away in the stone by St John, because he was old, of course, and needed help getting up from his bed. And here, look, the stone is worn away where he laid his head to sleep and here is the stone St John's disciple used to rest the book on while he was taking dictation from the saint. Up there is the three-way split in the roof of the cave which was made by God's trumpeting voice when he first addressed St John. Isn't it just like three fingertips bunched and ready to make the sign of the cross?'

Nikos then delivered a well-polished sermon of his own devising. It was an attempt to bridge the gap between the mind-sets of East and West by leavening the mysticism with scientific metaphors and accompanying gestures. 'Patmos was a minus [one finger stretched horizontal] for St John when he was banished here but he turned it into a plus [two fingers intersecting in a cross] by writing the Book of Revelation . . .' was how it began. He was not anxious to deviate from the subject of his lecture, but strongly recommended I go straight back down the hill and seek out his fervently Orthodox brother Tassos and his at least as fervently Orthodox Welsh sister-in-law, Elisabeth. I would find them near the harbour, at their gift shop,

Parousia, which means 'Presentation' or 'Second Coming'. I promised to do just that, but later in the day. I was on my way up the hill to visit the fortress monastery that old Christodoulos had built and dedicated to St John.

Pausing for breath on the way up the long flight of steep stone steps to the monastery, I stopped at a souvenir shop to purchase a mug with an icon of St John the Theologian – bent over his book, gold-haloed and furrow-browed – on the side. Some roughly sculpted figurines of black-robed monks riding mules, playing backgammon or fishing also caught my eye, but none more so than a horribly suggestive one of a seated monk with a woman kneeling in front of him, her head concealed under the flap of his robe. I was just asking myself why the monks had not descended from their grey citadel to put a stop to this lewdness on their doorstep, when a monk strode past the shop, throwing a cheery greeting to the smiling shop-keeper. Of course, I thought, the shop-keeper might have been a brother, cousin or nephew with a living to make.

There was something so forbiddingly massive about the great monastery that I was unconsciously putting off the moment when I would have to ascend the last flight of stone steps, walk through the great wooden door and ask to speak to one of its inmates. After a last cup of coffee I joined a straggle of other foreign tourists for a dutiful visit to its museum, then wandered across the courtyard to the postcard stall where I explained to the seller that I wanted to talk to a monk. He told me to sit down and wait.

Having lit a candle and stuck it in the tray of sand provided, I perched on the rim of a holy-water well. With its few pots of geraniums and whitewashed walls, the courtyard was a pretty place, not in the least threatening. It was the island's siesta hour and from the dark church came the sound of chanting, puffs of incense smoke and flickers of orange candle-light. A handful of monks were sitting in high narrow chairs in the porch, only half attending to the service, muttering to each other and chuckling through their grey beards.

When the service ended a flock of monks fluttered out of the church and sped off along corridors and up stairways leading off the courtyard. I waited. From all around came shouts of 'Vasilis!' and 'Symeon!' The splendid acoustics of the monastery had made a sort of central telephone exchange of the courtyard. 'Symeon! . . . Symeon!' shouted the postcard seller, until a thin young monk with thick spectacles came tripping down a stairway to attend to me.

He ushered me up another wooden stairway to the monastery library, a high-ceilinged gloomy chamber lined with half-filled bookshelves. Clearly, this was not *the* monastery library containing treasures dating all the way back to Christodoulos' founding chryso-bull but I explained my business and asked him if by any chance he had a book in English or French about the history of the monastery. He did not seem to hear me but kept his gaze averted and his head slightly turned from me. Such excruciatingly modest conduct must be thought becoming in a monk, I thought.

'Here is the wisdom of one holy *geront* of Mount Athos,' he said, handing me a paperback with a colour photograph of an ancient monk sitting in a sunlit glade on its cover. I had already bought a copy of it in the big religious book shop in Thessaloniki. Father Symeon seemed glad to hear that but then, still without looking at me, he riffled nervously though some church magazines, pointing out things of no possible interest. I wondered if he was a Hesychast and too busy with his interior prayer to attend to me. I tried asking him about the fate of the monastery during the Second World War. Somewhere I had read that the Abbot of the monastery had hidden wounded Germans, Englishmen and Italians in different nooks and alcoves of the place, without one guessing the presence of the others. But either he had nothing to say on the subject or he had not understood my question. It was not until I raised the matter of the Mount Athos monks' resistance to Greece signing the Schengen Agreement that he began to speak in coherent sentences, though only tangentially – as far as I could tell – about that agreement.

'The Bishop of Corinth is a good lawyer and he says no to this agreement . . . The holy *gerontes* on Athos use their spiritual TV to see things we can't see, angels and devils, which are everywhere. Look here in this book, St Paisius of Athos wrote, in 1987, "Sign of the Times = 666". The world is becoming full of sin.

If he could not or would not join me on my wavelength, then I would do my best to switch to his, I decided. 'Father Symeon, what is this 666?'

Fiddling with a magazine and still not looking me in the eye, he said, '666 is the Latin way of life, from Europe.'

From this I gathered that the almost eight-hundred-year-old memory of Constantinople's trashing at the hands of 'Latin' Crusaders from Europe, was still as vivid as the message of the Book of Revelation.

Father Symeon continued, 'A satanic attack against the Church is coming from the West, from the USA. New York is the Whore of Babylon. One *geront* used his spiritual TV and saw devils flying over all the western countries . . . But you must talk to my spiritual father who is the *geront*, Father Pavlos. Now the library is closing.'

'Oh,' I said, surprised and disappointed, but somewhat consoled by the prospect of a meeting with Father Pavlos. I had heard he was an exceedingly holy and famous old *geront*.

The door to Father Pavlos' room was open and the long-bearded old man was standing in his antechamber-cum-office. He was wearing a stripy pyjama top and a round black monk's cap with a tiny cross on the front and his old eyes were luminous with something I was beginning to identify as the love-of-God light. I was conscious of having encountered it on four previous occasions: once in the eyes of an old Romanian monk I had watched frying up wild mushrooms in a wood in the autumn of 1988, for a second time in those of the monk in the photograph stuck behind a dial in the captain's cabin of the boat in which I had sailed around Mount Athos, a third time at Dečani monastery in the eyes of the Serbian monk who had explained to me how Orthodoxy was like a great tree missing a large branch, and a fourth time in those of the Pied Piper Bishop Naum. It seemed to me likely that the light might be a distinguishing mark of a Hesychast on his way to 'becoming' God just as God became man.

Father Pavlos was not alone. A smartly dressed young woman with four small children and another middle-aged woman, who looked peeved to see me, were all crowded into that antechamber. I did not feel welcome. After a moment's uneasy hiatus the children and I received laminated holy cards from the trembling hand of the almost tangibly holy old *geront*, before being gently shooed out of the door. Suddenly close to tears, I ran downstairs again to the courtyard and bumped into Father Symeon. Flashing me a transformingly sweet smile, he said simply, 'It is Easter-time. Father Pavlos has many spiritual children who must make their confession to him. Come, there is someone I want you to meet.'

Back in the library he introduced me to a compatriot called Margaret, a native of Kent, a convert to Orthodoxy and a resident of Patmos. While Father Symeon lurked in the background, fiddling with his magazines, Margaret and I chatted about the monastery's recent painful schism. A young monk had wanted to abolish the Idiorrhythmic Rule in favour of a return to the stricter discipline of the Cenobitic one, but had encountered strong opposition from his older brothers. In the end, the reformer had had to decamp to Mount Athos with two of his spiritual children.

Margaret was dressed as nearly as possible like a nun, although without a veil or long black robe and she was as fervently religious a person as I had ever met. But she was not in any hurry to take the veil. 'As a nun you have to be absolutely obedient and I don't want some abbess sending me off on petty errands when I should be in church hearing the liturgy,' she confided.

Indeed, she seemed to have an aversion to convents because instead of attending services at one or other of the island's two women's houses she had attached herself to the monastery, where she was not always welcome.

'I have to pick my moment and sneak in,' she said, with a rueful smile, admitting she was much pained by the lowly status of women in the Greek Orthodox Church. 'It hurts me – it hurts me *terribly* that I can't take holy communion or kiss the icons when I have my period . . .'

'What are you talking about now?' interrupted Father Symeon, impatient for us to finish our conversation and leave. Have you spoken about the sacraments?'

'Yes, yes,' she said appeasingly over her shoulder, before returning to our subject. 'One of the Desert Fathers says something like, if you are walking on the edge of a precipice and there is a woman on one side and the devil on the other, you are safer erring on the side of the devil. Anyway, I'd better go home now to sleep.'

By my reckoning it was only seven p.m. I must have looked surprised because she explained, 'It's just that it's Holy Week, so there are a lot of church services. I find I have to spend all my time in church or asleep.'

Together we calculated that during that week leading up to the most important festival in the Orthodox Church calendar, she would be spending between four and six hours a day standing in church. Father Symeon was holding the library door open and jangling his keys.

'But most people don't stay for the whole service, they pop in and out, don't they?' I asked her.

'Yes, but they *shouldn't* – just like they shouldn't sit down in church. This modern way of providing chairs is *all* wrong.'

Margaret, I decided, was an Orthodox fundamentalist and it transpired that, along with the more religious aspects of the tradition, she had also imbibed that old Byzantine defensiveness born of centuries of encirclement by Muslim or Western heretic enemies.

'I wonder if the monastery would support a war against Turkey, over Cyprus, for example,' I mused aloud.

'Oh, yes, of course, because that would be a "just war". I would support it too, because Turkey, or Asia Minor, is the land that bred the saints, and every Greek has a soft spot for Constantinople . . .'

The wholeheartedness of Margaret's identification with her adopted faith and the Greek nation was daunting. It left me curious to know what another British convert to Orthodoxy, Nikos' Welsh sister-in-law, was like. Later the same day I made my way to the shop called *Parousia* and found Elisabeth dusting her icon display.

Brewing up a pot of English tea, she bade me draw up a stool for a chat. She had come to Orthodoxy, she told me, via her husband Tassos, but only after they had both dabbled in Buddhism. Despite Patmos' reputation as Greece's holiest isle it had not been easy to bear open witness to the True Faith, she told me. The locals had not been able to understand why she and Tassos did not frequent bars like other young people.

'We're *persecuted*,' she told me, 'but we remember that Christ said that the better you try to be, the more difficult people will make things for you.' Before long we were joined by a Scottish holiday-maker, a Presbyterian minister from Aberdeen. Another pot of tea was brewed, another stool drawn up and he and Elisabeth fell to sparring gently about the value of ecumenism. While he insisted that he bought icons and read Orthodox theology in the firm belief that all the Christian Churches have 'so much to learn from each other', Elisabeth stuck by her Orthodox guns. 'No. We have preserved the True Faith,' she told him, 'so of course we are not going to start compromising it with Churches that have deviated from it. We don't want to lose our treasure of the Truth.'

'But do you not think you run the danger of making the same mistake as the Pharisees, Elisabeth?' said the Scotsman, dunking his biscuit in his tea. 'You will remember how they were so busy observing the outward forms of the faith that they failed to recognize the Messiah when he came.'

Although speaking the same language they were a world apart.

The shop was filling up with evening custom when Elisabeth's husband, Tassos, breezed in. A radiantly happy-looking man, with bright eyes and a generous smile, he soon attracted his own circle of visitors – a group of three young Athenian schoolteachers, all women, whom he was gently guiding back to the True Faith. As I wandered over to inspect bookshelves filled with titles like *Orthodox Psychotherapy* and *A Night in the Desert of the Holy Mountain*, I overheard Tassos reminding his eager disciples that the Byzantines had called themselves *Romaioi*. He was telling them that it was the Franks – the Latin Crusaders of 1204 – who had first fixed on the name Byzantium, and that that was how the word 'Byzantine' had acquired such pejorative overtones. Tassos was urging them to rediscover the truth and glory about the empire of the *Romaioi*.

Later, when I was gently probing him for information on the influence of the monastery on the island, I discomfited him.

'If I hear bad things about the monks up there,' he said, with a sudden frown, 'I try to remember that the gospel tells us to look at the beam in our own eye before searching for the mote in anyone else's . . .'

Talking of eyes, I thought I detected in his a hint of the love-of-God light. 'Tassos,' I interrupted him, 'would you describe yourself as a Hesychast?'

'You must be joking!' He roared with laughter. 'How *can* I be a Hesychast when I have all the fuss and bother of the shop every day? The monks of Mount Athos are Hesychasts, not someone like me!'

Feasting off octopus in a taverna that evening, I remembered Tassos' reticence about the monastery and its inmates. He was not the first Patmiot to strike me as cagey on the subject. One person had grumbled to me about the shining black Mercedes limousines, with their red number-plates sporting silver Byzantine double-headed eagles, and about the amount of land the monks still own, but otherwise I had faced a wall of silence.* The obvious reason was that the monastery has reverted to what it was in Byzantine times, the goose that lays the Patmiots' golden eggs. Back then Christodoulos' miraculous relics were the goose. Today, the giant cruise ships, which drop by for just long enough to let their cargoes struggle up to the monastery then back down to the harbour for a spot of souvenir-hunting and a meal, would stop coming if the monastery closed its doors. In no time at all Patmos would revert to the parched wilderness it was before Christodoulos arrived. The

* In May 1999 the former abbot and two monks of Patmos' Monastery of St John Theologian were defrocked by the Patriarch of Constantinople. They are charged with embezzling 3.5 billion drachmas worth of monastery property and living in holiday villas built on church land.

monastery's ban on topless sun-bathing and night-clubs is a small price to pay for a livelihood. There is no living to be made from shipping any more.

But there was something else, too, behind that caginess. I thought I recognized in the Patmiots some traces of the defensive Greek nationalism of the Late Byzantium, the mistrust of the West and the mentality of a tribe closing ranks around their Church. I was aware again of that unresolved identity crisis that Greece's impressive dual heritage, of Hellenism from the Ancient Greeks and Byzantinism from the *Romaioi*, has bred in the hearts of its people. Patrick Leigh Fermor has called it 'the Helleno-Romaic Dilemma' and has listed the characteristics pertaining to each in parallel columns. On the subject of their different views of Orthodoxy and the rest of the world, he writes:

THE ROMIOS	THE HELLENE
19. Looking on Greece as outside Europe.	Looking on Greece as a part of Europe.
20. Seeing Europe as the region of alien 'Franks'.	Europe the region of fellow Europeans.
54. Belief in miraculous properties of certain icons.	Enlightened disbelief.
56. Indifference to ethical and mystical content of religion, but semi-pagan attachment to the Orthodox Church as the unifying guardian of *Romiosyne* in times of trouble.	Comparative indifference to ethical and mystical content of religion, but tolerance of Orthodox Church as symbol of Hellenism.
57. Strict observance of religious fasts and feast days and instinctive, tribal retentions of the external signs of Orthodoxy.	A tendency to disregard these except at holidays of Christmas and Easter.
62. Homesickness for the Byzantine empire.	Nostalgia for the age of Pericles.
64. The dome of St Sophia.	The columns of the Parthenon.[ix]

The Greek Orthodox Church is the mighty citadel of the *Romios* tradition and mentality – naturally since it guarded it closely through the centuries of Ottoman occupation. Leigh Fermor noted that in the 1960s Greeks did not even like references to this aspect of their heritage, but it is back in vogue today.

I would have to go to the Greek heartland – to the Peloponnese – to where Turkish rule was harshest and where the main battles of the early nineteenth century Greek War of Independence from the Turks were fought if I wanted to see more of the Greece of the *Romaioi*. But before leaving Patmos I had to unravel the tragi-comic story of one of the principal actors in that struggle for independence: the Patmiot Emmanuel Xanthos, whose grave John Kritikos had pointed out to me on our first meeting.

Xanthos was not a wealthy Patmiot. Although he attended the Patmos school his childhood home was not one of the white mer-chants' mansions, so it has not survived. Xanthos was just one of a large number of poor but educated young men who left the Greek islands to seek their fortunes in Russia at the turn of the nineteenth century because Russia was booming. The rising power in the East, Russia was the promised land whose Tsars, the Greeks believed, were as careful as big brothers of the Balkan Orthodox Christians still toiling under the Ottoman yoke.

Unfortunately, the Russians had already proved themselves incompetent saviours in their bid to rid Europe of the Ottomans. In the 1760s, Catherine the Great had sent an army to the Peloponnese to liberate the Greeks, only to see it massacred by Ottoman Albanian troops, and a second attempt had ended similarly. But both fiascos had been forgotten by the time Xanthos left Patmos to seek his fortune in Russia. Greeks of his era were dreaming the dream of a new Byzantine empire, ruled by Greeks, of course, comprising not only modern Greece but also Constantinople, Asia Minor and the rest of the Orthodox Balkans. The dream was lent substance by an Athos monk's best-selling compilation of prophecies, ancient and modern. One prophecy in particular foretold that 'a race with yellow hair, along with their coadjutors, should overthrow Ishmael.'[x] The

Athos monk and millions of Greeks became convinced that blond Russians were on the point of liberating their Constantinople for them.

The simple truth, that Tsar Alexander I had grown conservative with fright at Napoleon's bid to subjugate Europe and was far keener to preserve the imperial status quo in Europe than to reconstitute the Greeks' Byzantine empire for them, seems to have escaped people like Xanthos. The chaplain to the British embassy in Constantinople up to and during the Greek War of Independence marvelled at this Greek capacity for self-delusion. 'It is certainly remarkable that the Greeks, in their aspiration for liberty, should fix their hopes for aid only on that nation in Europe which is most hostile to the thing they seek . . .'[xi] he wrote. But he need only have turned to books about Byzantium to see that there was nothing very remarkable about it. Greeks tended then – as they had been back in Byzantium – to be divorced from reality where their empire was concerned.

Heading for the large community of Greeks in the southern Russian port of Odessa, Xanthos found work there as a humble merchant's clerk and joined a Freemasons' lodge, the enlightened thing to do at the time. This was probably where the plan to create a secret society devoted to freeing the Greeks was born. He and two compatriots began to dream up some of the most elaborate initiation ceremonies, code-words and hierarchies in the history of secret societies. The symbol of the Philiki Etairia, or Society of Friends, was a pair of flags joined in the sign of a Greek cross. On the flags were the initials of the slogan 'Freedom or Death'. The society was to have five ranks, they decided. A Greek could become an 'Adopted Brother' by getting down on his knees at dead of night and swearing to defend the interests of the homeland, and kill his nearest and dearest if he or she betrayed it. Adopted Brethren were allowed to know that there was a plan to improve the situation of the Greeks under Ottoman rule and might recognize each other by casually dropping the Albanian words for 'sandal' and 'pipe' into their conversation. Members of the next rank up, the 'Bachelors', knew there was going to be a revolution and marked their letters to each other with the name of their correspondent's mother. The 'Priests of Eleusis' were allowed to know that the period of struggle was close at hand and that there were higher ranks than theirs to aspire to. When two of them met they would have to make the joints of two of the fingers on their right hands creak, fold their arms across their chests and wipe their eyes. Some hundred 'Prelates' of the society had to go through a long rigmarole of shaking right hands while their heads rested on their left hands, rubbing their foreheads and reciting a litany of passwords. They were authorized to correspond with a mysterious 'Grand Archi', a top-secret committee which should ideally boast a patron as mighty as Tsar Alexander I of Russia himself.

Xanthos and his cronies did not give nearly as much thought to the less amusing but more practical details of precisely how a war against the Ottomans would be waged or what kind of Greek homeland would emerge from it. Nevertheless, when Xanthos got a job in Constantinople and one of his friends found work in Moscow while the other stayed in Odessa, they had the makings of a network and began recruiting in earnest. Soon Xanthos landed a big fish, a fellow Patmiot who had become the Patriarch of Alexandria, plus a couple of other Patmiot merchants who agreed to buy and transport ammunition and supplies. He evangelized Mount Athos and worked the Peloponnese, recruiting Archbishop Germanos of Patras who later started the war there by raising the standard of revolt at a monastery near what is now a ski resort. Serbia's nineteenth-century king, Karadjordje Petrović, joined up, but Greek merchants made up just over half the society's support, and clergy a further 10 per cent, including nine metropolitans, eight bishops and ten archimandrites. The recruiting drive was notoriously unsuccessful among ordinary Greek peasants. A western-educated merchant or intellectual fired up with high-falutin' foreign notions about something called nationhood and a peasant had little in common except hatred of Turks. It is reckoned that membership of the Philiki Etairia never stood above a thousand.

It was all very well using Alexander's ideally imagined patronage of the society as bait to land influential new members, but the time was rapidly approaching when the society would have to find a famous figurehead to convert the dream of revolution into reality. By 1820 Philiki Etairia had lowered its sights from the imperial heights of Alexander I and decided that Russia's Corfiot Greek foreign minister, Count Ioannis Capodistrias, would do almost as well. Xanthos set off for St Petersburg to recruit him, taking with him the society's impressive seal, with Capodistrias' initials already embossed in its centre, to boost his morale.

Count Capodistrias immediately refused the leadership of the society on the sensible grounds that he was the servant of the ruler of another country. He told Xanthos that he wished the Philiki Etairia well but only if its members could find a means other than violent revolution to achieve their aim. Xanthos seems to have wishfully, or wilfully, misconstrued his words as meaning that the society could count on Capodistrias' wholehearted support if only it could find another figurehead of a leader. Desperately, he cast around a wintry St Petersburg and found Alexandros Ypsilantis, a one-armed Greek general in the Russian army.

Ypsilantis was also a scion of one of the dozen or so fabulously wealthy Constantinople Greek families who, over the centuries since the fall of Constantinople, had made themselves indispensable to Ottoman Rulers by rendering them vital banking and interpreting services and taking it in turns to pay fantastic sums for the privilege of spending short spells on the thrones of the Danubian principalities. These few Greek families were the aristocrats of the patriarchate of Constantinople's empire-within-an-empire, and they concocted ancient Byzantine lineages for themselves. Known as Phanariots, since they had settled in the Phanar district of Constantinople close to the patriarchate, they soon controlled the incumbents of the patriarchal throne on account of their fabulous wealth. They were also champion dreamers of the dream of a resurrected Byzantium, which was looking tantalizingly close to realization by the early nineteenth century. Everyone could see that Ottoman Turkey was the moribund 'sick man of Europe', as Nicholas I of Russia once put it.

Alexandros Ypsilantis' father had occupied the throne of the Danubian principality of Wallachia for a while, but had been executed by the Ottomans on suspicion of assisting the Serbs' 1804 uprising. His romantic one-armed son's adoption of the cause of Greek Independence might have been motivated by impatience to see Byzantium reborn or, equally likely, by a desire to avenge his father's death. But when he delightedly accepted the honour Xanthos was offering, he was unwittingly planting a stick of dynamite under centuries of hugely profitable and mostly peaceful co-existence that generations of Phanariot families like his own had enjoyed under the Turks. Count Capodistrias had expressly warned him to beware of 'miserable merchants' clerks'[xii] like Xanthos, but Ypsilantis chose to set in motion a train of events that would bring the comfortably corrupted but still recognizably Byzantine Greek world of the Constantinople Church and the Phanariots crashing down around their ears.

Ignoring the unmistakable signs that the Philiki Etairia could expect no help whatsoever from Russia, Xanthos named Ypsilantis the 'General Representative of the Arch' and addressed him: 'Oh, my prince, God calls upon you to lead our people, the new Israel, to the land of promise. God has blessed the leadership which the nation offers you.'[xiii] No Greek would have balked at his messianic tone. Most had already married their customary religious fervour to the fashionable West-inspired creed of national liberation.

In March 1821, Ypsilantis dressed himself up in his Russian army uniform and set out on the first leg of his quest to liberate the Balkans with a mere twenty men. Crossing the river Prut from southern Russia, they arrived in the neighbouring Danubian Principality of Moldavia where they picked up a few more recruits. In so far as it had made any serious plans at all, the Philiki Etairia had reckoned that the Romanians, as heartily sick of Ottoman vassaldom as any other Orthodox Balkan people, would happily rally to the revolutionary cause and help liberate Greece. They had failed to notice, or had ignored reality in favour of the cherished old Byzantine myth, that those Romanians were at least as unhappy with Phanariot Greek rule over their lands as the Greeks were with the Ottoman *Turcocratia*. Like everyone else in that south-eastern corner of Europe at the time, the Romanians wanted to rule themselves. Instead of joining Ypsilantis' revolution, Romanian peasants rose up to stage their own revolt against their Phanariot Greek overlords. A fiasco ensued. Four months later Ypsilantis and the remnants of his army had sought refuge in a Wallachian monastery where they suffered a three-week siege by Ottoman troops. The Philiki Etairia fell apart, but not the revolution, which burst into flames in the Peloponnese.

THE PELOPONNESE

March 25, 1998, was Greek Independence Day and the important Orthodox Feast of the Annunciation, but a blizzard such as the northern Peloponnese had not experienced since the Second World War cut the electricity supply, the mountain railway line and all the roads to the ski-resort town of Kalavrita.

Crowds of Athenians who had ventured out from the capital in their neon ski-suits for a holiday weekend on the nearest piste were disappointed. But more to the point, as far as I was concerned, Independence Day celebrations up at the Aghia Lavra monastery a few kilometres out of the town had to be severely curtailed. There would be no open-air re-enactment of the gesture that is supposed to have started the ten-year Greek War of Independence in the Peloponnese: Archbishop Germanos of Patras' raising of the standard of revolt.

Instead there was only the usual service at the monastery, which provided a warmly candle-lit refuge from the flurries of snow. In the middle of the crowded church was a sort of easel on which the tired cloth banner of the revolt was displayed. Grouped around this sacred object, bearded priests and laymen, some in sailors' and air-force officers' uniforms, raised their voices in a stirring rendition of the shamelessly martial Greek national hymn.

> I recognize you by the fierce edge of your sword;
> I recognize you by the look that measures the earth.
> Liberty, who sprang from the sacred bones of the Greeks,
> brave as in the past, I greet you, I greet you! . . .[xiv]

After the service the local Bishop strode out into the curtain of flying snow, to pose with the warmly approbod faithful while som memorative photographs were taken. Then, with a smile and a general blessing, he climbed into his Mercedes and sped away down the mountain, just before the road became impassable.

Archbishop Germanos, the revolutionary standard-raiser of almost two centuries ago, was not quite the hero Greek history has made him out to be. A British philhellenist – one of hundreds, including Lord Byron, who were sufficiently fired with sympathy for the Greeks' plight to join their struggle against the Turks – described this pillar of Philiki Etairia as 'a very arch fellow, extremely careful of his own interest'.[xv] Germanos was apparently terrified when he found that his grandiose gesture at Aghia Lavra monastery had unleashed the uprising in Peloponnese. And with good reason: its repercussions were almost as instant in Constantinople as they were in the Peloponnese. It proved first acutely embarrassing then fatal for poor Patriarch Gregorios V of Constantinople, who was answerable to the Sultan for the misdemeanours of any of the Ottoman empire's 13 million Orthodox Christians. Patriarch Gregorios would probably have been delighted to see the Ottoman empire fall apart of its own accord to make way for a new Byzantium, but he did not relish violence and even less did he want to bring down the wrath of the Turks on the Greek minority of Asia Minor. So, on learning of the uprising in the Peloponnese, he issued a warning that any Greek who joined it faced instant excommunication.

But that old punishment had lost much of its power to terrify and, anyway, it came too late. The eastern Peloponnese had erupted in an orgy of massacre and forced baptisms of Turks. The local clergy, especially the parish priests who had not profited by Ottoman rule, were not just in the thick of the slaughterous fray, they were arming themselves and leading it, very successfully. They provided the revolution with its first heroes. The best known was a disreputable hothead archimandrite known as Papaphlessas who fought so fiercely that even the Turks were impressed and wished they had had him on their side. There was also the deacon, whose defiance in the face of impalement went down in Greek folklore: 'Go you and your faith, your filth, to hell with you! I was born a Greek and a Greek I will die!'[xvi] he is supposed to have replied when invited to save his life by converting to Islam. Half of Mount Athos' six thousand monks abandoned their *hesychia* to join the fray. It was a holy war against the infidel Turks, as sacred and righteous as the wars of old Byzantium. To the astonishment of the western philhellenes, the Greek forces even refused to fight on important Church holidays.

On a spring afternoon, ten days after the scene at Aghia Lavra monastery, Patriarch Gregorios was in his ceremonial best serving the Easter Saturday liturgy in St George's patriarchate church in Constantinople when Ottoman troops shoved their way through the crowd to seize him and sling a halter around his neck. Like a lamb to the slaughter, the *de facto* ruler of all the Ottoman empire's Orthodox Christians was dragged to the patriarchate gate and strung up from its lintel. A frail old man, he weighed too little to die quickly. Robert Walsh, the British embassy's chaplain, witnessed with horror how 'he continued for a long time in pain which no friendly hand dared to abridge, and the darkness of the night came on before his last convulsions were over'.[xvii] The corpse in its golden finery swung in the spring sunshine for three days, forcing anyone who needed to go through the gate to shove it aside. Cut down at last, it was dragged to the harbour, put on a boat, weighted and thrown overboard. Too light to sink, old Gregorios' body floated to the surface and was spotted by a Greek who was hiding on a Russian ship in the harbour. He fished it out of the sea and had it ferried across the Black Sea to Odessa, whose Greek community gave it a grand funeral. Gregorios' precious pectoral medallion of office eventually found its way west to Patmos where it was added to the monastery's treasury. More than any other, it was this gruesome episode that shocked the western powers into action on Greece's behalf.

The Ottoman yes-man of a patriarch who replaced poor Gregorios rebuked his flock for falling 'into such a state of weakness and madness as even to dare to form themselves into a Etairia, or Cabal, against this invincible government which has ever loved and cherished all alike'.[xviii] But it was far too late for U-turns. Twenty-eight Peloponnesian bishops and a thousand priests reviled him as a Judas and declared an independent Greek Church. Adamantios Korais, chief luminary of the Greek Enlightenment, wrote, 'From this hour the clergy of liberated parts of Greece no longer owe recognition to the ecclesiastical authority of the Patriarch of Constantinople . . .'[xix] Once the war was over it took only seven hours to complete the formal severance of the 1,500-year-old sacred bond linking the Greeks to their Constantinople. Thereafter the Greek Orthodox Church was autocephalous and self-governing, and the Serb, Bulgarian and Romanian Churches soon followed its lead.

The Turks were finally hounded out of the Peloponnese with the assistance of Britain, France and Russia, whose ships sank the Ottoman-Egyptian fleet at the battle of Navarino in 1827. Most philhellenes had been disappointed by the reality they encountered in Greece. The Greeks were not, of course, a race of heroes and gods, but a sadly fragmented people. There were a few western-educated romantics, ill-suited to waging a war or organizing a state, a handful of fearless outlaw chiefs, who became the war's heroes, the Phanariots and higher clergy who could not help but regret the passing of the Ottoman order that had elevated and cherished them, the bellicose lower clergy waging their holy war and, finally, the mass of suffering peasantry. The first category had nothing in common with the other three, the second turned on each other and terrorized the peasantry, while the lower clergy stoked the fires of war by blessing the slaughter. The dismal lack of cohesion among people who had only their Orthodox faith and language in common meant that the Greeks' war effort against the Turks had deteriorated into civil war amongst themselves. It had sputtered on for seven years.

Nevertheless, there was general rejoicing at the Turks' exodus and high hope that the brand new little Greek state would live up to the glorious ideals of its ancient namesake. In the chancelleries of western Europe it was tacitly understood that fifteen hundred years of Greek history – eleven hundred of Byzantium and four hundred more of Byzantium minus its emperor under Ottoman rule – were best forgotten. Those early high hopes were soon dashed. When Greece's first president sailed into Nafplio harbour aboard a British warship in early 1828, two rival outlaw chiefs were installed in its twin castles, firing off cannon blasts at each other.

The first president of independent Greece was none other than Count Capodistrias. In the elegant town the Venetians had built and originally named Napolia di Romania, in honour of the *Romaioi*, he was hailed like Jesus Christ on his entrance to Jerusalem, with shouts of joy and waving olive branches.

Nafplio, I thought, as I took the morning sun in the town's Venetian marble-paved square and watched a portly priest – proud as a ship under sail – glide past on his way to the bank, was an excellent choice as the first capital of the new Greek state. There were two castles on the hills behind the town to retreat to in case of attack but otherwise not a hint of anything but civilized peaceful living, nothing irksomely Ottoman whatsoever. Any number of gracious Italianate houses could be requisitioned as ministerial offices and residences. There was a wide marble square to promenade along in the evening, a respectable number of churches in which to worship and a busy harbour. A light breeze rustled through the spring green leaves on the lime tree by the bank as the priest emerged with a folder under his arm, and sailed across to the other side of the square. From an open-doored café came the sound of old men clicking their backgammon counters on Formica-topped tables. Nafplio must have seemed a provincial backwater to Capodistrias after the chill grandeur of St Petersburg, but I found it charming.

Capodistrias made an excellent start by persuading those quarrelsome chieftains to abandon their hilltop strongholds and devote themselves to the greater good by accepting him as their leader. But after that his new career went more or less downhill. There was something sad, in both the colloquial and literal senses of the word, about Capodistrias. From the start he seemed to be reaching for a martyr's crown and it took him only five years to win one. Having advised the Philiki Etairia members to wait for Divine Providence to

determine the fate of the Greek nation, he had accepted the invitation to become Greece's first president in the firm belief that the
same Divine Providence had ordained that he serve his country in
this later hour of need. On arrival he wrote to a Swiss friend:

> I will say without personal conceit that the confidence shown
> towards me by everybody, particularly the common people,
> enables me to endure with a sense of internal satisfaction the
> immense labour which is my portion every day. And certainly, if
> I am able to bear it, it is because I am strengthened by that
> sentiment and the protection of our Saviour.[xx]

A modest white statue of him, standing in a square around the
corner from the town's bus station, reveals nothing of the man's
profoundly Orthodox religiosity and celibate austerity, much less of
his secret dream to retire quietly to his native island of Corfu and
read theology for the rest of his life. To judge by that statue alone, he
was a typical cog in the wheel of the mighty Russian imperial civil
service. A small, neatly fashioned man with a high forehead, he must
have cut a rather stiff figure in his buttoned-up tail coat and throttling
high collar. The unpromising material with which he was forced to
work, coupled with his own taste for some of the most rigidly
authoritarian aspects of Russian imperial statecraft, seem to have
conspired to make Capodistrias a disastrously poor president. He was
impractical, slow to make decisions but obsessed with protocol and
detail. A good bureaucrat by training, he appointed the schoolteachers and devised their curricula; he decided the names of new streets
and the siting of drains. He distrusted Constantinople Phanariots, the
western-educated intellectuals, the outlaw chiefs and the higher
clergy, but warmed to the peasants when they started to call him
affectionately Barba Yanni, Uncle Johnny. The ideal Greece he
yearned for was a land inhabited by a race of peasant farmers who
would willingly submit to his brand of benignly paternalistic rule.

Capodistrias, as one historian has put it, wanted 'a nation with a
democratic society but not a democratic state,'[xxi] a desire he might
have conceived back in Russia where the same idealized brand of

egalitarian paternalism governed the autocratic tsars' relations with their people. All the peoples of the Russian empire were the Tsar's children, equally beloved in his sight, equally beholden and obedient to him. And where did this model originate? In Byzantium, in strictly ruled monasteries that aimed at reflecting Heaven on Earth more faithfully than the Byzantine empire was ever able to do. In those miniature societies all monks were equal in the eyes of the Abbot, who exacted devoted obedience from all. Property was held in common and all were equal in their poverty. After 1917 Russia may have seemed utterly changed without its God-appointed Tsar and Church, but it was soon clear that the basic relations between Russia's governors and governed had not changed at all. The new socialist order was just as paternalistic and egalitarian as the old one.

As Father Sava of Dečani had told me, the seed of Communist ideology fell on more fertile soil in the traditionally Orthodox countries of the eastern bloc. Communism's espousal of the old Christian ideal of a community in which the individual was sacrificed to the needs of that community in unquestioning obedience to the wishes of a supreme authority – a general secretary of the Communist Party, God, an abbot or an emperor – made powerfully familiar good sense in all these countries. Its appeal was naturally weaker in the traditionally Roman Catholic and Protestant countries of the Soviet empire – Czechoslovakia, East Germany, Hungary and Poland. Those countries all mounted at least one show of violent resistance to their Soviet-imposed Communist regimes. Even the Catholic Croats, locked into a Communist Yugoslavia dominated by Orthodox Serbs, raised a protest in the 'Croatian Spring' of 1972.

Largely thanks to western intervention in the Greek civil war of 1947 to 1949, Greece escaped Communist rule. Today, however, five in every hundred Greeks, including Sarandi the Patmiot fire-worker, is inclined to vote Communist. It seems to me likely that this strange fact may be due to a lingering Byzantine Greek feel for what an ideal Christian community should be, rather than to any respect for the reality Soviet Communism created.

Western-style democracy was not high on Capodistrias' agenda back in the 1820s but he did see eye to eye with his people when it came to favouring the speedy expansion of the little Greek state. Although modified by an acceptance that the Balkan Slav Orthodox did not want to be ruled by Greeks, the dream of re-creating a new Byzantine empire was not yet dead. This was perfectly understandable since at the time the country consisted of little more than the Peloponnese. In a letter to the British Colonial Office Capodistrias argued that Greece must grow because 'the Greek nation consists of people who have never ceased, since the fall of Constantinople, to profess the Orthodox religion, to speak their ancestral language, and who have remained under the spiritual or temporal jurisdiction of their Church . . .'[xxii] Greece's dream of re-creating Byzantium, their *Megali Idea*, continued to inspire all Greeks until 1922. In that year, the Greeks, having marched into post-First World War Turkey and retaken Constantinople with western assistance, overreached themselves by marching on alone towards Ankara where they were soundly defeated by Kemal Atatürk's forces. The Greeks of Asia Minor were forced to flee the land that had bred some of the earliest Christian saints. That *Katastroph*, as the Greeks still refer to it, was to sound the death-knell for the dream of a new Byzantium. The failure to join Cyprus to the rest of Greece, and the Turks' occupation of the northern part of that island in 1974, was only the last nail in its coffin.

Capodistrias had envisaged an important role for the Church in the new state. 'The first and most essential of the needs of the Greek government is that of procuring the religious instruction of the nation,'[xxiii] he had confided to a friend before arriving in Nafplio. However, the lower clergy were in no fit state to oversee the moral regeneration of the country. Some seven thousand had been killed in the war and only one in a hundred could write his own name. 'What could the president do to reform the clergy, to cure the ills of this rather large sector of the nation?' wrote his friend and apologist Mustokidis. 'To cut off all that was gangrenous would have left very little . . .'[xxiv] From time to time Capodistrias travelled about his war-wrecked domain to supervise works in progress. He always stayed with bishops or priests, whom he insisted on reimbursing for their hospitality. If he did not, his laboriously punctilious reasoning went, they could be guaranteed to take up a collection from the villagers when he left. Theodore Kolokotronis, the strongest of the outlaw chieftains, assured him that the priests would be sure to take up a collection anyway, the moment he was out of sight.

Kolokotronis, whose portrait today graces a Greek banknote of a higher denomination than the one bearing Capodistrias' sad face, cooperated with Capodistrias until he realized that he had introduced into the new Greece a favourite old Russian technique for controlling the population: a giant network of spies and informers. Private mail was being opened and the press censored. Making no allowances for Greece's dual Hellenic and Byzantine character, Capodistrias did not accept that the new Greece was looking to its own Parthenon rather than to Moscow for inspiration. Another outlaw chieftain and war hero, General Makrigiannis, warned him that Byzantine Russian ways might suit the Russians but would not be tolerated by the freedom-loving Greeks: '. . . this freedom, President, we didn't find it in the gutter and we shan't easily go back into the egg-shell; for we aren't a chicken to go back in, we've become a bird and we won't go,'[xxv] he told him. A third outlaw chieftain was the cause of Capodistrias' assassination in 1831.

At six a.m. on the crisp sunny morning of 27 September 1831 Capodistrias rose from his desk where he had already put in an hour's work, did up his double breasted coat with its silver buttons, fetched his hat and cane and headed off to the church of St Spyridon, in one of Nafplio's prettiest back streets, to attend the morning liturgy. He had been warned that his enemies were grouping but had said, 'Don't be upset. Holy Providence is watching over the life of the Governor of Greece.'[xxvi] He would have recognized the two young men lurking by the church door as the brothers of that third outlaw chieftain, Mavromichalis, who was languishing behind bars up in one of Nafplio's castles. He could have guessed their intention, especially as one had his right hand concealed inside his coat. But instead of turning tail, he greeted them affably and they respectfully raised their red caps to him. As he was removing his own top hat to enter the church, one shot him and the other stabbed him.

The president lay breathing his last on the church doorstep, while a scuffle broke out between his guards and the assassins, one of whom was shot in the leg and lynched by the mob. 'Don't dishonour me, boys! Better light a candle at the church door. Ho! Is there no *palikari* who will end me with a pistol ball?'[xxvii] he gasped. Most Greeks, especially the peasants who had loved their saintly Barba Yanni, were horrified at the murder but intellectuals and outlaw chiefs made heroes of his assassins.

Greece was still terminally incoherent in 1833 when Europe's Great Powers agreed to set a sixteen-year-old Bavarian princeling called Otto on a new Greek throne. To the Russians' and Greeks' fury he refused to oblige his new subjects by converting from Catholicism to Orthodoxy, then compounded the injury by taking a Protestant wife. His regents were a triumvirate of German ministers, one of whom, Gheorghe Maurer, set about demolishing any last vestiges of the Church's former power. It was he who promoted the severance of the bond linking the Greek Church to the Constantinople patriarchate, because he did not want Russia using universal Orthodoxy as a conduit to control Greece. He then set up a Holy Synod of government appointees to run the Greek Church. Well aware that the strongest opposition to Church reforms was coming, as it always had in Byzantine times, from the monasteries, he turned his attentions there. Noting that monks constituted a dangerously weighty pro-Orthodox Russia lobby on a political scene featuring parties called the 'British', the 'French' and the 'Russian', he ruled that any monastery containing less than six monks or less than thirty nuns must be dissolved. In 1833, 412 monasteries were closed. By 1840 Greece had only 128 monasteries and three convents. There was not much of an outcry. Bitter old memories of the Church hierarchy's four-hundred-year-long collaboration with the Ottomans outweighed fresher ones of the lower clergy's vital contribution to the war effort.

Enthusiasm for all things Ancient Greek, and modern and western, was at is height. Monasteries seemed to belong to a dark and ugly age, and to be the last thing the new Greece needed.

The little white church of St Spyridon, the scene of Capodistrias' murder, is still there and so is a bullet-hole, framed in brass and protected by glass, just to the right of the door. I went inside, lit a candle and read a notice announcing that a local archimandrite would be giving a lecture in a hall by the bus station that evening.

I had expected a handful of elderly to attend, but the place was full to overflowing with five hundred or so of Nafplio's most respectable-looking citizens, all of them – young and old – arrayed in their Sunday best as if for church. The atmosphere was charged with excitement when the ginger-bearded young churchman approached the rostrum, to declaim rather than speak his lecture. Capodistrias' name came up.

'Capodistrias was the original "spiritual man", who is described and defined by the Church. A "spiritual man" can only suffer for the world he finds himself in. Capodistrias *had* to be killed just because he was a "spiritual man",' he told his rapt audience.

Capodistrias' arrogance, his secret police and his chronic inefficiency had all been forgotten and a new myth was in the making, I thought. The Greek Church was repackaging Greece's first ruler as a perfectly Orthodox Christian who sacrificed himself for his people, just as Christ had sacrificed himself for man. In the short run, evil always triumphs over good, a good man's reward is always in Heaven rather than on Earth, and suffering is what makes a saint.

As I walked back to my hotel through the dark town I was thinking about Prince Lazar on the eve of the battle of Kosovo, about the Serbian Church's packaging of his myth and Goran's depressing assertion that Milošević's warmongering had gained Serbia saints as well as war criminals.

ATHENS

'NO TO 666!' read the blue graffiti on the concrete side of the ugly motorway linking the Peloponnese to Athens.

I had at last unravelled the contemporary significance of this silently bellowed protest that had haunted me every step of my way around Greece. At the Pantanassa convent in the centre of the ruined Byzantine city of Mistra, in the heart of the mountainous Peloponnese, I had met a young nun called Sister Agnes who, once she had finished hosing down the pots of geraniums in the convent's courtyard, had shepherded me into a dark parlour hung with portrait photographs of former abbesses, unlocked a cabinet to help herself to a couple of chunks of sugary *loukoumi* and then sat down on a hard bench to talk.

My request that she explain the 666 graffiti had caused her to frown and nod.

'What's that town in Holland where they made this terrible plan to register everyone in the European Community on a giant computer? . . . That's it – Schengen. Well, in the Book of Revelation it says that the mark of the Beast is 666 and that there will come a time near the end of the world when no one will be able to buy or sell without this sign. Well, that time has come with this Schengen Agreement. Thanks to the giant computer, everyone will have a barcoded identity card. The worst thing is that the Greeks' bar-code includes the number 666.'

'Oh, I see . . .'

I was recalling what Goran had once told me about a hermit he had encountered on Mount Athos. Goran had arrived at the holy man's hut bearing a gift box of German biscuits, and watched dismayed while the old monk hardly glanced at the present and instead went outside the door to throw it on what seemed to be a rubbish heap. It *was* a rubbish heap, he had told Goran, one especially reserved for all the satanically bar-coded goods he had ever been given.

Sister Agnes was asking me, 'You've heard of this new technology which will mean that everyone's details will be implanted as a microchip in people's hands, haven't you?' She burrowed through a pile of books and papers on the table. 'Here it is,' she said, producing a crumpled, badly printed leaflet with a picture of a bar-code in one corner. 'This will explain everything. You can have it.'

The material was not as illuminating as I had hoped. As far as I could make out, its main thrust was a warning to the Orthodox faithful not to use electronic cards or implanted microchips because they make one 'unable to resist the binds of the Anti-Christ's satanic magic and lead to eventual condemnation to the Fires of Hell'. Its author was a priest.

Athens' bustling crowds and a noisy Olympic Airways workers' demonstration outside the Parliament building were discomfiting after the vivid silence of Mistra and the ghostly quiet of the Peloponnese. But spring was in full swing, the trees decked in translucent green, and the pavement cafés full.

I settled in a hotel near the city's cathedral. It was quiet there, perhaps because all the shops along the narrow side-streets opening off the cathedral square were filled with *ekklesiastika* – church icons, furniture, lamps, books, crosses, vestments, lecterns, incense-burners. I spent hours in the square, sitting under a lime tree at an outdoor café, watching the priests glide or shuffle by. Sometimes there were noisy children playing tag around a statue of Archbishop Damaskinos, the churchman who had ruled Greece for a time after the Second World War and had been branded a 'wily medieval prelate' by Winston Churchill.

One morning I happened to run into a pair of young Romanian nuns at the hotel's reception desk, both of them modest, serious and delicately pretty in their black pill-box hats and veils. They told me that they had been planning to travel north to Thessaloniki and take a boat-trip around Mount Athos, but had unfortunately run short of cash. Assuring them that they were not missing much, I invited them to take coffee with me at my favourite café and the three of us walked to the cathedral square.

They had been in Athens a month, acquiring some further qualifications in icon-painting, they told me, but were now looking forward to going home because they had been sadly disappointed, even shocked, by the worldliness of the Greek Church.

'Honestly, we expected so much more. After all, Greece is the Mother Church,' said one, her eyes guileless but troubled behind their metal-rimmed spectacles, 'but now we have to believe that Romania is more advanced spiritually.'

I was looking forward to travelling to spiritual Romania in the autumn but the two nuns were in the throes of moving monasteries and could not tell where they would be by then.

Another dazzling morning I tarried long in the Plaka district of the city, at a café with a good view of the Acropolis and, at the same time, of a russet brick and frilly roofed Byzantine church shaded by trees. I found myself wondering which of the Greek traditions was likely to prevail in the next century: the western, with its old debt to the Ancient Greeks, or the Byzantine. They seemed to me to be growing more and more mutually exclusive. But perhaps not. I liked the way young Greek men on motorbikes took the trouble to cross themselves as they roared past that little church, their American rock-star T-shirts ballooning like reversed spinnakers behind them. I had been impressed by the lively evening scene in Thessaloniki's St Dimitri cathedral and by the Easter midnight mêlée of rich Athenians and locals at Patmos' monastery. On the other hand, 666 and the Schengen Agreement, which were exercising the Athos monks Father Symeon and Sister Agnes so much, seemed ominous signs that a serious clash might be in the offing.

Perhaps I was seeing trouble were there was none but my mood was sombre. That morning's edition of the English language *Athens News* had contained an astonishing story. Greece's 17 November terrorist organization, infuriated enough by 'American imperialism and internationalism' to have murdered twenty-two people, including a CIA chief, since 1975, had stepped up its activities with five attacks in the past three months. The group's latest manifesto, which accused the US of demonizing Greek nationalism, had opened with a startling parallel between a fifteenth-century Catholic pope's demand that Byzantium submit to Rome, and America's arrogant assumption of supremacy today.

Escaping from the suffocating *nefos* of downtown Athens one quiet Saturday afternoon, I ventured up into the hills, to the city's sprawling suburbs where the air is cleaner and the houses consequently whiter, to call on a Serbian friend of Bogdan's who was in Athens studying for a postgraduate degree in theology. For a while, until he began attacking western journalists for writing lies about the war in Bosnia, Mladen and I talked about his homeland.

'I think that the West is trying to make us forget our history,' he said, 'and how on earth can we do that? The Bible is also history, so that means we should forget our faith. That is terrible because it is only our religion which makes us Serbs! Of course, you western journalists knew nothing about us when the war started. You had to go and look up First World War history to see who we were!'

I asked him if he was finding Greek society more truly Orthodox than Serbian society.

'Greece is trying to achieve a proper harmony between Church and State, like in Byzantium. But it's not working. The state is winning. I can tell you something, more and more people – in all the Orthodox countries – are talking about re-creating a Byzantine empire to put a stop all this Western secularization.'

'Really? What sort of people?' I asked, extremely interested. I knew that Serbia's best-known contemporary novelist, Milorad Pavić, saw himself as the last of the Byzantines. In 1991 he had lamented in a newspaper interview, 'We have severed all the ties with our roots, with our civilization, with the Greeks, with the Romanians, and during the Communist era with Russia too, with the Orthodox Russia . . .'[xxviii]

A couple of years later, a prominent Russian intellectual had noted that 'geo-politically, the peoples of the post-Byzantine region have always constituted a continent between West and East'.[xxix] I would be fascinated to meet a neo-Byzantine Greek, and Mladen seemed willing to help me.

'My theology professor at Athens University, Father Giorgios Metallinos, is one. You should meet him, he's very influential, always on the radio and television chat shows. If you want to know about the 666 business, he should be able to tell you because he was in the thick of the protest. But he's a very busy man. You should call him after ten thirty at night.'

The following week Father Giorgios managed to find a tiny window of opportunity for me in his packed schedule. He told me he could give me half an hour the next day if I met him at six thirty p.m. sharp at the medical-faculty church of Athens University, just opposite the city's children's hospital. I took a taxi there but was almost late and not because of heavy traffic. Athens taxi-drivers, it seemed to me, are the unlikely practitioners of that originally Church-inspired egalitarianism. They will pick you up but then stop for anyone who flags them down. If that person's destination is even remotely on the way to yours, they will pick them up and make any necessary, time-consuming detour.

Father Giorgios was a power-pack of a man, bristling with bustling energy. We settled ourselves down in the little dark icon-hung office attached to the faculty church. My very first mention of Byzantium triggered an outpouring from him.

'Don't use that name, please,' he interrupted me 'Before Charlemagne Europe was united. There was the eastern Roman empire, which was known as Romania and its people as *Romaioi*. Therefore Byzantium's true name is Romania. In fact to call the old Danubian principalities of Wallachia and Moldavia Romania is just as if California were to start calling itself the US!'

'Yes, Father, but what about the Schism?' I interposed quickly, noting how he dated the rift between East and West a good 250 years before 1054 at the pope's coronation of Charlemagne in 800.

'That was the tragedy of the empire of Romania between the ninth and eleventh centuries, of course. Nowadays some people are trying to establish another united Europe, but it's a Franco-Teutonic empire. We don't want *that* and, by the way, I like you English just because you don't want to co-operate with the Germans and the

195

French in this united Europe. We Orthodox can't go along with this project because the West has lost the Greek part of civilization, the understanding of theology, which is the basis of civilization . . .'

'I see . . .'

'. . . and all the political and theological problems which we have today – eastern and western Christianity – they are all founded in this loss of Christian civilization by the West. I have been involved with many ecumenical conferences and I see that East and West are so far apart that we are speaking different languages. We have two words for church – *kyriakon*, which means something that belongs to the Lord, and *ekklesia*, which is the body of Christian society, of all those who are baptized with the Holy Spirit. In the West, the Church is either a building or it is an institution, a corporation. Look, another example. In the East, to be enlightened means to be filled with the spirit of God. In the West, it means to be educated!'

I imagined that today's ecumenical conferences must be spent gnawing exactly the same bones as were gnawed at the early Church councils and the 1438 Council of Florence. I wanted to ask him about 'the mark of the Beast', but he was already relaunched on an equally fascinating subject.

'A man called Huntington has written that Orthodoxy is a separate culture to the West. Do you know his book? *The Clash of Civilizations and the Remaking of World Order?*'

I did. I had been interested to find that Professor Samuel Huntington seemed to have rationalized my hunch that Orthodox countries of Europe constitute a world of their own, distinct from our western one, on account of their Orthodox culture. I had found his argument, that the wars of the near future would be fought over civilization borders rather than national, ideological or economic ones, very persuasive.

'This man wants to exclude Orthodoxy from the European tradition. We know that our Orthodoxy is offering a very difficult ideal to live up to, but western Europe must try to live up to it because Orthodoxy is the basis of Christianity. The model for our ideal is to be found in the Cenobitic Rule of an Orthodox monastery.'

But Capodistrias' Greece, pre-1917 Russia and the Soviet Union had tried that model, a democratic society minus a democratic state, and it had failed, I thought. 'What about the Hesychast tradition, Father Giorgios?' I asked quickly, aware that my time was almost up.

He leapt to the new challenge. 'We Greeks have been rediscovering this tradition in the last fifty years, and thank God! We are abandoning all that western scholastic theology and returning to the teachings of the Church Fathers. Salvation can *never* come from scholastic theology!'

Hesychasm, I was beginning to see, is something of a double-edged sword in the hands of an Orthodox Europe trying to secure a safe place for itself alongside the rest of the continent. On the one hand it is the repository of Orthodoxy's enduring spiritual vitality and a powerful means of attracting westerners to Orthodoxy. On the other, however, because it is the aspect of Orthodoxy most alien to the ways of the West, its effect has been to sharpen the Orthodox Church's antipathy to anything western, making it a divisive influence . . .

Father Giorgios was already off on another tack. 'Of course, Russian Communism was not real Communism. It arrived in Russia in 1917 with Lenin who was sent by the German Kaiser to destroy the true Orthodox kind of Communism.'

'Oh? I thought the Kaiser put Lenin on the train to St Petersburg because he wanted to knock Russia out of the First World War so that Germany did not have to go on fighting on two fronts.'

'Pah! No! Lenin's real job was to destroy Orthodoxy. This is the opinion of people all over the Orthodox world, not just mine. Now I must go, because the church service is beginning. You have had precisely forty-five minutes.' He chuckled, with a glance at his watch. 'If there is anything else, you can write to me.' He scribbled his e-mail address in my notebook.

I looked for Father Giorgios outside the doors of Athens' metropolitan cathedral the next day but failed to spot him in the crowd of clerics, identically robed in billowing white satin for the state funeral of the head of the Greek Orthodox Church, Archbishop Serapheim.

Serapheim had been ailing for the last two years of his twenty-four-year reign so his death at the age of eighty-five was not unexpected. Indeed, it was something of a relief to a handful of ambitious bishops who had dared suggest to him that he might like to step down, and to a large part of the laity who worried that he was failing to confront the challenges of the modern world. But Serapheim, as the similarly moribund ex-President of Greece, Karamanlis, put it on hearing of the prelate's demise, was always 'a fighter'. As a young priest in Nazi-occupied Greece he had joined one of the Greek resistance movements, given its members spiritual succour, blessed their flags and even fought as a mountain guerrilla. So it was that, on his deathbed over fifty years later, he had refused to resign and angrily likened those bold bishops to 'vultures', bluntly bellicose to the last.

But he had always been more diplomatic in his relations with the Greek State, compromising as advantageously as possible over Prime Minister Papandreou's scheme to deprive the Church of its enormous properties, assenting to the belated introduction of civil marriages but ensuring that church marriages were equally valid, procuring a decent degree of autonomy for the Church without riling the politicians. He was assured of a full State send-off, a funeral procession grand enough to warrant clearing the heart of Athens of all its roaring traffic for a couple of hours in the middle of a working day.

Stiff lines of paratroopers, sailors and soldiers, sweltering in full kit in the hot spring sunshine for hours, lined the road from the cathedral along which the funeral procession was to pass. A doleful tolling signalled the end of the church service and the appearance of a straggle of churchmen, who were followed by a glittering crowd of more than seventy bishops, most of them ancient and bowed under the weight of azure, burgundy, white and gold robes of velvet or satin, heavy icon- and jewel-crusted mitres and gilded staffs. They approached, like top generals of another impressive branch of Greece's armed forces, until they drew level at last, and I noticed that all was not as grand as it had seemed from a distance. One old bishop was muttering to another that he was striding unbecomingly fast. Another adjusted a brocade stole whose tassels were threatening to trip him up and yet another was limping along with his mitre askew, trying to mop his sweat beaded brow without forfeiting his grip on his crozier. I remembered reading about a western outsider, observing a Byzantine church procession, who had been similarly struck by the gulf between the gorgeous ideal and the homely reality.

At the approach of the camouflage-painted lorry towing a modern military gun carriage with the open coffin, the crowd of bystanders bowed their heads and crossed themselves. The dead 'fighter' arch-bishop – a fluff of his silver beard and sharp white nose translucent in the midday sun and just visible above the coffin rim – sailed past the ugly post-Second World War blocks of flats. An army of foot-soldiers followed, hundreds of priests in their white satin and black stovepipe hats.

Serapheim's successor, Archbishop Christodoulos, must have been among those seventy-odd prelates wilting under their weighty adornments. Younger than most, a churchman as bushily bearded and bustlingly energetic as Father Giorgios, with five European languages at his fingertips and the setting up of a Greek Orthodox Internet server and radio station to his credit, he was promising to take his place as a heavyweight on the Greek political scene. He would be wanting to restore a measure of Byzantine *symphonia* between Greece's Church and State. As I write, less than two months after his appointment, a public opinion poll has already pronounced him the most popular public figure in Greece today and he is wowing Greek youth with a catchy new slogan: 'Orthodoxy is cool.' But his inaugural speech – a hot blast of anti-West rhetoric – set alarm bells ringing in the chancelleries of European Union countries.*

---

* When Nato launched its Kosovo campaign in March 1999, Greece protested. Archbishop Christodoulos, nicknamed 'Thunderbolt', commented: 'The Nato strikes are not only unChristian but a strike against Orthodoxy.' (*Guardian* 29.03.99). Greece was the only Nato country that refused to participate in bombing raids against Yugoslavia.

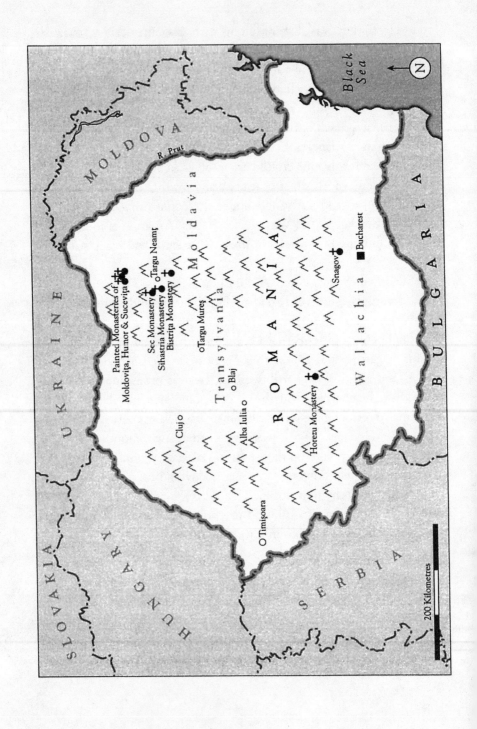

ROMANIA

Monastery of the Birth of the Mother of God
Transylvania

It had rained all afternoon but now the sky was clear and the sun setting in a blinding amber blaze over the wet road ahead. To left and right lay fields the hazy bluish hue of woodsmoke and, in the distance, dark mountains. But something startlingly bright lay just up ahead, in the lee of a low hill. Was it a shopping centre, a service station, or a giant McDonald's?

'No, no,' chuckled Viorel, as he swerved his old Mercedes jeep around a pot-hole in order to overtake a line of trundling horses and carts piled high with ragged cornstalks. 'That, my dear, is the brand new Monastery of the Birth of the Mother of God.'

That Eastern Orthodox Europe was hosting a grand monastic revival was no longer news to me, but that it should have spread as far as the country least able to afford such a development was astonishing.

Almost a decade after the collapse of her Communist regime, Romanians were still struggling to raise themselves from the abject depths to which Nicolae Ceauşescu had led them by the time he was shot on Christmas Day 1989. Most potential foreign investors had turned away in pity and horror from a country that seemed as brokenly dysfunctional as the neglected children filling its hell-hole orphanages. Ragged peasants were still travelling by horse-drawn carts along roads still dangerously uneven, unlit and unmarked. Most towns were still disintegrating messes of damp concrete, cracked pavements and weeds. Little had been achieved in the way of decentralizing the country or reforming its economy. Romania was still in urgent need of almost everything – except more monasteries to add to the hundred it had retained throughout the Communist period.

There had been some changes. All over Transylvania large signboards advertising the 'International Bank of Religion, for all Believers', (an outfit widely rumoured to be run by former members of Ceauşescu's Securitate police), had taken the place of rusting metal signs proclaiming 'Ceauşescu's Golden Epoch'. Peasants were toiling over their own small plots of land instead of conscript soldiers pushing horse-drawn ploughs through vast state-owned fields. The orphanages had been improved with western aid. New supermarkets selling a variety of foods had replaced dark shops stocked with only bad champagne and chicken feet, unless you happened to have a secret back-door arrangement with the shop-keeper. There were also reliable supplies of electricity and heating, instead of a freezing darkness so terrible that in the last winter of 1989 people had had to huddle around their kitchen gas-rings, reading by candle-light. There were a few new private restaurants, so that travellers no longer had to head for Orthodox monasteries if they wanted a kind welcome and an edible meal. In fact, so much had changed that I had begun to suspect that the country was losing the surreal quality that had so fascinated me on my first visit in the mid-1980s – until I saw that dazzling new Monastery of the Birth of the Mother of God.

Turning off left towards it and bumping along a rough track leading up to its gates, I stared aghast at an orderly vision of red-tiled roofs, multi-steepled church and pretty balconied buildings, which extended through well-kept gardens and on, up the hill towards more gleaming new buildings and another church, all of it surrounded by a neat red-brick wall. As confidently as any neon brand-sign, the Monastery of the Birth of the Mother of God seemed to be proclaiming, 'Come all you suffering sinners, to this patch of Heaven on Earth. Come, and refresh your souls!' Who could resist such an appeal?

Viorel had aimed to thrill me with this showpiece of neo-medievalism. 'Trust me, just trust me,' he had said, back in Targu Mureş, bundling me into his jeep and refusing to tell me where we were going. Officially named a hero of the revolution that rid the country of Communism and Ceauşescu, Viorel is a man of some standing in his home town, but he was chuckling as gleefully as a child at my astonishment and limbering up to another extraordinary revelation.

'And it's not the only new monastery around here. In Ceauşescu's time we had one in this county, now we can proudly say that we have seventeen!'

'*Seventeen* monasteries in Mureş?' For a moment I doubted my old friend's excellent grasp of English. 'You mean seven, don't you?'

'I mean just what I said – seven*teen*,' he repeated, and continued, 'I hope we'll find Father Ioan here. People say he's a very holy man, a *duhovnik*, and they come from all over the country to talk with him and receive his blessing. You should see the coaches here at weekends!'

The anxious young nuns I had treated to coffee in Athens had led me to suspect that the Byzantine tradition of holy men might have been better preserved in Romania than in modern Greece, but I had expected to find such people cloistered away in the heartland of Romanian Hesychasm, in a cluster of fifteenth- and sixteenth-century monasteries in the distant north-east corner of the country. There might even, I had thought, be some to the south, in the concentration of seventeenth-century foundations adorning the foot-hills of the Carpathians. To find one here, on a plain in the heart of Transylvania, at a new monastery a stone's throw away from a busy main road, was an unexpected stroke of luck.

As we walked through the gates I paused a moment. The monastery could not be a showpiece of neo-medievalism, I corrected myself, because the word 'medieval' pertains only to western Christendom and is used to demarcate the age of faith sandwiched between what used to be called the West's Dark Ages and its sixteenth-century Reformation. Orthodox Europe had no medieval era in that sense or, if it did, it is not yet over and done with. In a country like Romania therefore, building monasteries at the end of the twentieth century was not necessarily either bizarre or kitsch. If western Europe had not had its Reformation, it might be doing precisely the same because, for all the 1054 Schism and the Crusaders' 1204 sacking of Constantinople, pre-Reformation western Europe was not so very different from its Eastern Orthodox counterpart.

The Schism had caused a separation between East and West,

which the Fourth Crusaders' thuggery had hardened into an acrimonious divorce, but it was the Reformation that finally delivered the decree absolute. By preaching that there was no sense in trying to shorten one's stay in Purgatory with hefty donations to monasteries and churches, expensive saints' relics and indulgences, Protestants set out to expose the massive confidence trick played by the Catholic Church's greedy officials. God could not be bribed and only He could decide who deserved to be saved after death, they said. The Catholics' fabulously profitable insurance industry, feeding off popular fears of hell-fire and damnation, had nothing whatsoever to do with Him. Faith was the only soul-saving currency and only God could determine who had enough, said Martin Luther. In northern Europe, especially in what is now Germany and in England, monasteries were emptied and churches officially plundered of their treasures. In 1538 Henry VIII ordered the dissolution of most of England's monasteries.

Inevitably, the Reformation's revolutionary euphoria was followed by a Counter-Reformation. The Pope went back on the offensive and the Catholic Church came sweeping back through swathes of central Europe, including the Romanian province of Transylvania. With hindsight, one can see that it was too late to repair all the damage because the Reformation had irreversibly altered the mind-set of western man. His thoughts were never again to be so trustingly fixed on the life of the world to come, at the expense of his comfort and satisfaction here on Earth. The papacy was never to recoup all its losses. Catholic France was never again Catholic enough to prevent the violent break with the Church and the great leap forward of the 1789 Revolution. The Spanish civil war of the late 1930s was what finally broke the back of Spanish Catholicism.

Thanks to the conservative inertia of Turkey in Europe nothing quite like western Europe's Reformation or Counter-Reformation took place in the Orthodox world until the twentieth century. Then Communism, the fruit of Karl Marx's western mind, tried to force a leap further into a man-centred universe than any Reformation had, by explicitly substituting man for God. It failed, and a more graphic illustration of that failure than this brand new Monastery of the Birth of the Mother of God was hard to imagine. Only the best building materials had been used and no expense spared to make it a fitting slice of Heaven on Earth. The church steps were of gleaming white marble, the neat red-paved courtyard was freshly swept, and there were litter bins marked 'Order is easy to make, hard to keep!' dotted around flower-beds filled with marigolds. While a young nun hurried off to find the famous holy monk for us, Viorel and I wandered around the grounds. Peering in at windows, we marvelled at the elegant spaciousness of the place and especially at the laundry room's gleaming new washing machines. But Viorel had begun to look troubled.

'It's all very beautiful,' he said, with a deep sigh, 'but it worries me. Can you imagine the amount of money going into these places? I'm not saying that the government is spending tax-payers' money building them. No, they're mostly built on donations from good, faithful Romanians. Our national football team, for example, has just put up almost half the money for another new monastery in Alba county. But if I were to point out that we have plenty of other things to spend our money on – broken-down housing, orphanages, hospitals, roads, schools and so on – I'd be in trouble.'

'Why?' I asked. I had been thinking that this new monastery was a perfect illustration of what Orthodoxy's traditional emphasis on heart over mind, spirit over flesh and afterlife over this life could lead to. However, someone needed to raise the alarm before Mureș county boasted more monasteries than schools and hospitals and it seemed to me that Viorel, as the director of a local radio station, was well placed to be that someone.

'Why would I be in trouble? Because politics comes into it, of course. When the monks go round collecting money from local businessmen, you can be sure they're telling them that this part of the country needs monasteries to strengthen the Romanian Orthodox presence, to show the Hungarians that this is Romanian land and that we Romanians are here for good. The moment I complained everyone would say I can't be a true Romanian, that I must be being paid by the Hungarians.'

'Oh, yes, of course . . .'

Here we were on this plain in the heart of Romania, on the borderline between eastern and western Christianity again. The two Christendoms have been rubbing and chafing for a thousand years here in Transylvania and there is still no disguising the rift between the minority population of Catholic or Protestant Hungarians, and the majority of Orthodox Romanians. Neighbouring Hungary's loss of Transylvania in 1918 was Romania's proud gain, but this land – just like Kosovo or Bosnia or Macedonia – is another region whose possession is never secure, whose loss can never be compensated. With its fast-flowing rivers, snow-dusted mountain peaks, rich dark soil and mineral wealth, Transylvania is well worth having, of course.

Naturally bountiful, bucolic, woodsmoke-scented and hemmed in on all sides by a crown of the Carpathian mountains and the Transylvanian alps, the province sits like a bright rough jewel in its mountain setting. A world apart, Transylvania is a Bruegelesque-cum-Grimms'-fairy-tale place, dotted with little villages – some Hungarian, some Romanian and a few Saxon German settlements dating back to the thirteenth century. Its Orthodox churches, fat-bellied and squatter than the taller, sharp-steepled Hungarian Catholic competition or the few, now sadly crumbling, Saxon church-fortresses, embellish the countryside. Silver-roofed and freshly painted, they gleam in the cleavages between rolling green hills.

In Transylvania storks nest on top of the telegraph poles that line the roads, emblematic as rows of crucifixes. Wolves and bears roam the mountains and forests. Pigs, geese, cows and flocks of sheep wander the potholed highways. Shepherds in shaggy sheepskin capes snooze under trees, their felt flowerpot hats shading their faces. At this late autumn time of the year, the trees are a blaze of oranges and yellows and the fields full of corn stalks. Corn cribs are crammed with yellow gold to be spent fattening pigs for winter slaughter. The red peppers and cabbages have been pickled and the *ţuica* brandy bottled. Old men in high boots squat on benches outside their low blue- or green-washed houses, chewing their sunflower seeds and swigging their home-brew.

But the rustic idyll is deceptive because both peoples – the Romanians in the majority, Hungarians in the minority – persist in viewing their mini Garden of Eden as the cradle of their respective cultures. Armoured in their mutually exclusive versions of history, they mix uneasily, always on the alert for fresh injuries to tear the scabs off old wounds. The way they stereotype each other is strikingly similar to the way eastern and western Christians stereotyped each other after the 1204 sacking of Constantinople or, for that matter, the way Orthodox Serbs characterize the Catholic Croats. The Romanians say the Hungarians are clever but cruel, while the Hungarians dismiss the Romanians as lazy and dishonest.

Viorel's home town, Targu Mureș, was almost exactly half Hungarian and half Romanian by the time both tribes manned the barricades together to help overthrow Ceaușescu in 1989. The balance is shifting in favour of the Romanians now, but one hears both languages in the streets. Hungarian is cerebral-sounding and precise with its lengthy compound words and multiple sharp vowel-sounds. Latinate Romanian is flowing and emotional by comparison. Viorel speaks both languages perfectly, and one of his dearest friends is a Hungarian called Feri who has perfectly conformed to his national stereotype by establishing the pristine little hotel where I was staying. Viorel and Feri bonded for life, not on those barricades in December 1989, but three months later, in March 1990, on the day Romanians and Hungarians armed themselves with pitch-forks and crowbars and went to war with each other in a series of vicious running battles up and down Targu Mureș' main drag. Both men were in an office on the second floor of the town hall when the Hungarians decided to storm the building. Feri had had to intervene to save Viorel from a horrible death by defenestration. By sunset that day there were three dead, a famous Hungarian poet blinded and hundreds of injured. The first eruption of inter-ethnic violence in the new Romania had been the sad occasion of my first happy meeting with Viorel.

Despite his brush with death, Viorel is sufficiently relaxed about his Hungarian neighbours to consider that a degree of autonomy for Transylvania is now desirable. Most Romanians would not agree.

While recognizing that Romania is over-centralized and that Transylvania could do better alone, assisted by the Hungarians' work ethic and unburdened by the dragging weight of the rest of Romania, they will not hear of granting the region more autonomy. Ordinary Romanians suspect that would be the first step towards the province's eventual repossession by Hungary.

Viorel is an *extra*ordinary Romanian but even he bridled when I remarked that someone had spray-painted out the Hungarian place names on all the bilingual road signs. He told me that he sympathized with the vandal because the Romanian mayor had put up the new signs at dead of night, 'like a thief', when he might have held a referendum on the issue.

'I don't think you will ever understand how delicate this matter is – there's so much history,' said Viorel, as we strolled through Targu Mureş' in dazzling autumn sunshine. He was probably right, but I had understood something. Just to the north of his home town, in the eighteenth-century wall-paintings of a little wooden Orthodox church next to one of Ceauşescu's favourite hunting lodges, the evil Roman soldiers who crucified Christ had been recast as Hungarian soldiers. They were wearing red tunics and tight white leggings with a stripe down the side.

We paused on our walk to speak to a young monk who was collecting funds for the construction of another new monastery. My small contribution placed me eighty-third on his list of that day's donors for whom prayers would be said. It was that brief encounter that had decided Viorel to bring me here to this Monastery of the Birth of the Mother of God.

Climbing the white marble steps, we entered the church, a vaulting dark space whose new grey walls awaited frescoes. A party of schoolchildren walking hand in hand, two by two, followed us in and I watched the six-year-olds automatically cross themselves, some quite expertly. The young nun then reappeared, followed by Father Ioan, and we were shepherded into a little room to the right of the church door. Instead of the ethereal, burning-eyed ascetic I had expected, he was a spry and handsome old man, with vivid red cheeks and bright eyes. He was also boisterously cheerful, perhaps because for the first time in all his seventy-six years he was about to leave Romania to go on holiday. He had his new passport. Now only the wait for a Greek visa was delaying his longed-for departure to Patmos, courtesy of a well-heeled spiritual child.

'I am named after St John the Theologian so I must go to Patmos first,' he explained.

'I was there in the spring. I'm sure you will find it splendid, Father,' I said politely, and he continued in his exalted style.

'After that I will visit Mount Athos, the Holy Mountain! You haven't been *there*, have you now?' He slapped the gold-threaded green stole draped over his black-robed thigh and laughed. 'Thank God there are no women there – ha, ha!' and he winked at Viorel. 'Women are doing everything these days, going everywhere, wearing trousers, but have you noticed,' he said, again turning to Viorel, 'that men are carrying handbags? Ha, ha!'

I was beginning to suspect that Father Ioan had taken a drop too much plum brandy at lunch but, then, saintliness had never excluded a rollicking sense of humour. I tried to change the subject. 'Father,' I hazarded, 'Romanians seem to me the most devout of all Europe's Orthodox peoples . . .'

'Of course,' he nodded, instantly sober, 'because we were born Christian. We are Christians grown, like grass which has never been cut. Those Hungarians tell us that they were here in Transylvania before we were but it's nonsense! They were only christened a thousand years ago. We Romanians have always been here and we have always been Christian!'

Again and again I was to hear the same proud accounting for the Romanians' devotion to their Church. But what did it mean for a nation to be 'born' or 'grown' Christian 'like grass that has never been cut'? The assertion might be based on historical truth but it might not. Certainly, a few members of the pagan Dacian tribe, which occupied this land in about the fourth century, were christened by the Ancient Romans, but unfortunately there are no surviving records of either Dacians or anything identifiably Romanian for the next nine centuries. The true origins of today's Romanians, who speak a markedly Latin language but profess eastern Christianity, amount to what one historian has called 'an enigma of the Middle Ages'.¹ Such a sad dearth of documents has never stopped the Romanians pushing their claim to direct and proud descent from those ancient Dacian tribespeople who intermarried with Roman soldiers. For centuries a highly debatable truth – something akin to the Serbs' myth history – has been axiomatic in their argument with the Hungarians about which people is entitled to rule Transylvania.

What *is* known is that by the thirteenth century two embryonic Orthodox Romanian-speaking statelets had emerged, to be known until Romanian unification in the mid-nineteenth century as the hugely covetable and infinitely exploitable Danubian principalities. One of them, Wallachia, lay to the south of Transylvania, between the river Danube and the Transylvanian Alps. The other, Moldavia, was located to the east of Transylvania, between the Carpathians and the river Prut. Transylvania, the third of the three provinces making up the country that was named Romania when Wallachia and Moldavia were united in the mid-nineteenth century, was under Austrian or Hungarian rule until 1918, but most of its population was also Romanian-speaking and Orthodox.

Wallachians, Moldavians and the Romanian-speakers of Transylvania must have received a second, more effective christening from the disciples of those enterprising Macedonian missionaries to the Slavs, Cyril and Methodius, because the two little states came under the ecclesiastical jurisdiction of the Ohrid patriarchate, until the late fourteenth century when they both gained their own archbishops. Even though the Romanian language has nothing whatsoever to do with any of the Slav languages, Romanians' church texts were printed in the Old Church Slavonic lingua franca of the Balkans until the seventeenth century.

The fourteenth-century princes of Wallachia voluntarily surrendered to the encroaching Ottomans and were granted a measure of autonomy in Turkey in Europe. Instead of having to suffer Turkish occupation, Wallachia was made an Ottoman 'vassal' land.

Instead of delivering their best-looking children to the sultans' harems and armies every year and watching their churches acquire minarets, they were simply liable for huge sums of annual tribute. Otherwise there was nothing to prevent the principality's rulers styling themselves the direct heirs of the Byzantine emperors and they acted the part by calling themselves 'Autocrat', signing their documents in imperial red ink and building and endowing an enormous number of monasteries at home and abroad. They even had themselves depicted in new church frescoes, dressed in the formal finery of Byzantium's first Emperor Constantine.

One might say that the old Byzantine ideal of a universal, rather than narrowly national, Christianity was better and longer preserved in the Danubian principalities than anywhere else in Orthodox Europe. The fifteenth-century Prince Basil the Wolf of Moldavia was an exemplary Byzantine. Not content with endowing monasteries on Athos and churches in Constantinople, he paid off a Patriarch of Constantinople's debts and organized a Church synod to confirm Orthodox dogma. No more appealingly named than Basil the Wolf, the fifteenth-century's Prince Vlad the Impaler of Wallachia is better known to us today as the inspiration for Bram Stoker's Dracula, or as an unhinged sadist who delighted in creating forests of impaled Turks, but in his time he was also revered as a particularly generous patron of the Holy Mountain.

There is hardly a monastery on Athos that cannot boast treasures presented by Vlad the Impaler. The Orthodox world also remembers him as a doughty champion of Orthodoxy against Islam and Roman Catholicism. One chronicle has it that he once chanced to meet three barefoot and begging Roman Catholic Benedictine monks whom he invited to his palace at Targovişte for an initially light-hearted exchange of views, for he was fond of theological disputation. He asked them if he could not 'in the eyes of God be considered a saint, since he had shortened the heavy burdens of so many unfortunate people on this earth?'[ii] During his three reigns as Prince of Wallachia, a total of six years, he slaughtered at least forty thousand and perhaps as many as a hundred thousand. The first monk to answer his crafty question reassured him that the very moment of his death would not be too late to repent of all his sins and win salvation. The second monk was braver, indeed heroic. Lambasting him angrily for his crimes, especially against pregnant women and babies, he shouted, 'You mad tyrant, do you really think you will be able to live eternally? Because of the blood you have spilled on this earth, all will rise before God and His kingdom demanding vengeance ... your whole being belongs to Hell!'[iii] A shocked Prince Vlad lashed out in fury. Dispensing with the usual impalement procedure, he grabbed the monk, wrestled him to the floor and beat him to death. The victim was then hanged by his feet and finally hoisted on a stake in front of a Catholic monastery, alongside his similarly savaged donkey. The first and third monks fled Wallachia to seek refuge in an Austrian Benedictine monastery where they reported their narrow escape. The hair-raising tale bred the first Dracula horror stories, which had started circulating in western Europe by the 1460s.

By the late seventeenth century the rulers of the Danubian principalities fancied themselves more powerful protectors of Orthodoxy than the Patriarch in Constantinople himself. Prince Constantin Brancoveanu of Wallachia built a number of monasteries in the sunny foothills of the Carpathians, many of which are thriving again today, recolonised by pale, serious young nuns of the sort I had met in Athens. Brancoveanu was pious, learned and charitable but he was eventually discovered to be treacherously scheming with the West and Russia against the Ottoman empire. In 1714 he was deposed by a Turkish emissary of the Sultan who flung a black handkerchief over his shoulder. He was then taken by carriage to Istanbul and thrown in prison with his two sons and a son-in-law. His sixteen-year-old son was so terrified by the sight of his father and brother being tortured that he tried to save his life by offering to convert to Islam. In the words of a young nun of Horezu monastery, Brancoveanu's finest foundation, the prince stiffened the young lad's courage by telling him, '"If I could, I'd die a thousand times rather than lose my soul for a few years on Earth. None of our people has ever died as anything but a Christian. Follow your brothers" ... Oh yes, you can say poor thing, but they were saintly martyrs,' the pale young nun continued, her gaze passionate and shining behind the thick lenses of her glasses, 'and they were all canonized in 1992.'

After the Brancoveanu débâcle the Porte decided that Wallachia and Moldavia would be better and more reliably ruled by Phanariot Greeks, who would have to fork out giant sums for their thrones and be prepared to vacate them at a moment's notice. In exchange, they won the freedom to strut around their new playgrounds like Byzantine emperors. Needless to say, they bled the principalities dry to cover the costs of their thrones, while subversively dreaming of using them one day as a pad from which to launch a re-created Greek Byzantine empire. Inspired by their ambition, they set about Hellenizing the Romanians by opening Greek schools and, more importantly, by importing their own churchmen. Soon, hundreds of monasteries, which had originally been 'dedicated' for safekeeping from Ottoman tax-collectors to famous old Byzantine monasteries on Mount Athos, in Asia Minor and the Holy Land, were firmly in Greek hands. Their enormous revenues began flowing south out of the Danubian princi-palities, towards those distant older foundations. The loss to the two states' public purses must have been colossal when one considers that, by the time they won their independence and united to form the core of modern Romania in the mid-nineteenth century, a quarter of Wallachia and almost a third of Moldavia were in the hands of monasteries run by Greeks. Small wonder the principalities became renowned as 'the Peru of the Greeks'[iv] and that Romanians wanted no part in Alexandros Ypsilantis' hare-brained launch of the Greek War of Independence in 1820. As sometime Prince of Wallachia, Ypsilantis' father had not scrupled to squeeze the province dry in the customary fashion. The dispute over the 'dedicated monasteries' was finally solved in 1862 when Romania's first president abruptly stopped the haemorrhaging of his new country's lifeblood. The Holy Moun-tain registered a ruinously sharp drop in revenue.

So much outside interference in Romanian Church affairs greatly delayed the development of a Romanian national identity. And that is why, although there have always been Romanian monks on the

Holy Mountain, no exclusively Romanian monastery was ever built and endowed, so they have never had a say in the conduct of Mount Athos' affairs. They have a couple of large *sketes* instead. Today, Ecumenical Patriarch Bartholomaios of Constantinople is rumoured to be alarmed by the growing number of Romanian monks who have pitched up on the Holy Mountain since the collapse of Communism in their country. But the outflow may be slowing to a trickle. With an estimated three times as many monasteries and *sketes* as ten years ago, Romania needs its monks at home. Nuns it has a-plenty, about seven thousand. Thirty-five are here at this Monastery of the Birth of the Mother of God.

'Father Ioan, am I right in thinking that most of Romania's new monasteries are in Transylvania?'

'Of course, because here is where we need them most. In 1760, after the Habsburgs came to Transylvania to rule us instead of the Hungarians, their empress, Maria-Theresa, sent General Bukow to shoot his cannons and destroy one hundred and fifty of our monasteries – *one hundred and fifty!* We're just rebuilding now, over *two hundred* years later!'

If the fourteenth century was Serbia's defining moment, the early twentieth century Macedonia's and the early nineteenth century Greece's, then the eighteenth century was surely Romania's, and particularly Transylvania's.

In eighteenth-century Transylvania, Eastern Orthodox Europe faced one of its most testing moments. Roman Catholic Austria had no sooner acquired Transylvania from Hungary in 1698 than she started plotting to extend the borders of western Christendom eastwards, at the expense of Orthodoxy. Before General Bukow blasted Transylvania's Orthodox monasteries to rubble, Vienna had set about luring Romanian Orthodox bishops and their flocks away from Eastern Orthodoxy. Orthodox clergy were told that if they could only bring themselves to acknowledge the authority of the Pope and slip the filioque into their creeds they could keep their Slavonic liturgy, their married priests and their icons. Furthermore, they would also gain some basic rights denied to them for centuries by the Hungarian overlords. They would be educated and salaried instead of ignorant and enserfed, and their bishops would have the right to sit in the Transylvanian Parliament – the Diet. The bitter conversion pill was further sweetened by Vienna's assurance that in co-operating with the scheme the Orthodox clergy would only be belatedly implementing the decision on Christian reunion, the one taken at the Council of Florence three centuries before.

The Austrians had had some practice at this kind of religious aggression and had refined their technique after pulling the same trick a century earlier at the expense of the Russian Orthodox in what is now western Ukraine. In essence, the Uniate Church, as it came to be known in both areas, was a political manoeuvre of the Catholic Counter-Reformation, designed to win more souls for Rome and to counteract the effects of the Reformation. But it did little to consolidate the Habsburgs' hold on Transylvania. Instead, by granting converts access to a classical education, which revealed to them the link between Latin and their own language, it caused Romanians to start dreaming about an Ancient Roman lineage and steadily encouraged the growth of a Romanian national consciousness in Transylvania. That consciousness was to spread over the mountains to infect the Danubian principalities and bear fruit in the mid-nineteenth century. Uniatism also entailed a painful schism within Eastern Orthodoxy, whose marks are still visible today in both Transylvania and the Ukraine.

Mainstream Orthodox churchmen still regard the hybrid faith as the most grievous injury done to their world by the West since the Fourth Crusade of 1204. One Romanian monk I met sneered at it as 'a kind of artificial insemination'. Nevertheless, the sweetly forgiving and ebullient Father Ioan pronounced himself all in favour of reuniting the two halves of Christendom one day. Naturally a peace would have to be concluded on terms fairer to Orthodoxy than the decisions of the Council of Florence. The Uniate Church was no solution, but he could imagine the peace negotiations.

'The Orthodox Churches could tell the Catholics and Protestants, "Look we envy you your efficient organization, but in return you

should acquire our modesty." The western churches are so arrogant!
We could have a system of rotation for popes – one western, one
eastern. That's the way to do it!'

He slapped his thigh again.

TRANSYLVANIA

A little riot was in progress by the time I found my way to Alba Iulia
and the fortress hill where the 1920s Romanian Orthodox and the
thirteenth-century Hungarian Roman Catholic cathedrals stand side
by side, in eternal competition for the soul of Transylvania.

Three hours before, a large, shabby crowd had gathered in the
Orthodox cathedral's garden for a rare glimpse of Patriarch Teoctişt
of Romania and all his Transylvanian bishops. High up above the
crowd on their podium, those churchmen were a mesmerizing dazzle
of gold, pale blue and rose pink finery and, for a whole half-day,
elderly peasants, mothers with babies and denim-clad teenagers had
stood in reverent silence, crossing themselves and bowing their heads
at every 'Amen' and 'Lord have mercy'. But now they were tired,
hungry and disinclined to wait while a few callow monks proved
incapable of supervising the efficient distribution of blessed bread
rolls and free books. So they did not wait, and so it had come about
that, in the narrow archway leading out of the garden, the little riot
had broken out. Small peasant women were using their elbows, the
men their barrel chests and teenagers their lanky height to position
themselves to catch the rolls and books which the panicking monks
had been reduced to hurling into the air. There were roars of anger,
screams of pain and tugs of war.

'It's like a revolution,' grumbled one old woman, retiring from
the fray to readjust her worn coat and headscarf. Stuffing the glossy
book in her carrier bag and tearing a bite out of her roll, she headed
off through the groups of chatting monks and weedy seminarians
down the hill towards a car-park crammed with coaches from all over
Transylvania.

It was Wednesday, 21 October 1998, fifty years to the day since Romania's new Communist rulers, hand in glove with the Orthodox Church, had formalized the abolition of the Uniate Church and taken over its buildings. Uniates had been the most numerous denomination in Transylvania between the two world wars but the Orthodox had never forgiven the old Catholic injury. Anyway, Stalin – ever suspicious of Vatican influence in his dominions – had outlawed the Soviet Union's Ukrainian Uniate Church so it had behoved satellite Romania to follow suit. While the most faithful of the Uniates had mourned the imprisonment of their bishops and clergy and the confiscation of their churches, and gone underground, the majority had converted. Callously rejoicing at the lucky expansion of its flock and properties, the Romanian Orthodox Church had celebrated its heretic brethren's happy return to the 'True Faith' and extolled the virtues of 'unity'.

Today, most Romanian Orthodox clergy do not conceal their irritation that the Uniates have resurfaced after the collapse of Communism, demanding the return of their churches and clogging up the business of the law courts with their legalistic quibbling. The arguments soon spilled out of the law courts. Congregations of infuriated Uniates in some of the main towns and villages of Transylvania have been reclaiming their churches by force, smashing windows and breaking down doors at dead of night. Romania's, as well as Ukraine's, battles in Orthodox Europe's larger war against the West are being fought like this – intimately, one to one, over bricks and mortar.

Orthodox churchmen have continued to preach the need for unity, for one united Orthodox Church for all Romanians. Studiously, perhaps wishfully in that old Byzantine way, they are ignoring the plain truth that the Uniates never wanted and still do not want to reunite with them. Patriarch Teoctist and his bishops' seizing on the occasion of that sad fiftieth anniversary of the abolition of the Uniate Church to celebrate the virtues of unity in Alba Iulia that morning was, to say the least, tactless. The title of the free book being distributed read blatantly, *From Division Suffering, from Unity Happiness*.

Not the least of the problems between the two Romanian Churches is that back in the eighteenth century Uniates made up the cream of Transylvania's first intelligentsia. They were Romanians who had deemed their religious conversion to Uniatism a fair price to pay for the fine education they could receive in Jesuit-run Uniate schools. The Orthodox tend to forget that those early Uniates were passionate patriots, whose learned endeavours in the fields of history and philology would sow the seeds of Romanians' struggle for independence in the nineteenth century. That unique Uniate service to the nation is often ignored.

Another valuable service to the Romanian nation, performed by a Uniate university lecturer from the Transylvanian town of Cluj in the late 1980s, is similarly often forgotten. Doina Cornea's brave open letters of protest against Ceauşescu's mad scheme to destroy Romania's villages and move the peasants into tower-blocks were broadcast on the BBC and Radio Free Europe and constituted one of the first signs of popular revolt against the cruel regime. They got her sacked from her job at the university and placed under house arrest but she was to emerge in December 1989 as the revolution's only heroine. The persecution of another Transylvanian non-Orthodox, the Hungarian Protestant pastor László Tökes in Timişoara, was what provided the crucial trigger for the revolution. Another hero, he was soon as sidelined as Mrs Cornea.

Orthodox Romanians today tend to feel as hostile towards the Uniates as they do towards the Hungarians. They regard both as manifestations of the callously, cleverly scheming West, against which their Orthodox culture must be defended.

The 1989 revolution ate its Uniate and Hungarian children but it pardoned Patriarch Teoctişt, whose behaviour during those violently heady winter days fell far short of the heroic. Two days after the outbreak of the uprising, after the brutal but abortive military crackdown in Timişoara, Teoctişt saw fit to send Ceauşescu a telegram congratulating him on his re-election as leader of the Communist Party. In it he applauded Ceauşescu's 'wise and far-seeing guidance'. He hailed 'the golden age which justifiably bears your name and its

achievements which will endure for thousands of years'.ᵛ He resigned
in January 1990 but was coaxed back on to the patriarchal throne
two months later by his clergy. A single community of Romanian
nuns – as hard-line as the ones who rioted against the East's reunion
with western Christendom back in mid-fifteenth-century Byzantium
– has consistently protested his continued occupancy of the patriarchal throne. They heckled him during his 1997 Christmas service
and were dragged, kicking and screaming, from the church by police.
The Romanian government quietly esteems the Church and its chief.
In November 1998 it promised Patriarch Teoctist financial assistance
with building a brand new 'Cathedral of the Salvation of the People'
in the heart of Romania's capital, Bucharest. Large enough to hold a
congregation of fifteen thousand, it will set poor Romania back at
least five million dollars. Uniate Doina Cornea and Hungarian
Protestant László Tökes must be wondering what has become of the
revolution they risked their lives to make.

Eight years after the overthrow of Communism, the voice of that
single heroine was weak and plaintive at the end of a bad telephone
line from Targu Mureş to her hometown of Cluj, about an hour's
drive away. Mrs Cornea felt too poorly to receive any visitors and
suggested I visit Cluj's Uniate Theological College instead. Viorel's
devoutly Orthodox wife Carmen and I drove there one foggy morning, stopping off on the way at the Birth of the Mother of God
monastery, to light a candle and say a prayer for our safe journey.

'Did you know that Father Ioan once had a vision of the Virgin
Mary?' said Carmen, as we drove away. 'She told him that if he built
a monastery here he would help a lot of people.'

At the recently repainted college, a busy centre of operations for
the Uniate cause, a young assistant of the Uniate Bishop of Cluj
treated me to an account of the recent recapture of one of their
churches. Seated in front of a computer, he was a serious young man
dressed in black jeans and matching polo-neck sweater, with a large
wooden cross hanging around his neck.

'It was a Friday afternoon back in March. We had gone to the
supreme court to get our church back and the court had ruled in our

favour, but the Orthodox were refusing to hand our church back to us. That day some of our people decided they had waited long enough and broke in. The atmosphere was amazing, I know exactly how it was because I was there. It was like the revolution all over again! And then some Orthodox seminarians, led by one of their priests, showed up with wooden clubs and there was almost a proper battle in the church! I tell you, it was like the revolution. We were even talking about the Orthodox as terrorists! One of our priests was trying to get to the altar but the Orthodox seminarians were taking up positions. After about ten minutes they retreated and the police sealed off the area. Of course, we were wrong to take the law into our own hands like that. It was a big mistake, but people were tired of holding church services in the open air . . .'

We spoke about the current spate of Orthodox monastery-building.

'It's not just monasteries,' he interrupted me. 'Have you seen the new Orthodox church just opposite this building? It went up almost overnight. We think they want to have one of their spies fixed very near us. What you have to understand is that there is a kind of war going on here in Transylvania and the weapons are churches. If you can imagine, it's like the war between McDonald's and Burger King – wherever one is the other soon arrives.'

Viorel's wife and I repaired to Cluj's brand new but surprisingly empty McDonald's for lunch. Carmen explained that it was simply too expensive for the average Romanian to eat there, and soon we were back in the car, heading on towards the birthplace of the Uniate faith in Transylvania.

Blaj is a tiny Transylvanian market town, tucked away among hills almost half-way between Targu Mureş and Alba Iulia. Viewed from the hill above, the town was a pleasing sight on a bright autumn afternoon. On the edge of it the scaffolding-clad dome of an almost completed Orthodox church shone golden. In the tidily laid-out, distinctly Austrian-looking old centre were the twin baroque spires of the large Uniate cathedral and next door the freshly painted façade of the imposing Uniate seminary. Both buildings looked as if they

9A Bust of Bishop Germanos
of Kastoria, in Thessaloniki

9B Grand Lavra, the oldest
monastery on Mount Athos

10A Sarandi at Easter lunch on Patmos Island, April 1998

10B John Kritikos by the church his grandfather built after dreaming of a bush with an icon on it, Patmos Island, April 1998

11A Archimandrite
lecturer surrounded
by Nafplio society in
Nafplio, the Peloponnese,
April 1998

11B Count Ioannis
Capodistrias, Greece's
first president,
1828–1831

12A Archbishop
Serapheim of Athens'
state funeral, Athens,
April 1998

12B Archbishop
Serapheim's successor
Christodoulos – 'The
Thunderbolt'

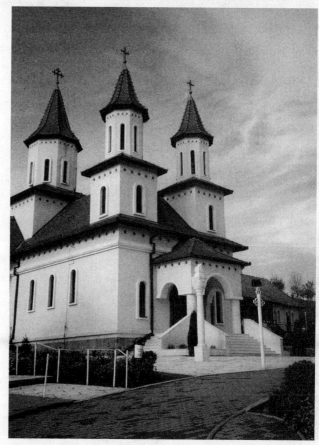

13A Approaching the Monastery of the Birth of the Mother of God, on the left of the road, Targu Mureş, Transylvania, October 1998

13B Monastery of the Birth of the Mother of God, Targu Mureş, Transylvania, October 1998

14A Young monks building
another new monastery, near
Targu Mureș Transylvania,
October 1998

14B Bread rolls and books
after the Union Day Service
at Alba Iulia, Transylvania,
October 1998

15A Ion-Innocentie Micu-Klein, the eighteenth-century first Uniate bishop of Transylvania

15B The eighteenth-century Ukrainian hesychast, St Paissy Velichkovsky

Ҟ ѿс: Пр: Ѿป: Паïсїє Сиар҄҄ ҃ Ст. ҃н҃с:

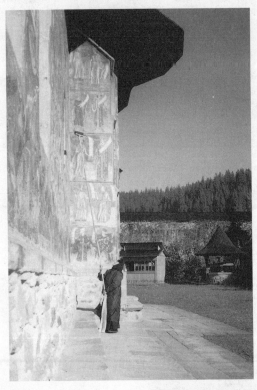

16A Nun cleaning the windows of the painted monastery of Moldoviţa, September 1998

16B Detail of sixteenth-century Petru Rareş and his family dedicating Moldoviţa monastery to God, Moldoviţa monastery

had originally been conceived as the centrepieces of an altogether more important and prosperous town – one the size of Salzburg in Austria, or Sopron in Hungary. They belonged in central not Orthodox eastern Europe, and they dwarfed their rather shabby surroundings.

Threading my way up some steps through a crowd of seminarians dressed exactly like the one I had spoken to in Cluj, I knocked at the seminary door and asked to see Father Nicolae Lupea, the college's spiritual director. A nun led me through a labyrinth of spotless linoleum corridors hung with sentimental nineteenth-century prints of the Virgin Mary in a blue veil, her head framed by roses, her cheeks pink, her blue eyes brimming with tears. There was no mistaking that strong Catholic influence. Although Vienna had only stipulated that Uniates acknowledge the authority of the Pope and use the filioque in the Creed, while allowing them to keep their eastern rite, their icons, their married priests and their liturgical forms, the emphasis here in the Uniate heartland seemed uncompromisingly Roman Catholic.

The room I was shown into was large, high-ceilinged in the Habsburg imperial style and painted a bright blue, the colour of the Virgin Mary's veil. Its occupant was a little old man, as spry and red-cheeked as Father Ioan at the Birth of the Mother of God monastery, but only half dressed. Slipping a shirt on over his vest, he apologized for his *déshabille* and explained that he had just had an injection.

Soon I was comfortably seated and telling him all about the Orthodox celebration of unity at Alba Iulia. When I mentioned the title of the free book I had seen being distributed there, he grimaced. 'To choose that day of all days to celebrate Church unity.' He shook his head in disbelief. 'Nothing changes. It's the same situation as in 1054 when the ambitiously worldly Orthodox East broke with Rome. Today that same ambitious worldliness is what makes them talk about unity, but really they only want to keep our church buildings,' he said, 'and that unity they talk about never existed because it meant the dissolution of our Church. I know how it was and it was not how they say it was! Look, about five hundred of our priests were arrested and then sent off to different Orthodox monasteries. Bishops were killed! I myself spent five years in labour camps and then went underground for ten years, moving from place to place, living with believers I could trust, holding services in bedrooms, in back yards, anywhere at all. Nobody can tell me it was different because I *lived* it!'

Reluctant to interrupt the old man while he was in full memory flow, I was, however, particularly interested in the early history of the Uniate Church. I wondered what he could tell me about the famous eighteenth-century Uniate bishop, the curiously named Ion-Innocentie Micu-Klein whom the fervently Orthodox Romanian historian Nicolae Iorga once memorably dismissed as 'a bad monk, a bad priest and a bad convert'.

'Ah! A great martyr of our Uniate Church,' was how Father Nicolae described him.

Ion Micu was the name he was born with as the son of a Romanian artisan. Innocentie was the name he took when he became a Romanian Orthodox monk and Klein, the German translation of his Romanian surname Micu, was what he added once he had converted to Uniatism and the Austrians had elevated him to the post of Baron-Archbishop of the Uniate Church in 1728. To Micu-Klein they delegated the dirty work of converting the Romanian peasantry to Uniatism, little knowing that his real vocation was as a Romanian politician. Micu-Klein's chief interest in espousing the Uniate faith was not the goal of reuniting Christendom or promoting the Counter-Reformation, but that of gaining more rights for downtrodden Romanians in a Transylvania ruled by a minority of Hungarians and Saxon Germans. Almost immediately he had fallen foul of the Hungarian landowners who controlled the business of the Transylvanian Diet and were prepared to fight to protect their privileges. Father Nicolae enjoyed the chance to recount a curious verbal skirmish between Micu-Klein and the Hungarians on the Bishop's first appearance in that parliament.

'One of the Hungarian nobles sneered at him, "What is Saul looking for among the prophets?" And his reply was, "I'm looking for donkeys lost by my father" – rights for Romanians is what he meant, of course. "We're going to throw you out of the window," the Hungarians shouted back at him. "I'm going to come back inside and defend my people's rights," he shouted back.'

Those Hungarians regarded the Romanians of Transylvania as being of about as much use as 'moths in clothes'. Mocking Micu-Klein's bad Latin, they stubbornly blocked any granting of rights to Romanians, except education for Uniate clergy. Nothing daunted, Micu-Klein bombarded Vienna with twenty-four lengthy petitions between 1730 and 1744. He wanted Romanians recognized as a people equal in status with the Hungarians and the Saxon Germans of Transylvania. For the first time ever, the Romanians' ancient-Dacian-cum-Roman heritage was used in political argument. 'We have been the hereditary masters of this land of kings since the time of Trajan [the Roman Emperor who conquered Dacia] . . .'[vi] he wrote in one of those petitions.

But the Austrians were not about to spoil their fragile relations with the fiery Hungarians for the sake of an uppity Romanian who was not making a very good job of their dirty work. A 1733 census showed that there were almost six times as many Uniate as Orthodox priests in Transylvania, but the impression that Romanian Orthodox were converting to Uniatism *en masse* was wildly misleading. If the artisan class could spot the material advantages to be gained from espousing the hybrid faith, the mass of the Romanian peasantry remained dead set against the innovation. Vienna correctly suspected that Micu-Klein had not troubled to explain it to them, but that was not the root of the problem. No amount of reasoning and argument was likely to sway a people reared in a faith that had never set much store by either skill. One peasant couched his objection to Uniatism in the following terms:

This coat which I have on is mine. But if the empress wishes to take it from me, I would give it gladly. I have worked day and night with these old arms and legs and with my whole body to pay the tithe. They belong to the empress and if she wished to take them from me I could do nothing. But I have only one soul, which I am keeping for God, and no earthly power may bend it.[vii]

In 1744 a Serb monk called Vissarion did irreparable damage to the Uniate project by roaming the Transylvanian countryside claiming he had been sent there by an angel to preach 'the ancestral Greek faith'.[viii] Because monks have always been better respected and more heeded by Orthodox peoples than priests or bishops, hundreds of thousands of Transylvanian Romanians harkened to him. Casting aside their nominal Uniatism, vast numbers reconverted to Orthodoxy. Vissarion had warned them that anyone baptized, married or buried by a Uniate priest was 'delivered into the arms of the Devil'. Uniate priests – dubbed 'devils from hell' – were hounded out of villages, their churches were repossessed by force and the sin scrubbed off their walls. Children were rechristened, couples remarried and the dead dug up and reburied. Vissarion's triumphal progress was shortly followed by another popular monk-led disturbance, which led in turn to the arrival of General Bukow and his cannons and the virtual extinction of Orthodox monasticism in Transylvania. Orthodoxy survived, however, and before long, at Russia's prompting, Vienna was compelled to recognize it legally. The Uniate faith also survived, but Micu-Klein's days were numbered.

In the year that Vissarion arrived in Transylvania Micu-Klein was summoned to Vienna by Empress Maria Theresa. He narrowly escaped imprisonment in a lunatic asylum there and fled south to Rome, where he found the Pope uninterested in his plight. Miserably destitute, paralysed in hands and feet, Micu-Klein was forced to pawn the pectoral cross of his office. He died in the Holy City, sadly unaware that he had successfully planted the seeds for Romanians' awakening to full nationhood in the nineteenth century. In Blaj, where he had set up his bishopric in a Hungarian noble's mansion, his nephew and a first generation of Uniate Transylvanian intellectuals devoted themselves to concocting a convincing history of the Romanians and a Romanian grammar. By 1848 the conflict between

Romanian Orthodox and Uniates had simmered down sufficiently for leaders of both Churches to meet at a field outside Blaj to demand their Romanian rights.

In the summer of 1997 Micu-Klein's bones came home from Rome to rest in the Uniate cathedral next door to this seminary. I wanted to pay my respects to the man who had found himself tragically trapped by the contradiction between East and West, between his desire for the material well-being of his people and the majority of that people's faithful cleaving to a religion and culture still steeped in the otherworldly universalism of the Byzantine era, rather than looking forward to the western nationalist age that was dawning. For better or for worse the new day would finally break with the French Revolution at the end of the eighteenth century. Western ideas of national self-realization and national churches would be the order of the new day. Greece led the way.

The huge wooden doors of the Uniate cathedral were locked, so I went in search of the key. On the far side of the park I found the palace of the Uniate Archbishop, the same Hungarian landowner's mansion that Micu-Klein had lived in two centuries ago. It was a damp-looking stone edifice with turrets and narrow windows, set in a distinctly un-Romanian formal garden. I rang the bell once and waited, then rang again. When the heavy wooden door finally creaked open I had no trouble recognizing Archbishop Lucian Mureşan himself. Arrayed in his black robes, red silk skull-cap and cummerbund he looked every inch a prince of the Roman Catholic Church. I had to stifle an urge to laugh because the grandiose Austrian buildings of Blaj, the Archbishop's palace and his august personage had suddenly assumed the exaggeratedly unreal quality of a comic-opera set. The Archbishop's expression was suspicious, but once I had explained my business he smiled and apologized for the church being locked. Despatching a plump young nun bearing a key the length and weight of her forearm, to open it for me, he bade me God speed. The Uniates of Blaj were on their guard, careful to whom they opened the door on a late-autumn afternoon, careful who entered their holy of holies.

The cathedral was large, light and spotlessly clean. An iconostasis separated the altar from the main body of the church just as it does in most Orthodox churches. But there were also rows of polished wooden pews and distinctly un-Orthodox statues of the Virgin Mary in her blue robes. On one side of the steps up to the altar was a plain slab of white marble under which lay Micu-Klein. His name and dates were chiselled on the surface and a small portrait of him, looking as handsomely bright-eyed and rosy-cheeked as Father Ioan and Father Nicolae, had been propped on top of it. It struck me that there would be no cult of Micu-Klein's relics in this church. All was grand but light and plain.

Back at home with Viorel in Targu Mureș that evening, I recognized the Archbishop of Blaj on the television news. That very day the Uniates and the Orthodox had informally agreed to dispense with violence as a means of resolving their differences. They would have to reach a formal agreement soon because the first visit ever by a pope to an Orthodox country depended on it. Pope John Paul II was scheduled to visit Romania in May 1999, at the Romanian government's rather than the Orthodox Church's invitation. No peace treaty between Orthodox and Uniates would mean no papal visit, and no papal visit meant no diplomatic kudos for the government and no diplomatic kudos for the government might mean no millions of dollars for Patriarch Teoctist's new cathedral in Bucharest.

Early the next morning I took one last look at the Birth of the Mother of God monastery, before turning right to the airport to catch my flight out of Transylvania, over the mountains to Bucharest.

Snagov Island
Wallachia

It was Transylvania's most infamous son, the fifteenth-century Vlad the Impaler who, as ruler of Wallachia for the third and last time in his long career, elevated Bucharest to a fortified city and set it on its way to becoming the capital of a united Romania in the mid-nineteenth century. But Vlad had felt equally at home at a fortress monastery on an island in Lake Snagov, about twenty miles north of the capital.

I set off there one drizzly morning with Dan Ciachir, a respected Romanian writer on religious affairs, who had assured me that we would be unable to reach Snagov monastery unless we called in at another monastery on the way to collect a certain Father Damaskinos, who happened to be a friend of the single monk now living on the island. I was back, I surmised, in the Orthodox world proper where personal contacts are the *sine qua non* of getting anything done. I would not be bowling around Wallachia and Moldavia knocking on doors and trusting to luck as I had in Greece and parts of Transylvania. Dan would be my guide in this latter-day Byzantium, just as Goran and Bogdan had been in parts of the former Yugoslavia.

All went according to Dan's plan and by mid-morning the three of us – Dan, Father Damaskinos and I – were standing in the rain on the edge of Lake Snagov, peering through a tangle of reeds into the mist beyond and shouting across to the island, 'Alloooo – alloooo!' Before very long the prow of a narrow rowing-boat appeared, followed by the form of a kerchiefed woman at the oars. Dan and I stepped aboard then Father Damaskinos, who gingerly lowered his portly bulk on to a narrow seat and drew his robes tightly about him. Soon we were skimming out through the reeds, on our way across the thick grey waters of the lake, making for the island.

'Now,' said Dan, as we passed one of Ceaușescu's pleasure palaces on the right-hand shore and the tower of the island's church became visible above the trees, 'please don't start asking questions about Dracula. Father Emilian is sick of all that tourist stuff.'

I nodded. I had been warned that Father Emilian Poenaru, almost the sole inhabitant of the island, was not the most genial of monks. The lay women who kept house for him – perhaps this very oarswoman – had even nicknamed him Dracula on account of his hot temper.

Arriving on the island I was disappointed to find no traces of the sturdy walls with which Vlad the Impaler had fortified the place, nor even any monastery. Instead there was just a little fourteenth-century church, in the same pretty, modest style as those I had seen in Macedonia. An equally modest wood cabin a few paces from the church housed Father Emilian. In Vlad's day those lost walls had extended down to the shores of the lake and, just like Constantinople's, deterred all invaders. Within them there had been three chapels, the monks' cells, guest-houses for visiting boyars and their servants, a modest palace for the prince, a small prison, a treasury and a mint. Snagov monastery had been a little fortress town and, given its location, a very effective refuge. Vlad certainly worshipped his God here, but he also – judging by the number of decapitated skeletons discovered since – tortured his enemies. Local peasant legends tell how he would invite his victims to a certain little cell, force them to their knees before an icon of the Mother of God then open a specially constructed trap-door for the pleasure of watching them disappear below, straight on to a forest of sharpened stakes.

Local legend also has it that, following his death in a battle against the Turks in 1476, Vlad the Impaler was buried here in the church, just in front of the altar. But there are suspicions that the Greek monks who ran the monastery in the eighteenth century dug him up and reinterred him in a less prominently privileged spot at the back of the church. Today there is a humble stone slab placed nowhere in particular in the church and marked with a print of the most famous portrait of Vlad. I was unimpressed and Dan was more interested in the prospect of an elevenses feast in Father Emilian's wooden cabin, whither Father Damaskinos had already repaired.

'One of the first points to understand about Orthodox monasticism,' Dan informed me, as we breathed the smells of freshly brewed coffee and roasting meat, 'is the tradition of monastic hospitality.'

The main room of Father Emilian's cabin was warmly heated by a tiled stove. It contained a large television set, icons and a table laid with all manner of Romanian delicacies – hot, cold and sweet meats, pickled red peppers and peanuts. The coffee cups were steaming. Out came a carafe of clear țuica and a bottle of wine. Gesturing towards us to be seated, Father Emilian, a bespectacled monk in his forties, settled himself down at the table with a packet of Marlboro Lights, an outsize ashtray and some knitting.

'*Ora et labora* – that's a monk's life,' he said, by way of explanation. 'In a single winter I can produce about twelve garments, some with sleeves, some without. Look, that's one, my creations,' and he pointed to Father Damaskinos, whose stout torso was cosily encased in a thick black version of the cream cardigan in progress. Father Damaskinos blushed.

Dan was in his element, relishing the opportunity to exchange church gossip, piling his plate and praising the wine. By quietly eavesdropping I learned that although Romania now boasts some three hundred more monasteries and *sketes* than she did in 1989, Dan and Father Emilian were worried about the inferior quality of young people flocking into them. They were convinced that the vast majority must be 'economic refugees' in search of a lifetime's meal ticket. Wasn't it proof enough that most of Romania's monks and nuns hail from Moldavia, the poorest region of Romania? Transylvanian Father Emilian did not care for the way so many of those Moldavian monks prided themselves on their holiness and even dared to call themselves Hesychasts, all because a great eighteenth-century Hesychast called St Paissy Velichkovsky came from Moldavia.

'If a person calls himself a Hesychast you can be 100 *per cent* sure that he is *not* one! If you know a man's a Hesychast then the *devil*'s already at work!' he said, jabbing the air with his knitting-needle for emphasis. Dan nodded, his mouth too full to answer, so Father Emilian continued, 'It was very different in Communist times. Back then you had to have a real vocation to become a monk. You had to be prepared for your family to suffer. My sister was an air hostess flying all over the world until I became a monk. Then it was domestic flights only for her. It's just too easy now to become a monk . . .'

'Father Emilian,' I dared to interrupt, 'how did you decide to become a monk?'

'One afternoon I was in Bucharest,' he said, pausing to lay down his handiwork and light another cigarette, 'and I went to see a British film about Thomas Becket – you know the one, with Peter O'Toole and Richard Burton. In fact, I saw it not once but six times in a row that afternoon. The next day was the feast of St Paraschiva. I went straight to a monastery and that was that. It was 1969.'

I found it poignant to think that the heart of this amusing but slightly cynical monk had once been so touched by a movie that he had left the world to join a monastery. As I lent half an ear to his bitter complaint against the West, which had exported to Romania all the world's evils – homosexuality, drugs and rock music – I wondered if he had once dreamed of heroically resisting the Communist state just as Thomas Becket had resisted Henry II. Was his failure to do any such thing the source of his bitterness? He *had* earlier admitted to having been friends with Ceauşescu's playboy younger son Nicu.

'. . . the whore of Babylon in the Book of Revelation is obviously America – a country without traditions, without history, without anything . . .' he was saying, as he stubbed out his cigarette and reached for the carafe. I was picking up the voice of Late Byzantium, which had come to prefer a sultan's turban to a cardinal's mitre. 'At least Islam has its traditions and doesn't try to export its point of view. I'll say that much for it. The Pope – for Heaven's sake – thinks he's Jesus Christ!'

'And those Uniates, they've got themselves up as princes of the Church, haven't they?' chimed in Dan. 'They're so proud of what they did for the Romanian nation but, really, what did they do?'

But Dan had hit quite the wrong note. He had forgotten that he was talking to a proud Transylvanian.

'No, no, no. You can say whatever you like about the Uniates,' said Father Emilian, in ominously measured tones, 'but there is no getting away from the fact that their intellectual contribution to the development of Romania in the eighteenth and nineteenth centuries was crucial – *crucial*, I say!'

Faced with another jabbing knitting-needle Dan shrugged his shoulders and helped himself to another piece of cake. When a dish of jam-filled pancakes arrived from the kitchen, he seized the chance to change the subject. 'Did you know,' he said, turning to me, 'that the word for pancake in Romanian is the same as the word for "tit" in Dutch?' That coincidence launched him on a bizarre new train of thought. 'I have an interesting theory,' he announced, 'that there is an important connection between lack of Orthodox belief and frigidity in a woman – it must be something to do with a passionate heart leading to other forms of passion, don't you think?'

To my astonishment, the two monks found nothing to quarrel with there. Far from it. While I furiously fantasized about Dan's chair, a trap-door and a forest of spikes, they nodded vigorously.

By the time we rose from the table the wine bottle was empty, the brandy carafe only half full and the rain still pouring down in the gathering gloom outside.

BISTRIȚA MONASTERY
MOLDAVIA

It was not until we had journeyed north together from Bucharest, up through Moldavia, to arrive one late afternoon at the monastery of Bistrița that I could be sure I had done the right thing by swallowing my female pride and retaining Dan's services.

The drive had been punishing. Moldavia's one decent road runs through some of the poorest towns in Romania. Buzau, Bacău, Barlad not only sound similar but, with their damply crumbling blocks, potholed roads, dirty shops and cracking pavements, they look the same. Foul-smelling diesel-belching lorries, sooty buses and horses and carts had hampered our progress every inch of the way. It was only once we had turned left off the main road, and begun to climb into the foothills of the Carpathian mountains which separate Moldavia from Transylvania, that the traffic thinned, the air cleared and the view started to improve.

'Go on, straight on!' said Dan, as I started to turn into the monastery's car park. 'Drive through the gates – you can park in the courtyard, over there, next to the church.'

'Are you quite sure?' I said, concerned to show a proper humble respect.

'Of course. Father Kiprian, who is my spiritual father, is also the *starets* – the abbot – here. We're staying the night here so the car will be safer inside.'

The chill autumn air smelt of woodsmoke. The monastery, tucked underneath a high hill sprinkled with trees and the white dots of a gaggle of geese, was a beauty. Monks were milling in and out of the church from which the sound of sung vespers was just audible. Lights were coming on in the monastery buildings. Their whitewashed walls and dark wood verandahs reminded me of those I had seen back at Dečani, the last monastery in which I had been permitted to stay the night. It was the church that was different, although it showed as many signs of western influence as Dečani's had. We were a long way from the frilly low domes of the Macedonian churches, the squat square form of the Greek cross and the fancy brickwork of a master-piece like the bubble-domed church of Gračanica. This church was built of pale stone. High, long and narrow, it had a steep black roof and a low steeple.

'We call this style Byzantine-Gothic,' Dan explained. 'One only finds it here in Moldavia. Poland and Hungary were very influential here in the Middle Ages so the architects drew their inspiration from the Catholic West as much as from the East.'

Its interior was equally un-Orthodox. While the dark frescoes, including one showing the Byzantine Emperor Constantine and his mother Helena at one of the early Church councils, were instantly recognizable as Eastern Orthodox, the layout of the church was not. Dan and I progressed from a carpeted anteroom containing a stall selling candles, Church calendars, incense and icons, through a low narrow doorway into a dark and empty pronaos, on, into a smaller chamber housing the stone tombs of former abbots and on again, through another narrow archway into the larger naos where the candles were lit and women were kissing the frescoes. The centre of attraction in the naos was a dark icon, lit like a Turkish market stall by a fluorescent strip and canopied in yellow nylon.

'The miracle-working icon of St Ann,' Dan hissed in my ear. 'You can ask Abbot Kiprian all about it. Come on now, or we'll be late for supper.'

To my chagrin I learnt that we would not be dining with the monks in their refectory. Dan and I had been billeted in a modern block, away from the community. Our dining room was a pompous, high-ceilinged, cold place with thick red velvet curtains. Its long table was set with a bowl of coleslaw and another of oily chips. It was not until Dan had explained the nature of the cosy relationship between the monastery and the local Communist authorities until 1989 that I was able to understand the room's original purpose. The block, with its formal reception rooms, had been built and used by local Communist Party grandees – factory and communal farm bosses, chiefs of police, party secretaries and the like – as a kind of private restaurant to which they would regularly repair for a decent meal in civilized surroundings. In this room the monks had happily laid out the best of everything they had, secure in the expectation of valuable rewards. One or other wife of a factory boss would be a furtive believer who would bully her husband into presenting the monastery with a lorryload of cement or bricks. Another would see to it that the monks lacked for nothing when it came to new furniture, and so on.

Just then Abbot Kiprian made his first, quietly impressive appearance from the direction of the kitchen. He was a Rumpelstiltskin of a monk, with a dusty cap set low on a head of straggling grey hair that reached his shoulders. His grey beard was ragged, but his eyes twinkled and he smiled toothlessly in welcome. The brown leather belt he wore high on his stomach was branded at the back with the word 'JERUSALEM'. In his arms he bore a large platter of fish drowned in thick brown aspic.

Dan jumped up from his chair and fervently kissed his *duhovnik*'s hand, before begging him to tell me how he had bravely outwitted the Communist authorities, flouting the ban on night-long church services and bell-ringing. Abbot Kiprian seated himself at the head of the table and smiled modestly. 'I just told them that night vigils and bell-ringing made sense since I was worried about robbers, what with all the valuable things in the church. That was all.'

'But . . .' Dan protested, eager for more of an anecdote.

'Oh, that was all a long time ago – you must have some of this *crap*,' he said, dredging me up a blind-eyed carp-head and piling my plate with yellow *mamaliga*. Impressed by his hospitality, modesty and serene good-temper, I was warming to Abbot Kiprian and asked him to tell me about Bistriţa's miracle-working icon.

It was almost six hundred years old, he told me. In 1407 the Byzantine Emperor Manuel Palaeologus – the same who had toured Europe and visited England in a vain last-ditch effort to drum up western Christian support against the Turks – had presented it to the prince who founded this monastery. A century later it had saved another Moldavian prince from certain death. Prince Petru Rareş had spent all night in church praying before the icon of St Ann when enemy Turks had rushed in, intent on chopping off his head.

'God saved him by miraculous transformation,' said Abbot Kiprian, 'Suddenly, before the very eyes of his enemies, he turned into a sultan – turban and all. The evil Turks threw down their weapons and started bowing and prostrating themselves before him.'

Thereafter the icon had been wheeled out whenever a miracle was needed. It had proved particularly useful in times of drought.

'In 1990 we went on pilgrimage with it for the first time in fifty years. It was early summer and the land needed water. By four in the afternoon it was raining – simply a miracle! Only last year the icon cured a woman of cancer of the colon.'

'But, Father, who is St Ann?'

'She's our defender – the defender of all Moldavians.'

'Yes, but I meant what did she do when she was alive?'

'Oh,' he said, with a toothless grin, 'you don't know that? She was Christ's granny, of course! St Ann was barren but one day found herself with child. When the baby girl Mary was born she took her from Nazareth to Jerusalem – not far, I know the lie of the land there because I've been to the Holy Land. Anyway, St Ann went straight to the temple, placed the baby Mary on the high altar and then went home. For twelve years Mary was brought up by an angel of God until she was told that she herself was going to have a baby.'

That, I thought, explained his souvenir Jerusalem belt, though not this story. I was later to discover that tales like this one, which are nowhere to be found in the gospels, were circulating throughout pre-Reformation Europe in the writings of a Roman Catholic friar called Jacobus de Voragine. Abbot Kiprian was no doubt equally familiar with the tale of the midwife who safely delivered Christ but was so doubtful of Mary's claim to be a virgin that she carried out her own internal examination of the Mother of God and gained a withered arm for her sceptical pains. The Protestant Churches and the Counter-Reformation Catholic Church did away with these lively folk-tales but this fairy-tale corner of the Orthodox world still loves and believes them.

Abbot Kiprian continued, and I began to recognize the story of the Annunciation. '"How can I be with child – I who have never known a man?" Mary asked the angel. She was ordered to accept the situation. You see now that the Virgin Mary wasn't born just any old how and she didn't give birth just any old how ... Have some more of our brandy. You need a good sleep because you have an important day ahead of you.'

Indeed we did. Abbot Kiprian had kindly armed us with a vital letter of introduction for presentation at the nearby Sihastria monastery, home to Moldavia's – indeed all Romania's and perhaps the whole Orthodox world's – most famous holy man and *duhovnik*, Archimandrite Cleopa. I had listened to an abbot of a Greek monastery sing this old Romanian monk's praises, and Bogdan had told me that his spiritual father, a Serb holy man called Father Tadej, regularly made his way to Sihastria to visit him. An ardent lover of the Jesus Prayer and the *Philokalia's* collection of the sayings of the saints, Archimandrite Cleopa, I had decided, was the only true Hesychast I was likely to meet.

Up in the north-eastern corner of the country we were deep in one of the old heartlands of Romanian monasticism. This was where Moldavia's greatest prince, the fifteenth-century Stephen the Great, built a church or a monastery in thanksgiving for every one of his thirty-four victories against the Ottomans. Stephen, honoured by Pope Sixtus IV with the title 'Athleta Christi', considerably delayed the Ottoman advance into Europe.

A glance at Dan's monastery map the next morning indicated a concentration of some twenty major monasteries within a forty-mile radius of Stephen the Great's capital, Suceava, a few miles to the north of Bistriţa monastery. This, I thought, was the closest I was likely to come to the atmosphere of the Holy Mountain. The black figures of monks and nuns were everywhere we drove through. There were nuns working in the fields, monks tending sheep, monks driving and fixing cars, nuns out shopping or walking along the road. We passed signposts to two of Romania's largest and best-known women's monasteries, Agapia and Varatec. During the nineteenth century they had been popular retreats for well-born widows and the daughters of churchmen or boyars. Romanian Orthodoxy was never just for the peasants. As in Byzantium, the upper classes played an important role in the life of the Church. In Romania there was never anything remotely *infra dig* about devoting one's life to God in a beautiful monastery set in salubrious surroundings. The youngest daughter of Queen Marie of Romania, herself one of Queen Victoria's granddaughters, is an octogenarian Orthodox nun living in America today.

We had turned off the main road and were following a winding way down a valley with a river and high wooded hills on either side. Passing Abbot Kiprian's *alma mater*, Secu monastery, on our right, we arrived almost immediately at Archimandrite Cleopa's home, Sihastria monastery. Founded in the nineteenth rather than the fifteenth century, it lacked the charm of Abbot Kiprian's Bistriţa monastery. Its buildings looked too new, its paintwork too dazzlingly bright, and it was expanding apace to judge by the cement mixers in the courtyard. But up a steep path, at the back of the monastery, stood a row of shabby little summerhouses with pale blue wooden balconies. One of these, the one with rows of wooden benches set out in front of it, contained the famous *duhovnik*.

A very handsome young monk wearing a thick leather jerkin over his cassock appeared on the balcony to inform us that the great Father Cleopa had just retired for a fifteen-minute nap. We sat down on one of the benches to wait. Was I just about to meet my first true Hesychast, I wondered. What would I ask him? What could he tell me about saving my soul and seeing the Uncreated Light? Had he ever seen an angel? Would he be like Father Ioan at the Birth of the Mother of God monastery near Targu Mureş – ebullient and given to slapstick? I hoped not.

The model Hesychast I had in mind was the eighteenth-century St Paissy Velichkovsky, the one mentioned by Father Emilian at Snagov, as the person who had overseen a startling revival of monasticism in this region by translating the writings of the Desert Fathers and Hesychasts from Greek into Romanian and Slavonic. An eighteenth-century Greek pilgrim who met St Paissy has left us a detailed description of the man. 'For the first time in my life I have seen holiness incarnate and unfeigned,' he wrote. 'I was struck by his luminous pale face, by his long abundant beard, shiny as silver, by the cleanliness of his clothes and his cell. His words are sweet and sincere ... He has the air of a man utterly detached from his flesh.'[ix]

A Ukrainian by birth, St Paissy Velichkovsky was still a schoolboy when he heeded God's call to leave the world. On visiting some monks at a hermitage near his home in Kiev he thought he was meeting 'God's angels' and wished that he, too, might one day be 'worthy of the holy angelic habit'.[x] Without more ado he began to search for a spiritual father, wandering from monastery to monastery in Ukraine, carving wooden spoons and saying the Hesychasts' Jesus Prayer. At last, disappointed in his search and harried by the Catholic and Uniate persecution of the Orthodox in the region, he trekked across the border into Moldavia where he developed a particular weakness for grapes, which had not grown in colder Ukraine. But he still lacked spiritual direction. At the age of twenty-four, his hunt for a suitable guide took him to Mount Athos.

Borrowing books from the library of the Serbs' Hilandar monastery and keeping a constant look-out for a spiritual father, he lived as a hermit on the Holy Mountain. Gradually twelve younger monks – seven Romanian-speakers, five Slav-speakers – were drawn to him. Instead of a spiritual father he had acquired some spiritual children, and soon he was lecturing the wider community of monks on Mount Athos on strengthening their spiritual lives by reintroducing the stricter Cenobitic Rule and constantly repeating the Hesychasts' Jesus Prayer, 'Lord Jesus Christ, Son of God, have mercy upon us'. He laid particular emphasis on that prayer because, he said, 'it is the work which angels and men have in common. In this prayer men can approach the life of angels'.[xi]

Paissy's fame spread, but the bigger his community became, the more buildings he needed to house his monks, and the more crippling were the Ottoman taxes. At last he and his bilingual brotherhood abandoned the daily struggle to survive on the Holy Mountain and set sail for Moldavia. There they came to rest in the tumbledown monastery of Dragomirna, a little to the north of Sihastria. It had no roof and few cells but it did have beehives, six oxen and fields. Like Mount Athos, it was out of bounds to women. Better still, there were no taxes to pay.

In 1774 the Austrian empire's acquisition of this far north-eastern corner of Romania, granted her by Russia as payment for her help in beating back the Turks, ruined that idyll. Paissy was appalled at the Catholic West's expansion this far east. It must have brought back bad memories of his tough times in Catholic-ruled and Uniate-infested western Ukraine. Before fleeing to Father Kiprian's *alma mater*, Secu monastery, he issued a stern warning to the monks who were staying behind at Dragomirna: 'It's impossible to escape heresies when one is surrounded by heretics. The Roman Pope is everywhere roaring like a lion and he's on the hunt for whatever he can devour. He leaves nowhere in peace, even places in the middle of the Turkish empire. He is constantly disturbing and offending the Holy Church of the East.'[xii]

Naturally, Paissy abominated the new Transylvanian Uniates. He once urged a Uniate priest who had sought his advice to 'leave the

Uniates as fast as possible, lest death does not overtake you and count you among the heretics and not among the Christians'.ˣᶦᶦᶦ

Just as St Christodoulos of Patmos and his monks had been harried from pillar to post in the Byzantine eleventh century until at last coming to rest on Patmos, so was St Paissy six hundred years later. By the last decade of the eighteenth century his community had grown so large that the then Greek Phanariot Prince of Moldavia asked him to take over Neamţ, a large old monastery a few miles from Secu and Sihastria. Paissy was averse to the idea. He feared there was no *hesychia* to be found at Neamţ because a miracle-working icon meant that the place was much frequented by women pilgrims. But he dared not refuse the Prince's gift. Later asked how life at Neamţ compared with that at Dragomirna, he lamented, 'It grows worse with every year, and strive though I do, it is impossible to prevent this in any degree. The cause of all this is the unrestricted entry of women into the monastery . . .'ˣᶦᵛ

Towards the end of his life St Paissy was spending entire nights translating the vital Hesychast texts from the original Greek into Church Slavonic. Lying in bed surrounded by grammar books, dictionaries, gospels and the sayings of the Desert Fathers, he scribbled away with a goose quill by the light of a candle, oblivious to his bedsore-encrusted body. Those nocturnal labours were to bear fruit not only in Moldavia, but in over a hundred monasteries in thirty-five dioceses in Russiaˣᵛ and inspire a long, slow monastic revival. Russia had 450 monasteries in 1810, but 1,025 by 1914. To St Paissy goes much of the credit for shoring up the prestige and vitality of Orthodoxy's Hesychast treasures, at a time when base nationalism was building up to a wave that would sweep over the whole of Europe in the nineteenth century.

But Paissy's personal memory was also revered. His biographer, a monk at Neamţ, monastery, concluded his version of the famous *duhovnik*'s life-story with a fond memory of having come upon him once, in the halcyon days of Dragomirna. Paissy had been snoozing in his room, 'his face as if ablaze'. The monk realized that 'the love of the fervent prayer in his heart had also filled his face with grace'.ˣᵛᶦ

Would Archimandrite Cleopa's face be ablaze with grace after his nap? Would I inevitably be robbing him of *hesychia*? I worried. The handsome young monk had reappeared to beckon us inside.

'Only ten minutes, please,' he whispered. 'Father Cleopa is eighty-seven years old and he has had six operations on his kidneys.'

On a high hard bed, inside a small, dim-lit, stuffy room, made smaller and stuffier by its wall-to-wall and floor-to-ceiling jumble of icons, candles and books, sat Archimandrite Cleopa. His face was not ablaze but strangely unlined. His eyes looked a little bleary, his gold-threaded stole somewhat worn, and in one hand he was clutching a large wooden cross emblazoned, like Father Kiprian's belt, with the word JERUSALEM. He was venerably, imposingly ancient and very still.

'Father,' I began falteringly, 'what is the work of a *duhovnik?*'

'A *duhovnik* is the soul of the monastery or the village. By his life and his sermons he should be the light of the world,' he began, but continued on a more practical note and in a louder voice. 'A *duhovnik* should know canonic law perfectly in order to be able to give people the right penance. A woman who has had an abortion cannot take communion for twenty years! But anyone who is ill can read Psalm 50 instead of performing fifty prostrations . . .'

His practical didacticism surprised me but as he embarked on his life-story it occurred to me that it was not incompatible with Hesychasm. During the nine and a half years he had spent in hiding from early Communist persecution after the Second World War, he must have found as much *hesychia* as any monkish heart could desire.

His memories of that time were crystal clear.

'Because I had worked as a shepherd monk for twelve years, I knew the forests very well so it was natural that I should choose to hide there in 1959 when the state began a new wave of persecutions. The new home I constructed for myself was three metres underground. It was three metres high, four metres long, three metres wide and insulated with tree bark. I camouflaged it well with pine branches. A person could have passed by a thousand times without ever suspecting that a man was living down there. I had a small hatch of a front door, with a wire to pull it open . . .'

'But how did you manage for food, Father?'

'Well, first I had a box in which I kept the holy sacrament and I also had a holy lamp. That was my real food, of course. But I had mushrooms, berries, nuts, and there was a faithful forester who visited me once a month. He used to bring enough potatoes for me to eat one a day, and perhaps some corn. It was dangerous for him so he always approached my den backwards – that way he left no traces.'

'What about wild animals?' asked Dan.

'Oh, yes, there were deer and bears. We avoided each other,' he said, with a surprisingly loud chuckle.

But what did you do all day in your den? Did you say the Jesus Prayer? Did you have any books – a copy of the Hesychasts' *Philokalia*, perhaps? Questions tumbled over each other in my mind but our time was up. The young monk was back, beckoning us out, and Dan was indicating that I should approach Archimandrite Cleopa to kiss his Jerusalem cross. I did so and felt the warm blessing of the old monk's hand on my bowed head.

Little more than a month after our brief meeting, as I sat down to write one morning, an e-mail arrived from Viorel, saying, 'Father Cleopa from the monastery of Sihastria died today. Because of the bad condition of the roads Carmen can't go to the funeral. I'm really sorry to send you this kind of news but – as a very famous stand-up philosopher from Transylvania used to say – death is a part of life . . .'

The demise of Romania's best-loved spiritual father was front-page news. In the manner of all the best Orthodox holy men he seems to have foretold his death a month before it happened. 'This is the last time I will preach to you. I have to prepare myself for death,'[xvii] he had warned a group of regular pilgrims. Whatever the weather, thousands of bereft spiritual children would converge on Sihastria to file past his open coffin and kiss his cold hand. He would be buried in a sitting position, as is the custom with Orthodox monks.

The Eastern Orthodox Churches are good at death. Viorel and

that curious-sounding 'stand-up Transylvanian philosopher' were only reiterating what the frescoes on the walls of Eastern Orthodox churches have been hammering home to the faithful for centuries. Those crowds of big-eyed, sword-wielding Byzantine saints, all those angels and kings in their Byzantine finery, and the living congregations, make up a single community – a single Church. No taboo attaches to death in the Orthodox world. Way back where I started, at Krka monastery, I had been offered the choice between planting a lit candle in the sand tray marked 'LIVING' or the one marked 'DEAD'. On that hot autumn day at Jovandol monastery in Montenegro we had prayed for very long-dead generations of the Nikčević family before their bones were doused in wine. The cosy communion between living and dead means that Orthodox cemeteries are not hushed, empty places but lively and bustling. Orthodox graves are crowded close together but often fenced off from each other with coloured railings like those of a child's cot. Usually there are little tables and a bench or two, set ready for the month, forty-day, three-month, nine-month or year anniversaries of a person's death. On those days family and friends repair to the graveside for a drink and a slice of *koliva* – a funeral cake. The pagan ancient Romans did exactly the same.

At the Reformation, the West lost not only her rich monasteries and profiteering priests but also this lively involvement of the living with the fate of the souls of those departed. By suggesting that there was nothing we could do about ensuring an easy life for ourselves or our dear ones in the next world, the Protestants seem to have encouraged us to concentrate instead on creating a good (virtuous or – more often, perhaps – comfortable) life in this one. We lost our connection with the dead. Death became first a sad prelude to a Judgement whose outcome was terrifyingly beyond our control, and then just a senseless end. Great fears are what breed great taboos.

Back at Abbot Kiprian's Bistriţa monastery the next morning I sat on a bench in the courtyard to enjoy the faint strains of the liturgy being sung inside the church. The sun, rising between the high hills, warmed the paving stones and illuminated a row of trestle tables erected against one wall of the church. Heavily laden with delicious-looking plaited breads, *koliva* dusted with cocoa powder and coloured beads of sugar, bunches of fat black grapes and bottles of wine and Coca-Cola, those boards were groaning. Local women in their church-going best bustled about sticking thin yellow beeswax candles in every bread and cake, lighting then relighting them when the wind blew them out. A handful of monks, the breeze flapping at their vestments, appeared to sing a blessing for the year anniversary of a local deceased.

We had spent another night at Bistriţa monastery because I wanted to do what the trickle of tourists to this remote north-eastern corner of Romania do, and visit the fifteenth- and sixteenth-century 'painted monasteries'. No other Orthodox country in Europe boasts anything quite as delightfully surprising as the churches of these five monasteries. Built by Moldavia's pious princes at a time when the rest of the Orthodox Balkans was groaning under the Ottoman yoke and constrained by law to make do with low hovel churches of the kind I had seen in Sarajevo, these churches are the same design as Bistriţa's – high, narrow and steepled. But it is the astoundingly preserved frescoes on their outside rather than just inside walls which have set them apart, won them world-wide renown and UNESCO's protection.

No one is entirely sure why those princes had the outside walls of their churches painted. Perhaps it was so that the filthy *hoi polloi*, forbidden to enter the church, might still benefit from religious instruction. Perhaps they were a useful indicator of their founders' huge wealth. But I prefer to think that they are a testament to the confidently fearless Orthodox spirits of those princes. Why confine frescoes and their holy instruction to the dark inside of a church when there is nothing to stop you advertising the True Faith on the day-lit outside? Whatever the truth of the matter, the rich vegetable paint colours of those frescoes – blue, red, yellow and green – have proved durable enough, on at least one wall of each church, to withstand five or six centuries of winters. Saints and kings, angels and devils, miracles, battles and Last Judgements are still as vivid as comic-book illustrations.

Hurtling from place to place in brilliant autumn sunshine, exclaiming at the flaming reds and golds of the beech-tree-carpeted mountains repeated in every scene of a red river of hell-fire and group of golden-haloed saints, we managed to see four painted churches in one day. At Humor we found a sixth-century Siege of Constantinople by the Persians, complete with Byzantine emperor and empress perched high on the crenellated pink towers of the city, next to a clutch of haloed clergy. Voroneţ's red river of hell-fire from the Book of Revelation was full of sinners – tricky merchants with their cheating scales, naked adulterous women chained together, turbaned Turks, patriarchal Jews and barbaric Tartars. At Moldoviţa we inspected a Fall of Constantinople with blasting cannons, archers in turrets and bishops in black and white chequered vestments, bearing bowls of boiling oil. The Byzantine soldiers defending the city were got up in something suspiciously like Moldavian folk-costume, we noted. We also encountered a nun called Mother Tatiana, who was sitting in Moldoviţa's sunny courtyard flicking through an Internet magazine. She told us that 'an avalanche' of young Romanian women were choosing the monastic life because 'the situation is so difficult outside'. I could quite see that a peaceful, ordered existence, either at the Birth of the Mother of God monastery, or down south in the foothills of the Carpathians, or way up here in one of these splendid old foundations was a barely resistible alternative to the sad and ugly chaos of today's Romania.

But Suceviţa was my favourite painted monastery. One of its outside walls is wholly given over to a scene of the Ladder of Virtue on which sinners are ascending to Heaven. To the right of the ladder are rank upon rank of identical angels. Golden-haloed and rosy-winged, they are flying in perfect formation, like a squadron of fighter planes. This was a divinely disciplined fighting force of the heavenly host, mustered to save sinners from tumbling into Hell on the other side of the ladder. The dark disorder of that other place looks as unappealing as most of Romania's towns.

To stand shivering in Targu Neamţ's main square for four hours the next gusty grey morning was a kind of Hell after the glories of the painted monasteries, but a small price to pay for a chance to meet the heir apparent to Romania's patriarchal throne, the youthful, forceful and darkly handsome Metropolitan Daniel of Moldavia.

Metropolitan Daniel happened to be consecrating a new church in that windblown dingy town. Hundreds had gathered in the square to hear the singing and receive their chief pastor's blessing. Although the singing was more plaintively melodious than the Greek or Serbian equivalent, the most constantly recurring words were the same. *Gospodi pomiluj* or *Kyrie eleison* had become *Doamne miluieşte* – Lord have mercy! Lord have mercy!

In a sermon that blared out, marred by a crackle of feedback, over the bowed heads of that impoverished crowd, Metropolitan Daniel referred to the painted monasteries. 'When we go into a painted church,' he reminded his flock, 'we think we are going into Heaven because a church is Heaven on Earth . . .' The thought that somewhere in the mêlée of glittering clergy by the church was Abbot Kiprian, who had kindly offered to present me to Daniel just as soon as the service was over, was equally comforting.

When the last 'Amen' and 'Lord, have mercy upon us' had sounded, the crowd surged forward like a tidal wave towards the spot in front of the church where free holy cards were being distributed. Then the current suddenly switched and swept the shining flotilla of churchmen – led by Metropolitan Daniel and hemmed about by police – across the square to the town's best restaurant. At its doors old women threw themselves at Daniel's hand, kissing his ring and weeping. Gypsy women with Austrian imperial gold coins dangling from their plaits grabbed at his robes and crossed themselves. Metropolitan Daniel, his hands dispensing blessings and his long-lashed dark eyes flashing with joy after the marathon four-hour-long service was a superstar.

Abbot Kiprian made a timely appearance to shepherd us swiftly into the restaurant just before the doors closed. About fifty of the town's notables, including the mayor and the chief of police, assorted abbots like Kiprian from nearby monasteries, a Dutchman and ourselves were honoured guests at a fabulous seven-course banquet. From the high table Daniel said grace and we all sat down to eat. For a time the only sounds were the tinkle of cutlery and an Ave Maria being piped over the restaurant's speakers.

I waited my turn to speak to Daniel until Turkish coffee, honey on the comb and cakes had been served. The Dutchman had slipped in quicker, between the stuffed cabbage leaves and steak and chips courses. By eavesdropping on his conversation with Daniel, I learnt that the Dutchman had spent the last nine years collecting funds to build the brand-new orphanage. Now that it was ready he was up against a last tangle of red tape and desperately needed Metropolitan Daniel to intervene and crack the whip. In fact, he was not going to go back to his seat at the end of the high table until he had extracted a firm promise to that effect. He did not get one. Metropolitan Daniel tut-tutted and sympathized but dismissed him with a holy card and a blessing before turning to me and strongly recommending – in excellent English – that I slip a piece of honeycomb into my coffee.

The best educated and most travelled of Romania's hierarchs, Daniel speaks a number of European languages. All that and his ecumenical sympathies have endeared him to foreign churchmen but alienated him from most of his peers in Romania. Rumour has it, these days, that his succession to the patriarchal throne after Teoctist is by no means a foregone conclusion. The elderly Bishop Bartolomeo of Cluj, who has taken a loudly uncompromising stand against the Transylvanian Uniates, is emerging as a strong rival for the post. I chose to avoid the murky waters of Romanian church politics. Instead, I began by explaining to Daniel that I was writing a book which would, I hoped, illumine the nature and history of Europe's Easter Orthodox culture. I mentioned that I was focusing on two of its chief characteristics: Phyletism and Hesychasm.

He spluttered into his coffee. 'No, no, no,' he said shaking his head vehemently. 'First of all, who are you to talk about nationalism when your Northern Ireland question is still unsolved? Second, your new division of Europe down the 1054 Schism line is all wrong. Look, it's not just the Orthodox countries which are being left out of an enlarged EU. Don't forget that Slovakia, a Catholic country, is not being allowed in either. The point is that East and West are complementary and *mustn't* become isolated from each other again.'

'Oh, yes, I quite agree, but . . .' I attempted mollifyingly.

'I know! You've been reading that dangerous man Samuel Huntington, haven't you?' he interrupted impatiently.

'Yes,' I admitted

'In his book about clashing civilizations,' said Daniel, his voice suddenly low and urgent, 'he is talking about blocs and ideologies, not about realities. The world is no longer divided into blocs. Look at Britain today – you have I don't know how many Asians and Africans living there. Huntington is *very* dangerous.'

The vehemence of Daniel's response shocked me. It seemed that I had touched a raw nerve. His being conversant with Huntington and EU expansion suggested to me that he had devoted a lot of time to arguing with his fellow Church hierarchs over the pros and cons of viewing Orthodox Europe as a separate entity. He sounded on the defensive, as if he were in the minority, with his desperate insistence that Europe – East and West – must remain one world.

'The Russians,' he grumbled, 'love Huntington's book because they see a role for themselves as the boss of his so-called Orthodox bloc. But the Greeks don't like it because they are already in the EU and Nato, and they feel they would not be boss in this Orthodox bloc. No, no, no. Huntington's idea is not right for Europe and it is certainly not right for Romania.'

I could understand his fear. The Romanians, pulled eastward by their religion and westward by their Latin language, are almost as schizophrenic a people as the Greeks. They have had their fill of Russian big-brotherliness after forty-odd years of Communism.

Thanks to Ion-Innocentie Micu-Klein and succeeding Uniate intellectuals and the Latin roots of the Romanian language, they have
long been anxious for close relations with the Latin countries of the
West – France, Italy and Spain. But the West has rejected their timid
overtures, and turned down their bid to join the ranks of the central
European countries entering Nato in 1999. A new partition of Europe
traps this fish-cum-fowl of a country. The Romanians' best hope is
that men like Metropolitan Daniel of Moldavia can turn a trap into
a bridge between East and West. This is presumably the sort of
thinking behind the government's invitation to Pope John Paul II.
But the level of anti-Vatican feeling I had encountered in the rest of
Eastern Orthodox Europe, let alone in Romania itself, made me doubt
the strategy's chances of success.

Without giving me a holy card, Metropolitan Daniel suddenly
turned away to address the assembled party. The restaurant fell silent
as he started. 'This Englishwoman has travelled to our country to
discover our Orthodoxy, but she is comparing the best of her western
culture with the worst of ours and that is dangerous,' I blanched,
suddenly scared by a sea of hostile faces, 'not that she is alone in
making such a mistake,' he went on mitigatingly. 'We Romanians are
often equally guilty of comparing the best of our culture with the
worst of the West.'

'Asa e – Absolutely!' I managed lamely, praying that a word or
two of Romanian would serve to deflect that hostility.

Fortunately the company was sufficiently mellowed by fine foods
and drinks to forgive me. Only Archbishop Petre of the neighbouring
former Soviet Republic of Moldova – the eastern half of Moldavia
that Russia annexed in 1941 – continued to look disgruntled. He
could be forgiven his glumness, I thought. The Moldovan Orthodox
Church is riven by factionalism. While Patriarch Petre's segment of
the Church looks to Teoctist in Bucharest for guidance, the rest,
which represents the majority, remains loyal to the Russian Patriarch
in Moscow.

As we emerged from the warm restaurant into the twilit empty
cold of the town square, I smelt the coming winter. All too soon I

would have to return to Russia, by far the largest Eastern Orthodox country in the world. I had already spent a harrowing month in the European part of the country that lies to the west of the Urals, but Russia without Siberia and snow is hardly Russia.

Barents Sea

Ural Mountains

FINLAND

Solovetsky Is.
Kem○ ○Belomorsk

R U S S I A

○Verkhoturye

○Yekaterinburg

✝
● Alexander Svirsky
Monastery

St Petersburg○
○Novgorod

EST.

Pskov○

LATVIA
LITH.
RUS.

○Sergeyev Posad
■Moscow

KAZAKHSTAN

POLAND

BELARUS

✝
● Optina Pustyn
Monastery

Aral
Sea

UZBEKISTAN

Kievo

U K R A I N E

SLOVAKIA

HUNGARY

MOLD.

ROMANIA

Chechnya

Caspian
Sea

TURKMENISTAN

YUGOSLAVIA

BULGARIA

Black Sea

GEORGIA

AZER.

ARM.

ALBANIA

MACE.

GREECE

TURKEY

IRAN

CYPRUS

Mediterranean Sea

CRETE

SYRIA

LEBANON

IRAQ

ISRAEL

JORDAN

N

EGYPT

SAUDI ARABIA

1000 Kilometres

Russia

Solovetsky Monastery
White Sea

A desert mirage in a cold climate . . .

Way below, between a heavy white sky and a grey White Sea, an archipelago of islands is drifting into view. The largest island, thickly forested and lacy with lakes, is dwarfed by an outsize white monastery complete with high walls and a cluster of grey onion domes topped with golden crosses.

The rickety little aeroplane banked and turned above this northernmost outpost of Eastern Orthodoxy on the edge of the Arctic Circle. Beginning its descent towards a temporary runway laid on tussocky grass, it landed with a skid and taxied to a juddering halt in front of a blue-washed wooden hut with a faded Aeroflot poster in its window. My Russian artist friend Vanya and I, a couple of Dutch biologists and a beatifically smiling deaf-mute with his mother clambered out into a howling summer wind, zipping up our anoraks and smiling with relief at having survived the one flight a week to Solovetsky from Archangel.

The smiles faded as Vanya and I set off down the track leading to the village and on, towards the monastery. A cloud of mosquitoes swarmed at us, a crazy old *babushka* cursed us from her vegetable plot, and a motorbike with side-car roared past on its way to the village of log-cabin houses set in weeds. Outside a darkened dirty shop a couple of men in tracksuits and grubby denim jackets were glugging at bottles of vodka. They turned away as we passed. Vanya broke our shocked silence with, 'It's so Soviet. I was expecting somewhere beautiful and unspoiled – a new Jerusalem . . .'

We should both have known that not even a tiny island almost a thousand miles north of the Kremlin could escape the dead hand of Soviet totalitarianism. That connoisseur of Russia's mutilated body and broken heart, Andrei Tarkovsky would have made something of this ravaged and sky-laden landscape. He would have liked the shabby monastery at the end of the rough track, the damp-warped log cabins and the shells of a few brick edifices that owed their dereliction to neglect and vandalism rather than to climate and time. Tarkovsky used to dream of somewhere like Solovetsky, and once noted in his diary: '. . . a terribly sad dream. I dreamed again of a northern (I think) lake somewhere in Russia; it was dawn, and on the far shore were two Orthodox monasteries, with amazingly beautiful cathedrals and walls. But I felt such sadness! Such pain!'[1]

He could have captured its not so much *fin-de-siecle* as *fin-du-monde* feel and told its apocalyptic history in soundless pictures: a fifteenth-century hermitage, a holy site of pilgrimage and an impregnable frontier fortress for five hundred years, the first Soviet gulag camp and a byword for senseless terror after 1917, a naval base after the Second World War.

Solovetsky is one of the most decayed and economically non-viable spots in post-Communist Russia. Its thousand inhabitants are fleeing to the mainland, escaping both past and present. Whatever future the island has is in the hands of couple of dozen young monks who, since 1991, have recolonized the massive monastery with its five tumbledown churches and eight-yard-thick stone walls. The derelict establishment is up and running on ritual-marked Orthodox time again. There are liturgies on Sundays, chanting processions around the monastery walls on saints' days, and daily prayers.

Vanya and I walked through its open gates into a debris-strewn courtyard, and paused to watch a few monks at work in their dusty cassocks, thick leather belts slung low on their hips and high velvet caps pulled down over their brows like helmets. One was wearing goggles and wielding a chainsaw in a storm of windblown sawdust. Another split logs with rhythmic blows of an axe. A few more stood up to their waists in a muddy trench, digging down towards a fractured water-pipe.

'It burst in April,' one told us, leaning on his spade and wiping his forehead on his cassock sleeve. 'We haven't had running water since then. Now at last, after four months, the earth has thawed and God willing . . .'

God's will and Orthodox time are all very well, I thought, but their lives are ruled by the eight dark and frozen months of the year, which they spend waiting and watching for the thaw. Then comes their race with the short, sharp summers when they must chop enough firewood, grow enough vegetables and fix burst pipes, before the freezing gloom descends again. Why did they have to reclaim Solovetsky, when mainland Russia – the European part that lies to the west of the Ural mountains and Siberia – is strewn with ruined monasteries in need of repair and habitation? Were these monks trusting that their daily battle against the elements up here could atone for almost a century of godless Soviet evil and somehow help set Russia back on the path along which it was travelling before the Bolshevik cataclysm?

Perhaps it could, but there may be centuries – not just decades – to atone for because one could argue that Holy Russia's fall from grace began not in 1917 with the imposition of an atheist power, and not even in the eighteenth century when the ruthlessly westernizing Peter the Great abolished the Russian patriarchate and Catherine the Great 'rationalized' the monasteries by dissolving most of them. One could argue that the decline began at least a couple of hundred years earlier, during the sixteenth-century reign of Ivan the Terrible and that that unhinged tyrant's murder of an abbot of this Solovetsky monastery was what marked the fatal turning-point.

But how, in the first place, did Byzantium come to assist at the birth of a state that managed to penetrate this far north and dared to style itself 'Holy Russia'?

Way back in the tenth century when Byzantium was the golden eye of world civilization, one of her trading, and sometime warring, partners was pagan Kievan Rus. Destined to become the kernel of a Holy Russia,* Kiev lay way to the south, a short hop across the Black Sea from Constantinople, on the banks of the river Dniepr, in what is now Ukraine. The main settlement on the trading route linking

---

* This is the claim of Russian historians. Ukranian historians dispute it, arguing that the Russian Orthodox Church was a separate organism.

the Baltic Sea in the north to the Black Sea in the south, it connected Byzantium to northern and western Europe.

The pagan Kievan Russians had long been in the habit of mounting pesky raids on the Byzantines, but these had almost ceased in 860 when the Byzantines' judicious airing of the Mother of God's veil had blown up a storm mighty enough to strike the fear of the Christian God into one of those raiding parties and send it scuttling home to Kiev. Peaceful trading in wax, furs, timber and amber dictated the general character of subsequent relations between the two powers. But the miracle of the Mother of God's robe had planted a seed of doubt in Kievan Russian minds as to the efficacy of their multiple home-grown gods of sun, thunder and birch trees. The future was obviously monotheistic.

So it was that towards the end of the tenth century Prince Vladimir of Kievan Rus came to be weighing up the merits of the various monotheistic religions of the day. Islam, he judged, was out of the question for his people since it forbade the consumption of alcohol. 'It is the Russians' joy to drink; this we cannot forgo,' he is said to have calculated. The humiliating homelessness of the Jews was sufficient to discount Judaism. He might have chosen western Christianity because, although the Schism was still over half a century away, the differences between the two halves of the Christian world were clearly visible. But it so happened that he had sent his ambassadors to Constantinople where they were so mightily impressed by the beauty of the Byzantine rite as performed at the Haghia Sophia that they did not know whether they were 'in Heaven or on Earth'. Furthermore, thanks to the ninth-century Macedonian missionaries Cyril and Methodius, the Greek Church texts had been translated into a Slavonic language, which the Kievan Russians could more or less understand. Orthodoxy's appeal was irresistible and Byzantium's power unrivalled. Its spiritual rather than military conquest of Kievan Rus, and so later Russia, was a glorious victory the like of which the western Church could never boast.

Prince Vladimir had himself baptized and satisfactorily married to a Byzantine princess in Constantinople before travelling home to

Kiev with his bride, a crowd of Greek clergy and the skull of St Clement. Once back, he lost no time in setting Byzantine churchmen to work conducting wholesale baptisms of his people on the banks of the river Dniepr. Realpolitik apart, Vladimir proved so passionate a Christian that he put the Byzantines to shame by abolishing the death penalty in his realm. Less than a hundred years after his conversion, Kiev boasted its own Haghia Sophia, decorated with frescoes and hung with icons by Byzantine artists. So did Novgorod, a city on the northern stretch of the trading route, up near the Baltic Sea. Although Vladimir's son, Svyatoslav, was far from pious, in 1015 he did Russia a valuable service by martyring his meek and mild younger brothers. They were Russia's first saints, Boris and Gleb.

But the monasteries were the most efficient channels of Byzantine influence. Less than thirty years after Vladimir's conversion, a Kievan Russian who was living 'the angelic life' on Mount Athos was ordered home by his abbot. 'Antonij, go back to Rus, so that you may strengthen others there by your success, and may the blessing of the Holy Mountain be with you,'[ii] he was told. Antonij did not go home to a life of active preaching. Instead, this first Russian ascetic followed the Byzantine Desert Fathers' example of dissident passive resistance to the evils of the world, the same example Romania's Father Cleopa was to follow a thousand years later. He dug himself a pit in which he spent the rest of his life. Fellow Russians, drawn by his example, dug and settled in their own caves all about him. At last, one of his spiritual children, the monk Theodosius, led the community above ground and founded Kiev's famous Monastery of the Caves. Out of it came the Kievan Russians' first efforts to discover their place in the world and history. A monk called Nestor is generally credited with the authorship of their early twelfth-century 'Primary Chronicle'. A history of the world starting with Adam and Eve in the Garden of Eden, it assesses the parts played by the Jews, Ancient Greeks and Romans, Byzantines and finally Russians in the ongoing historical drama of man's Providence-governed quest for salvation. The idea of Russia as a holy land, entrusted with a mission as divine as that of the Byzantines, dates back this far.

Because it was not in the Byzantine Church's interests to undermine the True Faith by muddying its clear waters with worldly
learning, the Russians inevitably developed their own religious myth-
history and a typically Byzantine Orthodox distrust of the intellect.
Their utter isolation from the rest of Europe during two hundred
years of Mongol rule was to fix the attitude that reasoning, as a
Russian divine once declared, was 'the mother of all lusts'.[iii] Russian
churchmen took pride in their ignorance of Latin and Greek learning
and the religious purity of their Christian culture. Reasoning's only
job was to confirm the truth of the Orthodoxy.

Philotheos, a sixteenth-century Russian monk, did permit himself
the luxury of reasoning that since the old Rome had fallen into
heresy and the new one, Constantinople, to the Ottomans, Moscow
must be the third and last Rome. But he scoffed at ancient learning.
'I was not born in Athens, nor did I study with wise philosophers,
nor did I converse with any such; I studied from the books of divine
grace by which I might save my sinful soul,'[iv] he wrote. Two hundred
years later Peter the Great was determined to drag his huge country
into the modern world by embracing the new western science, but
his subjects cursed him as the Anti-Christ. Catherine the Great
imported the values of the French Enlightenment but they only
penetrated as far as her French-speaking court. Between them, she
and Peter laid the groundwork for nineteenth-century Russia's fatal
divide between the brittle icing on the top of society and the vast
dark fruit-cake of the Orthodox peasantry. Until 1917 an ordinary
Russian's sense of himself and his place in the world and history was
probably more entwined with religion than that of a Greek or even a
Serb.

Kievan Rus still shines as bright as a lost New Jerusalem in the
popular Russian memory. That short blaze of glory, between Vladimir's conversion in 988 and the sacking of the city by the Mongols
just over two hundred years later, is to the Russians what fourteenth-
century Serbia is to a Serb or golden Byzantium to a Greek. As one
Russian Church historian has admiringly written: 'In the dramatic
and even tragic history of relations between the Christian Church

and state, the Kievan experience, in spite of its brevity and fragility, may be regarded as one of the best Christian achievements.'v

Kievan Russian princes humbled themselves before the throne of God. A mere monk could call a prince a 'usurper' with impunity, or keep his sovereign waiting outside the monastery gates. A holy old *starets* could put a sudden dampener on courtly revelling and reduce a prince to tears by asking a simple question like 'Will it be like this in *that* world?'vi Prince Vladimir of Monomakh, who married King Harold of England's sister Gytha after the Norman invasion, left instructions for their sons which were at least as much moral as political.

> My children, praise God, and love men . . . Forget not the poor but feed them. Remember that riches come from God and are given you only for a short time . . . Be fathers to orphans, be judges in the cause of widows and do not let the powerful oppress the weak. Put to death neither the innocent nor the guilty, for nothing is so sacred as the life and the soul of a Christian. Do not desert the sick; do not let the sight of corpses terrify you, for we must all die. Drive out of your heart all suggestions of pride and remember that we are all mortal, today full of hope, tomorrow in the coffin . . .vii

By the eleventh century Kievan Rus had taken its place as a full member of Europe's community of Christian states. The fact that the new Kievan Rus Church was dominated by Byzantine clergymen on loan from and closely backed by mighty Constantinople accounted in large part for why *symphonia* worked so well there. Out of twenty-three Metropolitans who headed the Church between Vladimir's conversion and the Mongol invasion two hundred years later, seventeen were Byzantine and only three native Russians.

In 1240 the city of twelve monasteries and four hundred churches, Holy Russia's first and finest incarnation, was laid waste and captured by the Mongols. Like the Ottomans in the Balkans after 1453, the Mongols did not persecute or even tax the Church, which left it as free as the Orthodox Churches of the Balkans to nourish the Russians' sense of a distinct and coherent Christian identity and myths of a golden age past. While the native princes in their myriad fiefdoms squabbled and skirmished and abased themselves before the Mongol khans with multiple prostrations and annual payments of tribute, Church hierarchs made themselves useful by representing their flocks at the Mongol court. From Vladimir's conversion in 988 until 1448, after the Mongols had been driven back south and Moscow had succeeded in uniting the other principalities under its rule, the usually Byzantine Metropolitan of Kiev was the only person in a position to represent all Russians.

Mongol rule in Russia lasted as long as it did because Byzantium and Byzantine churchmen decided that heretic western Christianity was by far the greater evil. Time and again the Byzantine Church exhorted Russian princes to defend Orthodoxy against the Roman Catholic Swedes and Teutonic knights who, by the beginning of the thirteenth century, were brutally engaged in extending the writ of the Roman Catholic Pope among the pagan tribes of the Baltic region. A long history of resistance to western incursion has left Russians with as ugly an opinion of western Christianity as the Byzantines gained after the sack of their city by the Fourth Crusaders in 1204.

One battle in particular has entered the Russians' collective unconscious and still resonates like a clanging alarm bell whenever western invasion threatens – be it seventeenth-century Polish, nineteenth-century Napoleonic, twentieth-century Nazi, or today's eastward-creeping Nato borders and influx of American Protestant or Jesuit Catholic missionaries. In 1242 Prince Alexander Nevsky encountered an army of Catholic Teutonic knights on Lake Chud, on ice too thin to take the huge weight of the western heretics with their iron armour and horses. To his great delight, and in the nick of time, the ice cracked and the lake swallowed his mighty enemy.

By the fourteenth century Byzantium was backing the grand dukes of Muscovy as the people best suited to unifying the Orthodox Russian lands and fending off the West. Moscow was conveniently situated among protective forests and at a crossing of trade routes up to Novgorod and the Baltic Sea, and south to the Black Sea. The

Metropolitan of Kiev set his seal of approval on the new capital by taking up permanent residence there, in a purpose-built stone palace next door to the Prince's humbler wooden one.

Hesychasm had reached Russia, reinforcing the new state's connection to the physically shrunken but spiritually expansive Byzantine empire. The monks at Sergeyev Posad's Trinity Sergeyev monastery, fifty miles north of Moscow, were feasting off the same soul-food in Slavonic translation as their brothers three thousand miles to the south in Constantinople, on the island of Patmos and Mount Athos, at the great Hesychast foundations of Bulgaria and Macedonia and the Serbian monasteries in Kosovo. Russia's favourite saint, Sergius of Radonezh, was particularly admired by Byzantium's Hesychast patriarch, Cyprian, who wrote a charming letter to Sergius and his brethren, saying: 'I hear of you and of your virtue, how you despise all worldly pursuits and concern yourselves only with the will of God: I thank God greatly for this and pray Him that He may grant us to meet together and receive the pleasure of a spiritual conversation . . .'[viii]

The saintly Sergius was abbot of his Sergeyev Posad foundation and spiritual father to the Prince of Muscovy at the moment the Russians became ready to rid themselves of the Mongols. Managing to marry spiritual endeavour with earthly efficacy, Sergius urged the Prince to fight the decisive battle of Kulikovo in 1380 and despatched two of his monks to open the hostilities. Legend has it that while the battle raged the holy man sat in his monastery over three hundred miles away, miraculously reeling off the names of the Russian warriors as they fell, and praying for the repose of their souls.

St Sergius, who had started out as a forest hermit with only a friendly bear for company, was the best-known of a small army of hermits who, nourished on the sayings of the Desert Fathers, followed their ancient lead by rejecting the world and escaping into the *pustyn*, the desert, in search of *hesychia*. They must have burned with the fire of faith and that old Byzantine capacity for ignoring reality in favour of the ideal, because the nearest things to deserts in Russia were cold, dark forests. They cleared trees, built their huts, mortified their flesh and prayed. Rather like Christodoulos on Patmos, or Paissy in eighteenth-century Moldavia, their *hesychia* was usually disrupted, if not by war then even more commonly by other monks attracted by their example. Before long a monastery would be established. A village would grow up around it and the monastery grow rich on donations. By the time it had fallen into lax worldly practices, another dissident Hesychast would be haring off into the forest in search of another, even more remote spot, and the whole cycle would repeat itself, again and again.

These dissident Hesychasts were the agents of Russia's expansion northward, off the old river trading route. Pioneers, engaged on spiritual rather than worldly quests, their motivation was the hope of salvation rather than greed for untapped natural wealth. The likes of St Sergius and St Alexander Svirsky – a famous Hesychast who spent seven years in a forest pit staving off starvation by eating handfuls of earth, while swarms of mosquitoes feasted off his naked torso in summer and the frosts turned his skin to hide in the winter – were Russia's founding fathers. And this was how two monks, Zosima and Savvaty, found themselves heading in the direction of the Arctic Circle. By 1429 they had reached the natural limit of the White Sea and its archipelago of little islands, the largest of which was Solovetsky. Ignoring the spot's numerous natural disadvantages and the advice of an Archbishop of Novgorod who said, 'Your monastery is so far away from people – who would go there? How can the Church be there?'[ix] they noted instead its curiously clement micro-climate, a gift of the Gulf Stream. Having scared off a few pagan Finns, they established a first hermitage, which gradually metamorphosed into a large fortified monastery. Pious donations of land and money were soon pouring in and before long the monks were landlords of thirty-two villages on the mainland. Ivan the Terrible, who came to the throne in 1547, favoured the place as a useful outpost of Russian power against the hostile Catholic Swedes and graciously donated a further two villages whose income was to be spent building the main Transfiguration cathedral.

*

Solovetsky monastery was the prime mover in northern Russia's economy and government when a certain well-born monk called Philip became its abbot. By halfway through the sixteenth century he had set in train the first major tussle between Church and State and with it Holy Russia's long decline.

A minor boyar's son, Philip was raised on the fringes of the royal court in Moscow, an experience so appalling that by the time he was thirty he could no longer endure the glaring contradiction between the world on offer in the Kremlin and that envisaged by Christ. Disguising himself as a humble peasant, he abandoned Moscow for Solovetsky Island and its monastery, which were as far as he could flee from the capital's contamination. The monastery was still make-shift, equipped with an altar of granite, a stone hammer and gong instead of bells and a huge crude crucifix carved out of walrus tusks. After a few years of menial labour there, and some astute spiritual guidance from a *starets* who had been the mosquito-bitten Alexander Svirsky's spiritual child, Philip became abbot.

Like St Sergius, Philip seems to have excelled on both the material and spiritual planes. The saintly Hesychast turned out to have a gift for big business and a genius for inventing labour-saving devices. He modernized the monastery into a hugely prosperous and efficient industrial corporation, whose interests included farms, shipping, salt-pans, timber, wax and tallow works, fisheries, a dairy and a brewery. Channelling between the island's lakes, Philip dug fishponds and improved the monks' diet with butter, fruit jellies and scrambled eggs. He built the biggest church and enriched it with one of the two new ruby-and-pearl-studded altar crosses Tsar Ivan had presented as gifts. Everything on Solovetsky prospered until Ivan decided that the Abbot of Solovetsky's talents were altogether too rare to squander on a remote outpost of his growing empire. In 1566, when Philip had been Abbot of Solovetsky for twenty years, Tsar Ivan invited him to Moscow to fill the post of Metropolitan of Russia. The Byzantine Church had started allowing the Russians to choose their church leaders almost a century before, but it was not until shortly after Ivan's death, in 1588, that they acquired their own patriarch.

Philip was far from keen to forgo his *hesychia* and accept the Tsar's elevation. 'Why are you putting such a heavy weight in such a small boat?'[x] he protested humbly. But the root of his reluctance was that mainland Russia was a helplessly horrible place to be. Tsar Ivan, apparently in the grip of an advanced paranoia, was seeing enemies and traitors everywhere. His *oprichniki* – a six-thousand-strong personal army of bloodthirsty paramilitary thugs blasphemously got up in monks' black cassocks – were rampaging around the country on horseback, with long knives, dogs' heads and brooms attached to their saddles. The second item symbolized Ivan's capacity to bite his enemies, the third his determination to purge Russia. The *oprichniki* were wholesale slaughterers. People looked to the Church to rescue them from this man-made plague, to churchmen like Philip. As one nineteenth-century Russian Church historian wrote, 'Terror reigned. People locked their doors, squares and streets were empty. In the horrible silence the unhappy people awaited only one voice, that of Philip.'

For all his abominable cruelty Tsar Ivan IV was the first to refer to his country as 'Holy Russia' and was a profoundly religious man, apparently tortured by the same dilemma that had sent Philip fleeing to Solovetsky: how to reconcile practical life on earth with the uncompromising dictates of true Christianity. In a letter to one of his chief critics Ivan wrote, 'Is it befitting for a Tsar when he is struck on the cheek to turn the other? Is not this the supreme commandment of Christianity? But how shall a Tsar without honour rule his country?'[xi]

The precariousness of his expanding empire, its vulnerability to outside threats from western Christendom and the Muslim world as well as to internal rivalries all seemed to rule out the old Byzantine luxury of ruling in divine *symphonia* with a churchman. Anyway, Ivan could reason, what good had *symphonia* done Byzantium? What good had come of caving in to the passive defeatism of Hesychast churchmen? The imperial city of Tsargrad had fallen to the Ottomans a century before, but the disaster was still fresh in Ivan's mind. Most Russians blamed Constantinople's fall on the last Byzantine Emperor's craven willingness at the Council of Florence to abandon the True Faith and submit to the Pope in exchange for western military support against the Ottomans. But Ivan seems to have reached a different conclusion. In the same letter he emerges as a man fully prepared to ditch the True Faith if the safety of the state depended on it. He wrote: 'Now you will never find a kingdom which does not fall to ruin when ruled by priests ... Thus the Greeks destroyed their kingdom and became tributaries of the Turks.'[xii] It seems that at the 1438 Council of Florence Ivan would have submitted to the Pope just as the Byzantine Emperor had, but he would not then have returned home and let Hesychast prelates, armies of hard-line nuns and monk-led mobs undermine and overturn that decision.

Ivan could comfort himself that no other European ruler was power-sharing with priests. The western states were forever warring with the Pope. The Reformation was under way. England's Henry VIII had dissolved some 650 monasteries. After England's short-lived reversion to Catholicism under Mary Tudor, Henry's second daughter, Elizabeth, was cutting loose from Rome again. Machiavelli's political philosophy was all the rage and, nearer home, the previous century's Prince Vlad the Impaler of Wallachia had set a fine example to follow. Ivan never dreamed the dream of reuniting a universal Christendom. He cared only for the security of his realm, but the gulf between heavenly and earthly kingdoms continued to irk him. Indeed, it seems to have driven him crazy. With a mind filled with brutally practical western notions of kingship but a heart still idealistically Byzantine, he was torn in two. He veered between savage excesses of slaughter and torture, and paying for prayers to be said for his victims while prostrating himself before icons until permanent bruises bloomed on his forehead. Although, thanks to the discovery of Siberia after 1582, Russia had doubled in size during his reign, the words Ivan croaked on his deathbed in 1584 were those of a man still tortured. The basic conundrum presented by the clash between the real and ideal allowed him no rest. 'The body is exhausted, the spirit is sick. The cords of my soul and my body have been stretched too tight, and there is no physician who can heal me . . .'ˣⁱⁱⁱ he is supposed to have said. As the end approached, his treatment of Philip twenty years before must have weighed heavily on his conscience.

Philip had eventually accepted the heavy burden placed on his shoulders, taken his leave of Solovetsky and installed himself in the Kremlin's stone palace. But, determined to exercise the old Byzantine patriarchal privilege of criticizing the Tsar, he had soon clashed with Ivan. One of their run-ins went something like this:

P: All-powerful Tsar . . . If you have such a high rank you should respect God because your crown and power comes from God – so you are the image of God. But you are also mortal. A ruler is one who can rule himself and doesn't serve his passions. If you forget yourself in your madness your state is disturbed.

I: It's none of your business. You're just a simple monk.

P: By the grace of the Holy Spirit, by the Holy Cathedral Council and by your wishes I am the shepherd of the Christian church. Together we need to look after the peace and piety of this Orthodox Christian realm.

I: Shut up!

P: I can't keep silent now. Silence could multiply the sins and defamation. What account will we be able to give when Jesus Christ comes again?

I: Philip, don't be against our state so that my anger does not throw you out of the Metropolitanate.

P: I didn't send any demands or messages, I didn't cross any palms with silver to get this post of Metropolitan. You deprived me of my *pustyn*. Do as you like!ˣⁱᵛ

One spring morning in 1568, Philip was standing at the altar of the Kremlin's Uspensky cathedral, venerating an icon of Christ the Saviour, when Ivan and a band of his *oprichniki* wearing their black robes and carrying drawn knives strode in. Philip did not appear to notice their arrival and continued his contemplation of the icon.

'The Tsar is in front of you – bless him,' commanded one, but Philip refused.

> P: Tsar, who do you think you're imitating got up like this and demeaning the real image of your rank? . . . I grieve for your soul.
>
> I: Are you going against us? I'll test your strength!
>
> P: I am a visitor on this Earth as were all my fathers . . . and I am ready to suffer for the Truth![xv]

Ivan turned on his heel and marched out to despatch his *oprichniki* about the task of gathering a group of churchmen willing to denounce Philip. His agents travelled all the way to Solovetsky where they found the new Abbot of the monastery more than happy to fabricate evidence against his saintly predecessor. A kangaroo court convicted Philip on trumped-up charges of black magic and moral turpitude.

Philip knew his fate was sealed and offered to hand over the gold-threaded stole and crozier of his office. It is some measure of Ivan's chronically sick mind and heart that he stopped him, saying no, Philip had to serve a last liturgy on an important feast day. But as soon as that service was over *oprichniki* stripped the old man of his vestments, bundled him up in a coarse monk's cassock, threw him on a sledge and hauled him away to incarceration in a distant monastery. His faithful flock wept to see him go and accompanied the sledge on its way. Philip was chained in a stinking cell. Ivan, still seething with guilty rage, had one of the disgraced churchman's nephews executed and the head sent to Philip with a message saying, 'This is your favourite relative – your sorcery didn't help him!'[xvi]

A year later, while Ivan was on his way to purge the too-independently minded towns of Novgorod and Pskov, the *oprichniki* chief visited Philip in his cell. The old monk was to be given a last chance to repent of his stubborn opposition to the Tsar and salve Ivan's bad conscience.

'Holy Bishop, bless the Tsar on his way to Novgorod,' commanded Ivan's henchman.

But Philip would not oblige. In the manner of all Orthodox holy men, like old Father Cleopa at Sihastria, he knew that his end was near. Three days earlier he had warned his keepers, 'The end of my *podvig* [Christian feat of endurance] is approaching.' He was suffocated with a pillow.

One might argue that Ivan's murder of Philip was equivalent to, and no more or less dramatic than, Henry II of England's solution to the same power struggle between Church and State with the murder of Thomas Becket on the altar of Canterbury cathedral in 1170. But Thomas Becket was allying himself with the temporal as well as the spiritual power of the Roman Pope, while Philip was a passionate patriot who never questioned Ivan's divine right to rule Russia. The only threat he represented was a spiritual one.

The high drama of Philip's murder could be said to mark the moment when Russia blatantly betrayed the Byzantine *symphonia* ideal. After Philip's death Ivan gave up any pretence of operating in harmonious partnership with the Church. The clergy trembled and retreated behind clouds of incense or escaped into the frozen wastes to build hermitages. The interests of the new Russian state and its autocracy were paramount, and subsequent attempts to right the old Byzantine balance ended more or less badly. A father-and-son kind of *symphonia* was achieved in 1613 when teenage Mikhail, the first Romanov tsar, appointed his father Patriarch and allowed him to misrule in his place. In the seventeenth century, Patriarch Nikon overruled a tsar and succeeded in provoking a horribly damaging schism in the Church. Peter the Great, who was inspired by the example of the docile Anglican Church of the eighteenth century, took Ivan's treatment of Philip and the Church to its logical formal conclusion by subjugating the Church to the State and abolishing the patriarchate. Without a translation of the Bible into the vernacular, which had played such a crucial part in the development of the individual's sense of right and wrong in most of Europe, Peter's reforms were a disaster. A first full translation of the Bible from Old Slavonic into modern Russian was at last printed in 1876, after Marx's *Das Kapital*. Peter's religious reforms turned the Russian Church into a withered arm of a brutally unjust state, so that by the nineteenth century there was an empty space in the hearts of Russia's new urban masses and educated intelligentsia especially – a space waiting to be filled by the more material consolations of Karl Marx. The Church, patently powerless to build Heaven on Earth in a country battling to catch up with the West's industrial revolution, could only promise justice in the after-life. Socialism, the new religion, promised justice here on Earth. An intrepid English journalist who accompanied hundreds of Russians on a pilgrimage to Jerusalem just before the outbreak of the First World War, witnessed a dramatic proof of the tragic divide in Russian society. He wrote that the human cargo on the boat sailing across the Black Sea was split: '. . . all the while the monk was preaching this true-blue sermon of Russian conservatism up above, the ship's carpenter was preaching red-hot social democracy below'.[xvii]

An eminent historian of Russia has recently and persuasively argued that the 'irremediable weakness of the Orthodox Church was the most fateful of the deficiencies of Tsarist Russia'.[xviii] The post-Communist Russian Church is weak still, but literally and metaphorically regaining lost ground.

Vanya and I had had to solicit the blessing of Patriarch Alexy II himself to secure an audience with Philip's modern successor as Abbot of Solovetsky monastery, Archimandrite Iosif. A satellite telephone link between the Moscow patriarchate and Solovetsky had brought him word of our impending arrival. A golden-bearded, ruddy-cheeked man in the prime of life, we found him in his office on the third floor of the monastery's only fully restored building. Seated on a carved-wood throne upholstered in purple velvet, he was flicking through some papers while, to his left, a computer endlessly scrolled the words of the Hesychasts' Jesus Prayer, 'Lord Jesus Christ, Son of God, have mercy upon us!', across its royal blue screen. Otherwise, his office was as functional as any Soviet bureaucrat's. His manner was, correspondingly, warily Soviet until I explained that I had travelled all this way to see him because Solovetsky seemed to have played a vital role in almost everything that has happened to Russia in the past half millennium. There was Philip of Solovetsky's brave stand against Tsar Ivan, Solovetsky as the stronghold of the Old Believers whose last hopeless gasp of resistance to the State tore the Church apart in the seventeenth century, Solovetsky as a monk-manned fortress against the Swedes in Peter the Great's time, Solovetsky's heroic resistance under a hail of cannonballs lobbed at it by British warships at the start of the Crimean war, Solovetsky as the first gulag camp, Solovetsky as one of the first monasteries to be reopened after the collapse of Communism in 1991, and in 1997, Solovetsky's monastery, depicted on a new banknote, but to all true believers' horror, bereft of its gold crosses – as it had been in godless Soviet times.

He liked that synopsis enough to define history for me in what I assumed for a moment was the old Orthodox way, until I recognized it as more in line with Soviet thinking. 'History, as a rule,' he began, 'is the voice of the people . . . and the voice of the people is God's voice,' he added quickly.

He was just warming to his subject with a lament for the continuous 'golden thread' of Solovetsky's spirituality, which Lenin had snapped by turning the place into a gulag camp where 'over a thousand' clergymen had perished, when I interrupted him. 'But surely something went very wrong for Solovetsky and the Russian Church long before the Bolsheviks took over?' I was thinking of Abbot Philip and Ivan the Terrible, but said, 'Even in Tsarist times this monastery, like many others, housed a dreadful prison, didn't it?'

'Yes . . .' said Archimandrite Iosif with a wary look in his eye. 'The monastery could not oppose the tsars' will . . . The tsars were probably not using the monastery in quite the right way . . .'

Just prior to our meeting with Archimandrite Iosif, Vanya and I had spent an hour in Solovetsky's little municipal library – a shambolic and dusty room without electric light because the bill had not been paid – struggling to sift some nuggets of fact from the dross of atheist propaganda in a Soviet-era work about the monastery. We had gleaned that for about 150 years, until the end of the eighteenth century, the monastery had enjoyed a reputation as the most dreaded penitentiary in all Russia. Prisoners were thrown into tiny underground cells with hay-covered wooden floors and left to rot there for decades, barely sustained by bread and water supplied by monks through a hatch in the ceiling. The author estimated that four hundred prisoners had perished in these holes, including a Roman Catholic Spanish monk sentenced for proselytizing, and a counterfeiter of banknotes. In the sixteenth century, Maksim the Greek, an Athonite monk who had lambasted the Russian clergy for being 'like some sort of blood-sucking beast', languished here awhile. 'Imprisonment here brought some people to repentance, of course,' Archimandrite Iosif was saying. 'Some people needed to spend a period of their lives like that in order to choose the right spiritual path afterwards.' Clearly, he was not about to plunge back into history with me, back as far as the collapse of the *symphonia* ideal and Philip's martyrdom. He seemed more inclined to reinforce the Russian Orthodox Church's later inglorious role as the withered arm of a repressive, rather than law-governed, state. But this was not all that surprising. Our meeting was taking place just a month before the catastrophic rouble crash of August 1998. His thoughts were naturally running on Boris Yeltsin's Russia, more terrifyingly lawless, even, than the tsars' version.

Without the vital underpinning of centuries of law, Russia's heady love affair with the West and democracy was fast coming to grief. Many Russian churchmen, like Archimandrite Iosif, were sneering at the new freedoms Russians were now able to enjoy, which seemed to amount to little more than committing crimes and consuming western pornography. They were beginning to crow, 'We told you so.' The three pillars of the late tsarist Russian state ideology – Orthodoxy, Autocracy and Nationhood – still figure prominently in the minds of the majority of Russian churchmen, even the youngest. The Communists had toppled one of those pillars, 'Orthodoxy', by declaring an atheist state, but they had preserved the other two by maintaining a recognizably autocratic system and by remaining hostile to Russia's traditional western enemies. In the eyes of Russian churchmen today,

Boris Yeltsin had committed a more heinous crime than the Soviets ever had by smashing those last two pillars. Since 1991, Russia's 'Autocracy' – the patriarchally repressive State – has dissolved into a scary chaos called democracy, and Russia's 'Nationhood' has been rudely violated by western consumerism, Nato's eastward advance and heretic Protestant and Catholic missionaries. Measured against that dreadful double demolition job, Yeltsin's reinstatement of the first pillar, 'Orthodoxy', and his return of all Church properties confiscated after 1917, count for almost nothing.

One begins to see how the apparently unreasonable closeness of atheist former Communists to the Russian Orthodox Church today has come about. Both groups are agreed that Russia must immediately rebuild the two missing pillars. A strong leader coupled with a self-imposed quarantine from the contaminating West would set Russia to rights, they believe.

'A Russian is made in such a way that he can never become a European, a westerner, in his habits and ways and character,' declared Archimandrite Iosif. Frowning as he tidied the papers on his desk, he added, 'I don't think the time has come for Russians to have close contacts with the West. It's no accident that our ancestors were always opposed to such contacts.'

So saying he rose to his feet and walked us back down to the courtyard where his monks were still hard at work, chopping and digging. Chatting about the island's frequent power cuts, his frozen waterpipes and the air service reduced to one flight in and out a week, the Archimandrite concluded apocalyptically, 'You see how it is. At the end of the twentieth century civilization is leaving us. And where will you be staying while you're here?'

'Oh – I don't know . . .' I said, casting a doubtful eye at the crumbling monastery buildings, 'We couldn't stay somewhere in the monastery, could we?'

'No,' he said and, whipping a mobile phone from the folds of his cassock, he called Solovetsky's only hotel.

The long log cabin that is Solovetsky's hotel is almost as improbable a sight as the monastery. Its proprietor Sergei and his wife Lyuba work as hard as the monks for the few light months of the year when the pilgrim boats arrive and, if they are lucky, a handful of dollar-bearing western biologists drawn here by the whales, which spawn off the island's north-east coast.

The little establishment was full, but kind Lyuba had told the archimandrite that she could accommodate us in a flat they owned at the far end of the village. She walked us there, back past the monastery and the ruin of the old naval-base building, which departing soldiers had stripped of anything useful before setting on fire. We skirted the Holy Lake, choppy and dark in the wind. I struggled to picture it as it must have looked at the end of the nineteenth century, heaving with the winter-pale bodies of pilgrims benefiting from the blessed waters, swimmers struck so dumb with sacred awe that if one dared to talk, another would admonish him, 'Quiet! Don't you know what sort of a place this is? Can you imagine how many saints have swum here?'[xix] A nearby signpost reminded those blessed bathers that there on Solovetsky they were 4,818 *versty* from Tsargrad, Constantinople. By the end of the century some thirty thousand pilgrims a year were sailing here on monastery-owned boats with gold crosses glinting on their mastheads. The excellently organized and exceedingly wealthy monastery, with its six hundred monks, fed and accommodated all those who made it to Solovetsky. Pilgrims bought vouchers – thirty copecks a prayer, one and a half roubles for a prayer with holy water, and so on. A narrow-gauge railway line ferried them around their holy holiday camp.

The novelist Dostoyevsky noted the Russians' extraordinary love of pilgrimaging. The Russian peasant, he wrote, in his *The Brothers Karamazov*, 'may suddenly . . . abandon everything and go off on a pilgrimage for his soul's salvation, or perhaps he will suddenly set fire to his native village, and perhaps do both. There are a good many "contemplatives" among the peasantry.'[xx] After the Holy Land and Mount Athos, Solovetsky was ordinary Russians' top holiday destination and the Holy Lake its chief attraction. Only the duty-free shops of Dubai and the beaches of southern Cyprus exert anything like the same pull on most Russians, these days.

Lyuba escorted us on past the island's clanking electricity gener-
ator, past sturdy log cabins built to house the gulag camp guards and,
still further, to some newer but already derelict-looking blocks of flats.
In one of these, a dismally dark place with barred windows, she
bustled about making beds and apologizing for the lack of hot water.
I peered out through the bars, at a yard filled with stray dogs, weeds
and a shed full of rusting iron.

'Lyuba,' I asked, 'does having monks in the monastery again help
the island?'

'Oh, yes, on the moral plane it helps. Little by little the dirtiness
in people's souls is being cleaned out. People are not against the
monks any more as they were when they first came back in 1991. You
have to remember that there were people living in the monastery
until then, with shops and so on . . .' When she left, Vanya and I
unpacked the emergency supply of Snickers chocolate bars and
consumed one with guilty enjoyment. Snickers have become the
symbol of everything so many Russians hate about this most recent
bungled attempt to westernize their country. *Snickerizatsiya* – Snick-
erization, is a pejorative term for westernization. Archimandrite Iosif,
I thought, had probably never tasted a Snickers.

It was eleven p.m. but still as light as a late-summer afternoon when
we set out for a walk along another dirt track, through the forest and
clouds of mosquitoes, lakes to our right and the sky-coloured sea –
just visible through the trees – to our left. Vanya wanted to find one
of Abbot Philip's finest innovations, the shoreside fish-ponds, which
had provided his monks with fresh protein when they were not
fasting.

There was something otherworldly about Solovetsky, although
not in the spiritually uplifting sense, we thought. It occurred to me
that the island might have been a rough sketch of the world,
discarded by God in favour of something better-proportioned and
more harmonious – something a little kinder to life. The rocks on its
shores are too big and a lot of the vegetation oddly stunted, presumably by the wind. There are too many lakes, far too many mosquitoes

in summer and too much wind. Its perpetually light summer nights are almost as unbalancing as a permanently strip-lit prison cell.

We never found the fish-ponds or, more disappointingly, as far as I was concerned, any sign of an Old Believers' cemetery. The vast number of devoutly Russian Orthodox faithful who staged a last doomed defence of Holy Russia against the overweening tyranny of the State in the seventeenth century, the Old Believers' violent objection to a high-handed patriarch's decision to force the Russian Church into line with the Greek Church of the time, was what brought about a schism in a Church already weakened by Ivan the Terrible's murder of Philip. Patriarch Nikon was a Byzantine imperialist who thought that the first step along the glorious way to reuniting Eastern Orthodox Christendom and winning Tsargrad back from the Ottomans was to eliminate the differences that had arisen between the Greek and Russian practice of Eastern Orthodoxy. But the Old Believers, as they came to be known, feared change like the devil himself and vehemently protested that his minor adjustments spat in the face of centuries of Orthodoxy – literally, Right Worship. How could the Russian Orthodox Church, entirely based on the rigorous safeguarding of the ancient Byzantine tradition, have been mistaken all that time? Had such a brave defender of Russia against the Mongols as St Sergius been wrong to cross himself with two fingers instead of three? Of course not, they reasoned. Was it possible to tamper with the calendar to make the year begin in January instead of September? No, blasphemy! The world and time must have begun in the autumn: how otherwise could Eve have picked an apple in the Garden of Eden? Apples do not ripen in January. To these arch-conservatives, Patriarch Nikon's reforms heralded the advent of the Anti-Christ and the imminent end of the world. St John the Theologian's Apocalypse was nigh.

It so happened that the obnoxious Patriarch Nikon had started his ecclesiastical career as an unpopular monk on Solovetsky, so that when his order to use the new church books arrived here from Moscow, the abbot of the time felt justified in replying in the following fashion:

There are many untrue things in these books ... nothing but the writings of the Servants of the Anti-Christ ... Why have you brought us this anti-Christian learning? ... Nikon is not a patriarch but a heretic. He's not a preacher to souls but a cruel wolf, a servant of Satan ... Russia has been Orthodox for all these years and it cannot be Un-Orthodox ... We don't accept this new faith ... We'll suffer great trials and we'll joyfully accept the end of life if the great Tsar wills it, and we'll decently appear at Christ's Last Judgement![xxi]

Some twenty thousand Old Believers, from the highest born to the humblest in the land, suffered death rather than change an iota of their Orthodox ritual. Twenty thousand locked themselves in churches and set fire to themselves rather than die 'un-Orthodox'. Others fled into the uninhabited wastes of Siberia, out of reach of persecution. Still others made their way to Solovetsky where, alongside the monks in the fortress monastery, they withstood a terrible eight-year siege by the Tsar's army. At last a monk betrayed their cause. The bastion of Old Belief was emptied and repopulated with followers of Nikon, but modern scholarship on the subject of the Old Believers suggests that they were right all along. Their old Russian forms of worship *were* truer to the ancient Byzantine original than those of the Greeks at the time. To this day, however, the Russian Orthodox Church has not apologized to the Old Believers, who continue, in shrinking pockets here and there, to hold their own services in their own churches. Alexander Solzhenitsyn has identified a lack of contrition in this matter of the Old Believers as one of the biggest ills besetting the Russian Orthodox Church today.

There is no graveyard on Solovetsky to tell the Old Believers' tale, not even a plaque to commemorate the siege. But, then, neither are there any tell-tale traces of Solovetsky's years as an annexe of Hell after 1917. Since 1996, the work of one devoted layman, a heartrending memorial of photographs, clothes, identity cards and implements of the thousands who perished in the Soviet Union's first gulag camp, has graced a room in the monastery's museum, and the monks have erected a couple of wooden crosses on the island. But there is no graveyard. No gulag survivor has stayed to make his home here and there are no graffiti on the thick stone monastery walls. One has to turn to Solzhenitsyn and to the memoirs of Russia's greatest living historian, Dmitri Likhachev, to begin to re-create the Solovetsky of that era. Solzhenitsyn's description of the hellish goings-on at the White Sea gulag camp in his *The Gulag Archipelago* is almost incoherent with rage against Soviet man's inhumanity to man. The words tumble over each other.

> Or in summer 'on the stump', which meant naked among the mosquitoes. But in that event one had to keep an eye on the culprit; whereas if he was bound naked to a tree, the mosquitoes would look after things themselves, And then they could put whole companies out in the snow for disobedience. Or they might drive a person in the marsh muck up to his neck and keep him there. And then there was another way; to hitch up a horse in empty shafts and fasten the culprit's legs to the shafts; then the guard mounted the house and kept on driving the horse through a forest cut until the groans and the cries from behind simply came to an end.[xxii]

The historian Likhachev served a sentence on Solovetsky in 1929 because a friend had cabled him a bad-joke birthday telegram from the Pope and someone else had reported him for owning a book entitled *International Jewry*. In his memoirs he recalls how the guards herding convicts off the ships and onto the island had gleefully warned them, 'The law here is not Sovietsky, it's Solovetsky,' then screamed obscenities, the mildest of which was 'I'll make you suck snot from dead bodies.' Likhachev had discreetly crossed himself on arrival before the gates of the monastery. 'I treated Solovki not like a prison but as a holy place,' he remembers.

Likhachev describes the monastery into which the vast majority of prisoners were crammed – a number greater than the population of Belgium, he says – as heaving like 'a giant ant-hill'. Prisoners were divided into fifteen units. The sixth unit was full of the clergy, who made up a fifth of the prison population and were the only people deemed trustworthy enough to guard the monastery gates. The eleventh was for workaday criminals, rapists, thieves and murderers. The seventh was full of members of the hated 'creative intelligentsia'. Likhachev was in the fourteenth, sleeping with his legs in the sleeves of his fur coat for fear of the teenage thieves who shared his cell. He only escaped death by firing squad by going missing the day he saw his name on a list of those sentenced. Solovetsky haunts him still. 'Clearly someone else was taken in my place and I would live for two – for me, and for the one they took for me . . .'[xxiii] he wrote in 1995. A fêted historian in the new Russia, Likhachev is in his nineties now and so well respected that he could pen a note to President Yeltsin in July 1998, urging him to forget politics for a day and join in a collective gesture of repentance by attending the long overdue St Petersburg burial of the last Romanov tsar, Nicholas II, and his family, whose broken skeletons had been discovered in a forest pit in the Urals in 1991.

During Likhachev's stay on Solovetsky a few monks were still there. Any prepared to toe the new regime's line were employed to show the prisoners how to fish for the delicious herring they shipped south to grace the Kremlin dinner tables. The mass of clergy imprisoned on Solovetsky were those who had eagerly participated in the Church's belated attempt to purge and renew itself in the tiny interval between Tsar Nicholas II's abdication in March 1917 and the Bolshevik revolution in November, so had repudiated the new regime's atheism. On Solovetsky four dissident bishops secretly ordained priests and heroically plotted ways of holding Easter services. Churchmen rendezvoused furtively, in a forest clearing they called the Church of the Holy Trinity, whose dome was the sky. By 1927 they had organized sufficiently to draw up a letter of protest to the new Patriarch who had reached an accommodation with the Bolsheviks. It said:

The Church recognizes the existence of the spiritual principle; Communism denies it. The Church believes in the Living God, Creator of the world, Guide of its life; Communism does not admit His existence ... The Church believes in the steadfast principles of morality, justice and law; Communism looks upon them as the conditional results of class struggle, and values moral questions only from the standpoint of their usefulness. The Church instils the feeling that humility elevates man's soul; Communism abases man through pride.[xxiv]

This was the voice of Abbot Philip, raised again four hundred years after his death in exactly the same cause. But this time the case was more urgent and much more hopeless. Ivan the Terrible had never tried to abolish the Church, only to overrule it. Westernizing Peter the Great had abolished the patriarchate and forced priests to turn spies in the confessional, but even he had not questioned the value of the Church. Early in his career he had fled to St Sergius' monastery at Sergeyev Posad for shelter from his enemies, and on a visit to Solovetsky, he had sung tenor in the monastery choir. But here were the Bolsheviks, not only abolishing the Church but proclaiming the death of God at gunpoint. Most of that protest's signatories died on Solovetsky or were killed soon after their release.

At half past midnight the sky was still a twilit pearly pink behind the shadowed monastery domes, the Holy Lake and the dark surrounding sea. Vanya and I were already weary of that prison island and its torturing perpetual light.

The next day was a blustery Sunday. Gusts of wind whipped at the surface of the Holy Lake and whistled through the holes in the monastery's walls, around which Archimandrite Iosif and his monks were ritually processing. Their rich vestments flapping, they were stopping at each of the eight wall-towers to chant and flick a holy-water blessing. It would have been a grand and glittering spectacle had the wind not shredded the thread of the monks' chanting, buffeted the holy banners they carried and blown clouds of incense back in their faces. Vanya spotted the beatifically smiling deaf-mute and his mother who had accompanied us from Archangel among the group of bedraggled pilgrims and locals who were tagging along behind, zipping up their anoraks and retying their headscarves. Waving to them, we split off from the procession and repaired to the warmth of Lyuba's hotel dining room, where we had arranged to meet one of the island's schoolteachers.

Oleg, a gaunt young man with a thin beard, bowed shoulders and the round, metal-rimmed spectacles of a Russian intellectual, looked sadder than anyone else we had encountered on Solovetsky, almost numb with the impotent loneliness of one of Turgenev's 'superfluous' men. It struck me that the lot of the intellectual in most of Orthodox Europe is unenviable. The Latin derivation of the term used to describe the class of higher-educated and politically engaged Russians in the nineteenth century – the *intelligentsiya* – is itself an obvious clue to these people's outsider status in a culture that traditionally prized a spiritual way of knowing and the soul way above the mere intellect. In Orthodox culture intellectuals are foreigners and misfits who, nourished on secular learning, have all but supped with the devil. Perverted by the heretic, humanist West, they ignore the mystery of the soul to take an evil pride in the power of human creativity and reasoning. The mystically religious last tsar of Russia, Nicholas II, was so little a westernizing intellectual he wanted the very word *intelligentsiya* erased from the language. 'How I dislike that word!'[xxv] he once exclaimed. Nicholas II and Stalin, the tyrant once destined for Orthodox priesthood, shared a distrust of intellectuals and Jews.

In the mid-nineteenth century there were attempts to heal the fatal divide in Russian society. Hundreds of well-meaning intellectuals rushed out of the universities to the provinces to explain to the peasants how they could go about improving their miserable lot, but they were met with distrust and scorn. Russia's nineteenth-century Slavophile movement was a part of the Russian intelligentsia's effort to get closer to the masses by reconciling Orthodoxy with the modern world of reason and science. The Slavophiles cogently argued against the modernizing westernizers of the time that, for all its material progress, the West had lost its soul and its spiritual way. Over-reliant on human reason and vaingloriously ambitious, the West was doomed, they said. Steeped in Byzantine history and Orthodoxy's democratically communal *sobornost* tradition, they believed that if Russia and her Church could only return to the era before Peter the Great she could be immeasurably superior to the West. Today, that old split in Russia's intelligentsia, between westernizers and Slavophiles, has reappeared and is getting wider by the day. The Westernizers are currently losing the battle. Slavophilia, of course, strays perilously close to and often blends into the heresy of Phyletism, Russian religious nationalism.

It was some time before I plucked up the courage to ask Oleg the question to which I had sought an answer from the moment we had arrived on the island. 'Oleg, why have the monks come back here? It still feels more like a prison than a holy place because so much evil has happened here. Wouldn't it be better to leave this place alone?'

'No, no,' he replied impatiently. 'The evil is exactly why there must be monks and life here again. Patriarch Alexy II thinks Solovetsky's so important that he's been here twice in the past seven years.'

Oleg turned out to be a devoutly Orthodox Slavophile intellectual. As much of a newcomer to Solovetsky as the young monks, he had moved here from St Petersburg two years before, hoping that he and his wife could live the good and virtuous life on Solovetsky, out of reach of the hideously westernized 'new Russia with the *mafiya* and so on'.

As we sat there taking tea, while the wind rattled at the windows, he told me how he had come by his Orthodox faith. In the early 1980s he had enrolled at St Petersburg University to study philosophy, intent on discovering the meaning of life. Force-fed a diet of Marxism he had soon sickened. It was too materialist to stomach. He and many of his classmates turned to other western philosophers, but soon found their rationalism equally nauseating.

'When we saw that science and philosophy could not help us, many of us came to religion,' he explained. 'We were not doing anything new, only what so many nineteenth-century Slavophiles and Russian philosophers did, even the ones who were Marxists to begin with. A lot of Russian intellectuals are now returning to the purity of the Hesychast tradition . . .'

That made perfect sense. Hesychasm's spiritual light burns brightest whenever Orthodox empires are threatened and dying. When the Ottomans were battering at the gates of fourteenth-century Bulgaria, Serbia and Byzantium, when Roman Catholicism was gaining its Uniate foothold in eighteenth-century Romania, when the Mongols ruled fourteenth-century Russia, and again, when the new Marxist creed was spreading in nineteenth-century Russia, there you found Hesychasm. Today, when western materialism and rationalism are the chief threats to Orthodoxy, it is thriving in the monasteries of Moldavia, among Russian intellectuals and on Mount Athos. Against all the odds and with all their hearts, the guardians of this tradition insist that the Almighty has a plan of which the Orthodox are privy to the details: there is hope of salvation on Earth because 'God became man so that Man might become God'.

But Oleg was tragically aware that his overdeveloped intellect was a barrier to finding peace in the True Faith. 'Most of the priests here on Solovetsky are not intellectuals so they can't understand my problems and my way of thinking,' he said, 'but recently I have begun to realize that my spiritual father at the monastery, old Father German, can help me even if he doesn't understand me . . . There was a time last winter when things were very bad for us here – very bad indeed . . . Somehow Father German knew that because he came to us and he helped. Maybe that is the energy of the Hesychast . . .'

I feared our talk was only deepening Oleg's misery.

Kind, motherly Lyuba was waiting to tell us that if we had really set our hearts on leaving Solovetsky before the next week's plane arrived, she had a friend who could sail us to the mainland on his home-made yacht that very afternoon. Vanya's delight at the prospect outweighed any qualms I had about the vessel's sea-worthiness.

By mid-afternoon the sky had cleared, the sun was shining and the yacht was moored by the pier in front of the monastery. Our skipper was a sunburned man in his forties, moonlighting from his job on the Russian railways. A sailor to the depths of his soul he had patiently, faithfully pieced together his boat, just as the Soviet Union was collapsing, just when everything he needed was either in short supply or of bad quality. With a piece of bathroom fitting here and something that belonged on a car or a train there, the *Antar* was an object of rare beauty.

Soon we were slicing out across the glittering sea, sails full, tiller steady and the sun in our eyes, free. The skipper put Vanya on the tiller and jumped below deck, to reappear with a tin mug of tea and an anorak for me. And, a moment later, the crackly strains of the Beatles hymn about Mother Mary's wise words in times of trouble floated out of the cabin and across the sea. I must have been simultaneously moved by the skipper's kindness, seized by nostalgia for the simple-hearted sixties, and overcome with relief that all Solovetsky's dark past and unpromising future were dissolving in the shining sea of a dazzling present, because I cried.

It was early evening by the time the *Antar* landed us at the desolate wasteland of Kem's shipyard, the infamous marshalling point for thousands of Solovetsky-bound convicts from all over the Soviet Union during the 1920s and 1930s. We hitched a ride into the equally desolate wasteland of Kem itself and found lodging for the night with the town's only priest, Father Igor. Like his church, which had been converted into a sports hall in the 1970s, his flat was undergoing extensive repairs, but he made us as comfortable as he could and seemed glumly glad of company. Father Igor was young, a Muscovite and a former producer for a pop band whose name – Mongol Post – rang a bell with Vanya. He had come by his faith by accident, he said. One day, after a particularly gruelling tour with his band, he had taken himself off to a monastery to rest and recuperate and somehow just stayed there, until he decided to become a priest and had then been sent here to Kem. 'Well, of course, nothing happens by accident. It's God's will,' he concluded morosely, dunking a cake in his tea.

'But what can you do for these people?' I asked him. 'This town is so poor and there are no jobs . . .'

Vanya and I had been dismayed by what little we had seen of

Kem, with its crumbling concrete blocks and cracking pavements. In its one open eatery, a dim-lit cavernous hall filled with angry young denim-clad drunks, as bowed and unsteady as very old men, we had kept quiet and eaten fast. On our way back to Father Igor's flat, the sight of a young woman, in a garish mini-skirt, impossibly high heels and sunglasses, stumbling around the potholes in the light northern night had filled us with a mixture of horror and admiration. Kem was like a person emerging barely conscious from an almighty drinking binge. It had the half-inhabited feel of a place barely surviving the aftermath of a nuclear attack.

'What can I do for these people? Nothing,' said Father Igor. 'Whole generations are lost. I can try to catch the children, and perhaps the ones under twenty, but all the rest are lost. I can only honestly serve the liturgy.' We fell to discussing the forthcoming reburial of the remains of Tsar Nicholas II and his family. As politely as I could, I asked him why, when scientists had confirmed the authenticity of the bones with exhaustive DNA tests, the Church was still stubbornly withholding its approval for, and the Patriarch refusing to officiate at, the funeral.

'Those DNA scientists were westerners, weren't they?' he replied, as if it stood to reason that being westerners made them incapable of objectivity where anything Russian was concerned.

'Yes?'

'We cannot trust those tests. There is the same risk with this as with accepting westerners' version of our history. In your history books it says that by 1917 Russia was too tired and disorganized to go on fighting the First World War. That is not the truth. No,' he said, pouring himself another cup of tea, 'that is only the western version. The truth is that the Russian army was easily strong enough to march to Berlin and even as far as Tsargrad, to win back everything for Orthodoxy. But we were forced to sign a cease-fire and then the Germans sent Lenin to St Petersburg to stop the war, start the revolution and destroy Orthodoxy. That's how it was.'

Where had I heard this before? Father Giorgios Metallinos, the bristlingly energetic Greek theology professor I had met in Athens in the spring, had sung me the same suspect song. The Greek rendition had shocked me. This Russian one – with its DNA prelude and minor embellishments – frightened me.

North Russia

Thump. Bang. Thump. Bang! My favourite Russian pop song again. 'My star is far away, and the night is so long . . .' Vanya and I had been on the road for days, sleeping on night trains, eating in squalid station buffets, snacking on Snickers, catching slow buses from one crumbling town to another through untidy, empty countryside, and developing a perverse taste for thudding disco beats.

In Belomorsk, a desolate town on the White Sea at the head of the Soviet convict-built White Sea canal, we had met another lonely priest, with vodka on his breath, tears in his eyes and a wide, gap-toothed smile. Father Sergei's predecessor had been shot in 1938 and his makeshift church was a barely converted savings bank. A grizzly bear of a man in an outsize cassock with a thick leather belt slung around his waist, he lived – with the two cats he wore draped over his broad shoulders – in a tiny broken-down wooden hut without running water. It was crammed with books, a set of crockery decorated with views of Solovetsky monastery, a pair of heavy iron weights, an old radio tuned to the BBC's Russian-language service and a large collection of rosaries.

We accompanied him on a walk through high nettles, down to the river to collect a bucket of water for our tea. In winter, he told us, he uses a wooden pole to break ice a metre and half thick, before hooking a little ladder to the rim and descending to the icy waters below for a dip. Just before squeezing around his kitchen table on low stools, the three of us turned to face the icons while he muttered five Lord-have-mercys. Inadvertently dripping strawberry jam from a tea-spoon on to his already spotted cassock, he complained of the crippling monthly tax he was required to pay to the Moscow patriar-chate. I was outraged on his behalf. Surely the Moscow patriarchate should be paying *him* to live in a place like this? 'Can't you ask to be moved to another town or at least to better accommodation?" I asked him.

'Ho, ho.' He chuckled grimly. 'No one would replace me up here – there's no money in a place like this. With a congregation of only about sixty poor people I can hardly afford the tax, let alone better accommodation. Anyway, this place is right for someone like me. These little houses are known as the hermitages. They were built for the town's widows and a few Old Believers at the end of the last century—'

'Are there any Old Believers still left here?' I interrupted him eagerly.

'No, the last old woman – a very good and educated sort of person – died last year ... You know, anyway, I'd rather live here than in one of the new blocks on the edge of town where some of my parishioners are. That's Hell!'

Slowly heading south, we had reached Lodeinoye Polye, the lakeside town where Peter the Great's navy was born, and hitched a ride out to the monastery, which had grown out of the hermitage of the mosquito-bitten Hesychast, St Alexander Svirsky. As hugely fortified as Solovetsky, it looked as anciently ruined as Pompeii. Seventy years of Communism in a climate like Russia's made it impossible to imagine its 1910 heyday. The roofs were caved in and the walls crumbling. Long grass covered the courtyard and a few patients from the psychiatric hospital that still occupied one of the monastery buildings were going about some menial tasks with seven young monks to oversee works. One happily informed us that, after almost eighty years spent mouldering in the bowels of St Petersburg's Museum of Military Medicine, St Alexander Svirsky's perfumed remains had returned home.

The entire back wall of the church was covered in a lurid eighteenth-century fresco of the Last Judgement. On the wrong side of the River of Hell were Russia's, and therefore the Church's, traditional enemies, a far greater number and far better detailed than those of Romania as depicted on the walls of Moldavia's painted monasteries. There were Germans in eighteenth-century brocade coats and tricorn hats, Tartars, turbaned Turks, long-bearded Old Testament Jews, Catholic Poles, Greeks (presumably on account of their willingness to betray Orthodoxy by contemplating union with heretic Rome back in fifteenth-century Byzantium), Finns and Arabs.

We had boarded another southbound night train and tarried just long enough in St Petersburg to catch a crowded suburban train out to leafy Pushkin, formerly known as Tsarskoye Selo, the eighteenth- and nineteenth-century tsars' country retreat. Wandering around an exhibition in one of the old imperial palaces of items pertaining to the lives of the last Russian tsars, we had attached ourselves to the fringes of a Russian tour group. Its guide was waxing passionate about Alexander III's golden helmet with its Byzantine double-headed eagle, about a plethora of military uniforms, about the last tsarevich's donkey's fancy harness and some fine white dresses. But it was the terrible fate of the last tsar and his family that inspired her to heights of eloquence.

'The last tsar's eldest daughter, Olga, was on the point of getting married when the Bolshevik revolution happened. She was so happy that she hadn't, so glad to stay and suffer with her family! And her mother, Tsarina Alexandra, declared that she would rather lower herself to washing floors in Russia than flee from her adopted country in its darkest hour. Then, of course, Nicholas II's life was simply one long *podvig*,' she was telling the group. 'His life and death can only be compared to that of Jesus Christ, who was also killed by Jews. I'm sure you all know that Jewish Cabbalistic signs were found on the walls of the cellar where they were murdered on that terrible night exactly seventy years ago . . .'

This talk of Jewish murderers and Cabbalistic signs is only a rumour but it is one that has gained especially wide credence among Russia's clergy. They are finding it extremely useful in their struggle to reconcile their hatred for the Communists who killed the Tsar with their sympathy for today's ex-Communists' determination to rebuild the lost pillars of 'Nationhood' and 'Autocracy'. By harping on the huge part played by Jewish Russian Communists in the early

Bolshevik movement, and therefore presumably the Tsar's murder, they can neatly exonerate ethnic Russian Communists and not embarrass their new allies.

From St Petersburg we had journeyed on west by train to Pskov where a new plaque affixed to the wall of the station building had reminded us again of Tsar Nicholas II. In March 1917 his train had stopped off at Pskov on its way to St Petersburg from Russia's criminally under-supplied and mismanaged western front. He had found no guard of honour waiting and an official disrespectfully wearing galoshes, both of which phenomena he interpreted as bad omens. And rightly, because he was soon informed that not only were the politicians in St Petersburg urging him to abdicate but his generals no longer trusted him as their commander-in-chief. In his luxury train-carriage salon he had resigned his God-given throne. 'What else could I have done,' he wrote at the time, eerily echoing the sentiments of both Jesus Christ and the paranoid Ivan the Terrible, 'when everyone has betrayed me?'[xxvi]

Nicholas II seems to have been faced with the same conundrum as his dreaded sixteenth-century predecessor Ivan: how to reconcile running a vast and vulnerable empire with the proper observation of Christ's commandments? How to be a God-appointed autocrat *and* a good Christian? How to rule a modern state in the style of a long obsolete demi-god? But instead of boldly challenging God, as Ivan the Terrible had repeatedly, Nicholas adopted a more passively fatalistic attitude than even Greece's first pious president when he had stepped into that little white church in Nafplio in 1831. A chief courtier has outlined Tsar Nicholas's state of mind at the time of his abdication. The Tsar, wrote Alexander Mossolov, had,

> ... an unshakeable faith in the providential nature of his high office. His mission emanated from God, for his actions he was responsible only to his conscience and to God ... Responsible to the elements that are not reason and at times are contrary to reason. Responsible to imponderables; to the mysticism that steadily increased its hold over him ...'[xxvii]

Russia's last tsar had done the very thing Ivan had always refused to do. Dashing off to the front to hamper Russia's war effort, he had left a 'priest', in the shape of the holy man Rasputin, to run the realm. But no emperor of doomed Late Byzantium, during the zenith of mystical Hesychasm, not even Emperor Andronicus II, who humbly submitted himself to the authority of a martinet Hesychast patriarch, had so carelessly relaxed his grip on the practical business of ruling. At the time of his abdication, the vast majority of Russians still held Nicholas II in precisely the same reverence as the Byzantines had held their emperors five centuries before. An entry in the diary of the imperial family's spiritual father at the time of the Tsar's imprisonment by the Bolsheviks at Tsarskoye Selo, attests to that. Archpriest Afanasy Beliaev considered himself '. . . favoured by God's grace to become the mediator between the Heavenly Ruler and the earthly one. Beside me was standing the one whom no one else living on earth rises superior to. Until this time, this was our God-given Anointed Sovereign, a Russian Orthodox Tsar . . .'[xxviii]

The trauma of seeing Russia's God-given Anointed Sovereign reduced to the status of a prisoner chopping his own firewood in the gardens of Tsarskoye Selo must have paled into insignificance beside the nightmare of the revolution and the civil war. But it was surely as great as that suffered by old Gennadius who, when Constantinople fell at last, could hardly tell who he was any more.

And that trauma is still unhealed. The beautiful dream of Byzantium, with its idealistic insistence on a Christian Orthodox emperor's duty to rule his dominions as God ruled Heaven, with the Church by his side, was smashed in Russia in 1917 – no matter that the reality had long ago ceased to tally with it. Having killed off the Emperor and God, the Communists then created a blasphemous caricature of what was left of the dream, until that too died. Now, when the natives of the largest Orthodox country in the world look into their past, they find only wreckage. It must, I decided, be the fall-out of all those broken dreams that has left the country looking like one giant Kem, like somewhere failing to recover from a nuclear war, or someone half dead of hangover.

The advent of Gorbachev and then Yeltsin had not just meant the simple overturning of a bankrupt Communist regime. They had set in train a far more radical and perhaps impossible reform. After almost a thousand years they were forcing Russians to jettison their Byzantine capacity for ignoring reality in favour of a dream. The world's second superpower was bankrupt and, with Ronald Reagan's America boasting about star wars, Russia's very existence was at stake. Russians could not afford to go on dreaming about holy national missions and salvation on earth.

In the past decade not only Russia but to varying degrees all Europe's former Communist Orthodox countries have been experiencing the same cruel awakening. Is it any wonder they are clinging on to the old dream and resisting efforts to draw them into the West-dominated version of a godless real world? The fact that the chief custodians of the old dream – the Orthodox Churches, but also former Communists turned nationalists – are refusing to wake up is not so remarkable. How can they rejoice at having won the freedom not to dream?

As Vanya and I wandered out of Pskov station and through the town's streets, we were depressed by the sight of a woman standing selling one dried fish and a pair of Chinese slippers outside a once-beautiful but now derelict church. My mood was bordering on the apocalyptic but Pskov is not far from the lake where, in 1242, Alexander Nevsky watched the ice crack obligingly under those heretic hordes of Teutonic knights. Since the demise of Communism, the lake has become a popular summer pilgrimage destination because, on a small island in the middle of it, lives the famous *starets*, Father Nikolai, whom we were counting on to lift our spirits. We hitched a lift to the spot on that lake's shore where a few locals were making a good living out of ferrying pilgrims back and forth to the island in narrow, motor-powered fishing boats.

Our boat phut-phutted out along a narrow channel through high reeds, heading for the open water and the island in the distance. The boatman, wearing smart sunglasses and a baseball cap advertising Marlboro, pulled a matching pack of cigarettes from the breast pocket of his denim shirt and lit up. Relaxing in the sunshine and cooling breeze I followed suit.

'No! No smoking!' he shouted to me, above the rumble of the engine. 'You're a pilgrim – Father Nikolai is very opposed to tobacco. You'll see!' Turning back to Vanya he yelled, 'Why isn't she wearing a skirt and headscarf? She's Orthodox, isn't she?'

'Catholic!' shouted Vanya.

'What the hell's she coming here for, then?' he bellowed back.

The island was verdant. With its village of low wooden houses, free-range cows and geese and freshly whitewashed church, it was less ruined than Solovetsky. At the end of the rough track that served as its high street was Father Nikolai's house. We knew that without having to ask because there was a small crowd of people – mostly women in headscarves and skirts – kneeling among the giant nettles growing high by his garden gate. Behind them stood a group of four young men chanting in harmony. A little further back, in the shade of some trees, a few young couples were lounging in the grass, snoozing or reading improving theological works. Learning that the *starets* was still resting after lunch, we joined the last group and discovered that one couple had travelled all the way from the oil town of Tyumen in Siberia in the hope of catching a glimpse of the eighty-nine-year-old monk. I remembered a Muscovite friend telling me that her daughter and son-in-law made the pilgrimage here every year. Last year Father Nikolai had told them to hurry up and have a child called Andrei. They had obeyed.

The holy man appeared at last at his garden gate, a tiny figure in the shadows cast by large trees. Ethereally pale in his long black belted cassock, with a thin silver beard, fierce deep-set eyes and large ears protruding on either side of a high velvet cap, he could have been a ghostly revenant from almost any century of Russia's history. He was almost as old as the twentieth century. Already seven when Nicholas II, with his wife, son and lovely daughters, was shot, doused in acid and dumped in a forest near Yekaterinburg, Father Nikolai was a survivor from another world.

People drew closer to hear his faint voice. Standing on the edge of the circle I could not catch most of what he was saying, except for the words 'tobacco' and 'vodka' and 'evil'. But the meaning of two episodes was clear. A well-dressed man with an expensive-looking camera approached Father Nikolai to ask if he would consent to have his picture taken with him and his wife. Father Nikolai answered him by angrily grabbing the camera and making as if to dash it to smithereens on the ground. Next, a middle-aged woman approached him, saying, 'Father, it's so hard. My husband refuses to go to church. What shall I do?'

'It's written in the Bible that you should respect your husband,' he told her sternly. 'You should obey and be afraid of your husband. I don't think you fear your husband enough!'

A Russian Orthodox priest from Manchester, now resident in Moscow, *had* warned me that 'one man's *starets* can be another man's cretin', but I was disappointed nevertheless. Just then something changed. Something about the sight of Father Nikolai's shaking hand, fumblingly dipping an unbent hairpin into a tiny phial of oil, about the way he slowly and deliberately traced a cross with it on the forehead of everyone there, touched me. Was it the desperate credulity of the people? Was it the tragic old Byzantine gap between the reality of an oil-smeared hairpin and the golden mystery of a holy *starets*' blessing? Or had I fallen prey to the sort of helpless sadness I had witnessed in Oleg back on Solovetsky and attributed to an intellectual's tragic incapacity simply to believe? Perhaps. I really could not say.

My protracted investigation of Orthodoxy in Europe was finally, here in Russia, beginning to take an emotional toll. In three years spent working in the country and those past two weeks of rambling around its north, Russia had eluded all my efforts to describe it. Although I had most of the rest of Eastern Orthodox Europe to measure it against now, no amount of reasoning was coming anywhere near to accounting for Russia's special soul-battering effects. Helpless tears seemed somehow nearer the mysterious mark.

Thump. Bang. Thump. Bang! 'My star is so far away, and the

night is so long...' Vanya hummed along as we hopped off a last night train. At seven o'clock on a bright Sunday morning, Moscow seemed as glamorous, as alive and fully functioning, as New York.

MOSCOW

All thanks to the city's energetic mayor.

In the decade since the Soviet Union and Communism gave up the ghost Mayor Yuri Luzhkov has established a quasi-Byzantine *symphonia* with Patriarch Alexy II. They have collaborated on a project involving hundreds of workers toiling by night and by day to resurrect the gigantic Cathedral of Christ the Saviour whose nineteenth-century original Stalin dynamited in 1931. Billed as a giant gesture of repentance for sins committed during decades of godless atheism, the new cathedral is estimated to have cost a billion dollars. In the summer of 1998 a Russian TV advertisement showed an old man, a cross between a *starets* and Leo Tolstoy, with his long white beard, strolling along beside his roller-blading grandson. The boy gazed up at his grandfather. 'Grandpa, people say that Moscow is the heart of Russia but where is this heart? In the whole of Moscow or in the Kremlin?' 'No,' mused the grandfather, 'it's something different. I think the heart is probably the cathedral.' The gold domes of Mayor Luzhkov's new Christ the Saviour cathedral then rose like a sun in the background, along with a bank account number for depositing donations. He might not have given Moscow back its heart but there was no denying Mayor Luzhkov had given the city a new lease of life.

On a warm summer evening the simple sight of Muscovites contentedly lounging on brand new park benches, in a brand new park, complete with a fountain and marble balustrades, was very heartening. Right there, in the shadow of the red Kremlin walls, those benches seemed at least as miraculous as the view of Solovetsky monastery from the air. Like the nearby new shopping mall with its fast-food outlets and even the capital's new bus shelters, they added up to a simple, humane concession to ordinary people's needs and comfort such as Russia, so long hooked on the postponement of pleasure until the hereafter, had rarely made before.

'Surely,' I said to my old friend Lena, 'all this means that the lot by the Lenin Museum have shut up shop?'

Lena knew exactly what I was talking about. Four years before, she and I had spent a cold winter evening down by the Lenin Museum consorting with angrily disaffected youths demonstrating against Yeltsin's West-inspired democratic reforms. They had worn barely disguised swastikas on red armbands and sold translations of Hitler's *Mein Kampf*, extremist nationalist and monarchist newspapers and reprints of the 'Protocol of the Elders of Zion', a proven forgery of a nineteenth-century document detailing the Jews' master-plan to rule the world. Lena – Jewish on her father's side – had been dismayed and frightened.

'Gone? You're joking! Well, I don't think so . . .' she said. 'Let's check . . .' We meandered through a crowd of happy families at leisure – children with shiny balloons and parents with cameras – that had gathered in a nearby square for an open-air concert, past peanut- and sweet-sellers in bright matching uniforms and peaked caps, and on towards the Lenin Museum, an ox-blood-red Gothic monstrosity on the edge of Red Square. It was late but Lena was right. Although there was no sign of the angry youths there were still a few old women selling the same old newspapers. I relieved one of a copy of a paper with a scarcely disguised swastika motif. It was called *Russky Poryadok* – Russian Order.

We found ourselves one of the new benches to sit on and enjoy the swirling mêlée. I flicked through the paper, mildly interested by an article claiming that Jesus Christ could not possibly have been a Jew. Another arguing that 'national socialism is the Tsardom of God on this Earth' and that Yeltsin and Co. were hell-bent on forcing Russia to 'integrate with the Tsardom of the Anti-Christ, the spiritless community of western countries, which is trying to prolong its luxurious existence by sucking the living fresh juices of our [Ortho-dox] nations and doing away with them' was more interesting. But my attention was properly caught by a large bar-code illustrating an article written by a certain Archimandrite Tikhon of Moscow's Sretensky monastery. The piece was all about the Greek Orthodox Church's opposition to the Schengen Agreement. While the West harps on about human rights, the article claimed, something more interesting is going on 'in the last country to have joined Schengen – small, poor Greece. A small, poor but Orthodox country ... something in the make-up of free Schengen, with its total, all-European and soon to be world control, has reminded them of the grand and final state of human history, as described in the Book of the Apocalypse'. It went on to quote a statement issued by the Greek Orthodox Church's Holy Synod of bishops.

'With regret we point out that achievements in the sphere of electronics in this situation are connected with the number 666, which is being used as the main code sign in the technology for making electronic passports. This number is absolutely directly stated as being the number of the Anti-Christ in the Apocalypse.'[xxix]

The fact that the Russian Orthodox Church was sensitive and sympathetic to movements in the Greek Church, its mortal rival for leadership of the Orthodox world, was interesting. But I was more shocked that a churchman should be writing for the anti-Semitic mouthpiece of a growing movement numbering an estimated ten thousand of those swastika-armbanded youths who hailed their Hitler-moustachioed leader with Nazi salutes. In a country that sacrificed some 20 million lives to halting the Nazi German advance on the eastern front in the Second World War, it seemed obscene. I understood how a majority of Russian churchmen could sympathize with the Communist-turned-nationalists' hopes of doing away with democracy and restoring 'Autocracy' and 'Nationhood', but surely there was no excuse for joining forces with neo-Nazis.

'Lena, let's go and find this Archimandrite Tikhon,' I said.

'Who?' she said vaguely. 'Oh, him, he's always on the television, on that weekly religious programme *Russky Dom*.'

'What's that?'

'It gives the conservative Orthodox view on events in Russia and the world, Russian history . . .'

Archimandrite Tikhon's monastery was no great distance away, behind a high white wall on one of the main streets radiating out in all directions from the Kremlin. A haven of tranquillity from the roaring traffic outside, its green-domed whitewashed seventeenth-century church surrounded by beds of blooming rose bushes was very pretty. Amidst the inhumanly monolithic high-rises of the Soviet city, such places, with their man-size proportions, rounded forms, gardens and colourful domes – green, azure with golden stars, gold, multicoloured swirls or red – are a vivid reminder of the Tsarist Moscow of 'forty times forty' churches. St Petersburg's West-inspired eighteenth- and nineteenth-century grandeur seems as unconvincing by comparison as a poor theatre set. Moscow belongs to Holy Russia, St Petersburg to Peter the Great's forced and half-grown modern state. It was no accident that the mystically religious Nicholas II always preferred Moscow to his northern capital.

Trowel in hand, an elderly monk rested from his labours on a chair by a rose bush, surveying his garden 'Everything here is for the Queen of Heaven.' He sighed happily, rubbing the small of his back.

Archimandrite Tikhon was a sharp-eyed, wiry young monk with a straggling flame-red beard. Mobile phone in hand, he shooed us into his office, warning us that since his time was so precious we could only claim five minutes of it. Swivelling on his chair behind an outsize desk and fiddling with his phone he chatted fast and easily about the tenfold increase in the number of monks at the monastery since it had reopened four years ago, about the prosperous printing works that earned them their keep and about how he had decided to forsake the world for the cloister. He had attended a film school and studied Russian literature.

'There I learnt that Dostoyevsky, Tolstoy and Turgenev were all believers in spite of their arguments with the Church. Brezhnev and Co. were atheists, of course, so soon I got to thinking that either the first lot were fools and Brezhnev and I clever or we were fools and they knew something we didn't. That was it,' he concluded, with a 360-degree swivel of his chair. He would make an excellent media-monk, I thought, as the conversation switched smoothly to politics.

'Russia today,' he was saying,' has two options. There are all the prerequisites for the country to fragment into three or four separate states which, of course, is what America hopes will happen. I'm not being melodramatic about this. If we don't fix ourselves up with a strong power right now, that's what's going to happen! What the West has to understand is that Russia can't be run in a vulgar democratic way. It can only be a huge country run by a mighty hand ... Of course, it would be very nice if that mighty hand was a kind one ...'

And what if it wasn't? I thought. The time for pleasantries had passed.

'Father Tikhon, I've come to see you because of your article in *Russky Poryadok* about Greece and the Schengen Agreement.'

'Oh, really? I don't know anything about that – they must have taken it from somewhere else and reprinted it.'

I was waiting for him to launch into an angry tirade at finding himself tarred with a neo-Nazi brush, but he continued nonchalantly, 'Well, never mind – I don't object since so far I don't have any quarrel with them and their aims.'

'But we're talking about a fascist movement!"

'Fascism? What fascism? Fascism is not possible in Russia because the mentality of Russian people is absolutely non-aggressive. Germans wouldn't have gone quietly to the gulag camps in their millions like Russians did.'

'Excuse me, Father Tikhon, but weren't the Russians who sent those millions of other Russians to the gulag camps aggressive?'

'No! What Russians? The gulag camps were not set up by Russians but by Jews. The Russian mentality is not capable of conceiving of any such thing! Ninety-three per cent of the early top Communists were Jews.'

I could sense half-Jewish Lena's shrinking discomfort, and I knew for a fact that sons of clergymen were at least as well represented as

Jews in the upper echelons of the Bolshevik Party, in much the same way as former Communist activists are well represented among Russian clergy today. This is not so surprising. I was thinking that the common denominator must be a predisposition towards didactic belief. Father Tikhon was the young, media-friendly, well-travelled face of the Russian Orthodox Church, but he was now using the same nineteenth-century anti-Semitic poison that was allowing churchmen to exonerate Russians from the guilt of massacring their last tsar, to obscure the home-grown character of Lenin and Stalin's death camps. I prepared to leave. 'Well, thank you, Father – I know you're very busy . . .'

'One minute, do you think I'm a fascist?' he said, with a sharp swivel round to face me square on.

'Since you ask – yes, I do.'

'Well, have a look at this,' he said. From the folds of his cassock he had whipped a crumpled American dollar bill. 'Read here, this Latin inscription . . . It says, 'Novos ordo seclorum' the new world order.'

'Yes?' I said doubtfully. Surely the Latin for world was 'mundus' and wasn't 'seclorum' something to do with centuries? The inscription said 'the new order of the centuries', but there was no stopping Father Tikhon now.

'This is the Jews' new world order. Look at that Jewish symbol of a pyramid with an eye in the middle of it. Everyone knows that America is controlled by the Jews. Now they want to control Russia too. In my article I wrote about the setting up of a fascist totalitarian police state connected with identification cards founded on the number 666. That's just one part of the new world order. The Anti-Christ is the leader who wants to unite the whole world into one state. That's the only kind of fascism I recognize!'

As far as I could make out, West + America + Jews = the Anti-Christ. Hatred and distrust of the Jews and the West is not confined to the Middle East, these days. It has seeped north into post-Soviet Russia and reached as far as Greece. I was remembering Sister Agnes, the nun I had met at ruined Mistra in the Peloponnese. I had not paid much attention at the time but she had also made the link between the Jews and 666 . . . Father Tikhon was in full flow.

' – and this disease, Aids, this is the breaking down of the immune system. Our national feeling is our immune system and it's also breaking down . . .'

'Yes, well, thank you,' I said. His mobile phone was ringing urgently.

A very shaken Lena, and I exited swiftly.

'Well, that's conservative Orthodox opinion for you,' said Lena. 'Can we do something else now? What about lunch at the church of the new world order of McDonald's?'

As we sat munching chips and burgers, Lena perused a daily newspaper, filled with commentary on the forthcoming reburial of the last tsar in St Petersburg, and the ongoing debate about whether President Yeltsin would or should attend the Romanov family funeral, whether Patriarch Alexy should or would officiate at the service.

'Look, here are some churchmen's comments. Let's see what old Father Dmitri Dudko has to say. He might be talking sense.'

'Who's he?'

'He was a dissident priest in the 1970s and early eighties whose cause was taken up in the West because he gave inflammatory sermons and called the church hierarchy "puppets of the atheists". He kept getting sent to jail – spent about eight years there – a bit of cause célèbre . . . Oh, no . . . listen to this . . . My God, I can hardly believe it. It could only happen in this country.'

Lena's laughter was teetering on the edge of the hysterical.

'Father Dmitri says, "Stalin was given us by God. He created such a powerful state that no matter how hard they tried to destroy it, it couldn't be finished off . . . If we look at Stalin from God's point of view he was really a special person, given by God and saved by God . . . That's why I, being an Orthodox Christian and a Russian patriot, am bowing low to Stalin." 'xxx

How could a man who had spent eight years in Soviet prison camps for his faith, have become an apologist not just for Communism but for its worst exponent? I wanted to meet him.

'Lena—'

'All right, all right. I'll find his number and call him tonight. I just hope he's not an anti-Semite as well as a Stalinist. I don't think I could stand that!'

'If you're lucky he'll be a misogynist and xenophobe too, and refuse to have anything to do with us!'

I had maligned Father Dmitri. Neither a misogynist nor a xenophobe, he welcomed us into his home, a single room in a small flat in a dreary Moscow suburb. Dim-lit and stuffy as a fox's den it was hung with icons and piled high to the ceiling with books. An elderly pink-cheeked and bright-eyed little man in shirt-sleeves and braces, with frizzes of white hair standing out above his ears, Father Dmitri received us from his bed, unable to rise on account of his gammy legs.

'I'm so glad you're writing about this,' he enthused. 'It will help people understand us Orthodox better. Catholicism and Protestantism have acquired such a secular character. Orthodoxy is more conservative but its spirit is always being renewed. God willing, with your woman's heart you can go to the roots of the matter.'

In all my months of travelling in Orthodox Europe this was the first time I had heard a good word about women. Father Ioan at the Birth of the Mother of God monastery in Transylvania had credited the Abbess of that monastery with all the fund-raising for the building, but had gone on to praise Mount Athos for not admitting women. As a married priest, Father Dmitri had some first-hand experience of women.

He made oddly light of his eight and half years in prison camps. 'The last time I was jailed, in 1980, I found I could appeal to the guards' finer feelings. When they tried to stop me celebrating the Easter liturgy I said to them, "Look, why are you destroying this? I'm a priest, doing my work." After that they brought me bread and wine for the service! One of them came up to me later and said, "What joy you've brought me! Can I shake your hand?"'

Father Dmitri's bright eyes had turned misty at the memory.

'What about in Stalin's time?' I asked.

'Of course, in Stalin's time nothing was allowed but, you know, when I see the destruction and decay all around me today, I know I'd prefer to be in prison, even in a Stalinist prison – really I would! In camp it wasn't so easy to be insulted or killed as it is today. I feel respect for Stalin. He wasn't so cruel. He just understood that in order to rule people one has to be firm. As the tsar, he was wielding the sword, you see. He was defending people by creating a strong state. Now we are without defences . . .'

I was hearing echoes of Ivan the Terrible's political philosophy. Father Dmitri was another churchman missing the old 'Autocracy' and 'Nationhood'. His bitter disenchantment with contemporary Russia and its regime was also clouding his judgement where the burial of the last tsar's bones were concerned.

'This whole matter is pure politics. Yeltsin and his democrats just want to make political capital from the funeral but I am one hundred per cent convinced that these are not the Tsar's bones.'

'But what about the DNA tests?'

'Pish! Look, this democratic government does not accept Russian-ness. There is a cover-up going on because the people who shot the Tsar were Jews. You know there were Cabbalistic symbols on the walls of the cellar where they were shot? It all makes sense when you see that the head of the commission that is arranging the funeral is a Jew.'

I was cringing on Lena's behalf.

'Democrats and Jews want to destroy the internal construction of a person. The Communists were better because they don't accept the deliberate destruction of Russia as a spiritual organism. You know, the West always tried to portray me as a dissident, but I was *never* against my country.'

It was time to go. Father Dmitri had heartily enjoyed our visit and presented me with his two-volume autobiography. On the flyleaf he scribbled: 'To Victoria – with deep respect. God grant that the West and Russia understand each other, bowing before the Cross of Christ.' I broke the sad silence in the car driving back into town with, 'I'm going to go and ask someone in the patriarchate about this anti-Semitism.'

The next morning I made my way alone across town to the Patriarch's headquarters at Danilovsky monastery which, with its high encircling walls, its blocks of office buildings, flower-beds and churches, resembles an entire Kremlin. A veteran Cossack in blue trousers with a red stripe down the side, a belted tunic, wide peaked hat and medals stopped me at the gate and ordered me to cover my head.

'But I don't have a scarf with me,' I protested.

'You can buy one here,' he said, pointing to a souvenir stall selling the flimsiest of leopardskin printed scarves. I selected the cheapest, draped it over my head and wandered off to find a bench in the gardens to relax on in the sun and wait for the time of my appointment with Father Vsevolod, chaplain of the Church's Department of External Affairs.

I tried to read but was hopelessly distracted by the antics of two Russians occupying the benches to left and right of me. One was an unexceptional-looking middle-aged woman who removed her shoes, lifted the skirt of her dress to unhitch her stockings, carefully rolled them down and then splashed a plastic bottle of water over her bare white shins, vigorously rubbing at each in turn. I reasoned that her shins might have been playing her up and the bottle just might have contained holy water. The second was a respectably dressed elderly man who took a cracked powder compact mirror, a comb and a pair of scissors out of a plastic bag, and set about trimming his beard, just as if he were in his bathroom at home. In his case I struggled to reason that he might not have a bathroom or even a home. Russia and Romania shared that oddly touching surreality. It was something I admired in both countries and I fell to pondering how much it might have to do with the old Byzantine Orthodox mistrust of the world's reason and logic, and trust instead in the wilder, wiser ways of heart and soul . . .

Every inch a bureaucrat with his briefcase open on the desk in front of him and a battery of telephones to hand, Father Vsevolod made distressingly light of my observation that anti-Semitism seemed rife among the Russian clergy.

'What can you expect? It's early days. Although, thanks be to God, we now have twenty-one seminaries instead of only three, even the new generation of seminarians are learning their history and theology from reprints of nineteenth-century textbooks. We must wait for the next generation of church historians and theologians,' he said with a shrug and a smile.

The good news he could tell me was that the Russian Orthodox Church, in all the former Soviet republics as well as in Russia proper, had succeeded in reopening over four hundred monasteries. Ten years before, in 1988, there had been only twenty-one. I asked him why Patriarch Alexy II was refusing to officiate at the Tsar's funeral in St Petersburg the next day, especially since Yeltsin had decided to attend after all, and it was common knowledge that Alexy had accepted the results of the DNA tests on the bones. Surely Russia's Patriarch ought to be there presiding over such an important gesture of collective repentance for the sins of the Soviet era? I refrained from saying that, given his past as a KGB informer code-named Thrush, wasn't it the very least he could do?

'No. The Patriarch will not go to St Petersburg,' he said. 'You've seen for yourself how most of the clergy feel about this government and that includes its arrangements for the reburial of these remains. The main thing for the Patriarch is to preserve the internal peace of the Church, to stay with the mood of his flock and his clergy.'

The last comment neatly confirmed my suspicion that Fathers Tikhon and Dmitri and even Archimandrite Iosif of Solovetsky and Kem's biscuit-dunking Father Igor were fair representatives of mainstream Church opinion.

While I was there in the Church's Department of External Affairs I dropped in on Father Ilarion, the priest in charge of relations with non-Orthodox religions. He treated me to a sharp critique of American Protestant missions, which had arrived in Russia to bribe people away from Orthodoxy with free Bibles, and followed that up with a hot blast of anti-Ukrainian Uniate rhetoric. Ukraine's religious affairs were in shocking disarray, the worst possible advertisement for Eastern Orthodoxy. Her glory days as Kievan Rus are just a distant memory, kept alive only by her Byzantine St Sophia cathedral and the first Russian Monastery of the Caves. Since Ukraine gained its independence, its Orthodox community has split into three fractious parts: one still loyal to the Moscow patriarchate and two independently Ukrainian with their own patriarchs, both unrecognized by Constantinople. The Ukrainian Uniates – like Romania's in their preoccupation with retrieving Church properties seized after the Second World War, but far more plentiful than the Romanian Uniates – are regaining ground in western Ukraine.

'The Uniates have seized back about a thousand of our Orthodox churches. Of course, it was a great injustice that Stalin abolished them in 1946 but you cannot cure one injustice with another.'

'Are you in contact with the Vatican about this?'

'Humph!' fumed Father Ilarion. 'The Vatican always tells us that the Uniates are somehow independent, that they have no responsibility for the Uniates. But of course they belong to the Catholic Church and this is one of the main reasons why our Patriarch Alexy has been refusing to meet the Pope for the past few years. By the way, there are far more Roman Catholic priests than are needed in a town like Novosibirsk. All this is plain proselytism aimed at converting people who are already Christians and we are categorically against it! Of course, it doesn't take the same shape as it took with the Crusaders but it's just the same mentality!

The Fourth Crusaders' 1204 sacking of Byzantium might have happened yesterday.

TRINITY SERGEYEV MONASTERY

Instead of helping to give Tsar Nicholas II and his family a decent and long overdue send-off in St Petersburg, Patriarch Alexy was going to be about fifty miles north of Moscow, at Sergeyev Posad's Trinity Sergeyev monastery, celebrating the feast of St Sergius.

Lena and I would be there too, filled with foreboding about the first serious division between the State and the Russian Orthodox

Church since the fall of Communism. By refusing to take part in the Tsar's reburial, the Church had lined up behind all the forces opposed to reform. The sudden collapse of the rouble and the Russian government was still a month away, but the signs seemed to point towards a centre incapable of holding. Lena, gamely racing her old Lada against new rich Russians' gleaming Mercedes and Cherokee jeeps, was betting me there would be serious political trouble by autumn when she suddenly swerved off the motorway running north out of the city towards a straggle of hopeful hitch-hikers.

'A monk!' she said, reaching behind me to open the back door. 'I bet he's going to Sergeyev Posad too. Let's give him a lift.'

Lena had been my office assistant but also my dearest friend during the three years I had spent in Moscow. This lightning abduction was typical of our happy old working stride. A sharp-eyed young monk, who was accompanied by a big cloth bag and a silent younger male companion, arranged himself on the back seat of the car and tossed a couple of holy cards into my lap. 'Can you drive?' he asked Lena.

'Well, we haven't travelled this far by miracle! My old Lada is no magic carpet!' she wisecracked back at him, swinging the car out into the traffic. 'Comfortable back there? We thought you must be making for Sergeyev Posad, but aren't you a bit late for the service? It began over an hour ago.'

'I know, I know. I set my alarm clock for six but I just couldn't get my eyes to open,' replied the monk distractedly, clutching the back of the driving seat and staring hard at the road ahead.

Before long I was wondering precisely what kind of monk Lena had succeeded in bagging. When I asked him which monastery he came from, he was evasive. When I asked him his name he replied with a riddle. 'I have the same name as one of St Sergius' favourite brother monks at Trinity Sergeyev . . .' he teased.

Zosima, Christodoulos, Paissy, Amfilojihe? I reeled off my current favourites but without success and soon gave up. How was I supposed to know the name of some lesser Russian monk of the fourteenth century? Suddenly I was feeling a sneaking admiration for that

Church-wrecker Peter the Great. As well as abolishing the post of patriarch and forcing priests to work as government spies, he had insisted that monks stopped wandering around the country like good-for-nothing beggar tramps, and stay in their monasteries to work their fields. Our passenger's footloose nonchalance seemed to me a sign that the Russian Orthodox Church might be slipping back into some of its lax old ways.

'Keep him talking, keep him talking,' said Lena in mumbled English. 'He's trapped. We're taking him all the way to Sergeyev Posad for nothing but a couple of cheap holy cards. He's got to talk. I bet he's wishing he'd walked now!'

I told the monk that I had been to Solovetsky. He had also been there, he said, before asking me what I had made of Archimandrite Iosif. His refusal to offer his own estimation of the man caused me to suspect that he had clashed with the Archimandrite. I guessed he had got himself turfed out of the monastery and off the island for some kind of turpitude. I told him how interested I was to meet him since I was writing a book about Eastern Orthodox Europe. His response to this information was a quick warning to Lena – delivered too low and fast for me to understand – to be careful who she talked to because there were armies of foreign spies and Jews about. Then he asked me, 'If you converted to Orthodoxy would you prefer the Russian or the Greek version?'

'That's a good question,' I said politely, although there didn't seem to me to be much to choose between them. 'I think I'm most tempted by Macedonian Orthodoxy actually,' I answered eventually, remembering that sad pariah Church and the Pied Piper Bishop Naum of Strumica with his happy nuns. 'I like Romanian Orthodoxy too.'

'No! You must choose Russian Orthodoxy! The Macedonian Church does not exist and the Greeks, the Serbs, the Bulgarians and the Romanians are all wrong because they have changed to the western calendar. Only the Russian Church has stayed with the old Julian calendar, and that is how we have kept the True Faith! By the old calendar, today is the fourth, not the seventeenth of July. We are always thirteen days behind.'

'Thirteen days? More like thirteen centuries,' muttered Lena.

Our passenger was probably unaware that the Holy Mountain is ruled by the old calendar and that there are thriving old calendarist movements in all the other Orthodox countries, but particularly in Greece where the sect, with its own hierarchy, churches and monasteries, is regarded by the mainstream Greek Orthodox Church as dangerously schismatic and fundamentalist.

'Russia,' he continued, 'is the only pure country left. Every saint there has ever been has said that Russia will save the world. Did you know that Russia has never suffered a single defeat on the battlefield? Nor has she ever attacked any other country. I have information that in the Vatican there is a document signed by Alexander the Great saying that Slavs should never be attacked.'

Which Church history books had *he* been reading, I wondered. Or was he just remembering his Soviet school history lessons? It was hard to tell. By the time we came in sight of Sergeyev Posad's giant white fortress monastery we were glad to be rid of him, and I know the feeling was mutual.

The monastery looked splendid. Its gold-starred blue domes were dazzling. That hot, bright blue summer morning was singularly unsuited to lurking in dimly candle-lit churches rendered airless by incense smoke so I was glad to see the service was already over. Headscarved women in ill-fitting Sunday suits were already streaming out through the monastery gates. A fleet of shiny black Mercedes and Cherokee jeeps with official Moscow number-plates was still parked outside, suggesting that a post-liturgy banquet for the Patriarch, some of his bishops and a few Church- (rather than government-) inclined politicians was under way somewhere inside. But there was no question of us gatecrashing that. This was not the occasion of a routine church consecration in a small town in Romania, but the celebration of the feast-day of Russia's number-one saint, at Russia's number-one monastery, Russia being the mightiest Orthodox country in the world.

We wandered through the gates into a shady courtyard dappled with sunlight. It was as lively and thronging as a small-town market-place. There were young seminarians in their smart black suits escorting their proud mothers. Women laden with heavy shopping bags full of gifts of food for the monastery – spring onions, tomatoes, cucumbers, eggs, sunflower oil for the holy lamps and honey – were bending priests' ears with impromptu confessions or consulting their spiritual fathers. Couples grabbed at the wide sleeves of some of the monks' black robes as they passed, fervently kissing their hands and ordering their children to follow suit. A throng, armed with plastic bottles, mobbed a gushing holy-water fountain. There were people leaning against trees scribbling requests for prayers on scraps of paper and counting out the requisite roubles to pay for them. Crowds swirled in and out of the monastery's many churches, kissing the glittering icons and relics and prostrating themselves, but also in and out of the monastery's shops to view a tempting assortment of priest's cassocks, fake-pearl-encrusted bishop's mitres that were retailing at around a hundred dollars, incense-burners, icons, books, videos and rosaries.

I was thinking that it must always have been like this, with a few breaks in times of war, especially during Russia's seventeenth-century 'Time of Troubles' when thirty thousand Catholic Poles besieged the monastery for sixteen months. When Ivan the Terrible came on pilgrimage here just before his coronation in 1547 and deposited lavish funds for a new church, when a youthful Peter the Great galloped up here from the Kremlin in a state of undress one night to seek refuge from his sister's dangerous scheming, when one after another the Romanov tsars of the nineteenth century heaped treasures on the place, this was all going on too, in exactly the same way. At one point in its history the monastery's total land-holdings were second only to those of the Tsar himself. Hesychast St Sergius, who so loved to send cartloads of bread to the poor at the monastery gates, might not have approved but he could not have failed to be impressed by all this holy hurly-burly.

I had never felt closer to the old Holy Russia and was pleased I had resisted the temptation to travel to St Petersburg for a distant glimpse of Yeltsin and the west European descendants of the Romanov tsars in their funeral-going best.

Wherever we went we encountered our strange passenger, still accompanied by his young sidekick, sweating under the weight of the mysterious cloth bag. But they were by no means the only curious sight in that colourful crowd. I spotted a bedraggled-looking young monk in a mud-spattered white robe with dangling red trimmings, striding around purposefully with a smoking incense-burner in one hand and a plastic bag advertising Marlboro cigarettes in the other. We watched while a pair of women caught him by his flying red-trimmed sleeves and set about kissing his hand. No sooner had they finished and the monk hared off again about his mysterious business than they were accosted by a stern black-robed monk. 'What the hell do you think you're doing kissing *his* hand?' he railed at them furiously. 'Can't you see he's not a monk? He's just a loony bum!' They fell to kissing his hand instead.

I felt for them. In a country with a long tradition of revering *yurodivy*, holy fools, they could surely be forgiven their lapse. One has to go back as far as that crazy grazing monk on Mount Athos to find another example of an Orthodox society taking a couple of sentences from the gospels quite so ludicrously literally. Christ's Apostle Paul is somewhat to blame. In his first letter to the Corinthians he says, 'If any one among you thinks that he is wise in this age, let him become a fool that he may become wise,'[xxxi] and he rams the point home again later in the same letter, 'We are fools for Christ's sake . . .'[xxxii] The Byzantines had also gone in for something like holy fools but their version, *saloi*, were never as histrionically extreme as the Russian ones. Of the forty-four holy-fool saints featured in the calendars of all the Orthodox Churches, thirty-seven are Russian.

A modern authority on Russia's 'fools for Christ's sake' suggests that they had more in common with Siberian tribes' pagan priests, the shamans, than with Byzantium's *saloi*. She has provided us with a thumbnail sketch of what was an astonishingly common phenomenon in Russia until 1917. Holy fools, she says, were 'characterized by a striking neglect of bodily needs, a marked fondness for iron objects, vagrancy, soothsaying, clairvoyance, and a tendency to commit apparently immoral acts, including sacrilege and even murder.'[xxxiii] As free from the constraints of the official Church hierarchy as *startsy* like Father Nikolai on his island in Lake Pskov they often enjoyed the same level of popularity and respect as them, but they were not contemplative loners, more often exhibitionist nudists – 'stark naked, save for a clout about their middle',[xxxiv] as one visiting Englishman noted four years after Ivan the Terrible's death. They loved crowds and the incomparable buzz of being licensed to say and do things no one else could hope to get away with. Holy fools are some measure of where Russian Orthodoxy's stubborn anti-intellectualism and the State's stifling of political dissent had led the country by 1917. Like those early holy hermits who signalled their rejection of the world by fleeing into the uninhabited northern wastes, they were an unorganized but remarkably effective dissident movement in a brutally autocratic state.

Ivan the Terrible loved and respected holy fools. The psychedelic whirligig-domed St Vasily's cathedral, which still stands at one end of Moscow's Red Square and graces every tourist's holiday snaps, was originally dedicated to the Mother of God but soon became a monument to the memory of St Vasily the Blessed. One of the six holy fools Ivan canonized during his reign, Vasily had thrown off all his clothes and set himself up as a holy fool while still a teenager. He had soon made his name by throwing stones at churches, blinding a group of girls who laughed at him and murdering a robber who had plotted to steal his new fur coat. Vasily once let rip at Ivan the Terrible himself, for allowing his thoughts to wander during a church liturgy. No less than the then Metropolitan of Moscow, the saintly Philip's predecessor, officiated at Vasily's funeral and Ivan himself was a pall-bearer. In 1569, the year Philip was murdered, Ivan was on his way to punish the too-independently minded town of Pskov, when he was accosted by another holy fool, known simply as Nikolai. It was Lent, so when Nikolai offered Ivan a chunk of raw meat to eat, Ivan piously refused it. 'Oh?' said Nikolai. 'But you *do* eat the flesh and drink the blood of human beings . . .' Ivan was horrified, and Pskov was spared a trashing. So enamoured of holy fools was Ivan that by the end of his frightful life he had gone so far as to dub himself 'Parfeny the Holy Fool'.

By the nineteenth century revisionist Russian historians were repackaging Ivan the Terrible as a holy fool rather than a psychotic madman. Ivan's holy foolishness explained away and atoned for everything, and his rehabilitation helped to make holy fools thoroughly respectable. By 1912, while the First Balkan War was raging in Macedonia, twelve of them were clanking around the northern Russian town of Novgorod in iron caps and heavy chains. At around the same time the daughter of a St Petersburg aristocrat caused a stir by marrying a 'holy fool' known as Mitya whom some sections of St Petersburg society would have described as a mentally retarded deaf-mute dwarf.

I was remembering the beatifically smiling deaf-mute on Solovetsky and wondering if he might qualify for the title of 'holy fool'. In Greece's northern Peloponnese port city of Patras I had met another likely candidate. A simple-minded, sweetly smiling youth, he had insisted on marching me right across town one evening to show me St Andrew's relics in the seaside cathedral there. Another teenage boy hanging around Father Kiprian's Bistriţa monastery in Moldavia had also seemed to answer the job description. Certainly the extraordinary rise of Russia's Grigory Rasputin – a character so often erroneously described as a monk or priest – is more clearly understood in the context of holy foolery. If in the eyes of some Russians, not least those of Nicholas II and his wife Alexandra, he was a *starets* on account of his miraculous healing powers, clairvoyance and wise counsel, for many in St Petersburg he was simply a power-crazed nincompoop masquerading as a dangerous cross between a *starets* and a holy fool. A Siberian upstart, who seduced women with his magnetic gaze and paraded his penis in public, there was nothing very remarkable about him, except that his home telephone number – 64646 – happened to contain the mark of the Beast of the Apocalypse.

Lena and I drove back to Moscow, well pleased with our expedition to Sergeyev Posad, despite our failure to catch a glimpse of Patriarch Alexy by crashing his banquet. While half watching the television news coverage of the St Petersburg funeral and glimpsing the former Solovetsky convict Dmitri Likhachev* there, holding a flickering church candle in his shaky hand, we set about planning another jaunt.

OPTINA PUSTYN

A visit to the monastery of Optina Pustyn, almost as famous as Sergeyev Posad but about a hundred miles south of Moscow, would cast a soul-stirring light on the mystery of how three nineteenth-century *startsy* became the sweet golden glue of marzipan on the thinly iced Russian fruit cake.

Their spirits nourished on the finest Hesychast soul-food of St Paissy Velichkovsky's translations from Greek into Slavonic, they did more than anyone else at the time to close the gap between urban intellectuals and aristocrats on the one hand and superstitious peasants on the other. One after another between 1828 and 1911 they managed to bring about what one historian has called 'a kind of formal reintegration of Russian culture, in both its high and low variants, in a way which neither the imperial state nor the intellectuals were able to emulate'.xxxv

The first of the saintly trinity, Leonid, immersed himself in St Paissy's translations and was renowned for the humility he instilled in his brother monks at Optina. When one confided to him a wish to wear chains as a special mark of repentance, Leonid dropped in on the monastery's smith and told him, 'If a certain brother comes to you asking you to make chains for him, tell him: "What do you want chains for? And then strike him hard on the face."' All went according to plan, but the unpleasantly surprised young monk

* Dmitri Likhachev died in September 1999, aged ninety-three.

smacked the smith straight back and a fight broke out. They finished up in the *starets'* cell, seeking his mediation in their quarrel. Leonid simply asked the monk, 'How can you dare wear chains when you are unable to endure a mere slap on the face?'[xxxvi]

The anonymous author of the famous Hesychast text *The Way of a Pilgrim* sat at the feet of Macarius, the second great Optina *starets*. The book he later wrote is a gripping and moving account of a Russian who sets out to save his soul by wandering around the country from monastery to monastery with a copy of St Paissy's translation of the *Philokalia* in his bag, and the Jesus Prayer so engraved on his heart that saying it becomes as natural as breathing. Finding helpful holy *startsy* everywhere he goes and seeing mini-miracles in everything that happens to him, he is flogged almost to death by Russian police for vagrancy, but befriended by a pious Russian landowner. We leave him in the company of a university professor, heading north towards Solovetsky, where he hopes to find 'a second Mount Athos'.

Russian nobility, renowned Slavophiles and luminaries on the Russian literary scene, including Dostoyevsky and Tolstoy, but also thousands of poor peasants – called simply *krestyane*, Christians, in Russian – were regular visitors to the cells of the Optina *startsy*. In his novel *The Brothers Karamazov*, Dostoyevsky modelled the character of his *starets*, Zosima, on Optina's third great *starets*, Ambrose. Dostoyevsky has one of the brothers tell an extraordinary story, which brilliantly illuminates the Orthodox Churches' basic objection to the Catholic Church. The tale is about Christ staging his long-awaited Second Coming in sixteenth-century Seville, at the height of the Spanish Catholic Inquisition. He appears, humble as a beggar, in a bustling marketplace, but is soon recognized as the Messiah. Having caused a stir by resurrecting a dead child, He is taken in for questioning by the city's Grand Inquisitor. Before long that Catholic churchman is convinced that he is indeed face to face with the Son of God, and the real drama starts. The Grand Inquisitor complains that on his last visit to Earth Christ burdened man too heavily with the terrible gift of freedom of choice.

I swear man was created a baser creature than you thought him to be ... Had you respected him less, you would have asked less of him, and that would have been more like love, for his burden would have been lighter ... We [Catholics] have corrected your great work and have based it on miracle, mystery and authority. And men rejoiced that they were once more led like sheep and that the terrible gift which had brought them so much suffering had at last been lifted from their hearts. Were we right in doing and teaching this? Tell me. Did we not love mankind when we admitted so humbly its impotence and lovingly lightened its burden and allowed men's weak nature even to sin, so long as it was with our permission?[xxxvii]

At last the Inquisitor is done with venting his spleen and boasting about the Catholic Church's matchless organization and efficiency. When he falls silent Christ replies by getting up and planting an enigmatic kiss on his 'bloodless, aged lips'. The Grand Inquisitor, He implies, is free to act and believe as he wishes. Exasperated, the Inquisitor releases Him, ordering Him to 'Go, come no more – don't come at all – never, never!'

That third Optina *starets*, Ambrose, had 'the gift of tears' – a sure mark of true repentance and humility in anyone pursuing the Hesychast path to salvation. Another Optina monk remembered, 'Sometimes I found him lying in bed in tears, which were always controlled and barely noticeable. It seemed to me that the Elder Ambrose always walked in the presence of God ...'[xxxviii] After rediscovering religion during a long spell in a Siberian prison and reacquainting himself 'with the Christ I had learned to know as a child but whom I had deserted when I became a liberal European',[xxxix] Dostoyevsky had sought comfort at Optina and Ambrose had approved of him: 'This is a man who repents,' he noted. Count Leo Tolstoy, a profoundly religious man but an arch enemy of the official Russian Church, which eventually excommunicated him, first met Ambrose in 1878. Because Optina Pustyn was only five days' walk from his country estate at Yasnaya Polyana, he visited the place often over the next thirteen years. Ambrose once wrote to Tolstoy reassuring, or perhaps warning him that 'one *can* save oneself outside a monastery, but with great difficulty'.[xl] In 1910 Tolstoy had just left Optina after visiting one of his sisters, a nun in a neighbouring convent, when he sickened and died at a nearby railway station.

We *had* to go to Optina Pustyn. The monastery was a major railway junction on Russia's soul-journey.

'I'll ring them right now,' said Lena, 'just to let them know we're on our way and that you need to speak to someone.'

Her telephone conversation with a monk called Father Vasily went splendidly at first. He sounded most welcoming, until he asked, just as an afterthought, 'She's Christian of course, isn't she?'

'Yes, she's christened,' said Lena, choosing her words carefully.

'I meant, is she Orthodox?' he answered sharply.

'Actually Father, she's a non-practising Roman Catholic,' she admitted.

Lena was fearing the worst, and heard it. 'No. We don't receive Catholics,' he said, and the line went dead.

After a moment's thought I suggested, 'Lena, let's go there anyway. We can always pretend that the line cut before the bad news. What are they going to do? Chuck boiling oil on us from the monastery's fortress walls?'

'Even worse if they find they've got a Jew as well as a Catholic on their hands!' said Lena, with a nervous laugh. 'But I'd like to see the place . . .'

Early the next morning, properly attired in scarves and skirts again, we set off south for Optina Pustyn. As we sped through the gently undulating green hills of southern European Russia it was easy to imagine Dostoyevsky and Tolstoy bowling along the rough tracks in their carriages on summer days a whole century ago, with the domes and white steeple of Optina in their sights and the hope of some 'spiritual conversation' in their hearts. The landscape was so much kinder than northern Russia's. We sped past the pretty little town of Kaluga on the bank of the wide river Oka and on, through the village of Kozelsk, passing a green marsh to our left, with Optina's domes just a gleam in the distance. To be on the safe side, we parked the car – not Lena's Lada this time, but another car with giveaway foreign number-plates – some way from the arched entranceway to the monastery, adjusted our headscarves and proceeded on foot.

It was a weekday but the monastery's car-park was full of coaches and the courtyard almost as bustling with pilgrims and monks as Sergeyev Posad's had been, but with additional signs and sounds of building works in progress. Unnoticed in that mêlée, we wandered past flower-beds bursting with marigolds and foxgloves into the main church to watch dozens of pilgrims patiently queuing to kiss a gold crucifix in the hands of a romantically handsome young priest with shoulder-length hair parted in the middle and a wax-pale face. One after another the pilgrims bowed over it then crossed themselves. I thought, as we wandered out again, that Russians might have learnt their famous powers of endurance from their Church. Putting off the dreaded moment when I would have to find and face Father Vasily, I mentioned to Lena that I wanted to see the holy Ambrose's cell. We asked directions to it from an elderly woman who looked as if she might know the place well.

'The *skete* where he lived is forty minutes' walk down that way,' she said, pointing out a path leading off through the forest behind the monastery, 'but you can't go there. No women are allowed unless they're attending the five o'clock in the morning service . . .'

There was nothing for it. It was time to find Father Vasily so the woman redirected us to the monastery's administration building. Standing waiting at the half-open door of his office we caught a glimpse of its inside. Done up in businesslike chrome and grey, and lit only by electric light, it was well equipped with computers, one of which had a flickering photograph of Nicholas II on its screen. There were printers, scanners and televisions. A huge improvement on Father Sava's cramped work-space back at Kosovo's Dečani monastery, it might have been a star-ship's flight deck. Father Vasily appeared at last, flushed with embarrassment at our visitation. Nothing was said about his parting telephone shot and I presented my project to him in as inoffensive a way as I could manage.

'So, you're taking a scientific approach to Orthodoxy,' he said, walking us out into the brilliantly sunny courtyard again.

'No, no,' I reassured him, knowing anything that smacked of science was guaranteed to alienate an Orthodox monk. 'I'm not a scientist. I love history, and my Catholic upbringing means that I know something about religion.'

'Pah! Catholicism!' he said. 'What is Catholicism? When Catholics go to mass they sit in rows just as if they were going to a performance at the theatre! I've heard that some Catholics are receiving the holy communion bread by post these days!'

He was not won over, but I thought the fact that he was speaking to us at all boded well. He walked us as far as the monastery's refectory building where hundreds of pilgrims, young and old, male and female, rich and poor, hale and infirm, sane and insane, were queuing to have lunch in shifts of about a hundred. Lena was astonished by the sight of teenage boys in jean jackets and trendy trainers patiently waiting their turn to eat and kissing Father Vasily's hand. The nineteenth-century pilgrimage season at Solovetsky monastery or at the Holy Mountain's St Panteleimon would have been just like this, I decided, as Father Vasily commanded us to join the line and promised to find us again after lunch.

Herded into a gloomy hall filled with long tables and benches, we moved in single file to take our places. In a matter of seconds our shift was packed in, tight as a tin of sardines, with our backs touching those of the people at the next table. Overworked nuns in high black velvet caps and veils plonked buckets of watery soup, tubs of buckwheat porridge, black bread and giant teapots on each table. On the wall was a sign with the text of prayers to be said before and after eating. We all stood for the first prayer, chanting the words in time with a tapping pointer wielded by a bearded man in a white doctor's coat. Two teenage boys were sharply reprimanded for talking while grace was being said. 'No one has forced you to come here. Either be quiet or get out!' barked the white-coated master. We ate in silence until an elderly drunk sitting opposite me noticed that I refused a plate of buckwheat porridge, realized I was not Russian and remarked testily, 'I suppose you think you have better food than this where you come from.'

The sweetly smiling teenage boy sitting next to me whispered, 'I know it looks like the same old buckwheat but somehow it's tastier here in the monastery. Try a little.' He piled my plate high and I ate.

Father Vasily was as good as his word. He was waiting for us outside the refectory and led us off towards a graveyard and garden nearby. There we inspected the finely engraved tombstones of the three great holy men, lying close together in a line. But my eye was soon distracted by the sight of three new graves, marked with simple new wooden crosses and covered with flowers. They belonged to three young monks named Ferapont, Trofim and Vasily. All three had died five years before, on the same Easter Sunday – 5 April 1993 by the old calendar, 18 April by the new.

'How did they die, Father Vasily? Was there a flu epidemic?' I asked.

'No, no. The monastery had only been reopened two years before and it was just coming back to life, like the countryside after winter. It was Easter Sunday morning and everything was bright and joyful, and all the bells were ringing out, calling people to the liturgy. My namesake, Father Vasily, and one of the other two were ringing them over there in the bell-house, when suddenly the pealing slowed and stopped. The third monk ran over to see what had happened and found that a terrible, terrible crime had taken place, and that he was next to die . . .'

'What had happened?' I asked, gripped by his tale.

'A satanic murderer slaughtered all three of them. The weapon, a huge knife half a metre long, was found later with the number 666 engraved on its blade. The criminal is in a lunatic asylum now because the court had to declare him mad. There is no category of "ritual satanic murder" in Russian law, but he wasn't mad . . . The strange and beautiful thing about it was that Father Vasily had always said he would love to die on an Easter Sunday morning when the bells were ringing – and that's just how God arranged it for him.'

Lena and I were speechless with horror. Leading us over towards a bench where we all sat down in the hot afternoon sunshine, Father Vasily went on, 'You see, death doesn't frighten Orthodox people very much and death on Easter Sunday not at all. Those three have gone straight to Heaven, of course. Before you go I'll give you a copy of the video which the father of one of the martyr-monks made all about it.'

We sat there in contemplative silence for a while. I hardly dared to ask more questions, for fear they would sound intolerably banal after this tale of dark horror oddly leavened by redemptive joy.

'Father, do you think the monastery is now much the same as it was before 1917? You seem to have a lot of pilgrims.'

'About six hundred a day at the moment,' he said. 'Probably you can't feel the divine energy here but our pilgrims feel it – even when our *starets* Ilias is away, as he is at the moment, resting. Before the revolution people brought different kinds of problems to the monastery, problems of a more spiritual nature. Now people come here to research books.'

I laughed at his gentle teasing. He gave me a first ironic smile, and thereafter we got on very well indeed.

'It doesn't matter what kind of problem a person comes with – the important thing is that God has pushed everyone to come here for a reason,' he said.

Father Vasily took my quest, but more particularly my soul, more seriously than any other monk, nun, priest or bishop I had talked to during my long travels. In a fervent bid to win me for the True Faith he asked as many questions of me as I did of him. For three hours or so, until the sun started to set behind the forested hill at the back of the monastery, we talked as honestly as possible, arguing, joking and soul-searching by turns. Sadly, my notes of our 'spiritual conversation' are sketchy but I do remember that he asked me point-blank why I was writing a book about a religion I did not believe in.

'Intellectually I can explain why,' I answered carefully. 'I like all these countries very much and, after living in three of them for the best part of a decade, I am convinced that they cannot be properly appreciated or understood without taking Orthodoxy and all that it entails into account.'

'Yes, that's intellectually,' he interrupted, frankly bored by my laborious explanation. 'And otherwise?'

'Well, I'm sure that somehow I'm on the right track with this because I feel I've been lucky with every step of my travels. I seem to arrive in the right place at the right time, meet the right people, see and hear the right things. There's no skill in that. It seems like purest luck, which you would call a blessing,' I answered.

I was remembering that Bogdan had once attributed our safe and smooth progress around Serbia and Montenegro to a blessing he had extracted for us from his spiritual father, Tadej. Father Vasily was nodding approvingly so I continued, 'And here's a perfect example. You told me not to come because I'm a Catholic and look at us now! I'm glad to be here and very pleased to have met you.' The poor man was blushing and concentrating hard on flicking the dust off his cassock, so I changed the subject. 'But how did you become a monk, Father? What were you doing before?'

'Monks are not supposed to talk about their past life. All I can say is, I was a real outlaw – like Opta, the founder of this place, who was a common brigand in the thirteenth century when the Mongols ruled Russia, but who repented of his sins. I was like the thief who hung beside Jesus Christ on the Cross. Like every other monk, I came to the monastery as one would go to a hospital – to get well in spirit and become a saint, to give up passions and become free. Our kind of freedom is so different from the western idea of freedom, which is the freedom to take drugs, drink and have sex.'

Anxious to avoid a downward slide into an attack on the West, I quickly changed the subject again to ask him if he was a Hesychast, and was touched by the sad sincerity of his answer. 'No, I'm not – nowhere near. You've seen all the monks walking around with their prayer ropes in their hands. They're all saying the Jesus Prayer in their hearts. I can't seem to do it . . . I wish I could.'

I thanked him profusely for his time and interest.

'Well, I think our next meeting will take place under different circumstances,' he answered slowly, studying me through narrowed eyes.

'Do you mean that you'll be out of your cassock, or that I'll be in a nun's habit?' I joked back.

He just smiled his ironic smile, and said, 'I'll get you a copy of that video I promised.'

At the gates to the monastery he heaped us with gifts of books as well as the video. I said a final goodbye and rather awkwardly shook his hand. What happened next was quite unexpected. Lena approached him, bowed her headscarved head and kissed his hands. I stood a few paces away, astonished by and a little envious of whatever it was that had moved her to humble herself like that.

Back in the car, I asked her why she had done it.

'I kissed his hand because I think I'm too proud,' she said simply, as if it were the most natural thing in the world.

At Lena's flat in Moscow that evening we sat down to watch the *New Martyrs of Optina Pustyn* video. It showed footage of the murderer, his face blurred, being interviewed by a criminal investigator who asked him if he repented of committing the crime.

'No, I don't feel any repentance . . . I just wanted to get at God through those monks. They were not my enemies. I feel sorry for them. I know that they're in Heaven now, that they exist as clearly as I see you now,' said the devout murderer.

VERKHOTURYE
SIBERIA

The Beatles again. A song about bright stars shining in a dark sky and love never dying comes piping over the train's Tannoy.

Birch trees are running by in the opposite direction, their trunks like silver legs of snow. Trees, snow, trees and snow. The train sways and sways around a long bend, howling like a wolf. We have been carousing for hours. A blurred Vanya, vodka glass in one hand and caviar-stuffed pancake in the other, is telling me that the train is a 'dream machine' and a hangover 'a form of religious ecstasy'.

As the train slid out of Moscow's Yaroslavsky station he had started conjuring up a feast. Out of his bag had come a stack of still warm pancakes wrapped in silver foil, three pots of red caviar, two bottles each of vodka and beer, a half-loaf of black bread, smoked ham, oranges, four Snickers chocolate bars to remind us of summer and Solovetsky, and a cucumber.

'Tomorrow's the first day of Lent so we're having my birthday party a day early,' he had announced. 'Did you notice that Patriarch Alexy celebrated his birthday early for the same reason? ... Oh! I forgot to pack any glasses – wait a minute!'

Outside in the corridor he had immediately run into a travelling saleswoman and asked her if, by any chance, she had glasses for sale. From the depths of her sports bag she had produced an attractive set of six thimble-sized glasses.

'Exactly what we need! You must be an angel sent by God!' exclaimed Vanya, handing her a fifty-rouble note.

Once again, I marvelled, it was just as I had told Father Vasily at Optina Pustyn in the summer – right person, right place, right time, right thing.

We were journeying east, across European Russia, over the Ural mountains, into Siberia, a region so vast we would have to have ridden that 'dream machine' for more than a week to reach its easternmost limit at Vladivostok on the Sea of Japan. Calculating that one could fit roughly five European Russias inside a single Siberia, I was almost forgetting that European Russia was already about ten times the size of any Western European country ... My head grew dizzy with the effort of trying to reckon infinity.

Fortunately a mere thirty-five hours separated us from our destination, a tiny town just the other side of the Urals called Verkhoturye. Founded at the turn of the sixteenth century by Fyodor, Ivan the Terrible's holy fool of a son, Verkhoturye was known as the Gateway to Siberia. Because all the 'soft gold' of Siberian sable pelts had to pass through this outpost to be taxed, valued and transported west, it had soon grown into a wild, bustling town full of soldiers, free-booting Cossacks, and churchmen. Verkhoturye thrived until the late seventeenth century, when suddenly it found itself staring ruin in the face. Peter the Great's new post road from European Russia across the Urals into Siberia, and with it the sable 'soft gold', of course, would be running away to the south, bypassing the old Gateway to Siberia and cutting off Verkhoturye's life-blood. The town desperately needed a new goose to lay her golden eggs and, as if by a miracle, one appeared in the unlikely shape of the relics of Siberia's first saint.

Sadly, little is known about this first economic-miracle-working saint of Verkhoturye. It seems that in the early seventeenth century, in a village about three days' walk from Verkhoturye, there had lived a poor, God-fearing man called Simeon who enjoyed a spot of fishing on the river Tura and made his living stitching fur coats. Simple Simeon would doubtless have rested in eternal peace and obscurity had his coffin not risen out of the earth a few years after his demise and, naturally, invited inspection. Its contents were judged unmistakably sweet-smelling and uncorrupted, which meant only one thing: Simeon was a saint. Canonized and credited with a string of miracles, he began to feature in icons, always grey-haired, always standing by a river with his rod at the ready.

The astute churchmen of Verkhoturye soon recognized that St Simeon's scented relics were guaranteed to draw the pious with their generous donations. Before long what remained of the humble fisherman was transported in solemn procession the thirty-five miles or so from his home village to Verkhoturye. A holy fool called Kosma accompanied the procession on its way, covering the entire distance on his knees. Whenever he tired, the story goes, Kosma prayed to St Simeon who prevented the crowd from taking another step until he was rested.

What with a saint's relics and a canonized holy fool, as well as generations of *startsy* who busied themselves saving their souls in *sketes* and hermitages in the surrounding woods, Verkhoturye – much like Solovetsky – was attracting thousands of pilgrims by the end of the nineteenth century. Quite by chance, one of these was Siberia's most infamous son, Grigory Rasputin, who was to discover his fateful vocation as a freelancing holy man at Verkhoturye and visit the place regularly until he died in 1916.

I knew something of Verkhoturye's colourful pre-Soviet past but little of its present. I had heard that the monastery had reopened, but not whether St Simeon's relics had survived the Soviet era. Would anyone there have heard of Rasputin, I wondered.

By late afternoon the following day Vanya and I were clambering off the train into three feet of snow. Verkhoturye's little station was freshly painted pistachio green, yellow and white but it was in the middle of nowhere. There were no houses, people or cars, just pine trees, snow, a heavy white sky and silence. Seconds later an army-surplus jeep came hurtling down the road towards the station and crunched to a halt in front of us. Out jumped a pleasant-faced young man in a black leather jacket.

'Do you need a lift into town? It's seven kilometres away,' he said, with a winning smile.

We decided he must be another 'angel sent by God'. I was climbing into the passenger seat to face a dashboard covered with icon stickers when he introduced himself as Sergei, the press secretary of Abbot Tikhon of Verkhoturye's Nikolayevsky monastery. He handed me a shiny crimson business card covered in fancy gilt Cyrillic lettering and a gilt-embossed monastery motif. The jeep, he explained, was monastery property. He was having to shout above the wildly doleful din of the soundtrack to one of Quentin Tarantino's movies that he was playing on a portable cassette-player.

'Of course, if you need to speak with Abbot Tikhon I can easily arrange it,' he offered, 'but don't you love Tarantino's films?'

'Why are you so keen on them?' I asked him, simply because I suspected his answer would surprise me. It did. Instead of grunting something vague about knowing where Tarantino was coming from, Sergei said, 'I feel that in the depths of Tarantino's soul and my soul there is the same substance.'

Sergei's reply made perfect sense in the light of the Tarantinoesque life-story he began to tell us. Since leaving school at fifteen, he had spent an uneasy year as a novice monk at the Nikolayevsky monastery before escaping to do his military service in Russia's brutal and still unresolved war against the Chechens. Despite seeing the mutilated remains of his two best friends sent home in potato sacks, he had prolonged his service in Chechnya by becoming a contract soldier, but soon afterwards suffered a near fatal motorcycle crash and lain in a coma for months. Somewhere along this hellish way he had married and divorced. He could not have been older than twenty-five.

'Did you ever feel that you were fighting a religious war against those Muslim Chechens?' I asked him, as we sped along a snowy road through a forest of pine trees.

'Of course,' he said, as if I had asked not so much an odd as a stupid question.

We were climbing the last hill towards the town. On our left up ahead was the colourful gateway of the Nikolayevsky monastery. Behind its high white walls towered a gigantic dun-coloured cathedral almost as massive as Mayor Luzhkov of Moscow's Christ the Saviour cathedral and spiky with scaffolding. Sergei informed us that it had standing room for eight thousand people and 137 windows. But, judging by its design, it could not have been even a hundred years old and I wondered who, back at the beginning of the twentieth century, had deemed the former Gateway to Siberia deserving of such a grandiosely outsize house of worship. There had been the three-hundredth anniversary of the Romanov dynasty to commemorate in 1913, but I suspected that Rasputin, with his powerful Petersburg court connections and a lingering affection for the place that had launched him on his fatal career, might have masterminded the immodest display.

To the right up ahead stood a second and more modestly proportioned eighteenth-century cathedral. Crowned with a mush-room cluster of little golden domes, it was gleaming as white as the snow in the dying golden afternoon light. Even when measured against Kosovo's heavenly Gračanica, against Macedonia's modest brick churches with their frilly domes, against Patmos' Hovis-loaf ones and Romania's Byzantine-Gothic painted treasures, it was a gloriously persuasive argument for Orthodoxy. I could quite understand why the Slavophiles had dreamed of returning to a pre-Petrine age, but Russia would have lost this jewel in the process.

The town of Verkhoturye, spreading along both banks of the frozen river Tura, lay before us. A car was driving slowly down the frozen river, under a bridge, past a tiny black figure of a woman who was filling two water buckets from a hole in the ice and hooking them to a yoke she balanced on her shoulders. In this climate, to have no running water but two richly restored cathedrals! I was remembering Romania with its hundreds of new monasteries, but hellish orphanages and crumbling housing blocks. The old Orthodox priorities had weathered all that materialist Communism astonishingly well. The next world, not this one, is what counts. A church, not a water system, and the spirit, not the flesh, still come first. The first scaffolding-clad Cathedral of the Exaltation of the Cross dwarfed the jumble of dark wood houses, each with a generous icing of snow on its roof, a puff of smoke rising from its chimney and glowing orange light in its windows. It occurred to me that if Marc Chagall could have ignored that modern cathedral, he might have felt inspired to paint that town, with an angel hovering low in the sky above it. 'This is Siberia!' exclaimed a delighted Vanya. We overtook a horse and sledge loaded with hay, and saw women, wearing elegant sable hats and long fur coats, plodding home through the snow. There were some drunks staggering around in their knee-high felt boots in the slush outside a cellar bar, their fur hats pushed well back on their heads, their throats bared. Curly-tailed dogs yapped and chased around.

'Because the cathedrals are both being restored we're using another big church in the monastery now,' Sergei was saying.

Yet another big church! I asked him what had become of the monastery and all those churches in Soviet times.

'The monastery and the big cathedral were one big borstal for around six hundred boys until 1990. Look, up there you can still see the guards' watchtowers and some barbed wire,' he said. 'The nuns' monastery on the other side of town was an orphanage. Their church was turned into a public bath, with a beer bar and even toilets inside! See that over there? That was a church they used as a bakery – just ripped the domes off and replaced them with corrugated iron – but you can still see a bit of fresco inside. The white cathedral, Trinity, was just a warehouse ten years ago. Abbot Tikhon has taken less than a decade to transform this town. Without him there would be nothing to see here!'

Sergei, I was learning, was quite as passionately devoted to Abbot Tikhon as he was to Quentin Tarantino. The Abbot of Nikolayevsky monastery was his spiritual father, mentor and hero.

'What's that monument over there?' I asked, pointing to a slab of red inscribed marble. It was in the middle of what – underneath that thick blanket of snow – must have been the town square.

'Abbot Tikhon erected that last year to commemorate the four-hundredth anniversary of the town's foundation. He also placed a big gold Byzantine double-headed eagle on top of it but someone stole that – damned hooligan! Now, here we are,' he declared, pulling up in front of a large, brand new red-brick building. 'This Hotel Sable is an important part of Abbot Tikhon's and the regional governor's strategy to restore Verkhoturye's reputation as a "religio-touristic complex". You're almost the first guests.'

To more mournful yowling of Tarantino soundtrack we bowled out of town the next morning in dazzling sunshine. Sergei was full of regret that Abbot Tikhon would not be able to see us on account of some trouble with his liver, but he was doing his best to assuage our disappointment by taking us to St Simeon of Verkhoturye's home village.

'We'll visit Abbot Avraam there. He's got a community of nuns in Yekaterinburg but they have a *podvor* out here,' he explained.

Abbot Avraam sounded like a poor substitute for the heroic Abbot Tikhon, I thought glumly, as we drove the same route, although in the opposite direction, that the holy fool Kosma had covered on his knees back at the end of the seventeenth century. But

I wanted to see what a modern Russian *podvor*, the equivalent of a Greek or Serbian *metochia*, was like. Crossing the frozen river Tura again we reached a gleaming white church with a black dome and golden spire, improbably set in a village so poor it looked abandoned.

'The people here are very jealous of the Church,' said Sergei.

I could quite see why that should be the case once he had parked the jeep outside the *podvor*, a large, new red-brick mansion surrounded by a defensively spiked metal fence. Any Muscovite new Russian would have rejoiced in the ownership of this mini-Kremlin, I thought, stepping inside. It was lavishly decorated in the style Russians call *yevro-remont*, a term meaning built to western European standards and finished with imported fittings.

'This must have cost a fortune! Where did the money come from?' I got Vanya to whisper to Sergei – Russian man to Russian man – as we waited to be ushered into the presence of Abbot Avraam.

'One of Avraam's spiritual children is the director of Uralmash in Yekaterinburg. He paid for everything,' said Sergei, and then, as if loyally to correct any adverse impression, added, 'But the nuns here are so holy they're like angels – always saying the Jesus Prayer.'

Uralmash is the biggest heavy machinery factory in Yekaterinburg, and Yekaterinburg is to Russia what Manchester was to Britain in the last century. The director of Uralmash was bound to be wealthy, even in these desperate times. But what astonished me was this startling evidence that the old Byzantine threads of influence between a spiritual father and his children were being spun again here at the end of the twentieth century, in post-Soviet Russia. Father Ioan at the Birth of the Mother of God monastery in Transylvania, and his quick holiday to Patmos and Mount Athos courtesy of a spiritual child, had hinted at the survival of this tradition, but that perk now seemed paltry when measured against this palace of a convent hung with chandeliers and velvet curtains. Vanya and I marvelled at the marble floors and the carved wooden doors with their brass handles.

Abbot Avraam, who must have been in his early forties, was not like any other Orthodox churchman I have ever encountered. First, he was dressed in a light brownish robe, which almost matched his long, strawberry-blond hair and the tinted lenses of his gold-rimmed and fancily engraved spectacles. Second, he wore his hair loose, cascading about his shoulders, and could easily have passed for an Indian guru of the suspect sort some westerners revered in the 1960s and seventies. The room in which he was lolling in an armchair – apparently recuperating from a minor indisposition – was the most sumptuously decorated of all. He rose to welcome us, a huge man but friendly and easy to talk to. Before long I was sharing my impressions of the Russian Orthodox Church with him and naturally broaching the subject of anti-Semitism.

'You know, I'm a Jew,' was Abbot Avraam's astounding comment, 'a baptized Jew from Odessa. It's not something I shout about but nor do I hide the fact.'

I imagined he must be feeling extremely uncomfortable in the modern Russian Church, but if he was, he took care not to show it. The only complaint he would allow himself was that people like him, Jewish intellectuals who had converted to Orthodox Christianity back in the 1970s, were hugely distrusted by their ethnically Russian peers who had converted much later, during Gorbachev's *perestroika* or after. He even laughed at my outrage on his behalf. 'Of course, you won't find a single Russian who doesn't blame the Jews for killing the Tsar and his family. That's as clear as daylight to everyone! Ha! Ha!'

'I hope you're right to be so sanguine,' I said, bewildered by his attitude. 'I find it another worrying aspect of the anti-West feeling I've found in every Orthodox country I've visited.'

He was interested to hear what I had discovered elsewhere, so I told him how the Greeks were worried about 666, and computers and bar-codes controlling the world, how badly the Romanians felt about the Transylvanian Uniates and the Hungarians, how no Orthodox Church would recognize the Macedonian Church, and how the Serbs viewed America and the West in general and the Muslims too of course . . .

'Well, I can easily understand how Serbia feels, as a sovereign country threatened with an invasion of Nato troops,' Abbot Avraam interrupted.

I did my best to present the, then common, western view of the Kosovo question, to impress upon him the extent of the slaughter occurring and the danger of chaos spilling into a state as non-viable as the Former Yugoslav Republic of Macedonia and then into all-out war in the Balkans.

He listened politely, before commenting, 'There is that saying, "Nobody helps the Serbs, except God in Heaven and Russia on Earth." Ha! Ha! Well, well! In accordance with the ancient prophecy everything will soon fall apart and then the Anti-Christ will appear to resurrect the Roman empire.'

When we got up to leave, Sergei approached him, bowed down low to the plushly carpeted floor, and kissed his hand. The gesture suggested ancient eastern luxury, the courts of the Mongol khans, Constantinople and Romanian Phanariots, Byzantine emperors.

Tarantino serenaded us back to Verkhoturye and the setting sun touched the pristine snow with gold. Back in the basement café opposite the Hotel Sable, we met a young man with exceedingly bright blue eyes. He was wearing the standard outsize fur hat and felt boots, and he was as drunk as a lord, swaying, blinking and burping.

'What is your *randy?*' he attempted in English, opening those eyes very wide. 'My *randy* is 'Risha!' (Burp!)

'Your name is Richard?'

'No, 'Risha! Like 'Risha Rasputin!'

'Oh, Grisha!' I laughed, suddenly recalling that was the short form of Rasputin's first name, Grigory.

Vanya judged that this Grisha had been blind drunk for two days. While I concentrated on my plate of home-made *pelmeni* with sour cream and he on his Lenten dish of fried potatoes, Grisha the Second performed an ecstatic shuffling dance around the empty tables, arms in the air, hips gyrating slowly. Grisha the First would have attracted little notice in this place, I decided.

Rasputin had started out as a horse-whisperer, a drinker, a petty thief. He was also a cart-driver, regularly plying the route between his home village of Pokrovskoye and Siberia's main town of Tobolsk about two hundred miles south-east of Verkhoturye. Sixteen when he first ventured this far west, he had liked the place and returned a few years later, happily married but soul-sick. His first child had died, aged six months, and a vision of the Virgin Mary granted him in a freshly ploughed field one spring day was troubling him. Just like Sergei, he had entered Verkhoturye's Nikolayevsky monastery as a novice for a year or so. Someone there had taught him to read and write after a fashion. A *starets* called Makarius, who had squandered a princely inheritance but was then saving his soul in a riverside *skete* called Aktai, became his spiritual father.

On our second day in town Sergei drove us the few miles to Aktai. A Soviet orphanage and then a trade-union-run rest home after 1917, it was now a holiday camp. Along with a three-foot-thick blanket of snow it had pretty garden lights and an open-air dance pavilion. Bereft of its domes, the original little wooden church was unrecognizable but the air smelt pure, of snow and woodsmoke. It was not too hard to imagine the soul-doctor Makarius, hung with his penitential iron chains, taking Rasputin's spiritual temperature and telling him, 'God has chosen you for a great achievement. In order to strengthen your spiritual power you should go and pray to the Virgin at Athos.'[xli]

Rasputin had prepared to obey his spiritual father, although it meant abandoning his home and family to live as a wandering *strannik*, off charity and monastic hospitality. Fortunately, his planned departure met with no opposition from his wife, who always rejoiced in her husband's spiritual prowess. Only his peasant father grumbled that Grisha had turned pilgrim out of bone idleness. Rasputin set out to walk the thousands of miles out of Siberia, across the Urals, down through Ukraine, through Moldavia, Romania and Bulgaria, all the way to the then still Ottoman Turkish province of Macedonia, and its southernmost point on the Aegean Sea – Mount Athos.

But Makarius' prescribed cure failed. Shocked and disgusted at the high incidence of homosexual activity among the monks of the Holy Mountain, Rasputin declared the Garden of the Mother of God to be a place filled with 'moral dirt and vermin'.[xlii] Instead of becoming a monk there, he fled the place and hurried home where Makarius calmly pointed out that monasteries were bound to be hotbeds of temptation. 'Remember your mission,' he counselled him. 'Since you have not found salvation in the monastery, try to save your soul in the outside world.'[xliii]

Historians have often wondered how Russia would have fared in the twentieth century had the boy-heir to the throne not been a haemophiliac. But it is perhaps worth wondering what might have happened to Russia had the monks on the Holy Mountain been capable of denying their sinful flesh. Rasputin might have quietly joined the Russian monastery of St Panteleimon there and never have travelled back to St Petersburg to haunt high-society drawing-rooms, win the trust of Nicholas and Alexandra by halting the Tsarevich's bleeding, and hasten the empire's end. As it was, he returned to Russia where his closeness to the famous *starets* Makarius and his vision of the Mother of God hugely commended him to highly placed members of the Church hierarchy. These included Tsar Nicholas II's spiritual father Theofan, whom Rasputin first met with Makarius in Verkhoturye but later visited and used as a ladder to reach the high windows of St Petersburg aristocratic social circles.

The time was exactly ripe for a giant Siberian peasant with long greasy hair, ragged beard, piercing blue stare and heavy boots to stride out of the Siberian cold into the overheated luxury of St Petersburg's palaces. Rasputin's peculiar blend of sexual and spiritual energy seems to have acted like an icy shot of vodka on a class that was jaded, sated, decadent and, deep down, probably scared to death by the terrifying impasse that Russia had reached. While fast becoming a modern industrial power, Russia was still run as a police state by a medieval autocrat who believed he was God-appointed. Polite society's lionizing of rough Russian peasants was a bizarre and kitsch last ditch attempt to heal the fatal rift dividing western-educated Russians from the mass of the peasantry. Wise men like the *startsy* of Optina Pustyn were doing the real work.

But this was how Rasputin's trajectory into the bosom of the

17A Solovetsky monastery,
Solovetsky Island, July 1998

17B Sunday church parade
around the walls of Solovetsky
monastery, July 1998

18A Ivan the Terrible

18B Tsar Nicholas II and Tsarina Alexandra
in medieval Muscovite fancy dress

18C Rasputin

19A Moscow's new cathedral of Christ the Saviour, begun in 1994

19B Sretensky monastery's rose gardener, Moscow, July 1998

20A Igumen Tikhon of Nikolayevsky
monastery, Verkhoturye, Siberia,
February 1999

20B Verkhoturye's
eighteenth-century
cathedral, February 1999

21A Archbishop Makarios,
President of Cyprus 1960–1974

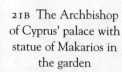

21B The Archbishop
of Cyprus' palace with
statue of Makarios in
the garden

22A Ariko, the 'mukhtaris'
of Kambos at Easter lunch,
Kambos, April 1999

22B The Russian chapel
at Limassol

23A Archbishop Chrysostomos of Cyprus, April 1999

23B Monastery of Apostolos Andhreas, Karpas peninsula, North Cyprus

24A Ecumenical Patriarch Bartholomaios I of Constantinople (left, bottom row) and Archbishop Christodoulos of Athens (centre, front) at the monastery on Heybeliada Island, Turkey, June 1998

24B Father Dorotheos at the empty theological seminary on Heybeliada Island, Turkey, June 1999 imperial family at Tsarskoe Selo could happen, even before he had proved himself the only person capable of stopping the Tsarevich's bleeding bouts. When he first met the Tsar and his wife at the Petersburg palace of two Montenegrin princesses in 1905, he was just a modishly devout peasant of the kind Nicholas and Alexandra were always inclined to be sentimental about. There was nothing so very remarkable about him when he showed up at the Tsarskoye Selo palace with a twelve-inch-high wooden icon of St Simeon of Verkho-turye to give to the Tsar. It was not so strange that he soon had the run of the teenage grand duchesses' bedrooms and the Tsarevich's nursery. But outside the palace his name began to spell scandal and there were periods when the bad odour surrounding him penetrated beyond the palace walls and the Tsar tried to distance himself from Rasputin.

During one such period in 1911, Rasputin made himself scarce for a while by going on a pilgrimage to the Holy Land and stopping off at Patmos to see St John the Theologian's cave. During Easter in Jerusalem he found himself pondering the superiority of Orthodox over Roman Catholic Easter and wrote, for later publication,

> With us, not only do we True Believers rejoice, but our faces are lit up with joy. But with them, even within the Church itself, there is no joy. It is as though someone had died ... How can this be compared with Orthodox Easter? It is something entirely different! Oh! how happy we True Believers are! There is no faith to compare with the Orthodox! ... I do not wish to be critical but I am just giving my opinion and am comparing the Catholic Easter with ours ... I do not pretend to plumb the depths of wisdom.[xliv]

As he sailed around the Ottoman-occupied Greek islands he expressed again that Russian disdain for the workings of the intellect. As he saw it, 'the Greeks were proud of their philosophy. And the Lord was angered and gave over to the Turks all the works of the Apostles.'[xlv] That, he reckoned, was the obvious reason why Asia Minor, Constantinople and most of the Balkans had fallen to the

Ottomans by the end of the fifteenth century. And most of Ivan the Terrible's contemporaries would have agreed with him.

The First World War broke out. After the Tsar rushed off to the front to make his ineffective contribution to the war effort, Rasputin's way was clear. The Tsarina relied on him for help with hiring and firing a succession of progressively less able government ministers, although he had never been a good judge of people. His daughter Maria, who shared her father's St Petersburg flat, and later fled to the United States, has written laconically of this period of her father's life, saying, 'Rasputin's clairvoyance seemed to desert him when it was a question of judging people where his own interests alone were concerned.'[xlvi] By 1916 Rasputin was pursuing his own curious agenda by bringing political pressure to bear on the French Ambassador to St Petersburg. Were the allies going to keep their promise that in exchange for her part in defeating the Germans, Russia could have Constantinople after the war, he tactlessly asked Monsieur Maurice Palèologue who was himself a descendant of the last great Byzantine dynasty. Monsieur Palèologue assured him the promise would be kept. 'Then the Russian people will not regret having suffered so much, and will consent to suffer a great deal more,' replied Rasputin.[xlvii]

Rasputin had acquired a fawning retinue – a development that especially worried his wife. The Siberian holy man who had hated vodka so much at the start of the war that he had advised the Tsar to ban it for the duration of hostilities had developed a taste for fine Madeira wine. The ascetic who had always refused meats and sweets was enlivening his diet with both. In place of a sober caftan he favoured baggy velvet breeches, bright yellow or azure silken blouses embroidered by his lady admirers, soft leather boots and a jewelled cross given him by the Tsarina. He loved speaking on the new-fangled telephone, travelling by car and the new Trans-Siberian Railway, and dancing with gypsies. He was living like a pampered pop star, but never forgetting God.

In a curious local newspaper, put out by the seemingly omnipotent Abbot Tikhon, Vanya discovered a marvellously vivid account of one of Rasputin's regular twice-yearly visits to Verkhoturye. The author of the article, a certain Shishkina-Berezovskaya, had been a girl of ten in the summer of 1916 when she had travelled to Verkhoturye with her mother and grandfather and found the place in a ferment of excitement because Rasputin was due to arrive. The popular Petersburg press at the time was full of cartoons implying that Rasputin was enjoying the German Tsarina's sexual favours while plotting Russia's ruin with her. His blood-freezing murder and dumping in St Petersburg's Neva river were only months away. But at Verkhoturye that summer he was received like a lord. Rasputin and his retinue attended the liturgy in that gigantic and, at the time, brand new cathedral of the Exaltation of the Cross.

the crowd in the cathedral is enormous. Rasputin and his retinue are standing in the middle of the church. Everybody is dressed well, everybody is important . . . people have come from all over the Yekaterinburg region and some from even further away. Everything is shining. All the chandeliers are lit and the icons and the shrine of St Simeon the Miracle-worker of Verkhoturye. All the icons are decorated with flowers . . . Rasputin is standing in the most important place, at the head of his retinue, on the carpet. He's in a light yellow Russian shirt, a fringed sash, wide velvet breeches and shiny knee-high boots. His hair-style is like Jesus Christ's in the icons, parted in the middle, chestnut hair, cut to shoulder-length. He's passionately praying, with all his retinue . . . the generals with their all their medals, the grand ladies . . . His face is blissful-looking, very calm, concentrated and nice. At the end of the service the cross is brought down from the altar and put in the middle of the church so that everyone can kiss it. First comes Rasputin to kiss this cross, then his retinue but after them a big crush. All the pilgrims, all the people praying, rush to kiss the cross so as to be near Rasputin and to observe the *starets* better and to touch him . . . Then this crowd pushes me right up against the *starets*, right under his right arm, and making a wide sign of the cross he brushes my head with his elbow . . . The deep prayerful mood was absent in the priests, parishioners and pilgrims . . .[xlviii]

Sometimes, as in this setting, Rasputin seems to have shone out like a rare beacon of sincerity and goodness. During those last years of riotous high-living and ruinous politicking, he could still have flashes of perfect good sense. A bigoted anti-Semite without any experience of Jews since there were so few in Siberia, he encountered some while living it up in St Petersburg and tried to convince Nicholas II to give them equal rights with Russians. Similarly, with knowledge gained from his Balkan wanderings on the way to Mount Athos, he dared to go against the tide of public opinion and told a St Petersburg newspaper that the Orthodox Christians fighting their wars in the Balkans were not altogether deserving of Russia's support against the Ottomans. In fact, he had noticed that 'the Turks are more fair and peaceful on religious things'.[xlix] He had foreseen that entry into the First World War would spell Russia's eventual ruin and tried hard, with bloodcurdling prophecies scrawled in letters to Nicholas II, to stop the inevitable.

I had not satisfied my curiosity regarding Rasputin's involvement with the giant dun-coloured cathedral so when a rumour reached us that Sergei's guru, the great Abbot Tikhon, had risen from his sickbed, Vanya and I went to the monastery's museum to call on its curator, Raisa Nikolayevna. We quizzed her on the subject of Rasputin in the hope that she would refer us to the Abbot.

'Well, Rasputin cannot have been only bad or only good, that much is clear,' she opined slowly.

'Raisa Nikolayevna, I hear that Abbot Tikhon is a great historian,' I said.

'Oh, yes, he's passionate about history and he knows all there is to know about Rasputin! *He*'s the one to talk to,' she said, in worshipful tones.

This retired schoolmistress chattered on about how working in the monastery had made her happy and healthy and how, since her christening by Abbot Tikhon in the autumn she had never felt fitter, until Vanya gently returned her to the subject of a meeting with Abbot Tikhon. 'Raisa Nikolayevna, we have asked Abbot Tikhon's press secretary, Sergei, to arrange us a meeting with him but without any result. Do you think you might be able to help us?' he begged, with a winning smile.

The mere mention of Sergei had caused her to grimace disapprovingly. It seemed, after all, that our friend was not so much a press secretary as a handyman around the monastery. Indeed, he seemed of the same order as the couple of loutish Cossack monastery guards with their ornamental *nagaika* whips and shaggy sheepskin hats and we had reluctantly dubbed him our 'fallen angel' after he had shown up at the hotel that morning, late and hung over, with a swollen, lacerated right hand. 'It's broken,' he had mumbled, 'got into a fight down the bus-station disco – at least, the other guy left with half his teeth missing. But I don't want Abbot Tikhon hearing about it. Christians shouldn't get into fights.'

Meanwhile, Raisa Nikolayevna was looking from me to Vanya and then back again, as if weighing our worthiness to experience Tikhon's full glory. 'He's a very busy man – only thirty-four but his beard is already grey. Look, I'll give you this photograph of him as a souvenir. There, you can see the grey. Poor man! Now, I'll see what I can do,' she promised, and left the room.

The souvenir photograph showed Abbot Tikhon to be a man as huge as President Yeltsin, who also happens to hail from this region of Russia. His startlingly direct dark-blue gaze reminded me of that French ambassador's description of how Rasputin's eyes had shone with a 'strange brilliance, depth and fascination'. His eyes were set in a big face, two-thirds of which was concealed by a beard that reached to his waist. Like Abbot Avraam's, his long hair hung loose over his shoulders and he was wearing a leather belt positioned high on his chest, just like Abbot Kiprian of Bistriţa monastery's Jerusalem one. Gazing at that awe-inspiring image, I found myself half hoping he would refuse to see us, after all. Since discovering that he had started out as a married builder before becoming a priest, then abandoned his family to become a monk, before finally rising to become abbot here at Verkhoturye, I imagined him to be another in the mould of that Bosnian Bishop Vasilije of Tuzla and Zvornik. I did not want to be bullied, or have to suffer those dark blue eyes boring into my soul.

Too late. Raisa Nikolayevna was back, all of a fluster. 'Quick! Here, put this on your head!' she said, tossing me a green nylon scarf. 'He's said he'll see you *now*! RIGHT NOW! Come along! Hurry!'

Abbot Tikhon, his long hair tousled, bristled with an energy that seemed more managerial than either spiritual or sexual. Waving aside my polite noises about his swift restoration of the spiritual capital of Siberia, he reminded me that he was extremely busy.

'Father, I'm interested in history,' I said.

And that was it, of course, because Abbot Tikhon loves history. His blue eyes lit up, a wide smile appeared in his beard and he sat well forward in his armchair. His amateur historian's heart, he told me, had 'filled up with blood' on seeing Verkhoturye for the first time in 1990. 'I could imagine exactly what it had been and what it could be again!' he said.

We argued about whether there had been any *symphonia* between the Russian Church and State after Philip of Solovetsky's murder in the sixteenth-century. He claimed that such an ideally delicate balance had indeed been attained. Did I know about the seventeenth-century patriarchate of Nikon? Of course I did. How could I forget the fanatical hierarch who had caused the schism and those Old Believers to set fire to themselves in their tens of thousands?

'Nikon? *Symphonia*? No!' I remonstrated. 'He just set himself up above the Tsar. That wasn't *symphonia* – that was megalomania. Surely his schism was a disaster for the Russian Church!'

'No, no, you're *wrong*!' said Father Tikhon, wagging a fat finger at me. 'Nikon was a great patriarch. Anyway, sooner or later changes would have been made because the Church was rotten with superstition at that time. For example, after having a baby a woman would come to church and place her afterbirth on the altar, where it would rot and stink for forty days.'

'Oh, no!'

'They believed it would bring their babies good luck.'

'All right, there was superstition,' I conceded, but insisted that Nikon was rather like Rasputin since both of them had ruled and ruined Russia.

'Aha! Rasputin! Now that's someone I've been thinking about and puzzling over these past twelve years, especially since all the archives were opened in the nineties.'

'Was he a *starets* or a holy fool, do you think?'

'Neither. But my impression is that he's been badly misunderstood as a force of evil. In fact, I'm dreaming of devoting a whole room in the monastery museum to Rasputin the believer, Rasputin the spiritual person.' I said I would happily return to see it, and proceeded to ask if there was any connection between Rasputin and the half-restored dun-coloured cathedral.

'Certainly, I think we can see a very close connection,' he replied, with satisfaction. 'I can't be sure that the funding for its building came directly from the Tsar at Rasputin's request, but I do know that it was thanks to Rasputin that the imperial family came to revere our St Simeon of Verkhoturye. Are you aware that Tsarevich Aleksei used to pray to St Simeon when he suffered a bleeding attack? Did you know that there were plans to bring the boy here, in the hope that St Simeon would effect a miracle cure? Did you know that after the massacre in the Ipatiev House in Yekaterinburg St Simeon medallions were found around the necks of each member of the imperial family?'

'Extraordinary!'

'I expect you know that the Tsar donated a precious casket and shrine for St Simeon's holy relics. It was made of silver and weighed over a hundred kilos but unfortunately it seems to have ended up in America. The Tsarina Alexandra and her daughters embroidered beautiful cloths for it. We also have a record of a telegram sent by Rasputin to the Tsar from here in the summer of 1916, assuring him that St Simeon was praying for him.'

'The imperial family never came here?'

'No. The Tsarina's sister, who was a nun, visited in 1914. If the First World War had not started the imperial family would have brought the Tsarevich here because Rasputin even had a house built for them. It's now the town museum. But I'm proud to say that last year the heir to the Romanov throne, Georgy Mikhailovich, was here with his mother.'

Oh, yes. The chubbily teenage Georgy and his mother had been on a pilgrimage around Russia in July 1998. While, like Lena and I, his grandmother had gone to Sergeyev Posad to side with Patriarch Alexy and the Church against President Yeltsin on the day of the Tsar's funeral in St Petersburg, Georgy and his mother had journeyed to Verkhoturye. The teenager and his womenfolk, who all hail from Madrid, have been branded pushy pretenders by other branches of the Romanov clan. But they are fairly frequent visitors to Russia and therefore a natural focus for whatever monarchist sentiment there is.

'Would you describe yourself as a monarchist?' I asked, remembering what Sergei had told us about the golden double-headed Byzantine eagle Abbot Tikhon had erected in the town square.

'Certainly I would. I think we should have a referendum on bringing back the monarch. But then, perhaps Russia is not worthy of having a tsar again yet. I believe that only when we have a tsar can we be the Third Rome. Only then can we truly claim to be the heirs of golden Byzantium.'

During the reign of Ivan the Terrible's father a sixteenth-century Father Philotheos of Pskov had cleverly noted that since the old Rome had fallen to the heretic Pope, and the new Rome of Constantinople to the Muslim Ottomans, Moscow must be the third and last Rome. That dubious dictum then became integrated into a powerfully imperialist ideology geared to winning back both Constantinople for Orthodoxy and access to the Mediterranean for the Russian navy. For centuries that dictum and the pretext of defending the Orthodox Christians had given Tsarist Russia a pretty excuse to meddle in the Balkans. One might say Philotheos of Pskov played his part in making the Balkans the lethal 'powder-keg' that it was at the turn of the last century and is again at the turn of this one. The other, more established, Great Powers were always exerting themselves to curb mighty new Russia's appetite for influence in the region. It was fear of Russian expansionism that led the ailing Ottoman empire, for example, to cede control of Cyprus to Britain in 1878. The British foreign secretary, Lord Salisbury, telegraphed a warning to his ambassador in Istanbul: unless Turkey immediately handed Cyprus to

Britain for use as a naval base, 'the capture of Constantinople [by Russia] and the partition of the Empire will be the immediate result.'[1] It is very hard to believe that Britain, France and America would have kept their promise – the one Ambassador Paléologue had reiterated to Rasputin, about giving Russia the 'City of cities' as a reward for her part in defeating the Germans.

With his talk of the Third Rome, young Abbot Tikhon had reduced the entire Soviet period of Russian history to a negligible twinkling of an eye. I protested that Russia was not the only power claiming the right to lead the world's Orthodox Christians. 'The Greeks—' I began.

'Pish, pah!' he said, impatiently flicking his long hair over his shoulder, suddenly thuggish as a Hell's Angel. 'Greece, Romania, Serbia, Bulgaria, Macedonia are all itsy-bitsy little countries! You have to understand only one thing: Russia alone is great enough to bear God!'

When I laughed in disbelief, he frowned.

That night Vanya and I set off on our long journey back west over the Urals to European Russia and Moscow. Trudging back down the old pilgrims' road from the monastery in a swirling snowstorm, we were having to hitch-hike to the railway station because Sergei's offer of a lift had fallen through at the last minute and the bus had broken down.

My thoughts were far away. As soon as it was spring I would be off to that old pawn in the Great Powers' games, Cyprus. A place that has never – to my knowledge – claimed to be great enough to bear God, Cyprus nevertheless supplies Mount Athos with more monks per head of its population than any other Orthodox country in Europe.*

---

* Abbots Tikhon and Avraam played leading roles in the denunciation of their local Bishop Nikon to Patriarch Alexy. By summer 1998 they had collected ninety separate reports of Nikon's infamous homosexual activities – including one by Sergei who alleged that Nikon had paid him the equivalent of a thousand dollars in 1996 for 'playing the man's part' in sex with him. Two months after my visit, the Holy Synod of the Russian Orthodox Church voted to retire the Bishop from his post, but also Tikhon and Avraam from theirs. By July 1999 Abbot Tikhon was in charge of another monastery in the diocese of Nizhny Novgorod.

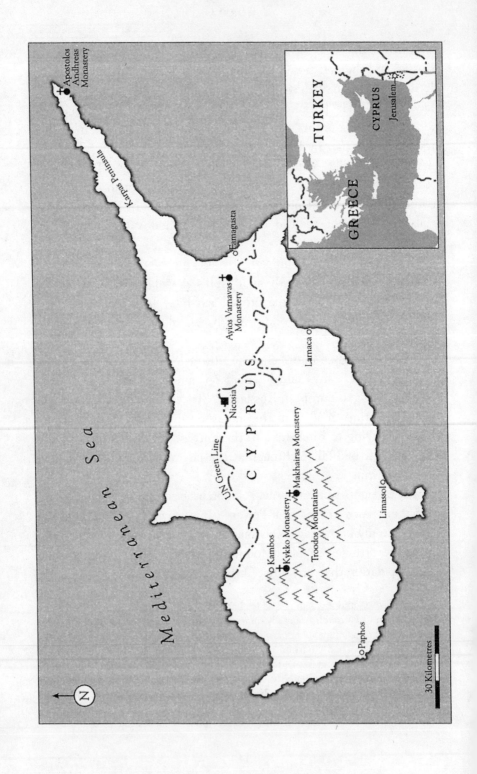

CYPRUS

I was in a taxi, speeding away from Larnaca airport, past holiday apartments and a night-club called 'BYZANTIUM' and on, inland from the coast, down a modest motorway running north between low, pale green hills dotted with bushes. While a warm breeze blew in at the window, a lone palm tree, emblematic against those background green hills, conjured up the world of the Crusades.

In 1191, England's favourite Crusader, Richard the Lionheart, had been on his way to the Third Crusade to recapture the Holy Land for Christendom, when a grievous insult to his sister and his fiancée forced him to drop anchor off Cyprus. The women had narrowly escaped first a shipwreck and then being taken hostage by the island's Byzantine ruler, before being refused supplies of fresh water. Richard came to their rescue, effortlessly conquered the island and – in a 'jocose and affable' mood – married his princess, Berengaria of Navarre, in the fortress of Limassol, before resuming his journey to the Holy Land. Shortly afterwards he dealt with a shortage of cash and worrying reports that the Cypriots were in revolt by selling on his new acquisition to the Knights Templar. In 1196, a furiously insulted Cypriot Orthodox monk recorded that Richard, 'the wicked wretch, achieved this only, that he sold our country to the Latins for two hundred thousand pounds of gold'.[i]

By overtaxing the island, the Knights Templar provoked so much unrest that they soon lost control and returned it to Richard, who found he still had no use for the place. Cyprus changed hands for a third time that year when Jerusalem's redundant Crusader king, Guy de Lusignan, bought it. Gradually it was settled with refugee knights of the lost Crusader kingdoms. Bolstered by the feudal system, which enserfed the native Orthodox Greeks, and settling Catholic church-men in place of the native Orthodox ones, Guy and his descendants ruled Cyprus for the next three centuries. In a curious twin ceremony they were first crowned kings of Cyprus in the vaulted Gothic cathedral they had built themselves in Nicosia, then anointed kings of Jerusalem in the equally gigantic Gothic cathedral of Famagusta, the nearest point on the island to Jerusalem.

By the beginning of the thirteenth century the crusading spirit was not what it had been and Cyprus was contributing to its waning. It seems that en route for the Holy Land to recapture Jerusalem from the Infidel, Crusaders sometimes broke their sea voyages for long holidays on the island and did nothing to endear themselves to the native Greeks. Gambling and quaffing the local wines which, as one chronicler complained, 'intestina et cerebrum destruunt et comburunt',[ii] they brawled. Many reached the Holy Land sick, penniless and good for little on the battlefield.

A centuries-long public-relations catastrophe, the Crusades projected an image of the West that neither Muslims nor Orthodox have ever forgotten. Richard's early conquest of Cyprus acted as a broad hint to Orthodox Byzantium that western Christendom had abandoned any scruples it might have had about seizing territory that was already Christian. The adventure ominously prefigured the Fourth Crusaders' abominable capture and sacking of Constantinople just over a century later. And that crime of a Crusade was what scuppered any hope of reuniting eastern and western Christendom.

I had to force myself back into the present because the car radio's tinny Greek music had faded into a news bulletin and fresh tidings of what sceptics in the West were already beginning to call a new western crusade. Launched on a high moral note like its medieval predecessors, Nato's campaign to stop Serbian police, army and paramilitaries ethnically cleansing Kosovo of its native Albanians was mired in moral ambiguities. Two weeks in, it seemed to be failing.

Bombardismos . . . Yugoslavias . . . was all I could understand of the bulletin.

'So,' sighed the taxi-driver in English, 'the Americans and British are performing their miracle.'

'Miracle?' I asked, bewildered. The bomb-word had made me wince. I had been expecting the taxi-driver to launch a bitter attack on Nato so his mention of miracles confused me.

'Here in Cyprus,' he explained, 'we say "miracle" for a joke, when we are talking about a one hundred per cent bad or stupid thing.'

'Oh, I see.' I was beginning to see something else too: an uncomfortable fortnight on 'enemy' Orthodox territory stretching ahead of me.

Less than a decade after the end of the Cold War the conflict was dividing the continent again. To the west of the 1054 Schism line lived the peoples who believed Nato to be engaged in an action aimed at ridding Europe of an evil warmongering tyrant. To the east lived peoples convinced that Nato's talk of 'humanitarian intervention' on behalf of Kosovo's Albanians was a fig-leaf badly disguising the United States' ambition to rule the entire world. Archbishop Christodoulos of Greece was describing Nato's efforts to protect the Albanians as 'a war against Orthodoxy'. The Cypriot Orthodox Church was collecting aid for the Serbs. From the Bosnian Serb Republic in the west to Vladivostok in the east, from Solovetsky in the north to Cyprus here in the south, the clock-hands were whizzing back on Orthodox time. Nato was wearing the colours of every force that had ever come out of the West to threaten the East – Crusaders, Teutonic knights, Napoleon's armies or Hitler's Nazis. In that Holy Week leading up to their Easter, Eastern Orthodox Europe was remembering Christ's betrayal, suffering and death with more passionate empathy than usual.

We were ploughing through rush-hour traffic in downtown Nicosia already but the taxi-driver had not concluded his appreciation of the West's 'miracle'. 'Haven't we all had enough wars in this century? America wants to control the whole world!' he was telling me, as he set me down at my hotel.

It was dark when I went out for a first stroll around an old town smelling emphatically exotic, of some kind of sweet blossom and drains. Narrow, unlit, flanked by high dark buildings and almost empty, the streets echoed eerily with the distant metallic screech of shutters coming down around a corner and the clip-clopping of high heels a few streets away. After half an hour or so I arrived in a more open space containing some trees and a large two-storey building with a high spiked fence around it. This, I deduced from my map, must be the Archbishop's palace. But what was that? A gigantic black figure, perhaps thirty feet tall, stood opposite me on the other side of the fence. Had I been anywhere in Russia I would have recognized a left-over Lenin statue or a monument to the socialist worker. But who were the Greek Cypriots honouring like this? I could just make out that the giant was bearded and wearing something other than trousers.

It could only be Archbishop Makarios III of Cyprus, the most famous Orthodox churchman ever and the most troublesome religious and political leader Cyprus' British colonial masters ever had to deal with. The outsize monument commemorated a man whose activities dominated world headlines for the best part of the 1950s and 1960s and severely tested the Cold War superpowers in the 1970s.

Makarios, of course, was not just Archbishop. He was 'Ethnarch', which meant that, like generations of Orthodox churchmen through-out centuries of Ottoman rule, he was the political as well as spiritual leader of his Orthodox flock. Cyprus had something as archaic-sounding as an ethnarch in the middle of the twentieth century because, almost a hundred years after the rest of the Orthodox Balkans had thrown off the Ottoman colonial yoke, the island was still under British rule. Ethnarch Makarios could have walked the old tightrope, promoting the interests of his flock while keeping in with his colonial British masters as old Gregorios V of Constantinople had been doing on the eve of the Greek War of Independence. But, no, Makarios' dream of *Enosis* – uniting Cyprus to Greece – left no room for compromise. Taking his cue rather from that standard-raising Archbishop Germanos of Patras in the Peloponnese, he blessed and backed the Cypriots' violent *Enosis* struggle in the second half of the 1950s. A guerrilla movement called the Greek Organization of Cypriot Fighters, but known by the acronym EOKA, did the violent, dirty work.

A year before EOKA's violence started, one British broadsheet admiringly described Makarios as a person possessed of at least as much natural star quality as the young Macedonian Bishop Naum of Strumica, the personable Metropolitan Daniel of Moldavia or Abbot Tikhon of Verkhoturye: 'He is a character as warming as he is striking. His dark dignity and garb make him seem much taller than he is. His beard is flecked with grey, his features are most handsome. Though in conversation he shows a thorough grasp of politics it is with the underlying spiritual issues that he seems concerned . . .'[iii]

That rosy assessment soon changed. By the mid-1950s wives of British servicemen were being blown up and the British tabloids had dubbed him 'Black Mak'.

The British, loath to lose their strategic toehold in the Middle East and reluctant to abandon the Turkish Cypriot minority to the whims of the Greek majority, stalled and stonewalled over relinquishing the colony. The religious fervour with which the Greek Cypriots were prepared to pursue their archbishop's dream of uniting the island with Greece appalled them. *Enosis* made no economic sense whatsoever because Cyprus was a better ordered and more prosperous place than mainland Greece in the aftermath of the second World War. Nor did it make better political sense. Turkey was never going to allow an island that was less than fifty miles off her shores, one on which Turks made up 18 per cent of the population, to become a part of Greece. A clearer instance of Orthodox heart ruling mind than the Greek Cypriots' insistence on *Enosis* in the 1950s is hard to imagine.

When the British discovered that EOKA was backed by Archbishop Makarios, financed by inexhaustible Church funds and reliant on a network of monastery safe-houses, they at last understood that their enemy was Greek religious nationalism. Desperately, they calculated that the EOKA killing machine could best be disabled by removing its spiritual engine. In 1956 Archbishop Makarios was arrested and, along with three other turbulent Orthodox churchmen, bundled aboard an RAF plane bound for the Seychelles.

There he languished for a year in a former British governor's mansion named Sans Souci. He filled the idle hours by studying English and the exotic native insect life, playing ball with a dog called Bimbo, exercising with a skipping rope, listening to news of his homeland on the radio and holding church services under a tree in the garden. From time to time the local Anglican archdeacon and the Catholic bishop paid visits, for tea and some theological chit-chat. His captors warmed to him. The British officer employed to guard the four Cypriots judged Makarios a frightfully good chap. 'It is difficult to understand why a man with such a sporting nature has not condemned the unsporting tactics of the EOKA terrorists,'[iv] wrote Captain de Geyt. His wife, Makarios' English teacher, was charmed by her pupil: 'Makarios has the most remarkable eyes,' she wrote. 'They suddenly begin to glow as if a lamp were lit, when he is amused, interested or enthusiastic.'[v]

Britain's cure for its EOKA ills spectacularly failed. Makarios' exile only made him a martyr back home, and EOKA continued its campaign of violence. When Cyprus was finally granted its independence in 1960 Makarios swept to presidential power with a resounding two thirds of the vote.

Makarios seems to have run Cyprus as an abbot would a monastery, or a father his family. But his style of politicking – elegantly evasive in the old Byzantine way – was at odds with a modern world dominated by two ruthless superpowers who possessed the means to blow up a world they were busy carving up between them. To Makarios' way of thinking, Cyprus was the equal of any superpower. The tone of his 1960 inauguration speech-cum-sermon is telling: 'We are a small people strong only in its spiritual power, which can assert itself only in its moral stature . . . The role of the Republic of Cyprus will be immense and its mission significant and sacred . . . the uneasy ambitions of three continents and the conflicts of two worlds stretch around our seas . . .'[vi]

Greek and Turkish Cypriot relations rapidly deteriorated after independence. Neither people trusted the other nor exerted themselves much to make the new constitution work. When the Turkish Cypriots refused to agree to Makarios' planned alterations to the constitution in 1963, the remnants of EOKA provoked street fighting and the Turkish Cypriots fought back. The troubles escalated. In

1964 George Ball from the US State Department flew in to trouble-shoot after Greek Cypriots had killed fifty Turkish Cypriots in Limassol. On the second day of polite meetings with Makarios, Ball told the Archbishop-President that the violence had reached an intolerable level. He reported the following exchange with Makarios.

> *Makarios:* But, Mr Secretary, the Greeks and Turks have lived together for 2,000 years on this island and there have always been occasional incidents; we are quite used to this.
> *Ball:* Your Beatitude – I've been trying for the last two days to make the point that this is not the Middle Ages but the latter part of the twentieth century. The world's not going to stand idly by and let you turn this beautiful little island into your private abattoir.
> *Makarios:* Oh, you're a hard man, Mr Secretary, a very hard man.[vii]

In 1964 United Nations troops arrived to try to restore peace.

A decade later Makarios fell dangerously foul of mainland Greece, whose right-wing military junta was backed by America. The colonels and their American friends feared and hated Makarios' independent-minded chumminess with the Soviet Union. Makarios, desperate to retain his independence from both superpowers, probably spent a lot of time discussing the Orthodox heritage that Greek Cypriots shared with Russians, rather than planning how to emulate the Soviet system or hand the Kremlin control of his island. But America's President Nixon once wrote off Makarios as simply 'Castro in a cassock'. Assisted by America, the Greek junta started plotting to remove the Archbishop-President and join Cyprus to Greece. *Enosis* was a good idea, after all.

Early in the morning of 15 July 1974, Makarios was at home in his archiepiscopal palace having a breakfast meeting with a delegation of schoolchildren, when a shell slammed into the building. Outside in the car-park was a line of firing tanks. An aide, one of Makarios' nephews, persuaded him of the urgent need to escape. Much to his chagrin – for Makarios was an extraordinarily fastidious man – he was hatless and unrobed when he and his nephew plunged out of a French window at the side of the building, through a tangle of bushes, across a dry river-bed and out on to a small back road. There they managed to commandeer a Morris 1500, which almost immediately ran out of petrol. Along came a battered Vauxhall, whose pious and handicapped driver selflessly donated his car to the Church.

Makarios and his nephew headed west for the cooler heights of the Troodos mountains. They were bound for Kykko, the ancient monastery where the Archbishop had begun his training for the priesthood at the age of thirteen and held meetings with EOKA leaders in the 1950s. When they arrived Makarios' brother monks informed him that his death had already been reported on the radio news. With no time to waste, Makarios switched to yet another getaway vehicle and drove on south towards the coastal town of Paphos. From a radio station there he broadcast to his stricken people: 'Cypriots! You know this voice. You know who is speaking ... It is I, Makarios. I am the one you chose to be your leader ... I am not dead as the junta in Athens and its representatives here wanted. I am alive. And I am with you, to fight and carry the flag in our common struggle. The junta's coup has failed.'[viii]

On hearing his familiar voice, some believed that their beloved leader had died and risen again in an uncanny imitation of Jesus Christ himself, others simply that a miracle had saved him.

A United Nations contingent in Paphos then arranged with the nearby British army base to have Makarios rescued by helicopter and flown off the island to safety.

Four days after Greece's clumsy coup Turkey wrought a terrible revenge by invading Cyprus. Turkish troops overran the wealthiest, most beautiful northern half of the island, and a horrible bout of two-way 'ethnic cleansing' ensued. A hundred and eighty thousand Greek Cypriots abandoned their homes, their orange and lemon tree plantations, their wheatfields and hotels in the brand new holiday resorts, and fled south. Thousands of Turkish Cypriots were bussed in the opposite direction. A UN-patrolled Green, or Attila, Line with its dead buffer zone, razor wire, sand-bags, flags and sentry-posts was established. It is still there, slicing right across the island, through the heart of the capital, Nicosia.

Archbishop Makarios was reinstated as president, but only of southern Cyprus. After two heart attacks he died in 1977, aged only sixty-four. Some said his maimed country had broken his heart. His successor, Archbishop Chrysostomos, has never put himself up as a presidential candidate but little else has changed. As soon as I started talking to people I found that 1974 was not a quarter of a century ago but yesterday, a moment ago, now. Nothing has healed. At the start of the twenty-first century Nicosia is the only divided city left in Europe and the United Nations force, which arrived for six months in 1964, has clocked up thirty-five years. With Orthodox slaughtering Muslim in Kosovo, the prospect of a solution has seldom seemed more distant. In the continent-wide war that Orthodoxy is waging to defend its traditional territories against Islam and the West, the Cyprus front is an important one. Greece and Turkey are both members of Nato.

From time to time there are skirmishes. In August 1996 members of a patriotic Greek Cypriot motorcyclists' club, whose activities were handsomely subsidized[ix] by the Orthodox Church, roared into the UN buffer zone at various points along the Green Line. In Nicosia their provocation was met by Turkish Cypriots armed with sticks and lengths of piping. Battle was joined. There were seventy casualties, including twelve injured UN soldiers, and one Greek Cypriot death. A week after the rally another Greek Cypriot was filmed running into the buffer zone, shimmying up a Turkish flagpole and being shot by Turkish Cypriots. While the UN peacekeepers fretted and fumed, and cursed the Greek Cypriots for their provocation, Archbishop Chrysostomos gave a funeral oration in which he praised the young hotheads on their metal chargers. He told them: 'Your demonstration proved that you have Greek fighting spirit which directs you. You helped the political leadership promote the fair demands of Cyprus for justice and the restoration of human rights ... Soon you will show that you are Greeks, descendants of heroes and martyrs.'[x]

I stopped marvelling at the giant Makarios and wandered on

towards a shining light a hundred yards away at the far end of the spiked fence. It flooded out of a little yellow stone church, so full that there were faithful spilling out of the glass swing doors into the courtyard. It seemed to me suddenly that on the first night of Holy Week the city's entire Orthodox population had compressed itself into this dazzling, vibrant little space. I was happy to be back east of the Schism line. Squeezing inside, I decided that Rasputin was more than justified in boasting of the superiority of Orthodox Easter. I lit a candle for Bogdan a few hundred miles to the north in Belgrade and another for the Kosovo Albanians.

The church was stuffy from the heat of candles, bodies and the lights of a film crew ambling up and down the nave, trailing flexes and swinging their cameras around the frescoed ceilings. Around the altar was a group of men singing the service in chorus. In the front half of the church were high pews filled with men sweating in suits. In the back half were elegant women fanning themselves. I watched as one of the cameramen zoomed in close on a silver-bearded churchman with doleful brown eyes. Dressed in red and black with a jewelled sceptre in one hand, he was seated on a carved golden throne just to the right of the altar having his ringed hand kissed by members of the congregation. A quick query to the woman beside me confirmed my suspicion. He was Archbishop Chrysostomos.

I squeezed out of the church and walked on. At the end of a pitch-dark street lined with almost derelict buildings was a guard-house, just a wooden shed painted with the stripes of the Greek flag, marking the border. On my side, up high, the blue and white-crossed Greek flag fluttered. Across the dead silence of the United Nations' buffer zone flapped the Turkish crescent moon. I heard the young Greek guards chatting in their box as the Muslim muezzin's pre-recorded call to prayer came floating across the Green Line. The sights and sounds belonged to another time, to the squalid grandeur of the Crusading age.

Wandering back a few streets, I found a vine-covered taverna with lights on and something that sounded improbably like church music drifting out of its open front door. Inside there was only the weary-looking proprietor. Sitting at one of the white-plastic-covered tables with a heap of diced meat and some skewers in front of him, he was slowly threading his pork *souvlaki,* and droning along to the church chant blaring from a television in the corner. A glance at the screen and I recognized the dazzlingly lit church interior I had left a few minutes before. The film crew had been broadcasting live.

Because Dimos left his *souvlaki-*making to prepare me some extraordinarily delicious meat with fresh lemon, some stuffed vine-leaves flavoured with mint, and chips, I found myself patronizing his establishment every evening of Holy Week. Usually I was his only customer because, he explained, most people were reluctant to venture this close to the Green Line after dark. We established a companionable routine. Night after night we watched first a Holy Week church service relayed live from one or other famous Cypriot church or monastery, followed by the late news about *Yugoslavias* and Nato's *bombardismos* before debating the question of the day. Was Milošević's offer of a unilateral cease-fire for Orthodox Easter sincere? Could Cyprus' ex-President persuade Milošević to release the three American soldiers? Were Russia's threats of military action in defence of the Serbs to be taken seriously? Dimos shared the taxi-driver's opinions on the war. 'Most people here think that America is not right,' he told me.

On Holy Thursday we ate and watched, then went on chatting together long after the news was over. The subject of Archbishop Makarios came up.

'You wanna know how much he smoked a day? Guess how many?'

'Forty?'

'Pah, forty! One hundred and fifty!'

'I don't believe you, Dimos.'

'I'm one thousand per cent sure of this – and he had a skinny girlfriend. You wanna know her name? And another girlfriend, a policewoman.'

'You didn't think of much of him, then,' I said, laughing and helping myself to another Coke from his cooler cabinet.

Dimos told me that in the late 1960s and early 1970s he and his father had had blistering rows about where Makarios was leading independent Cyprus. His father had loved the Archbishop so much he had called him 'the Second Jew', meaning that he was another Christ. He had once given his son a gold ring engraved with Makarios' face but Dimos had never worn it. Dimos had been twenty-one and already working in this same restaurant when the Turks invaded on 15 July 1974. The shooting had started at around eight o'clock in the morning and the radio news had confirmed his worst fears.

'You wanna know what I did? The first thing I did? I came out of the kitchen and I pulled the picture of Makarios – it was hanging right there over the door – straight off the wall. And you wanna know what I did with it? I *smashed* it on the floor.'

He had then been called up to fight but the gun supplies had run out just as it was his turn to be given one. Everyone ahead of him in the queue had been sent off north to do battle for an area called Kyrenia.

'None of those men came back. I think a miracle saved me,' he said. Dimos' visceral hatred of Makarios had never interfered with his belief in God and miracles.

'Makarios made a big, big mistake with *Enosis*,' he sighed, staring into his little coffee cup, 'and, you know, the problem with many of us Greeks is that we think history only started in 1974. We don't remember all the bad things we did to the Turks before that. Nobody's gonna talk about that! But now my daughter reads about Cyprus on the Internet and she says to me, "Dad, is it true that we killed the Turks?" and I must say, "Yes, it's true."'

Dimos told me how unfairly Makarios had behaved towards the Turkish Cypriots after independence in 1960. He told me that he remembered the last decade or so of the Makarios era as being like living under a Soviet regime. 'You couldn't say nothing against Makarios because the next day you were gonna get a bomb through your window – Paf!'

'But, these days, it's all right to say anything you like.'

'Well,' said Dimos, looking pained, 'I wouldn't say any of that to the people who come in here to eat every day because some are gonna boycott my restaurant or even plant bombs.'

'Do those kind of people still want *Enosis?*'

'No. I think only Archbishop Chrysostomos still wants *Enosis.*'

KYKKO MONASTERY

On a bright, warm Good Friday morning I set out from Nicosia to drive due west towards the Troodos mountains, along the route Makarios took in that Vauxhall on the morning of 15 July 1974. I was thinking how natural it was that, fleeing for his life, he should have headed straight to Kykko.

The most famous Orthodox monastery on the island, Kykko was Makarios' real home. From the moment the monks there took the bright village boy in to be educated and primed for exalted office in the Cypriot Church hierarchy, they became his new family and he exchanged his surname Moukhas for 'Kykkotis'. For seven years he studied hard, attended church services, fetched water from the well and kept the church stocked with candles. But he also larked about, feeding his master's favourite sausages to the cats and scrawling *Zito I Enosis* – Long Live Union – on the kitchen wall. When Makarios was twenty, the Kykko monks sent him to grammar school in Nicosia and lodged him at their *metochion* there. Next, the monastery subsidized his further theological and law studies in Athens, and finally it blessed his departure by ocean liner to Boston, on a World Council of Churches scholarship. It was Cleopa, Abbot of Kykko and Makarios' spiritual father, who subsequently promoted his elevation to bishop and cut short his stay in Boston. By 1950 Makarios was the thirty-seven-year-old Archbishop of Cyprus. Kykko became the venue for secret meetings with EOKA leaders, and a favourite place to entertain foreign guests on hot summer evenings. I imagined I would have no trouble finding a monk who remembered Makarios at Kykko and calculated I would be there within the hour.

The road ran straight past UN forces bases and loosely strung-out villages of new two-storey white houses until, after about half an hour, it began climbing into the foothills of the mountains. My spirits soared at the first signpost to Kykko monastery. Higher and higher I went, around the forested mountains and past a sign pointing off into the woods in the direction of an old EOKA hide-out, until the road suddenly opened out into a car-park filled with tour buses and hire cars like my own. There, at the crossing point of two shallow mountain valleys with two mountains, lay a sprawling red-roofed monastery flying a Greek flag.

Glittering modern mosaics and a posse of police surrounded its arched entranceway. In its courtyard were three different guided tour groups viewing some very new frescoes. One showed St Paul being tipped headlong into a ditch, over the head of an almost cartoon-style horse. My heart ached for Gračanica, alone on the Kosovo plain with its solemn dark masterpieces, and the little charred church of Veljuša monastery in the mountains of the southern FYROM. Kykko's gold-and-red-liveried museum attendants and its church's shiny marble floor resembled the lobby of the luxury hotel down the road from my own in Nicosia. There was the well Makarios must have drawn water from but it had been prettified with a shiny new pail hung beside the neatly wound rope. I remembered the ruined disorder of Solovetsky or Verkhoturye's work in progress. The closest thing I had seen to this glamorous palace was Transylvania's brand new Birth of the Mother of God monastery and that was modest and restrained by comparison.

Kykko has grown fabulously rich on donations made and land bequeathed to it on account of an icon of the Mother of God said to have been painted by St Luke from life. Possession of such an icon – one of only three in the world – made the monastery as important a stop-off as Mount Athos for generations of Russian pilgrims en route to Jerusalem before 1917. How exactly the monastery came by its holy money-spinner is a dramatic tale of casual violence and miracle cures.

It is said that an eleventh-century Byzantine Duke of Cyprus called Mihailis Voutomedes was out in the Troodos mountains hunting the island's native *moufflon* one day when he lost his way in the forest. After a time he chanced upon an old hermit, of whom he haughtily asked the way. The hermit protested this unkind treatment by acting as if he had not heard the Duke and this in turn so infuriated Voutomedes that he gave the old man a good hiding. The hermit retaliated with a curse, which returned to haunt the Duke when he fell dangerously ill shortly afterwards. Voutomedes had the hermit brought to his bedside and promised to fulfil any penance the old man cared to set him in return for lifting the curse. 'Go to Constantinople, ask the Emperor for an icon of the Mother of God painted by St Luke and bring it back to Cyprus,' ordered the hermit. The Duke set sail for the City of cities, with the hermit in his entourage. Not surprisingly, the Emperor was reluctant to see one of Constantinople's most valuable icons removed to an obscure island. After much wrangling, the hermit at last received the icon as thanks for his success in curing the Emperor's daughter of some terrible affliction. Back home in Cyprus, the Duke had the treasure installed in a church he had built near the hermit's cell. The very trees bowed down to venerate the icon as it passed on its way to its new home.

Unlike the original monastery buildings, that icon has emerged unscathed from three monastery fires. During one it was stuffed into the hollow trunk of a pine-tree by a handicapped man whom the Mother of God told to 'Arise quickly and take my icon and save thyself.'[xi] The icon also acquired a reputation for savage acts of violence. An eighteenth-century Greek monk was punished for daring to draw aside its protective covering with a hot blast in the face. Once it tore the arm off an impious Turk who was trying to light his cigarette from a holy lamp. Kykko has known gentler wonders. In February 1997 another of its Mother of God icons, a sixteenth-century work, began to weep. A novice monk was the first to notice tears flowing down the faces of the Mary and her Christ-child. Archbishop Chrysostomos of Cyprus lost no time in declaring the miracle to be a sign of impending disaster, but the monastery's Abbot

Nikiforos was less pessimistic. He thought it was probably a gesture of sympathy towards Greek Cypriots for the tragic division of their island.

It being Good Friday, all the icons were draped in dark cloths of mourning for Christ's death on the Cross, so I could not check for droplets or damp spots on the icon. Instead, I located the monastery's shop, which was doing an excellent tourist trade in clear *zivania* brandy made from grapes. At the cash desk I asked a friendly-looking young man's help with finding a monk who remembered Makarios and the EOKA era. He kindly escorted me across the courtyard towards a corpulent older man who – to judge by the way he stood in a doorway surveying the scene and fiddling with a string of silver worry beads – held a position of responsibility in the monastery. He told us that I needed to speak to a certain Father Kirillos, who was down at the tourist restaurant, drinking coffee. By the time I located the vast single-storey glass and concrete building that was Kykko's tourist restaurant, the corpulent man with the worry beads had arrived there too. Coffee in one hand, beads in the other and mobile phone on the table he was sitting with a group of people, including a grey-bearded monk wearing a royal blue cassock and a businesslike couple of pens clipped to his breast pocket. I guessed this must be Father Kirillos. The corpulent man invited me to join them for coffee.

An exceptionally fit-looking seventy-four-year-old, Father Kirillos had an evenly tanned face and bright dark eyes. A hint of a smile was just discernible through his beard. My project puzzled him but he obligingly told me a story about the old days, about one day in particular – 28 January 1956 – when he had assisted the cause of *Enosis*. Makarios had urgently needed to visit Kykko to liaise with Giorgios Grivas, the commander-in-chief of EOKA whose hide-out headquarters I had passed on my way up the mountain. But the Archbishop never went to Kykko in mid-winter. Such a conspicuous departure from the norm was guaranteed to raise British suspicions. At last it was decided that only an occasion as momentous as the anointing of a new priest could adequately explain a sudden January jaunt to the mountains. Twenty-five-year-old Father Kirillos was unexpectedly upgraded from deacon to priest.

But the British were clamping down and closing in. Makarios was deported to the Seychelles that year and a series of forest fires smoked EOKA activists out of their mountain hide-outs. When British soldiers broke open the monastery safe and found it full of dynamite, Kykko was emptied of all but three old monks. Father Kirillos and most of his brothers were removed to the monastery's *metochion* in Nicosia. The British calculated they could keep a better eye on them there, but they had reckoned without Father Kirillos' devotion to the cause.

'I am proud to say that there on the edge of the city, with my own hands, I dug Grivas the hide-out, which was his last residence,' he said, with the ghost of a smile. We chatted on about Kykko's supplies to EOKA's hide-outs and the difficulties involved in co-ordination and communications.

'The EOKA men had to be like postmen,' interjected Father Kirillos' corpulent friend, reaching for his mobile phone. 'Nobody had these in those days. Now we all have them. Ha! Ha!' With another hint of a smile the old monk drew from the folds of his royal blue cassock a perfectly matching little royal blue phone.

Wishing the company a happy Easter, I asked directions to the grotto where Makarios had wanted to be buried in sight of his home village of Panayia about fifty kilometres to the south. It was five minutes' drive away at the very top of the mountain. Outside a crazy-paved mausoleum and a tomb adorned with Makarios' portrait and some fresh flowers, two boy soldiers in camouflage were eating their lunch.

Early the following morning I drove back to Kykko from the nearby town where I had spent the night. It was Easter Saturday. The local foresters and fruit-farmers were bound to be attending a morning service, I thought. I arrived to find Kykko's car park filled with rows of shiny new Japanese and American four-wheel-drives and pick-ups but the inner courtyard was thronging with the faithful in dark

Sunday suits. The service was almost over. A boy hammered on a *semantron* hanging from the balcony. A line of black-robed monks exited swiftly from the church, climbed the stairs to the second floor and swept along the balcony. Pursued by part of the congregation they then disappeared behind closed doors. The atmosphere was clannish, and I was a conspicuous intruder.

I left and followed a long line of those pick-ups making its way home to the village of Kambos. The Green Line lay a few miles north of Kambos and the territory stolen by the Turks in 1974 north of that. The road, bordered with hedgerows full of yellow flowers, wound down the mountain, into a green valley misty with blossoming cherry trees, around another mountain and on to the village, which lay tucked into the cleft between mountains, in a space so narrow that the houses looked as if they had been stacked one on top of each other up the mountainside. Descending a steep road to its heart I reached a little bridge over a stream and a tree-shaded outdoor *kafeneion*. The gurgle of running water, the cool leisure of men sitting smoking and drinking coffee under a plane tree reminded me of a Bosnian town I knew well. What Kambos and Travnik had in common, I decided, was the easy old Ottoman atmosphere, the restfulness lent a place by running water, wood, shade and plenty of time. I stopped for coffee at that *kafeneion* and was just about to drive off again when who should pull up in an Isuzu jeep with tinted windows and 'Big Horn' emblazoned on its rear but Father Kirillos' corpulent friend. I noticed how enthusiastically the old men idling over their coffee hailed his arrival. More coffee was ordered.

Ariko, short for Theokharis, which means God-bearer, was huge enough to bear anything. Almost as broad as he was tall, his air of accustomed authority was enhanced by a fine toothbrush moustache and impassive blue eyes. The news that Ariko was *mukhtaris* of Kambos – the village mayor or headman – did not surprise me in the least. I later discovered that both the word and the position it denotes are a direct legacy of almost four hundred years of Ottoman rule. Ariko had been *mukhtaris* of Kambos for twenty years, he told me, but spent most of his time helping out at the monastery. So charmed was I by the similarity between Kambos and Travnik, and the survival of Ottoman headmen, that I was starting to see Ottoman influence everywhere I looked. I suggested to Ariko that his beautiful worry beads must be another Ottoman legacy. 'No, no – nothing Turkish!' he corrected me sternly, 'They're *kombolloi* – only Greek! Only Christian! A present from Father Kirillos!'

But instead of resenting my insult, Ariko told me that I must spend Easter in Kambos. After ordering the *kafeneion* owner to rent me a room for the night, he commanded me to be waiting for him at eleven thirty p.m. when he would honk his car horn, pick me up and take me to the local church for the midnight service. The following day, he informed me, I would be having Easter lunch with his wife, two married daughters and six grandchildren. Then, *kombolloi* in one hand, mobile phone in the other, he heaved himself back into his Isuzu jeep and roared off up the mountainside.

I passed a pleasant day, driving from one to another little stone church, each with hardly a bell-tower, let alone a cross, to betray its function. Instead they had the steeply pitched snow-repellent roofs of Romania's painted churches. Most of these little jewels were built just after the Crusader Lusignans arrived on the island to impose their Catholic establishment. Replacing the native Orthodox bishops with their home-grown Catholic ones, the Lusignans had palmed off the Orthodox with ludicrously remote and unimportant sees. The little barn churches of the High Troodos were the precious products of a culture and society forced to take to the hills. The flaking frescoes of their interiors are mostly later than those I had seen in Macedonia and Serbia. The apostles' lively expressions, the insertion of a *moufflon* or a hunting dog – figures unknown to Byzantine art – are tell-tale signs that the Orthodox were not immune to the first seismic stirrings of the Renaissance. The island's almost four centuries of Catholic rule meant that, with time, accommodations were reached and odd syntheses achieved between eastern and western Christianity. Ayios Ioannis Lambadhistis even has a fifteenth-century Catholic chapel opening off its much earlier Orthodox church.

Outsiders were sometimes shocked by such symbioses. When a

German Catholic monk called Felix Fabri visited Cyprus in the fifteenth century, he was disgusted to find that a single priest was serving two churches, one of them Orthodox, the other Catholic. In the first, he noted, the priest dispensed leavened communion bread, in the second unleavened. Fabri denounced the priest as 'a heretic of the worst kind, leading the people astray hither and thither'.[xii] The Cypriots' religious tolerance usually favoured the Latins, of course. A favourite Orthodox story goes that once upon a time two Orthodox monks were happily arguing with two Catholic monks about leavened versus unleavened communion bread, until one of the Orthodox monks suggested they put the matter to the test. An Orthodox monk and a Catholic monk would each take his communion bread in his arms and walk into the middle of a fire with it. Whoever emerged unscathed would win the argument, said the Orthodox monk. The Catholics were so terrified by the challenge they ran off to report the Orthodox monks to the Catholic authorities. Charged with heresy, the Orthodox monks found themselves tied by their feet to horses' tails, and dragged over cobblestones in a marketplace until the flesh was torn from their bodies. They were finally burnt at the stake. The little matter of the hefty taxes the Orthodox clergy had to pay to their Catholic counterparts also rankled with the former. In the middle of the sixteenth century the Orthodox Archbishop was having to find 12 measures of rose-water and 12 ropes of garlic in summer, while in winter he was liable for 600 walnuts, 4 measures of figs, 6 measures of sack, 12 pigs and 12 hens.

Delighted by my day, and looking forward to Easter with Ariko and his family, I turned back towards Kambos. The light was pinkish and fading fast as I rounded a long bend on one of those empty mountain roads and was shocked to see a white placard marked with the word Nato and a swastika sign fastened to a tree. I had grown used to the occasional glimpses of a target sign, modelled on the badges the Belgrade Serbs were sporting in their daily demonstrations against Nato's bombing campaign, in the back window of a car, on an office desk or even a T-shirt. But I found the idea that someone had made the placard, deliberately brought it to this remote spot, and climbed up above the road to tie it to a tree, disturbing.

While I was eating dinner in Kambos' grandiosely outsize restaurant later and half watching a video of the *Life of Christ* on a giant screen, the helpful young man I had encountered behind the cash desk in Kykko's gift shop appeared. He introduced himself as Kyriakos, ordered himself a beer and sat down. It transpired that he and Ariko were related, via his brother who had married Ariko's elder daughter. Kyriakos, who spoke excellent English, told me that Ariko's prosperity was the result of a lottery win. The *mukhtaris* of Kambos had claimed his prize, thrown in his forestry job and offered his services to Kykko where his qualities of leadership were highly appreciated. He was first placed in charge of the team of women who cleaned the guest rooms but soon promoted to more responsible duties. Now he was famous as the right-hand man of Father Kirillos, himself the right-hand man of Abbot Nikiforos. Just as Verkhoturye had for Sergei thousands of miles to the north in Siberia, Kykko had acted as a magnet for Ariko. Both men, it seemed to me, were energetic sorts, on the look-out for a purpose in life that was grander than profit. Assured of God's blessing and plenty of patriotic kudos, men like Ariko or Sergei could take a real pride in their association with their monasteries.

One of the reasons why Ariko was such a popular *mukhtaris* was that his indispensability to Father Kirillos meant he was excellently placed to find jobs for Kambos people as museum workers, restaurant staff, guards, cleaners and shop attendants.

'In fact, because of Ariko Father Kirillos gave me my job in the gift shop,' Kyriakos admitted. 'Abbot Nikiforos wants young people to stay in the villages, so he is helping by creating jobs for us. Some people complain that Kykko is like a second government of Cyprus, with jobs in its own civil service to hand out – but I think it's a good thing.'

Kyriakos had just proceeded to astound me with the news that the large restaurant we were patronizing had been a gift from Kykko to Kambos, when we were joined by his brother Louka and then, very briefly, by the *mukhtaris* himself. Ariko sauntered in, nodded at us, ordered the restaurateur not to let me pay for my meal, and sauntered out again.

I was finding Cyprus friendlier even than Patmos. In Kambos on that Easter evening, the war over Kosovo and the widening crack between Eastern Orthodox Europe and the West seemed a world away.

At eleven thirty I was ready and waiting at the *kafeneion* when Ariko honked the horn on his Isuzu. I climbed in beside two of his granddaughters and his serenely friendly wife Niki, for the couple of hundred yards' drive to the church. Modestly built of stone, single-storey and steep-roofed, it was already full. As befitted a *mukhtaris*, Ariko headed towards the front of the male preserve up near the altar, while his wife made sure I was provided with a candle to light at that death-defying midnight moment before shepherding me to the back of the church. It was crowded with women and small children. All around me were bowed widows in their black, young mothers with freshly washed hair and formal clothes, teenage girls in mini-skirts and tight blouses. One toddler demanded that her fancy candle be lit early while another slept, feet dangling and mouth open. While Niki bowed her head in prayer, her teenage granddaughter cast a coldly critical eye over every young male who entered.

From where I was standing I had a good view of the back of Ariko's shiny pate, of the gilded iconostasis and of the priest in his glittering robes. The choir sang badly but lustily for a while, and then, at five minutes to midnight, all the lights except the icon lamps were extinguished. An icon's gold background gleamed in the gloom. There was a low buzz of childish excitement but silence when the priest emerged from behind the altar with lit candles in his hands to announce that Christ had risen. Then he passed his lights on, and on and on and on, as far as the back of the church until all the children's faces were glowing golden. The singing was lustier than ever.

And then it seemed to be over. People were standing in line to kiss the icon, make a donation and have their hands sprinkled with rose-water before leaving the church. Outside, the noisy celebrations had already begun. The chilly night air was being ripped by the rackety random ack-ack of firecrackers while the men of the village stood in a circle around a roaring bonfire, their faces red. All day I had been seeing piles of logs rising outside village churches in preparation for this moment – the burning of an effigy of the apostle who had been prepared to betray Christ for thirty pieces of silver. Kambos' Judas was shrivelling and falling at the centre of a raging inferno. Orange sparks shot up to challenge the stars and the village boys roared with glee. Ariko and his son-in-law, Louka, greeted me with 'Christos anesti!' – Christ is risen! Remembering Patmos I replied hesitantly, 'Halithos anesti!' – He is risen indeed.

The next morning everyone greeted everyone like that. Drinking my coffee under the shady tree by the bridge, I watched a teenage girl shout the good news of Christ's resurrection to the kafeneion-owner. An old man mumbled it to an old woman in black as they passed each other shuffling along the road. Men rolled down the windows of their pick-ups and shouted it at each other. A woman shrieked it from her wooden balcony to the neighbour living opposite, who was sitting on his doorstep basting his Easter meat with margarine as it turned on a spit over charcoal. By late morning everyone must have heard the news and agreed it was the truth. The whole village was wrapped in the incense of roasting meat.

I wandered back up the road towards the church, past the cemetery and the monument to the five villagers who had sacrificed their lives for the Greek cause when the Turks invaded in 1974. Another service seemed to be in its last stages when I arrived because the door swung open and out tumbled some altar-boys in blue and silver satin robes. They were pushing and shoving at each other in their eagerness to do a clumsy job of carrying out and setting up a wooden stand before loading it with a large icon of the church's patron saint. At last it was done and the icon's gold background looked dazzling against the green-clad mountainside behind. Hot spring sunshine warmed us all while a woman threaded her way through the crowd handing out chunks of communion bread from a large basket. With a shy smile she gave the last crust to me. Touched and very pleased, I sat on a bench with a row of old women in black and munched, watching everyone else approach the icon, kiss it, have their hands sprinkled with rose-water and greet the priest.

Honk! Honk! It was Ariko in his Isuzu, come to collect me for lunch. I climbed aboard and we charged through the village centre. Turning off the main road through the village he raced the car up an almost vertical incline then swerved sharply towards a large white family house. Its front garden was filled with children and smoke from the barbecue. When lunch was served at a table set for fifteen in the kitchen, I was seated in the place of honour, up at the men's end, near Ariko and his sons-in-law. While Ariko and his wife squabbled about whether the rules of the Lenten fast had permitted her to eat olive oil on Easter Saturday and the children boomeranged noisily from the table to the blaring television and back again, Ariko's son-in-law Louka confided to me that he had been among the first witnesses to the miracle of Kykko's weeping icon. 'I was so scared by it, I can tell you,' he said gnawing on a bone, 'but Abbot Nikiforos has told us not to be frightened.'

Once the meat dish was emptied and everyone's greasy hands wiped clean with paper napkins from a china dispenser decorated with the word JERUSALEM, a basket of painted eggs was placed on the table. This was the moment the six children – three girls belonging to one daughter, three boys to the other – had been looking forward to. Each member of the company selected an egg and we began a game of conkers. My yellow egg fought off an especially strong challenge from a dark red one wielded by Ariko's eldest grandson. My egg was champion.

Ariko read the victory as a sure sign that I must never get married. I told him there was usually more than one way of reading such portents. After all, Abbot Nikiforos and Archbishop Chrysostomos had not been able to agree about the meaning of Kykko's weeping icon, had they?

TROODOS MOUNTAINS

Back in Nicosia I had spent a day or two at the Archbishop Makarios Library in the basement of the Archbishop Makarios Cultural Centre, just behind the cathedral church I had visited on my first night in Cyprus. There I had found an account of a Ukrainian monk's travels around the island in the early eighteenth century when the Ottomans held sway, and a British travel writer's tale of his walk around the island in 1972, when Cyprus was uneasily independent, ruled by President Makarios and only two years away from division. As I drove out of Kambos, I decided to let Father Vasily Barsky and Colin Thubron guide my subsequent explorings.

Barsky was of almost the same generation as his fellow country-man St Paissy Velichkovsky but less the saintly Hesychast, more the rigorous scholar. Born and brought up near Kiev's famous Monastery of the Caves, he was at school in Kiev when a suppurating ulcer on his leg threatened to ruin his career prospects. Fortunately for him, the ulcer was cured by a miracle and he set out on a pilgrimage of thanksgiving. He roamed as far afield as Mount Athos, Patmos, Cyprus and Jerusalem and found a religious vocation. Thirty-three when he became a monk, Barsky visited Kykko and pronounced the island's flagship monastery 'perfect in every detail'.

About two hundred years later Thubron had been depressed to find Kykko neglected and almost empty. Convinced that Orthodox monasticism in Europe was doomed to extinction, he wrote, 'I thought of the dying monasteries of Meteora and the Peloponnese, the emptied sketes of Athos, the dispersed Russian fraternities, cloisters falling quiet in the Balkans . . .'[xiii] He could not possibly have predicted the wholesale collapse of Communism at the end of the twentieth century, or that one aspect of Orthodox Europe's defence against an encroaching West would be a startling monastic renaissance.

For a number of reasons I decided to go first to the Monastery of Chrysorrhoyiatissa, a name that translates as Our Lady of the Golden

Breasts. Barsky wrote it off as a 'very small and poor' dependency of Kykko, with only its 'healthy location'[xiv] to recommend it, but it had been the monastery nearest Makarios' home village and a boyhood haunt of his, and in 1956 EOKA had suspected the Abbot of Chrysorrhoyiatissa of treachery. One evening a posse of EOKA operatives dressed in cassocks and masks had barged their way into the monastery while the Abbot was sitting in his parlour listening to his radio and pumped him full of bullets. Almost twenty years later Thubron heard no mention of this horrible deed when he spent a night at the monastery.

Much more authentic-looking and prettier than Kykko, Chrysorrhoyiatissa still commands an excellent view over the plain stretching south of the Troodos mountains towards Paphos. But it lies on a busy road. A terrace restaurant and stalls selling cheap icons and sweets of Ottoman origin clutter its entrance. A monk sped out of the monastery church and across the courtyard, scowling and averting his eyes from the sight of some German tourists in shorts. I paused to read a potted history of the place, which I found, framed, behind glass and nailed to a stone wall. Beginning in the twelfth century with the tale of a miraculous icon from Constantinople washed up on a beach near Paphos and spotted from afar by a hermit, the account moved on to some pillaging by Turks and a fire in 1967, to culminate in August 1974 with: 'The Turkish hordes again bombarded the monastery, this time from the air . . . The damage done by their planes to the roof, to the solar heaters and to the arches of the monastery can still be seen.'

I drove on down the road for a mile or so to Ayia Moni, another *metochion* of Kykko, where Father Kirillos had told me I would find a pair of Romanian monks. As carefully restored as Kykko, although not as opulent, Ayia Moni was also located on the main road. Inside, a young monk wearing what looked like a pair of Marks & Spencer's tartan slippers was sweeping the courtyard with long, leisurely strokes. He was Father Dumitru from Suceava monastery in Moldavia, he told me. The initial contact between his monastery and Kykko had been made when his spiritual father had accepted Abbot Nikiforos' invitation to convalesce at Kykko after an operation on his prostate gland.

That first invitation had led to others, to young monks to come and learn Greek and man Kykko's multiple *metochia*. We chatted about Romania for a while and he asked me if I knew that the Pope was due on a visit there in May.

'Oh, yes and I think it's wonderful that Romania should be the first Orthodox country to welcome a pope since the Schism of 1054,' I enthused.

'Hmmph! But we're not letting him go to Transylvania where the Uniates and the Hungarian Catholics are. He's only allowed to go to Bucharest,' countered Father Dumitru.

From Ayia Moni I journeyed back north into the mountains to Troodhitissa monastery, about which both Barsky and Thubron wrote at some length. Both had been treated to the same story of how the monastery's precious icon of the Most Holy Mother of God had acquired a lump of stone in its wooden back. Once upon a time a boy had fallen mortally sick. As was the custom in those days, his distraught parents had promised they would dedicate him to God as a monk if only he could be cured. In the excitement surrounding the patient's miraculous recovery the promise was soon forgotten. One day the family was in the church making a donation when a stone suddenly threw itself off the roof of the church. Hurtling towards the boy, it was about to kill him when the icon flew to his rescue by hurling itself off its stand, into the path of the flying stone. The stone had lodged in its back. This miracle swiftly removed any resistance to the idea of dedicating the boy to God's service.

Barsky, faithful Orthodox though he was, had had serious doubts about the veracity of this tale. An inspection of the icon's wooden back and the stone lodged in it had brought out the closet rationalist in him. He wrote that the missile, 'appears not to be embedded but cleverly attached to it. Apart from this, a stone, naturally falling, cannot become embedded as the church is low, the stone is small, and the wood is hard, so that this could not happen naturally.'[xv] Two centuries later Thubron patiently listened to the same tall tale and then to the moral his monk-guide drew from it. '"You see, God is justice as well as love," said the monk ... "You will not find everybody in heaven. Not the Jews, no, nor the Arabs nor the Russians who believe in nothing, nor ... but the Americans are Christians, aren't they?"'[xvi]

Intrigued by the icon story, I followed all the signs to Troodhitissa. Almost at the top of a mountain, a last sign directed me off to the right, to a very large and empty car-park where once-garish stalls selling snacks and cold drinks were now broken down and rusting. I concluded that the monks had imitated their Lord by throwing the merchants and money-lenders, so to speak, out of their temple. Just then a line of monks, walking four abreast, appeared at the far end of the car-park. They approached me, passed and were just about to disappear through a high wooden gate when one of them glanced back at me and pointed to a brass plaque on the wall. It informed me in underlined English that Troodhitissa no longer welcomed tourists.

After enjoying the run of Russian, Macedonian, Serbian and Romanian monasteries I felt unreasonably peeved for a moment. But both Cyprus and Greece have been inundated with tourists in the past thirty years or so. I could easily imagine that seeing troops of non-Orthodox holidaymakers trailing through one's beloved spiritual workshop would severely strain a monastic community's willingness to dispense hospitality. My temporary disgruntlement on this occasion was mild in comparison with some of Thubron's long miserable moments, when his feet were raw with walking and his clothes soaked through by rain. Barsky, too, had his bad times. At one point in his wanderings, the brainy but often ailing Ukrainian monk got lost and fell in with a couple of foresters. They looked after him but he spent a miserable night:

> ... tossing and turning, like a lamb on a spit unable to endure on one side the heat of the fire, on the other the cold of the mountain, which I felt because my clothes were wet from sweat ... As soon as I started to fall asleep I would once more wake up, sometimes from the howling of the wind and the cold, or the biting ants, or fear of snakes, or the wonderful scent of burning wood ... tossing backwards and forwards I recited the vespers and matins ...'[xvii]

Leaving the High Troodos, I had just joined the stream of Easter Monday traffic heading back towards Nicosia when I remembered that a friendly bookseller I had met in the capital the week before had strongly recommended I visit the monastery of Makhairas. It was on my way. 'Don't delay,' the woman had urged, 'because they're likely to ban women soon. The Mount Athos influence is getting stronger and stronger there.' In her office at the back of her excellent Moufflon bookshop, she had begun in an urgent whisper, better suited to disclosing state secrets or military intelligence than to sharing Church gossip, to divulge that Makhairas' former Athos-bred abbot, Athanasios, had led a startling revival of the place before being elected Bishop of Limassol.

'What you have to understand,' she went on, in her intent and slightly breathless way, 'is that there's an all-out war going on in our Church just now. On one side you have people like this truly spiritual Athanasios who, many people hope, will become archbishop when Chrysostomos dies. But on the other side you have people like Athanasios' scandalous predecessor as Bishop of Limassol – Chrysan-thos. You must have heard of him? . . . No? . . . Over thirty allegations of fraudulent business dealings have been filed against him since your New Scotland Yard first sounded the alarm about a bad investment scheme. He's a crook, and I'm talking millions of dollars! He finally had the sense to resign last November but there are others who belong to this tendency too. You must have heard how the Bishop of Paphos tried to destroy Athanasios' good name and stop his election to Limassol by claiming that his spiritual father – an Athos monk in his eighties now – had slept with eleven Cypriot nuns and infected them all with a venereal disease . . .'

'Wait a minute,' I said, unable to take in anything but the most lurid highlights of the woman's lightning survey of the present state of the Church of Cyprus. 'When did this scandal happen?'

'Some time in the 1970s but it's only just come to light. Oh, yes, another thing, he claimed to have proof – the nuns' prescriptions for the medicines they needed to cure their infections. Mount Athos and even the patriarch in Constantinople finally intervened to defend the old monk ... Anyway, I've got away from the point with all this filth. What I meant to say was I think it would be worth your while to go to Makhairas.'

My traveller guides had both called in at the famous monastery, so there was every reason to go there. Barsky's visit to Makhairas had happened to coincide with that of an Athos monk whose fund-raising for his monastery was going well because he was able to entertain everyone he begged from with 'his wonderful and artful singing' and glimpses of a 'part of the skull of martyr Sergios' and a piece of 'bone with some flesh from the great martyr St Panteleimon'.[xviii] But the Ukrainian was particularly impressed with Makhairas' illiterate Abbot Parthenios who contrived to carry in his monk's cap 'various little implements, like fine and thick awls, drills, knife, an iron for striking fire, comb, nails, a thick needle, needles and thread, wax, string and other different things'.[xix] Thubron, footsore and exhausted a couple of hundred years later, had had the misfortune to reach Makhairas on Easter night, just when he could count on all the monastery's guest rooms being taken. After almost sleepwalking through the midnight service, he was invited to bed down in the cloister.

When I finally caught sight of the monastery, after many hours of mountain driving, it looked as if it was clinging – rather like the bird's-nest Athos monasteries – to a sheer green mountainside bathed in late afternoon sunshine. Again more reminiscent of an Athos monastery than of Kykko, Makhairas was whitewashed and timbered in the old Macedonian Ottoman style. Makhairas, I thought, would not have looked out of place in the FYROM's Ohrid or in Greek Macedonia's lakeside Kastoria.

A plaque by its gate read in English,

THIS MONASTERY IS NOT A PICNIC AREA. ENTRY IS PROHIBITED TO ANYONE IN SHORTS AND TO WOMEN WEARING TROUSERS. PLEASE ENTER THIS HOLY PLACE IN PEACE, QUIET AND WITH SELF-RESPECT.

But a young man at the gift shop where I bought two pamphlets (one about the Hesychasts' Jesus Prayer, the other about holy fools) plus a tub of monastery-made marzipan smelling of roses, assured me that I *could* risk entering in trousers. He said most of the monks were napping.

Just inside the front door of the monastery was a mosaic floor with a double-headed Byzantine eagle in the centre, but that was the only hint of Athonite influence I could discern. Perhaps I was too soon distracted by something far-removed from the spiritual. Just to the right of the door was a little museum celebrating the life and death of an EOKA martyr called Grigory Afxentiou who, after refusing to surrender to the British, was blasted out of his hide-out in 1957. On display were his gun (with the acronym EOKA carved on its stock), a faded Greek flag, a couple of hand grenades, some binoculars, a greying cassock, some underwear (dingy vest and baggy drawers), a photo of him, another of a monk (bearing an uncanny resemblance to him) and – oddest of all – a gold tooth. I begged a Cypriot woman who was standing next to me, studying each item as carefully as I was, to tell me the story behind this collection of relics. She said that at the height of the EOKA era Afxentiou had needed time and good food to recuperate from an operation so, seeking refuge at Makhairas, he had disguised himself as a monk. He had been almost well and ready to take up the struggle again when some British officers dropped by on a routine patrol. Just for the hell of it, the guerrilla chief, alias Father Chrysanthos, had bustled about, humbly serving his sworn enemies glasses of lemonade and water. He smiled but never opened his mouth for fear his one gold tooth would give him away.

A little way up the road from the monastery stood a gigantic bronze statue of this jester whom the British martyred. In March 1970 Archbishop Makarios had travelled up here to this very spot to celebrate the thirteenth anniversary of his death, doubtless feeling somewhat shaken after the first of many attempts on his life. Only a few hours before, his helicopter had been taking off from the grounds of his palace in Nicosia when a remnant of fighters who resented Makarios' willingness to make do with independence instead of union with Greece peppered its underbelly with bullets. The helicopter had plunged back to earth. Makarios had picked himself up, dusted himself off, resumed his journey by car and made it here only slightly behind schedule.

LIMASSOL

The only unpleasant minutes of my entire fortnight in Cyprus were the result of my asking one innocuous question: 'Excuse me, could you tell me where the Bishop's palace is?

I had arrived in Limassol, booked myself into a hotel with a view of the sea and set out for a walk. My guidebook had suggested that just to the right of the hotel I would find the old metropolitan cathedral. It was there, although utterly concealed from public view by a blue glass skyscraper belonging to the Hanseatic shipping company. Inside the empty little church I cast around for a candle to light and then became aware of something moving about behind the iconostasis. A thin elderly man eventually drew aside a curtain on the left of the altar and descended to ask me my business. I had asked him that simple question. 'Are you Orthodox?' he had replied suspiciously.

I shook my head but explained what I was about and why I was interested in knowing the whereabouts of the Bishop's palace.

'Are you married? No? ... Pity. You should have married an Orthodox man in one of the Orthodox countries you have travelled in. Where are you from?'

'London.'

'Tell me something, why is your country against all the Orthodox countries now? Russia, Greece, Cyprus – we're all opposed to what Nato is doing to Serbia.'

'I know.'

'But why? *Why* is Nato attacking?' he said, suddenly urgent and poking at my forearm with his finger. 'Can you explain this to me?' He almost dragged me out of the church.

'I can try,' I said, little suspecting that he wanted an argument not an explanation, 'but will you please stop prodding me and shouting?'

He wanted to know why Nato had not lifted a finger to stop people like him being ethnically cleansed from northern Cyprus by the Turks in 1974. He demanded to know why the BBC was only showing footage of weeping Kosovor Albanian refugees instead of pictures of Nato's bombing raids. He believed that the West was planning to conquer a line of the major Orthodox powers – Serbia first, then Greece and finally Russia. With his fine, drawn features and burning black eyes the old man was beside himself with fear and fury. I had had encounters like this before, but only with Serbs in Bosnia during the war, or with Russian ultra-nationalists, or Romanians in Transylvania in 1990. On a spring Sunday evening at a holiday resort in Cyprus, this terrified and angry old man had caught me off my guard.

'What Clinton is doing in this war is worse than what Hitler did!' he shouted at me, with another sharp dig at my arm.

'Now you're talking rubbish,' I said. 'I can't listen to any more of this.'

'Rubbish, you say? [Prod, dig.] *No! Go!*'

Angry, shaken and convinced that only my gender had saved me from a beating, I left.

I did not have much more to do with Cypriots while in Limassol. I was only there because I had been led to believe that if Mount Athos is the spiritual capital of Orthodox Europe, Limassol – a busy port and holiday resort – could be said to be its secular antithesis.

The simple fact that citizens of Orthodox countries of the former eastern bloc do not need visas to visit Cyprus, as they do for anywhere else in western Europe, has made the island, but especially Limassol, a honey-pot for Russians, Ukrainians, Serbs, Romanians and Bulgarians seeking work. Women easily fall into prostitution. In the early 1990s especially, Cyprus' unregulated banking system was making money laundering here delightfully easy for Serbian black-marketeers or for Russians in need of a safe place to deposit giant sums earned from selling off the old Soviet Union's assets.

I found Limassol's dirty-sex business easier to spot than its dirty-money business. The first Russian I saw was a marvellously long-legged blonde in hot pants and a tight T-shirt. She was escorted by a Cypriot the shape and size of Ariko. He lowered his head and scowled as he climbed out of his pick-up and followed her to a table in the hotel restaurant. On my first morning in town a kerb-crawler hissed at me through his car window, 'Russia? Romania? Yugoslavia?' Later the same day I was sitting reading a book on Limassol's stony beach when a voice called, 'Dyevushka!' – the familiar Russian greeting to an unmarried female. I looked up to find see a small red motorboat called Rendezvous bobbing in the shallows a few yards from the beach. Aboard were three Russian males acting out life in a Martini advert, with their sunglasses atop their heads and bottles of vodka to hand. The one who had hailed me had blond hair, tight red swimming trunks and a fine suntan.

'What?' I shouted back to him in Russian.

'Are you on holiday here?'

'No, I'm working.'

'Working?' he said, pausing to turn round and have a good laugh with his friends. 'And what kind of work would that be?'

'I'm writing a book.'

'Writing a book no less! Ha! Ha! About what if I might ask?'

'About Orthodoxy.' I was getting tired of shouting and hoped they might be intrigued enough to step ashore for a proper chat.

'Orthodoxy?' he bellowed in disbelief. 'Good luck! Bye!'

The Rendezvous with its 'jocose and affable' cargo sped off towards the horizon and the setting sun.

It was probably just as well that they did not join me because, sitting there on that beach, listening to the roar of traffic behind me on the road and watching the sun set, my mood swung from contented to fearful. It struck me that less than a decade had passed since the Russians had gained the freedom to come to Cyprus and enjoy themselves alongside their western counterparts, but already one long-term result of Nato's war with Serbia was a continent divided again, down the Schism line. What if such jolly encounters with Russians on holiday in Cyprus, let alone more fruitful exchanges, were to become impossible again? What if the 1054 Schism line turned into something like Cyprus' Green Line? What if Eastern Orthodox Europe was to cut itself off from the soul-destroying West? What if the various Eastern Orthodox churches started demanding a real *symphonia*, and all their monasteries started closing their doors to heretic unbelievers, and archbishops began doubling up as presidents like Makarios? I had a vivid flashback of Goran, reclining in a chair under the yellow awning of Bijeljina's Café Byzantium, telling me that Serbia needed someone like a patriarch 'to get us out of all this shit'.

The following day I encountered yet another kind of Russian, one who was neither selling his flesh nor on holiday but who spoke the sort of carefully perfect English I had learnt to associate with former KGB men. Head of something called the Association of Russian Businessmen in Cyprus, Yuri Pyanikh had lived on Cyprus for almost ten years, so I asked him why Russians seemed to feel so at home on the island.

'Well, first, the word taverna is written the same way in Greek or Cyrillic script,' he said smoothly, 'but, more seriously, did you know that seventy per cent of the light fittings in Kykko's church came from Russia and that before the Bolshevik revolution Kykko had a *metochion* in Russia? ... No, I can't remember where. The links between the Russian and Cypriot Churches go back a long way.'

It was Yuri who told me of a plan to celebrate these ancient and now revived links between the two countries by building a mighty Russian Orthodox church somewhere in the hills above the town. He then arranged for his business associate Vladimir, a gigantically tall man driving a long black Mercedes limousine, to transport me up there to view the site.

We sped out of town together along a new motorway and up into hills scattered with brand-new or half-built mansions. It looked to me as if the Cypriots had fled up here – rather as they had fled to the

Troodos Mountains in the twelfth century – to escape the invasion of western tourists, after resigning themselves to the loss of their town and its sea-front.

Vladimir entertained me with the story of the Russian church project. The idea had begun to take shape in the mid-1990s when the Russian embassy in Nicosia had presented it to the Cypriot Orthodox Church. The now disgraced Bishop Chrysanthos of Limassol had lost no time in donating a prime plot for the church. A donation of 715,000 dollars from an anonymous Russian businessman had been enough to make a start on the foundations. The indefatigable Mayor Yuri Luzhkov of Moscow then became involved and decided that Limassol must first have a chapel to serve as a house of worship while the big church was being built. He ordered the construction of an exact replica of Russia's oldest wooden church. It was to be built in Moscow, dismantled, shipped to Cyprus and reassembled.

The project could not have wished for better godparents than that single wealthy Russian businessman and Mayor Luzhkov but it soon ran into trouble. The scandal of Bishop Chrysanthos of Limassol's myriad murky dealings first exploded in early 1998. It was remembered then that the entire anonymously donated sum of 715,000 dollars had been made over to that prelate for safekeeping and Patriarch Alexy II of Russia's formal enquiry yielded no news of its whereabouts. The money had vanished. Meanwhile, work on the little prefabricated chapel was falling behind schedule. A grand blessing of both the site and chapel was planned for Easter 1998 but there was no time left to ship the chapel to Cyprus. It would have to travel by air. A giant Antonov transport aeroplane was chartered from the Russian Ministry for Emergencies and the chapel loaded aboard. No sooner had it touched down in Cyprus then a wild and dangerous rumour swept across the island. 'The missiles have arrived.'

For many months the Greek Cypriots had been eagerly awaiting the arrival of a consignment of Russian-made surface-to-air missiles, so the unheralded arrival of a giant Russian transport plane with what looked like military markings was guaranteed to trigger thoughts of these weapons. People nodded and winked, and agreed that Russia's handling of the delicate delivery – knowing how much Northern Cyprus, Turkey and the West opposed the siting of such weapons in what was already the most heavily militarized country in Europe – had been marvellously discreet. At last, Russia's ambassador to Nicosia had had to douse the rumour's raging wildfire with an official denial. 'The Antonov's cargo is not SAM-300s, but a far more powerful weapon – a Russian church,' he sheepishly informed a news conference.

Chuckling at the memory of this fiasco, Vladimir stopped the car on a windy hill-top, in front of a wooden Russian church the colour of an old donkey. It looked a little like the churches Vanya and I had seen near Archangel, in their natural habitat of high bright skies, silver birch trees and water. This sweltering hill-top, just a few stony yards away from a half-built villa, was quite the wrong setting.

Transplanting buildings was a mistake. But what about transplanting people? Father Dumitru back at Ayia Moni had admitted to feeling homesick for rain and the beech forests of north-eastern Romania. How, I wondered, had Kykko monks fared while manning their *metochion* in distant Russia?

NICOSIA

How had Kykko come by that Russian *metochion*? Where was it and what had become of it?

Back in Nicosia, the day before a scheduled audience with Archbishop Chrysostomos, I heard of a historian capable of answering these questions. He was based at Kykko's main *metochion* in Nicosia, a monastery-cum-business-headquarters-cum-historical-research-centre set in lush green gardens in some of the city's finest real estate.

The man was at his desk, more than willing to help me with my enquiry, but unfortunately unable to speak any English. 'No problem,' said a plump young monk, with long-lashed blue eyes and shiny black hair scraped back in a bun, 'I am going to translate.' But no sooner had I phrased my first question then the poor historian was forgotten.

'But I'm the one you need to talk to about this,' said the monk with an incredulous laugh. 'I'm the only one who's been to our so called "Russian *metochion*". I know *everything* there is to know about it! I spent five years of my life in Russia! And you know what? You're lucky to find me here because I'm off back to college in Thessaloniki tomorrow.'

After two years of being astonished and delighted by every happy coincidence I experienced on my travels, I was more blasé than Father Isaias about our fortuitous meeting, although it turned out that he was quite as interesting as any Russian *metochion*.

In the early 1990s Kykko's mighty Abbot Nikiforos had ordered Father Isaias to leave Mount Athos and transfer to Russia for a five-year course at Sergeyev Posad's famous seminary. He had just completed his second year there when another order had arrived from Kykko. His free time, he was told, was to be spent discovering the whereabouts of Kykko's pre-1917 Russian *metochion*. A succession of wild-goose chases and false dawns followed but, three years later, when he had almost given up the hunt and left Russia to pursue yet more theological studies in Thessaloniki, Father Isaias had made some progress at last. Someone informed him that Kykko's Russian *metochion* was not in Russia at all but in the newly independent former Soviet Republic of Georgia.

A sunny, fertile land lying to the north of the Black Sea, Georgia had been converted to Christianity a whole four centuries earlier than Russia by a woman saint called Nino. At some point in the eighteenth century a couple of Kykko monks on a begging expedition had succeeded in wandering all the way to this jewel in the crown of Eastern Orthodoxy, into the court of a pious King Heraklitos. With hair-raising tales of Ottoman raids on Kykko, fires and devastation, they had encouraged the monarch to dig deep in his royal pocket. The alms he donated to Kykko took the form of not only an entire monastery but also of the revenues deriving from whole forests, vineyards and mountains. Although royal munificence on such a grand scale was remarkable, it was not unheard-of at the time. The monasteries of the Phanariot-ruled Danubian principalities were fulfilling the same kind of golden-goose function for the similarly harassed Orthodox monasteries of Greece and Asia Minor. In 1811 the Russian empire swallowed both independent God-fearing Georgia and its autocephalous Church, without however touching Kykko's *metochion* at a place called Vartzya.

'Getting there was like going on a safari,' said Father Isaias. 'You know what it's like travelling anywhere in the former USSR. When at last we arrived, we found a big party going on in the village – a wake for someone who had just died. There was a lot of wine and toasting – you know how the Georgians are . . .'

I did. The closest thing to a Mediterranean country that the former Russian empire or Soviet Union had to offer, Georgia must have been something like a home from home for the Cypriots, not a place of exile. Father Isaias had been magnificently received there like a home-coming hero and royally entertained. To his amazement he discovered that distant Kykko was perfectly preserved in local memory, as was the history of the *metochion* and the story of the last archimandrite of the monastery, who had arrived from Cyprus with his nephew in the late nineteenth century. That nephew, Father Isaias was told, had put down roots by learning Georgian, marrying a local woman and raising a family. Father Isaias was then introduced to an old man who turned out to be his son.

'As soon as I mentioned Cyprus the old guy started crying – it was a very emotional moment for me as well,' said Father Isaias shyly, fiddling busily with the buttons on his smart chrome mobile telephone. 'He was telling me that all his life he had wanted to talk about Cyprus but hadn't dared because of the Communists. He told me in Russian that his family came from Nicosia and it turned out that the recipe for *zivania* – you know, that clear brandy we make and sell up at Kykko – had been passed down from his great-uncle to his father to him!'

Father Isaias had found the monastery church in a shocking state of disrepair but been gratified to learn that every 8 September, the feast day of the Virgin Mary, a secret religious service had been conducted there. Vartzya's schoolmaster had been able to indicate to him precisely which 'thousands and thousands of acres' of forests, vineyards and mountains had once belonged to Kykko.

'The old archimandrite and his nephew started selling off parts of the *metochion* before 1917. You can tell by the letters they wrote back here to Cyprus that they felt something terrible was about to happen . . .'

Our conversation was interrupted by the harsh clanging of the monastery's church bell. Still talking, Father Isaias got up and walked me down the shady cloister towards a group of monks. One of them was a small man, wearing a brilliant purple cassock, pens in his breast pocket, a well-trimmed beard and something like pomade in hair coiffed high enough to give him a couple of extra inches.

'Please meet our Abbot Nikiforos,' said Father Isaias, leading me first to this striking figure whose hand I shook, and then onward to another monk who was the very antithesis of the abbot. A thin old man in a droopy, greying cassock, he was Father Gavriil, Father Isaias' spiritual father.

'Why is the West throwing bombs at Serbia?' he enquired of me in a thin shaky voice, his dim eyes focusing on an eternity located just behind my right shoulder. 'That which has been built up over hundreds of years – all the physical as well as the spiritual ties – must not be destroyed!'

Father Isaias led the way into the cool of the monastery's refectory, a high room furnished with a shiny marble table long enough to seat twenty and a lively fresco of Christ surrounded by his Apostles at the Last Supper. Up by Abbot Nikiforos at the head of the table were four or five monks dressed in sober navy blue or plum-coloured cassocks. Each had a neat haircut and a pen or two in his breast pocket. Next came the ancient Father Gavriil and an equally shabby youngster, with wild, dark eyes. Then there was the ebullient Father Isaias, myself, and finally, a handful of laymen. Once Abbot Nikiforos had said grace, a monk waiter appeared at my elbow proffering a bottle of Kykko's own red wine, swaddled in a starched white napkin.

Father Isaias heaped my plate high with bean stew, the finest chips I have ever tasted, perfectly *al dente* Brussels sprouts and prime-quality tinned tuna steak. On top of this odd assortment of foods he poured a generous helping of what he called 'the best' olive oil – Kykko's very own. I recalled Thubron's description of his meal at Kykko, almost thirty years before. 'The refectory table stretches for forty feet in jointed marble, and a feeling of plenty surrounds the monks who assemble there. Even the beans are washed down with olive oil and lemon juice, and bolstered by onion-flavoured croquettes.'[xx]

'Usually we listen to some spiritual reading at meals,' Father Isaias muttered with just a hint of an apology, 'but this is the administrative centre of Kykko. When the abbot is here in Nicosia he has business matters to attend to.'

I would have loved to enquire into Kykko's business affairs but did not think it polite to do so in the circumstances. There was no doubting that the monastery was fabulously wealthy and busily resisting mounting pressure to pay taxes. But equally my experience in Kambos suggested that the Abbot took the monastery's responsibilities to the community very seriously. If some Cypriots hated and feared their country's religious establishment, describing it as a giant untaxed and untouchable Mafia owning about half the island in land, television and radio stations, hotels and factories, others insisted there was plenty that was good about it. A woman academic who had spent weeks at Kykko studying its ancient foundations swore to me that she had been a violent critic of the place until with her own eyes she had seen Abbot Nikiforos scribbling £2,000 cheques for hard-up locals.

While the business monks talked business and the wild-eyed young monk gobbled his food, Father Isaias and I continued our conversation. He explained how he had come by his spiritual father and a monastic vocation. On completing his military service he had been about to go to a prestigious American business school his father had chosen for him when his mother had suggested that he meet her spiritual father. 'I met Father Gavriil and in a moment my whole life was changed. That was it,' he concluded, with a happy smile.

Something about Father Isaias was reminding me of both the FYROM's Pied Piper Bishop Naum and of Father Sava. All three men had the sort of confident intelligence I had met only in the products of top British public schools or Oxbridge colleges. None of them was shy of looking a woman in the eye. They did not talk about the whore of Babylon or the mark of the Beast. None of them was angrily defensive, bitter, aggressive or puffed up with pride. They shared youth, intelligence and education, but there was yet another common denominator. All of them, I realized, must have drunk deep of the confident new spirit of the Holy Mountain's renaissance. My forebodings of a few days before were forgotten. I was suddenly buoyed up by a surge of optimism. What if the Holy Mountain was teeming with Savas, Naums and Isaiases? What if they constituted a vanguard movement devoted to proving that heart and mind could work together, that the intellectual traditions of the West and the spiritual traditions of the East need not exclude each other, that East and West could be joined again?

When lunch was over Father Isaias took a mobile phone call in fluent Russian, but then seemed as happy to continue our conversation as I was. He showed me into what he might have called his cell but which was really a small apartment made up of a sitting room furnished with a desk, bookshelves and a sofa, a bathroom and a bedroom. Lolling in a swivel chair behind his desk, he continued to toy with the buttons on his mobile phone while I settled down on the sofa. The subject of Kosovo was unavoidable. I soon gathered that this jolly vessel of the spirit of the Holy Mountain's renaissance was quite as marked by Orthodoxy's sad history, as any of his older or less-educated brothers.

'I know the gospels tell us to love our enemies but we Orthodox have always trusted other people too much, and always been betrayed. Now, when one of our family is suffering, we are all suffering because Orthodoxy is like a body. If one part hurts the whole body is affected. Where one Orthodox people is being persecuted, all feel threatened, spiritually but also territorially. Even a child can see that America is trying to strangle Russia by first destroying a country which might act as a strong ally . . .'

In the words of a twenty-eight-year-old perfectly trilingual monk being groomed for high office and responsibility in his Church, I was hearing the old cry of the eternal Orthodox victim modelled on the crucified Christ, the fearful misery of shrinking Late Byzantium and a 'my people, right or wrong' attitude that was more tribal than religious.

'The real problem is that America has not convinced us that they are acting for simple humanitarian reasons. History shows us that America never does things for humanitarian reasons. If they did, we say, why didn't they stop the Turks ethnically cleansing us Greeks from the north of our country in 1974?'

'The world was different back then, there was a Cold War on,' I protested, but I was seeing the chasm of understanding that separated a culture founded on the careful preservation of collective memories of past suffering, from one founded on forgetting and starting afresh.

Father Isaias told me that a few days before he had taken to the streets to join a demonstration against Nato's attacks on Serbia. 'I was out there with my Greek flag shouting, "Stop the bombing! Stop the bombing!" Abbot Nikiforos had given me a blessing to shout that but not anything like "Down with America!" Of course, just because I was a monk, all the western TV news cameras were zooming in on me!'

'Talking of Greek flags, Father Isaias, why are there Greek flags flying above all the monasteries and near the Archbishop's palace? Why aren't they Cypriot flags?'

'That's easy for me to answer – we are the Church of the Greek *ethnos* – here, see this?' he said, jumping out of his swivel chair, taking a Greek flag off his bookshelf and unfurling it with a flourish. 'Aren't the colours wonderful? The blue so blue, the white so clean. I am going to recommend to the Abbot that we buy this kind in future. The cotton ones fade too fast. This is good strong nylon.'

Father Isaias kindly offered me a lift back into town. We were just leaving his apartment when he paused a moment, frowned, grinned then set me to solve an ethical problem of the kind his professors posed him at theological college.

'OK, imagine you're a monk, and that you've got a gun,' he began, 'and suddenly there is a Turkish enemy – could be any enemy, of course,' he added quickly. 'Anyway, this Turk is about to kill a group of children. Are you going to use your gun to kill him first?'

'If I was a good monk I think I would throw down my gun, stand in front of the children and beg the Turk to kill me instead,' I answered.

'No, no. That's no good at all,' said Father Isaias, 'because you know he's going to kill the children anyway.'

'But surely if I was a good monk I would never think the worst of anyone, so I would have to trust that he would spare the children?' I countered.

'No, no, no! You know for sure, for *sure*, that he will kill *everyone*!'

'I give up, then. What's the right answer?'

'I think I would have to say, at my age, knowing what I know right now, I would certainly kill that Turk,' he said. His blue eyes were gleaming, although whether with enjoyment at solving the puzzle or at the idea of despatching the Turk, it was hard to say. 'But then I would ask for God's forgiveness, go to confession and be prepared to do whatever penance I was given, however hard.'

We were down in the monastery courtyard and Father Isaias was unlocking the passenger door of a large silver Mercedes for me when he added as an afterthought, 'Of course, another solution could be, "God will guide me at the time. The answer lies with Him. That is the answer of a true believer."' That is also the answer of someone abdicating responsibility, I thought.

As we idled in a Nicosia rush-hour traffic jam I quizzed him on the subject of Hesychasm and was impressed by his quick and clear definition. 'Hesychasm is a state of the soul and a way of praying,' he told me. 'The task of my life as a monk is to achieve *hesychia* – quiet in my soul. I can do that if my soul is constantly connected to Christ.

At Kykko we try to combine Hesychasm with a life of service in the community, but you'll find that the monks at Makhairas and Troodhitissa are more devoted to Hesychasm.' We were approaching the ancient Paphos Gate to the old city, which is almost on the Green Line, when he spotted a Turkish flag fluttering high above the old city wall and abruptly changed the subject, 'You know I find that red flag very, very annoying . . . Phew! That's better!' he gasped, as we turned a corner and a Greek flag twinned with a Cypriot one appeared. Father Isaias was from the north of the island, from Kyrenia. He had been three years old in 1974 when his family had abandoned everything and fled their home.

The next day, the archiepiscopal palace – next door to the little cathedral church where I had seen Archbishop Chrysostomos on my first night in Cyprus – seemed empty, quiet as a grave after Kykko's bustling Nicosia *metochion*.

I was shown straight up a staircase whose walls were painted with biblical scenes, into an anteroom hung with portraits of Makarios and Chrysostomos and then on, into a parlour so grandly overfurnished and dimly lit that at first I failed to notice that it also contained His Beatitude Chrysostomos. More portraits of Chrysostomos and Makarios caught my eye, along with a marble-topped side table on which were two photographs, one of His Beatitude with President Clinton, the other of His Beatitude with Benjamin Netanyahu. Motioning me to be seated on a moss-green velvet sofa, the Archbishop began.

'You should know that the Church of Cyprus was the first Christian church after Jerusalem . . . the first people to spread Christianity outside Jerusalem were Cypriots . . . St Lazarus, whom Our Lord raised up from the dead, was the first Bishop of Larnaca . . . St Paul came to Cyprus and converted the Roman governor of Paphos to Christianity . . . His companion St Barnabas led the Cypriots to Christ . . .'

I was reminded of how another Beatitude, Archbishop Mihail of Macedonia and Ohrid, had sung me a similar hymn in praise of his Church's proud history. But although Chrysostomos was over a decade younger than Mihail, he seemed older and confused. Twice he explained the rules for electing an Archbishop of Cyprus, concluding with the same punch-line. 'It is exactly like the system for electing a president of the United States! When Americans come here I say to them, "We are older than you so you stole our system!" Ha, ha!'

At first I mistook his lack of clarity on the subject of Kosovo for an elegantly Byzantine evasiveness of the sort Makarios might have practised in similar circumstances. He mumbled something about Albanians – Kosovo or otherwise – being 'a problem', but he was not well.

The Archbishop was perfectly lucid on only one famously controversial point. Turkish Cypriots, he claimed, were not ethnically Turkish at all but poor Orthodox Greeks whom the Ottomans forced to convert to Islam when they could not pay their taxes. Way back in Bijeljina, the bad-tempered Bosnian Bishop of Tuzla and Zvornik had outlined the same sort of Orthodox origins for Bosnia's Muslims. Both churchmen seemed to be implying that their Muslim neighbours should snap out of their apostasy and return to the Orthodox fold which had retained a claim on their souls and, naturally, on the land they inhabited. The truth of the matter is that some Turkish Cypriots and some Bosnian Muslims are descended from mainland Turks, while some are the heirs of Greeks or Serbs converted to Islam *in situ*. That might not make any difference since we are talking about a religion, a matter of private conscience, not of ethnicity or land. But it makes all the difference in the world to men like Archbishop Chrysostomos and Bishop Vasilije Kačavenda of Tuzla and Zvornik. Here, it seemed to me, is some of the deadliest poison infecting a faith that, way back in Late Byzantium, learnt to identify itself utterly with an *ethnos*.

An aide appeared, bearing a large coffee-table book about Cypriot icons, which he gently laid on the Archbishop's lap. Out of an inner breast pocket of his cassock the old man carefully drew a fine-looking fountain pen. I was very much hoping that it was filled with red ink because, way back in the fifth century, when the Church of Cyprus first established its right to independence, Constantinople had conferred on it a number of privileges. One of these was the right to sign documents in red ink, like Byzantine emperors. I held my breath while beneath a pre-inscribed dedication saying, 'To remember Cyprus which is suffering from the invasion of Turkey and fighting for its Freedom, for Justice and Human Rights, with best wishes' the Archbishop slowly signed his name – in blood red.

On our way out of his parlour the Archbishop pointed to a worn and faded Greek flag hanging from a pole in pride of place by the door. It was, he told me, the standard raised by another ethnarch archbishop, in the Greek Cypriots' uprising against the Turks in 1821.

APOSTOLOS ANDHREAS MONASTERY
NORTHERN CYPRUS

In the passenger seat of a spacious Mercedes, I dozed and woke, dozed and woke again to views of blue-green mountains and white-gold fields of wheat. All was quiet and the road empty.

By half past eight in the morning I had cleared the Greek border post and walked the no-man's-land stretch of road – past the Ledra Palace Hotel, which the United Nations had commandeered, past shop-window displays of clothes dating back to 1974, past orange trees burdened with overripening fruit and empty lots. Arriving in the self-declared but still unrecognized Turkish Republic of Northern Cyprus, I had produced my passport, filled in some forms and haggled over the price of hiring a taxi for the day. My driver was a shy young Turkish Cypriot who had been eight years old when mainland Turks had invaded the island in 1974 and could remember how he and his family had been loaded on to buses and driven away from their home town, Paphos, across the Green Line, to the north, where none of them had ever set foot before. He lived in a village called Good Houses whose old name was St Mola and whose mosque was an old Orthodox church.

But he had not really wanted to talk politics with me so, in an effort to satisfy my appetite for information, he had tossed me a dog-eared brochure entitled *The Cultural Heritage of Cyprus: Its Protection and Preservation* – a publication of the Republic's Defence and Foreign Affairs Department. It was the Turks' irritated response to the Greek Cypriots' stricken complaints that they had looted and desecrated dozens of their precious Orthodox churches. Its main, rather shaky, line of defence seemed to be that when Greek Orthodox churchmen had had the chance to see to the upkeep of their precious monuments they had preferred to play at politics until, by the end of the last century, the state of those monuments had been 'an open scandal'. There was also a bitter reminder that the modern-day wealth and power of the Greek Orthodox Church was directly derived from 'the material favours and tolerance which it received from the Ottoman Turks'.[xxi] Soon the hot sunshine streaming through the windscreen was forcing my eyes shut, and I slept.

We stopped first at Famagusta where the driver rightly insisted that I view the ruins of the very splendid cathedral the Lusignan kings of Cyprus and Jerusalem had built themselves at the end of the thirteenth century. Standing on the thick city walls the Lusignan and later Venetian rulers of Cyprus had erected to keep the Ottomans out, I gazed out over a low sprawl of ugly modern housing blocks towards the old cathedral's massive but broken Gothic grandeur. With its fine golden stone arches, porticoes, twin decapitated towers and rose window it belonged far away in the other Europe – in France or Germany, in Reims or Chartres. Dazzled at first by the Catholic Crusaders' taste in Gothic pomposity and gigantic proportions, the Orthodox Cypriots had copied some of the decoration in their own little churches but never the severe spirit that produced the style. When the Ottomans conquered the island in 1571 and put Orthodox churchmen in charge of the *Rum-millet*, as they had in the Balkans, all signs of Catholic influence soon faded. The golden stones of this cathedral, where generations of Lusignans were crowned kings of Jerusalem, whose nave had been filled with Latin chants and whispered French, became a mosque with a single minaret and a darkened interior spread with carpets. Today, red and white Turkish crescent flags adorn its splendid façade.

We motored on through the quiet bright morning to the monastery of St Varnavas, named after the Apostle of Christ who had stayed behind on Cyprus after St Paul's short but high-profile visit to convert the natives to Christianity. Four centuries later St Varnavas had helped to secure Cyprus' ecclesiastical independence by allowing the site of his grave to appear to an archbishop in a dream. This led to him being dug up and found with a copy of St Matthew's gospel clasped in his skeleton hands, which in turn constituted sufficient proof that the Apostle Varnavas had worked and died on Cyprus. The Cypriot Church was declared old enough to retain her independence, in fact old enough to take precedence over every other Orthodox Church except those of Constantinople, Jerusalem, Alexandria and Antioch. Russia might be the only country great enough to bear God, as Abbot Tikhon of Verkhoturye had told me, but the tiny Cypriot Church has the edge over the Russian one when it comes to formal precedence. It is Archbishop Chrysostomos, shepherd of about half a million Greek Cypriot souls – not Patriarch Alexy II with some 125 million Russian ones in his charge – who may sign his name in red ink and carry a golden sceptre studded with rubies.

The white stone monastery was empty of monks and converted into an archaeological museum so we did not linger. Instead we headed on east, up the thin cocked gun-barrel shape of land pointing straight across the sea at Syria, the Karpas peninsula. I saw white churches missing doors and windows and sprayed with black graffiti, pink flowers and poppies, three high palm trees, two wild donkeys cavorting in a glade, a snoozing snake, a cloud of butterflies and the glittering silver sea. Behind the Cypriot Greeks' hatred for the Turks, who have stolen almost half of their homeland, must lie a bitter recognition that they have carelessly forfeited their own half of the island too by overdeveloping their tourist industry. The unspoiled landscape of northern Cyprus – low-hilled, scattered with flowers and dotted with palm trees – kept reminding me of the background scenes of medieval illuminated manuscripts showing pilgrims riding donkeys in the Holy Land. It was as unselfconsciously beautiful as a prelapsarian Paradise.

We were driving the single road to the end of the gun-barrel, to the monastery of Apostolos Andhreas named after Christ's Apostle Andrew, who stopped off here once on his way from the Holy Land. It is also where Richard the Lionheart is said to have teased the island's defeated Byzantine governor by ordering him bound in silver chains after he had fallen to his knees begging to be spared the humiliation of iron ones.

Three times a year the Turks allow a convoy of coaches loaded with a thousand Greek Cypriot Orthodox pilgrims, and accompanied by an armed UN escort, to journey up here. There had been such a trip on the Easter Monday before my visit so that on arriving at the sprawling nineteenth-century monastery with its view of rocks tumbling straight to the sea, we found a priest with his sleeves rolled up and some of the tiny number of Greek Cypriots who had stubbornly stayed on in the nearby town after 1974. They were sloshing pails of water across the monastery church's tiled floor, or on their knees scrubbing in whirlpools of soap suds. A couple of Turkish policemen stood by and watched the humble industry, their arms crossed, ties loosened and peaked caps tilted back on their heads. Another sat on a folding chair behind a picnic table under a couple of red and white Turkish flags. He demanded to see my passport and noted the date and time of my visit. I was the first, and very likely the last, visitor that day, to a place that in Colin Thubron's day had been as bustling as Russia's Trinity Sergeyev monastery on St Sergius' feast day.

There was not much to see, and what there was transported me straight back, full Orthodox circle, to where I had started about eighteen months before, to the misty green valley in Croatia and the abandoned, war-wrecked Krka monastery. Here where the Orthodox and Islamic worlds had collided until 1974 was almost a replica of there, where the worlds of Orthodox and western Christianity had collided until 1995. There were no monks in residence here, and nothing beautiful about the place. Rows of pilgrims' cells – a cross between bathing huts and motel rooms – had been daubed with red-painted numbers back in 1974, when invading Turkish troops had used the monastery as a barracks.

With the living heart ripped out of it, the monastery was as unimpressive as a discarded theatre set. I hated to think that the same fate might be in store for Kosovo's Dečani, Peć and Gračanica.

As I write now, in July 1999, Nato's *bombardismos* of *Yugoslavias* is over and hundreds of thousands of Albanians are returning to a Kosovo the Serb army and police have left lumpy with shallow mass graves and charred ruins. In this other place where the Orthodox and Islamic worlds have collided for centuries, the West is now in charge. A British general heads a Nato protectorate on a mission with no defined end. Father Sava is a brave Serb, back there insisting that Kosovo Serbs have a future in the province, but the long-term prognosis is unpromising. The monasteries of Dečani, Gračanica and Peć are sheltering terrified Serbs from Kosovo Albanian revenge. Today one of Father Sava's e-mails is simply a list of damaged or destroyed Serbian Orthodox churches. Another complains that, 'All around Kosovo everything which belongs to the Serbian people is exposed to merciless destruction. In fact, besides many outrageous murders, looting, expulsions, rapes, burning of homes, we are experiencing a culturocide of our people.'[xxii]

Greek Cypriots know all about that, and about how a quarter of a century can pass with nothing resolved and western soldiers keeping the peace along a line dividing Eastern Orthodox Christians from Muslims.

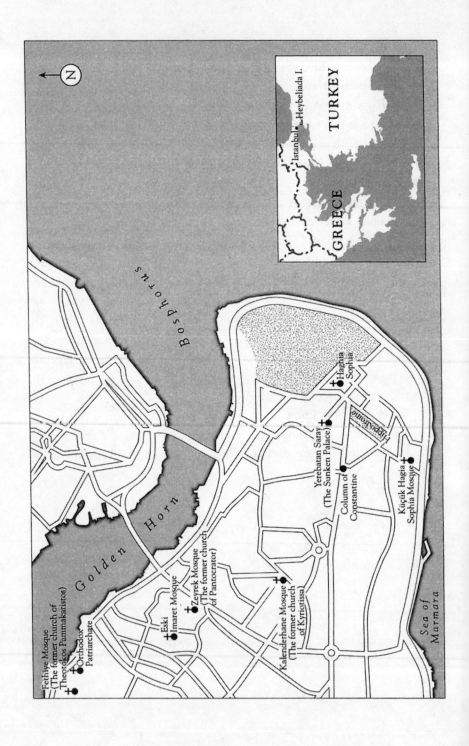

Istanbul

ISTANBUL

A good sunset, when the surface of the Sea of Marmara looks like the scuffed gold background of an old icon, can almost bring Byzantium back. But on a sweltering summer day when the sky is a prosaic off-white and rain buckets down into the grey Bosphorus where a Russian oil tanker is hogging the shipping lane, there is just the present.

The dual carriageway running down the west bank of the Golden Horn was flooding fast, its gutters turned to brown rivers bobbing with plastic flotsam. Buses roared past, spraying mud and diesel steam. My new acquaintance trudged on ahead of me, his bowed shoulders and trouser bottoms soaked, swearing there was not much further to go. The custom was to visit three churches on the first day of every month, he said – but on foot rather than by taxi whatever the weather. A young antiques dealer of mixed Greek and Russian ancestry, Çem was a Turkish citizen by birth but a Byzantine by heart. The double-headed eagle on his business card and a passion for fifteenth-century Byzantine church music advertised that fact. Every forgotten fragment of Byzantine wall, every derelict Greek merchant's house, every damply rotting Orthodox church we passed, and every triumph for gimcrack modernity offended him. He paused to point out a fragment of ancient masonry, about three foot high and sprouting weeds. 'Look, ancient wall of Byzantium. You see that excavator – it will smash the wall and they will build a shop or petrol station, or maybe nothing. Everything is breaking and broken.'

At last the rainstorm eased and we arrived behind a damp concrete shopping centre at a building that might once have been an Orthodox church but was no longer. It had neither iconostasis nor altar, just some identifiably Orthodox brass candle-stands planted with enough candles to make the already broiling heat insufferable. Hundreds of people, of every age and kind – Muslims, Christians, Armenians, Jews, so Çem pointed out for me – were queuing all the way down some stairs into the basement where they washed their faces and hands and made a wish at a marble fountain. On their way down they passed a seated Orthodox priest, who asked their names and murmured a prayer over them.

'Wait here,' said Çem, unscrewing the top of a small plastic bottle. 'I promised a friend of mine I'd get some of the holy water to sprinkle in the four corners of his insurance office . . .' He sped away from me, down the opposite stairway to jump the queue for the fountain.

I was all at sea, bewildered by my companion, astonished by the bizarre inter-faith ritual I was witnessing, and defeated by the constant struggle to discern the distant past in a city whose processes of change and decay flouted all the usual rules. That a Byzantine cathedral could survive fourteen centuries but an elegant turn-of-the-century mansion be an ancient ruin was mystifying. Small wonder a great fourteenth-century Turkish mystic like Bedreddin had once felt moved to muse that 'Everything is in the process of creation and destruction . . . there is no here or hereafter, everything is a single moment.'[i] I was longing for Eastern Orthodox Europe, with its ever-present past.

The Haghia Sophia, the Emperor Justinian's sixth-century wonder of the world, the Great Church of the *Romaioi*, where they lit their candles and prayed together on the eve of the Ottoman conquest of their city, had been used as a mosque and then as a museum for far too long. The morning I visited, a group of Russian tourists were glumly surveying their beloved Tsargrad's emptied heart, frowning over the Islamic inscriptions. Nothing I saw there answered the fulsome description of the place that the Byzantine Procopius had written soon after its completion:

> Within it is singularly full of light and sunshine; you would declare that the place is not lighted from without, but that the rays are produced within itself, such an abundance of light is poured into it. The gilded ceiling adds glory to its interior, though the light reflected upon the gold from the marble surpasses it in beauty. Who can tell of the splendours of the columns and marbles with which the church is adorned? One would think that one had come upon a meadow full of flowers in bloom . . .[ii]

The Great Church of the Byzantines could be a giant warehouse, a decommissioned railway station or an empty covered market now, and it was noisy with the hellish din of metal striking metal. Workmen were knocking together a giant scaffolding tower for some long-overdue repairs. Fifteen storeys high and equipped with a lift, the new structure was still only about two-thirds as tall as the cathedral's dome.

The Hippodrome where the *Romaioi* used to yell, 'Victory to the Blue [or Green] – Yes, Holy Mother of God, Victory to the Blue [or Green]', looks far too small to have accommodated horse-races so spectacular that their outcomes led to riots. These days, carpet salesmen lurk in patches of shade and haunt the teahouses around its rim, competing in the soft and tedious game of luring tourists into their nearby shops. Worse still, when I hired a taxi to take me to the 'Rum Patrikhanesi in the Fener' – in other words, to the patriarchate of the *Romaioi* in the Phanar district of the city, Istanbul's last living link to Byzantium, I discovered that it is a sad mini-microcosm of embattled late Byzantium and the surrounding area a slum.

Half an hour early for my meeting with the 270th Ecumenical Patriarch of Constantinople, I found a teahouse a few steps away, down a street strewn with muddy plastic bags, sunflower seed husks, bright crisp packets and cigarette butts, and settled on a low baby blue plastic stool to drink a Coke. The ambience was not pleasant. Two headscarved and long-skirted Muslim women with their identically dressed small daughters were kicking at the locked door of a grocery shop and a man on the opposite street corner looked from me and my notebook to a ruined house I was staring at. He frowned and shouted something. I put away my book after noting that the hollow ruin must once have been a Greek mansion.

A hundred years ago there were almost two million *Romaioi*, or Orthodox Greeks, in Ottoman Turkey, a quarter of a million of them in Istanbul itself. Some of the most influentially wealthy, the Phanariots, lived here in the area that gave them their name, until many fell from the Sultan's grace and were executed during the Greek War of Independence. The collapse of the Ottoman empire in 1918 and Greece's failed attempt – endorsed by Britain and France, but also by the Ecumenical Patriarch of the time   to win Byzantium back for Greece meant further decline. The *Katastroph* of 1922 was caused by the Greeks confidently marching on Ankara – with the ill-judged encouragement of Britain's Prime Minister Lloyd George – until they were halted, defeated and their *Megali Idea* smashed for ever. Massacres, the razing of large parts of Smyrna, now Izmir, mass drownings as that city's Greeks scrambled to board too few boats were horrors only halted when the 1923 treaty of Lausanne authorized the ethnic cleansing of almost all Turks from Greece and all Greeks from Turkey – with the exception of those living in Istanbul. Relations deteriorated still further when the Greek Cypriots launched their headstrong campaign for *Enosis* with Greece in the mid-1950s. In September 1955, the modern Turkish state exacted a horrible revenge for the Greek Cypriots' treatment of the Turkish minority by turning a blind eye while bands of thugs plundered and destroyed the vast majority of Istanbul's eighty Orthodox churches. They torched houses, smashed shop windows, desecrated graves and raped Greek women. Immediately it was over, thousands more Istanbul Greeks took the heavy hint and fled. While the Cyprus question rumbled on through the 1960s and into the early 1970s the patriarchate's printing press and its grand nineteenth-century theological school on the nearby island of Heybeliada, or Halki in Greek, were closed. Istanbul's tiny Greek community – all that was left of Constantinople and the Christian empire that had lasted more than a thousand years – dwindled to almost nothing.

By 1990 less than five thousand descendants of the *Romaioi* lived in the city. The last decade of the twentieth century would be uncomfortable, thanks to the after-shocks caused by the collapse of Communism all over the former eastern bloc. The Orthodox Serbs' crimes against Bosnia's Muslims between 1992 and 1995, the Orthodox Russians' crimes against the Muslim Chechens between 1994 and 1996, and a decade's worth of Orthodox Serb crimes against Kosovo's Muslim Albanians, culminating in the brutal mass expulsions and massacres of spring 1999, proved a powerful filip to

Turkish Islamic fundamentalism and helped foster a more nationalist climate.

The Greeks' toehold in the city is slipping all the time. The words 'Patriarch, you will die!' are regularly sprayed on the patriarchate walls and stones aimed at its windows. In 1994 a bomb big enough to blast the entire place sky-high was planted by the gateway from which Patriarch Gregorios V was strung up and left swinging like a doll in the sunshine for three days at the start of the Greek War of Independence. The explosive was defused in the nick of time but a note discovered nearby warned that a group named the Fighters of Light would battle 'until this place, which for years has contrived Byzantine intrigues against the Muslim peoples of the East, is exterminated.'[iii] In 1997 another bomb bounced on to the roof of the patriarchate church. The sudden thud caused a monk in his office on the third floor of a building adjacent to the church to abandon his computer and dash to the window. The bomb exploded and injured him so seriously that he remains paralysed in one arm. Only a day or so before my visit some Greek gravestones had been desecrated.*

That there should still be a patriarch residing in this city more than five hundred years after the fall of Constantinople seemed to me the poignantly unrealistic epitome of all that I had learnt about Byzantium and its heirs in the past two years. And it is not as if His All Holiness Bartholomaios I can console himself for his powerlessness in Constantinople by throwing his weight around in the rest of the Eastern Orthodox world. *Primus inter pares* among all the other patriarchs, he is not a supreme authority, so nothing like as powerful as a Roman Catholic pope. He cannot singlehandedly recognize the new Church of Macedonia, or order a purging of nationalists in any Church or impose a consistent Eastern Orthodox line on his fellow patriarchs and archbishops. If he could, the Orthodox European scene might look very different today because he has spoken out strongly

---

* In August 1999, both Turkey and Greece suffered serious earthquakes. Disaster brought them closer. The thaw meant Turkey was accepted as a candidate for EU membership.

against the heresy of Phyletism. As it is, they are perfectly at liberty to ignore such pronouncements and all his ecumenical endeavours, and he must handle them with care because they are all jealous of their independence and possessive about their territories. They are also always on the watch for signs that he is affecting and assuming papal airs and prerogatives. The Patriarch and his predecessors have been struggling to organize a 'Great and Holy Council' of all the Orthodox Churches since just after the First World War, thus far without success. For all the depth of their common cultural inheritance, Europe's Orthodox Churches remain more like separate and sometimes competing enterprises than branches of a single supranational conglomerate – like the Roman Catholic Church.

Relations between Patriarch Bartholomaios of Constantinople and Patriarch Alexy of Russia, who both claim to lead the Orthodox world, were badly strained in 1996 when Alexy deliberately omitted Bartholomaios' name from the dyptychs – the list of other Orthodox Churches with which an Orthodox Church is in communion. For a time the Russian Patriarch seemed prepared to bring Moscow to the brink of schism with Constantinople simply in order to register a protest at the way only one of two rival Estonian Orthodox Churches had been officially recognized by the little Baltic country's government then claimed by Patriarch Bartholomaios. His Holiness of Russia was furious that His All Holiness of Constantinople presented the stealthy theft as the action of a 'tender Mother' who must accept 'the free and unanimous request of her children.'[iv]

'Tender Mother' Constantinople's chicks have almost all flown the nest. The Ecumenical Patriarchate's spiritual jurisdiction has shrunk so dramatically over the centuries that it now extends to only 6 million Orthodox souls. Russia's Patriarch Alexy can boast over twenty times that number, about a third of all the world's Orthodox believers. Nor is Bartholomaios' little flock safely gathered in one majority Orthodox country. Half of them live in the United States and the rest are scattered across the face of the earth. Diaspora Greeks of Australia and America, other diaspora Eastern Orthodox including the Russian Church in Exile founded by White Russian refugees from the Bolshevik revolution, members of the autonomous Orthodox Church of Finland, Greeks on Crete, Patmos and the other islands of the Dodecanese, and the monks on Mount Athos make up his motley flock.

The large red and white Turkish flag flying at the gates to the patriarchate is a shock, but easily explained. The Turks question the loyalty of their tiny Greek minority to the extent that their law requires any Patriarch of Constantinople to be a Turkish citizen who has completed Turkish military service. Given the size of Istanbul's Greek community today, the patriarchal succession is becoming a source of great anxiety to the Greek Orthodox. To find a suitable candidate for the job, when the field of choice is necessarily narrowed to perhaps a handful of monks, might prove impossible. For decades the pressure has been mounting on the Greeks to evacuate the patriarchate and abandon the city for good. It tends to vary according to the state of relations between Greeks and Turks on Cyprus.

I gained admittance to the patriarchate through a side entrance and a bleeping metal security door. A tight cluster of ten buildings behind its high walls, the place consists of a nineteenth-century residence for the Patriarch, office buildings, another devoted to the production of *myron* – the holy mix of oil and herbs used in the sacrament of chrismation, which is performed when a person is received into an Orthodox Church – and an eighteenth-century church graced by a third of the wooden post against which Christ was flagellated prior to His crucifixion. Following a guard into the main building, I was led through an impressive entrance hall decorated with mosaics, into a lift and up to an anteroom heavily furnished in the bourgeois Balkan style.

His All Holiness Bartholomaios I – brightly blue-eyed with a neatly trimmed white beard – was like a genial university tutor. For the duration of our meeting I was to feel like a student whose essay topic had been judged interesting, even amusing, but not altogether academically sound. His replies to the five questions he had requested me to fax him from London filled four pages. He had spent, he told me, 'a very long time' pondering both questions and answers and, since in his delicate situation he could not risk even the slightest misunderstanding or misquotation, he had had all his answers translated from Greek into perfect English for me. On his desk was a pile of books he proposed to lend me for my 'further studies'. At a glance I could see that most of the weighty volumes were in English, but a couple were in Greek and Russian. When I confessed to an inability to read either language, I thought I saw him shake his stovepipe-hatted head despairingly. Behind his metal-rimmed glasses his eyes were kind, though.

For half an hour or so we managed to make 'off the record' small-talk in English, one of the eight foreign languages His All Holiness speaks fluently. Everything proceeded smoothly until I enquired as to whether he felt safe in his stoutly walled patriarchate. When he gestured that he was not at liberty to speak his mind on the subject I concluded that he must be working on the assumption that his office was bugged. Instead, we spoke about a cause dear to his heart: the theological school on the island of Heybeliada in the Sea of Marmara. Closed in 1971, it had been lovingly preserved and maintained during the intervening thirty years and kept in a state of perfect readiness for the moment the Turkish government deigned to allow it to reopen.

Bartholomaios chuckled over the sad fact that the patriarchate was spending large sums of money subsidizing putative future patriarchs' theological studies in Thessaloniki only to discover that by the time they had completed their studies they had met and married Greek girls and would not return home to Istanbul. He was praying that Turkey's recently elected new government would allow him to reopen the island school and nurture his successor closer to home.

'By the way, would you like to go to Halki, or Heybeliada, as the Turks call it? I studied there myself, you know. The island is cool and quiet and there are no cars. You must travel up the hill to the school by pony and trap. I will arrange everything.' He rose from his desk to present me with a heavy crystal paperweight engraved with the patriarchal cross. The audience, or rather tutorial, was over.

*

The following afternoon one of the Patriarch's assistants, an earnest young Greek-American called John, escorted me on the rickety ferry-boat, which sailed out of the Golden Horn into the Bosphorus and the Sea of Marmara. An hour and a half later we reached the island which, after the steamy heat and ugliness of central Istanbul, looked sunny but as green and pleasant as Patmos in spring. Its cafés, white holiday homes and languid atmosphere were all delightful. We rode in a comfortably dilapidated open carriage all the way up the pine-wooded hill behind the harbour to the theological school, anxious when the way was so steep that the poor horse had to slow to a walk.

'Does the Patriarch visit here often, John?' I enquired of my companion.

'Very often. His All Holiness takes a carriage up this hill, just like we're doing.'

I was happy to think of the Patriarch being able to escape from his slum-surrounded fortress to this pocket of the past.

The monastery of the Holy Trinity, which houses the theological school, was a giant imposing establishment built at the end of the nineteenth century by a wealthy Greek banker. An original school, built in 1844, had collapsed in an earthquake, miraculously while all the pupils were out in the garden waiting to be called in for lunch. Father Dorotheos, a gangly crow-like monk with an enthusiastic manner and a loud, happy laugh, let out a joyful hoot as he recounted this instance of God's ineffable grace. And then he continued his guided tour.

The school, which had three floors and two wings, was large enough to house 120 boys and their teachers and pristinely prepared for reoccupation, just as the Patriarch had promised. Its wooden and linoleum floors were polished and the high wooden desks in the empty classrooms dusted. The avocado washbasins in the communal bathroom were clean, and the dormitories with their neat rows of iron bedsteads properly aired. In the sickroom with its icon of St Nicholas on the wall, Father Dorotheos breathed in deep and his eyes lit up with delight. 'You can still smell a general sort of medicine smell, can't you? It could be just yesterday that everybody left . . .' he said wistfully.

Next he took us to the ground-floor library where room led through to room and on, into yet another room filled with mighty, mostly leatherbound tomes. 'You can easily be forgotten down here,' he informed me. 'Once, a visiting professor found himself locked in for a whole day and a night. When at last he was found he said he loved books so much that he did not suffer at all. Only the toilet . . . Hoot! Hoot!'

Father Dorotheos was full of hilarious tales of the unexpected, the happiest monk I had met on my travels.

'Next week we have a couple and their thirteen children coming to stay. The father and all the boys will stay here and sing in our church. The mother and the girls will be sleeping in the village.'

As our footsteps echoed down the long corridors I wondered if he was lonely in this empty mausoleum of a school. His companion monks were both youngsters.

'I waited forty-one years to become a monk,' he confided, as he led us outside for a tour of the school grounds, 'because I was planning to get married. But I never did so now I am a monk at last . . . Hoot! Hoot!'

There was a flourishing vegetable garden and row upon row of flower-pots filled with marigolds. From a terrace we admired a wonderful view across the sea to the neighbouring island. Strolling on, we paused at 'the monastery farm', as Father Dorotheos called it, to watch a single donkey bray and a goat clamber out of a stable window.

'When the Patriarch visits he always comes out here to chat to Leo the donkey and give him something to eat before he himself sits down to lunch. He loves animals and all the natural world so much.' Father Dorotheos told us, hand on his heart.

I was grateful for this tender new dimension to my picture of His All Holiness, whose written answers to my questions I had been putting off reading for fear I would be forced to rethink my entire thesis.

*

Back in Istanbul, the roof terrace of my small hotel near the Haghia Sophia was a haven of quiet, cooled by soft breezes. I also liked its view of the glittering Sea of Marmara and the sounds of children playing in the jumble of crumbling houses just below, so I settled there that evening, with a cold drink to hand, to read those four pages of replies.

To the first question, 'What had eastern and western Christianity each lost by the Schism of 1054?' he had replied that it depended whether I was approaching the matter from a 'theanthropic' stand-point or not. Was I appraising Christianity in terms of its true religious content or merely its 'epiphenomena'? It seemed that, as Patriarch, he would only answer my question from the first standpoint, the strictly religious one. 'We can say,' he had written, 'that the Christian life in western Christianity became anthropocentric, while in Eastern Orthodox Christianity it remained theanthropic.' If I had understood him right, Orthodoxy had lost nothing whatsoever by the Schism because it had held firm to the True Faith. I shuddered to think what he would make of my bold assertion that the Schism had proved catastrophic for both western and eastern Christianity: one had lost its heart, the other its mind.

My second question concerned the significance of the monastic revival I had witnessed everywhere in Eastern Orthodox Europe. He characterized monasticism as 'a genuine and sincere search for Christ as a God-man, as a friend and brother who is approachable, tangible, incarnate, and who shares our human nature in a way that is parallel, unconfused and undivided with divine nature.' Once again, I would have preferred a less 'theanthropic' appraisal of a material phenom-enon. In his answer to my question about whether Hesychasm and Phyletism could safely be described as the best and the worst aspects of Eastern Orthodox civilization, I sensed his criticism of that typi-cally western habit of thought that seeks to manufacture crudely clashing antitheses at the expense of a deeper understanding of any subject. 'In the Orthodox Church we are not accustomed to absolutiz-ing one good or evil,' he stated, before going on to explain that Hesychasm was simply one kind of monasticism and Phyletism a heresy as grave as any other since all heresies caused people 'to stray away from Christ and his Church'. My last question, a suggestion that the wars in former Yugoslavia had dangerously re-accentuated the division of Europe down the 1054 Schism line met with a firm, almost impatient denial. 'The war in Yugoslavia resulted from typical, small human causes. The attempt of some people to intermix Ortho-doxy among these causes is an attempt to conceal the reasons for the conflict,' he had written, and added magisterially, 'This perception is not based on a thorough analysis of the facts.'

Well, I thought – pausing to listen to the amplified tape-recording of the call to the day's last prayer to Allah – His All Holiness had stated at the start that he would take a 'theanthropic' line. He would not want to view the Eastern Orthodox countries of Europe as sharing a culture that remains steeped in the traditions and outlook of Byzantium, despite centuries of Mongol, Ottoman, Roman Catholic or atheist Communist oppression. Bartholomaios was first and fore-most a monk and a patriarch. In the end, I reasoned, there is no debating with believers – certainly not with the Orthodox – because they can always refuse to meet you on level ground, and head instead for the mountain-tops of dogma and absolute truths where you cannot follow. In the introduction to his book about the Orthodox Churches during the Ottoman era, *The Great Church in Captivity*, Sir Steven Runciman has stated the problem more elegantly: 'Of all the roads that a historian may tread none passes through more difficult country than that of religious history. To a believer religious truths are eternal.'ᵛ

Relaxing on that terrace, watching the blinking white light of the lighthouse over on the shore of Asia and the setting sun turning the sea its old-icon gold, I pondered my two years of travel through 'difficult country'. I felt like a pilgrim who, by the time he or she reaches his or her destination, has discovered that the thing desired or – as in this case – the question originally posed, was only a part of the point.

The answer to the original question Why Angels Fall, why Europe's Eastern Orthodox Churches have fallen so far from the

sublime ideal dreamed up in Byzantium that they are hotbeds of
nationalism, a factor weighting every Eastern Orthodox country's
political spectrum towards the xenophobic right and an obstacle
impeding European unification on western Europe's terms, lies with
history. Deadly pride, in the form of a religious nationalism that had
its heyday in the nineteenth century but can be traced back to
medieval Serbia and Late Byzantium, is why angels fall in Eastern
Orthodox Europe. But that much was clear to me when I started out
on my journey. What I did not know was the extent of western
Christendom's, or the West's, contribution. The manner of the
Schism, the Fourth Crusade and the way in which successive popes
bullied the Byzantines into recognizing Rome's supremacy were a bad
start, but the Habsburgs' Uniate project, the lethal Great Power
rivalries of the nineteenth century and the trouble caused by Britain
holding tight to Cyprus for too long were all grievous injuries too. I
had not expected that my encounters with Orthodox Church people
would also modify the final picture. Father Sava at Dečani, young
Bishop Naum and his happy nuns, Patmos' *geront* Father Pavlos,
Abbot Kiprian at Bistriţa monastery in Moldavia, *Starets* Nikolai on
his island near Pskov, Father Vasily of Optina Pustyn's earnest
humility, and even happy Father Dorotheos had all touched my heart
instead of just exercising my mind. Those people forgot I was a
western female, born a Roman Catholic but no longer a believer.
They made me wish I could believe as they did.

Some places had a similarly soul-stirring effect. Kosovo's Gračanica pink church on a clear early autumn morning, off-season Lake
Ohrid and its homely churches, Patmos' spring green hillsides dotted
with white mushroom chapels, Romania's painted monasteries among
beech forests turning flame orange, the dazzling White Sea viewed
from a home-made yacht, the holy hurly-burly of Sergeyev Posad on
St Sergius' feast day, the pristine perfection of Verkhoturye's seventeenth-century cathedral in the snow, Holy Week in Nicosia and
Easter in the High Troodos . . .

Everything I have seen and heard has convinced me that Eastern
Orthodox Europe may be physically shrinking but it is certainly not

dying. The various national Churches, and the common culture they have guarded and nurtured through the centuries are not about to disappear. Indeed, if the monastic revival is anything to go by, the reverse is the case. The best and the worst of the legacy of the great empire born here on the shores of the Bosphorus 1,700 years ago has survived into a new millennium. But there is much to be done on both sides of Europe if the continent is to be united and peaceful.

The Orthodox East will have to cut away the crust of kitsch that has been doing such a fine job of concealing its spiritual treasures from the world. That heinous religious nationalism, with its persecution and martyr complexes and longing for death and suffering, that targeting of enemies and dangerously emotive habit of spinning pretty patterns from the past – mythologies instead of histories – will have to go. *Symphonia* was almost always too high and vague an ideal to be entirely practical even among a people as fervently religious as the *Romaioi*, let alone in this secular age. However, in its dissident hermits – the filthy famished holy men of the desert and hardy pioneers of Russia's north who thundered away about the evils of the world – the Orthodox Churches have a fine and ancient tradition of curbing the excesses of corrupt governments and cruel regimes.

Some of these changes might happen if the western half of our continent could begin to acknowledge Orthodox Europe's separate history and vital differences. The West's belated backlash against soulless materialism suggests that an awareness of what we lost by tending our bodies and brains at the expense of our spirits is growing. The step towards appreciating the best of Orthodoxy is not such a big one to take, even for the unbeliever. We should then find it easier to understand that Orthodox Europeans' mounting protests against the West and its values are not just a temporary burst of anger aimed by the continent's 'have-nots' at its 'haves'. The roots of those protests can be traced as far back as the 1054 Schism and they are not objections to be swiftly silenced by large injections of cash loans and consumer goods. It is hard to imagine how the eastern Balkans and Russia can be integrated with the rest of Europe, unless both sides of the continent set about changing and understanding. Without more mutual recognition of what East and West tragically lost of each other by the Schism, without an effort to right the balance, there is everything to fear. As Professor Huntington warns in the conclusion to his book, *The Clash of Civilisations and the Remaking of the World Order*, 'The future of both peace and civilisation depend upon understanding and cooperation among the political, spiritual and intellectual leaders of the world's major civilisations.'[vi]

The breeze is blowing harder. The playing children have fallen quiet and the Sea of Marmara is a deep violet. Watching a dark boat hung with strings of white lights like the seed-pearl trimmings on Byzantine royal robes head west across towards the Dardanelles and the wide Aegean, I am imagining it sailing on, around the dark north Greek coast all night, up to Greek Macedonia. I can see it reaching the Holy Mountain at daybreak, when the early-morning sun is glinting off the Byzantine monasteries' crosses and the sea is turning from base metal to gold.

A mind can close the circle like this but a heart can stay open . . .

GLOSSARY

babushka	Grandmother, old woman (Russ.)
chetnik	Royalist nationalist Serb fighters in Second World War, against Nazis and Tito's Partisans. Resurrected in Croatia and Bosnia 1991–5. (Serb.)
crap	Carp fish (Rom.)
duhovnik	Orthodox holy man, elder (Rom.) or spiritual father (Serb.)
enosis	Union, of Cyprus with Greece (Greek)
ekklesia	Church, as community of believers (Greek)
ekklesiastika	Orthodox church accessories, e.g.icon, incense-burner (Greek)
flaunas	Traditional Easter cheese pie (Greek)
geront/gerontes	Orthodox holy man, elder (Greek)
hesychia	Inner silence needed for prayer (Greek)
inteligentsiya	nineteenth-century urban intellectuals (Russ.)
kafa	Coffee (Serb.)
kafeneion	Café (Greek)
katastroph	Catastrophic defeat by Turks in 1922 (Greek), evacuation of Asia Minor Greeks.
krestyane	Peasants (Russ.)
kellia	Hermitage
koliva	Funeral cake made of boiled buckwheat, sugar and nuts. Eaten at Orthodox gravesides and on anniversaries of deaths. (Rom., Greek, Serb., Russ., etc.)
kombolloi	Worry beads (Greek)
komitadji	Macedonian or Bulgarian freedom fighter (Mac.)

kyriakon	Church, as building, home of God (Greek)
loukoumi	Greek version of Turkish delight (Greek)
mafiya	Organized crime (Russ.)
mamaliga	Polenta (Rom.)
Megali Idea	Great Idea, plan to unite all Greeks in one nation state (Greek)
metochion/metochia	Orthodox monastery lands and estates, acquired by donation and legacy. Often valuable real estate in city (Greek)
metojiha	As *metochion* (Serb.)
mira	Chrism used in the sacrament of chrismation for accepting a person into the Orthodox faith (Serb.)
myron	As *mira* (Greek)
mukhtaris	Greek Cypriot mayor or village headman
nefos	Athens smog (Greek)
novo pecheni	Newly baked (Serb)
oikumeme	The Inhabited Universe (Greek)
oprichniki	Tsar Ivan the Terrible's praetorian guard of thugs dressed as monks (Russ.)
palikari	Fighter in Greek War of Independence (Greek)
paratesis	Free of logic and reason (Greek)
parousia	Christ's Second Coming, or Presentation (Greek)
pelmeni	Ravioli native to Siberia (Russ.)
perestroika	Restructuring of Russia undertaken by Mikhail Gorbachev in spirit of openness, after 1985 (Russ.)
Philiki Etairia	Society of Friends devoted to freeing the Greeks from Ottoman rule in the early nineteenth century (Greek)
Philokalia	Love of the Good. Title of collected sayings of the fathers of the early Christian Church. Textbook for Hesychast mystics (Greek)
podvig	Feat of spiritual or physical endurance (Russ.)
podvor	Orthodox monastery lands and estates, acquired by donation or legacy. Often valuable real estate in large city (Russ.)

pustyn	Desert, wilderness, hermitage (Russ.)
Romios/Romaioi	Roman. The Byzantines' name for themselves (Greek)
Rum-millet	Orthodox peoples of Ottoman Empire – literally, Roman nation (Turk.)
saloi	Fool for Christ, holy fool in Byzantium (Greek)
semantron	Wooden board struck with hammer to summon monks and nuns to church (Greek, Serb.)
slivovic	Clear plum brandy (Serb.)
souvlaki	Char-grilled chunks of meat on skewer (Greek)
srpska	Serbian (Serb.)
srpstvo	Serbdom (Serb.)
starets/startsy	Orthodox holy man, elder (Russ.) or abbot/manager of monastery (Rom.)
strannik	Wandering tramp pilgrim (Russ.)
symphonia	Harmony governing relations between Byzantine Church and State (Greek)
theosis	Process of becoming God (Greek)
tsargrad	Constantinople (Russ.)
ţuica	Clear plum brandy (Rom.)
turcocratia	Period of Ottoman rule (Greek)
turkska	Turkish (Serb.)
verst/versty	1.07 kilometres (Russ.)
vladika	Montenegrin prince-bishop, bishop (Serb.)
yevro-remont	Redecoration in west-European style (Russ.)
yurodivy	Fool for Christ, holy fool (Russ.)
zivania	Clear grape brandy in Cyprus (Greek)

CHRONOLOGY

4th	320	Roman Emperor Constantine converted to Christianity
	330	Constantinople founded
5th	410	Fall of Rome
6th		Haghia Sophia built
9th	800	**Charlemagne crowned Holy Roman Emperor by Pope**
	843	First recorded mention of Mount Athos monks
	860	Failed Kievan Rus raid on Constantinople
	864	Sts Cyril and Methodius arrive in Moravia with Slavic gospel
10th	957	Grand Lavra monastery founded on Mount Athos
	988	Kievan Rus converted to Christianity under Prince Vladimir
11th	1014	Fall to Byzantines of empire of Tsar Samuil in Macedonia
	1015	First Russian Sts Boris and Gleb martyred
	1054	**Schism between east and west Christianity**
	1088	St Christodoulos given island of Patmos by the Byzantine emperor
	1095	**First Crusade proclaimed by Pope Urban II**
	1099	Jerusalem captured by western Crusaders

12th	1191	Richard the Lionheart conquers Cyprus before Third Crusade
	1197	Women banned from Mount Athos by forged order of Patriarch of Constantinople
13th	1204	**Fourth Crusaders sack Constantinople and rule Byzantium**
	1219	Serbia's St Sava wins independent Church from exiled Byzantine Church at Nicaea
	1240	**Mongols sack and conquer Kievan Rus**
	1242	**Teutonic Knights attack Russians from west, near Pskov**
	1261	Byzantines retake Constantinople from Latins
14th	1321	Serbian Gračanica church built
	1346	Tsar Dušan crowned King of the Serbs and *Romaioi* in Skopje and Serbian patriarchate proclaimed
	1350	Serbian monasteries of Krka and Dečani founded
	1355	Tsar Dušan dies on way to invade Constantinople
	1380	Russian defeat of Mongols at battle of Kulikovo
	1389	**Battle of Kosovo and Prince Lazar's choice of a heavenly kingdom**
15th	1429	Russian Sts Zosima and Savvati reach Solovetsky island in the White Sea
	1438	Council of Florence, formal, but unsuccessful reunion of east and west Christendom
	1453	**Fall of Constantinople to Ottomans**
	1476	Death of Prince Vlad the Impaler of Wallachia, (Dracula)
16th	1538	Henry VIII of England decrees dissolution of monasteries
	1547	Tsar Ivan the Terrible crowned in Moscow
	1569	Assassination of St Philip of Solovetsky, Metropolitan of Russia
	1570	Ottomans conquer Cyprus
	1582	Exploration of Siberia begins

	1584	Death of Tsar Ivan the Terrible
	1588	Russia gains independent patriarchate
	1596	**Uniate Church of western Ukraine created**
	1598	Verkhoturye, Siberia founded
17th	1642	Death of St Simeon of Verkhoturye, Siberia
	1699	**Uniate Church of Transylvania created**
18th	1714	Last native prince of Wallachia executed in Istanbul. Phanariot Greeks rule the Danubian principalities for a century.
	1728	Ion-Innocentie Micu-Klein made Archbishop of Uniate Church in Transylvania
	1744	Serb monk Vissarion reverses conversions to Uniate Church in Transylvania
	1794	Death of St Paissy Velichkovsky
19th	1815	End of Napoleonic Wars
	1820	Greek War of Independence starts, first in Danubian principality of Moldavia, then Peloponnese Hanging of Ecumenical Patriarch Gregorios V of Constantinople
	1827	Defeat of Ottomans by western alliance in battle of Navarino
	1828	Count Ioannis Capodistrias first president of independent Greece First of famous trio of *startsy* at Optina Pustyn Monastery, Russia
	1830	Greek Church declares independence from Constantinople patriarchate
	1833	President Capodistrias assassinated in Nafplio Bavarian Catholic prince, Otto, becomes King of Greece 412 Greek monasteries and convents dissolved
	1870	Bulgarians win independent State and Church, known as Exarchate
	1872	Patriarch of Constantinople coins new heresy of 'Phyletism'
	1878	**Britain gains Cyprus from the Ottomans**

20th	1910	Death of Tolstoy
	1912	Outbreak of First Balkan War, Ottomans expelled from Europe
	1912/3	Second Balkan War, with partitioning of Macedonia
	1913	Archbishop Makarios of Cyprus born
		Completion of Church of the Exaltation of the Cross, Verkhoturye, Siberia
	1914/18	First World War
	1916	Grigory Rasputin assassinated in St Petersburg
	1917	Bolshevik Communist Revolution in Russia
	1918	Murder of Romanov imperial family at Yekaterinburg
	1922	Greeks' *Katastroph*. Attempt to create a neo-Byzantium by winning back Asia Minor ended in disaster, massacres, population exchanges and the death of the *Megali Idea*
	1927	Solovetsky gulag-camp bishops protest against Communism
	1939–45	Second World War
	1948	Abolition of Uniate Church in Transylvania
	1955	Anti-Greek riots in Istanbul
	1956	Cypriot EOKA fighters begin violent campaign for independence from Britain and *Enosis* with Greece
	1958	The Yugoslav Republic of Macedonia wins independent Church from Tito
	1960	Cyprus wins independence from Britain. Archbishop Makarios becomes first president
	1964	United Nations troops arrive in Cyprus
	1968	Roman Pope and Constantinople Greek Patriarch lift anathemas declared with 1054 Schism
	1970	**Population of monks on Mount Athos drops to a low-point of just over a thousand**
	1974	American-backed Greek coup against President-Archbishop Makarios of Cyprus
		Turkish invasion of Northern Cyprus. Population exchange. United Nations Green Line established
	1977	Death of President-Archbishop Makarios of Cyprus
	1980	Death of Tito in Yugoslavia
	1987	Slobodan Milošević comes to power in Serbia and tells Kosovo Serbs he will not allow anyone to 'beat' them

1989	Six-hundredth anniversary of the battle of Kosovo
	Fall of the Berlin Wall
	Romanian uprising and execution of Nicolae Ceauşescu on Christmas Day
1990	Removal of Kosovo's autonomous status within the Yugoslav Republic of Serbia
	Restoration of Uniate Church in Transylvania
	Battles between Romanians and Hungarian minority in Targu Mureş, Transylvania
1991	Ecumenical Patriarch Bartholomaios I of Constantinople elected
	War in Croatia
	Hard-line Communist coup against reforming Mikhail Gorbachev in Russia, Boris Yeltsin and the collapse of the USSR and Communism
	Remains of Romanovs discovered in forest pit near Yekaterinburg
	Solovetsky monastery and Optina Pustyn re-colonized by monks
	The Yugoslav Republic of Macedonia wins independence as the FYROM
1992–5	War in Bosnia
1994–6	Russia loses war against separatist Chechens
1995	Dayton, Ohio, peace agreement splits Bosnia between Muslim Croat Federation and Bosnian Serb Republic Nato-led peacekeeping force
1997	Exhibition of 'Treasures of Mount Athos', Thessaloniki Greece joins the Schengen Agreement
	Kosovo Liberation Army (KLA or UČK) formed by Kosovar Albanians
1998	Death of Archbishop Serapheim of Greece, election of Archbishop Christodoulos
	Romanovs reburied in St Petersburg
	Decision to site Russian surface-to-air missiles on Crete instead of Cyprus
	Collapse of rouble and government in Russia
	Serbia's ethnic cleansing of Kosovo begins
1999	**Expansion of Nato to include Central Europe: Hungary, Poland and the Czech Republic**

**Three-month Nato bombing campaign in Serbia to
reverse ethnic cleansing of Kosovo Albanians**
Pope John Paul II bridges the 1054 Schism with a visit
to Bucharest, Romania
Nato-led troops occupy Kosovo
Twenty-fifth anniversary of partition of Cyprus
Russia's second war with Chechnya begins
Boris Yeltsin resigns on New Year's Eve

2000   Fourteen Eastern Orthodox leaders gather to celebrate
Eastern Orthodox Christmas in Jerusalem

NOTES

MOUNT ATHOS

i Choukas, Michael, *Black Angels of Athos*, London, 1935, p. 224.

ii Dawkins, R. M., *The Monks of Athos*, London, 1936, p. 104.

iii Byron, Robert, *The Byzantine Achievement*, London, 1929, p. 133.

iv Lossky, Vladimir, *The Mystical Theology of the Eastern Church*, London, 1957, p. 18.

v Fletcher, Richard, *The Conversion of Europe: from Paganism to Christianity 371–1386 AD*, London, 1998, p. 22. Quoted from Eusebius, Bishop of Caesarea, c.260–c.340.

vi Morris, Rosemary, 'The Political Saint of the 11th Century,' in *The Byzantine Saint*, University of Birmingham 14th Spring Symposium, ed. Sergei Hackel, 1981, p. 47. Quoted from Symeon le Nouveau Theologien, Cathecheses, ed. B. Krivocheine and tr. J. Paramelle, 1963–5, ii, 335.

vii Psellus, Michael, *Fourteen Byzantine Rulers*, Penguin, 1966, p. 269.

viii Fortescue, Adrian, *The Orthodox Eastern Church*, London, 1911, p. 110, note.

ix Liddell, Robert, *Byzantium and Istanbul*, London, 1956, p. 36.

x Ibid., p. 29, quoted from R. Henn, *The Lonely Tower*, 1950.

xi Sherrard, Philip, *Byzantium: Great Ages of Man*, Holland, 1966, p. 34.

xii Ibid., p. 36.

xiii Meyendorff, John, *Byzantium and the Rise of Russia*, St Vladimir's Seminary Press, 1981, p. 5. Quoted from the Russian Primary Chronicle, tr. S. H. Cross and O. P. Sherbowitz-Wetzor, 1953, p. 111.

xiv Philips, Fr. Andrew, 'Orthodox Christianity and the Old English Church', Greenprint and Design, 1996, p. 30.

xv Ware, Timothy, *The Orthodox Church*, (new edition), London, 1997, p. 37. Quoted from Gregory Nazianzus, Letter 124; Poems about Himself, xvii, 91.

xvi Runciman, Steven, *The Great Church in Captivity*, Cambridge, 1968, p. 85.

xvii Ware, T., *op.cit.*, p. 21. Quoted from St Athanasius, 'On the Incarnation'.

xviii Golitzin, Hieromonk Alexander, *The Living Witness of the Holy Mountain*, St Tikhon's Seminary Press, Pennsylvania, 1996, p. 20. Quoted from St Symeon the New Theologian, The Practical and Theological Chapters, 3:4.

xix Botsis, Peter A., *What is Orthodoxy?*, Athens, p. 14.

xx Johnson, Paul, *A History of Christianity*, London, 1976, p. 178. Quoted from Luitprand of Cremona.

xxi Sherrard, Philip, *The Greek East and the Latin West*, Limni, Evia, 1959, p. 87.

xxii Todorovich, Slavko, P., *The Chilandarians*, New York, 1989, p. 105.

xxiii Norwich, John Julius, *Byzantium: the Decline and Fall*, London, 1996, p. 171. Quoted from Geoffrey of Villehardouin, *La Conquête de Constantinople*, ed. E. Faral, 2 vols, Paris, 1938–9.

xxiv Ibid., p. 179. Quoted from Nicetas Choniates, *Historia, in Corpus Scriptorum Historiae Byzantinae*, Bonn, 1828.

xxv Gibbon, Edward, *Decline and Fall of the Roman Empire*, Penguin, abridged, p. 177.

xxvi Billings, Malcolm, *The Cross and the Crescent*, London, 1987, p. 137. Quoted from Gunther of Pairis.

xxvii Davis, R. H. C., *A History of Medieval Europe: from Constantine to St Louis*, London, 1957, p. 349.

xxviii Schmemann, Alexander, *The Historical Road of Eastern Orthodoxy*, London, 1963, p. 252.

xxix Norwich, J. J., *op.cit.*, p. 201. Quoted from George Pachymeres.

xxx Meyendorff, John, *The Byzantine Legacy in the Orthodox Church*, St Vladimir's Seminary Press, 1982, p. 69.

xxxi Boojamra, John Lawrence, *Church Reform in the Late Byzantine Empire*, Thessaloniki, 1982, p. 61.

xxxii Ware, Kallistos, *Act out of Stillness: the Influence of Hesychasm on*

Byzantine and Slav Civilization, Toronto, 1995, p. 21. Quoted from F. Miklosich and I. Muller, *Acta et Diplomata Graeca Medii Aevi Sacra et Profana*, vol. 2, Vienna, 1862, pp. 190–1.

xxxiii Norwich J. J., *op.cit.*, p. 243.

xxxiv Ibid. p. 357. Quoted from Ducas, *Historia Turco-Byzantina, Corpus Scriptorum Historiae Byzantinae*, Bonn, 1828.

xxxv Runciman, Steven, *The Fall of Constantinople 1453*, Cambridge, 1965, p. 1. Quoted from *Chronicon*, (ed. Thompson), p. 57.

xxxvi Ware, T., *Eustratios Argenti: A Study of the Greek Church under Turkish Rule*, Oxford, 1964, p. 111. Quoted from Gill, *The Council of Florence*, p. 227.

xxxvii Schmemann, A., *op.cit.*, p. 254.

xxxviii Norwich, J. J., *op.cit.*, p. 388. Quoted from Michael Ducas.

xxxix Tr. Melville Jones, J. R., *The Siege of Constantinople*, Amsterdam, 1972 pp. 74–75. Quoted from Michael Ducas.

xl Runciman, S., *op.cit.*, p. 136. Quoted from Symeon the New Theologian, *Divinorum Amorum Liber*.

xli Meyendorff, J., *op.cit.*, 1982, p. 185.

xlii Winkler, Gabriele, *The Jesus Prayer in Eastern Spirituality*, Minneapolis, 1986, p. 19.

xliii Talk given to Friends of Mount Athos Society, Oxford, May 1998.

xliv Curzon, Robert, *Visits to Monasteries of the Levant*, London, 1916, p. 414.

xlv Rycaut, Paul, *The Present State of the Greek and Armenian Churches*, 1678, 1679, p. 262.

xlvi Kwop, Marcia, 'Orthodoxy's Modern Appeal', *Christian Science Monitor*, 28 July 1997; and Steve Crawshaw, 'Incense, Icon and Faith', *Independent*, 19 March 1998.

xlvii Runciman S., *The Great Church in Captivity*, Cambridge, 1968, p. 121. Quoted from Georgius Scholarius Gennadius, *Contre les Juifs*, in *Oeuvres Complètes*, III, 252.

xlviii Economides, Irene, *The Two Faces of Greece: A civilization of 7,000 years*, Athens, 1990, p. 84.

xlix Greek folk song tr. Constantine Trypanis.

THE SERBS

i Bulgarian Academy of Sciences, *Macedonia: Documents and Materials*, Sofia, 1979, p. 86. Quoted from *Monumenta Slavorum Meridionalium II*, Zabrabiae, 1870, p. 278.

ii Baynes, Norman H. and Moss H. St. L. B. (eds), *Byzantium: An Introduction to East Roman Civilization*, Oxford, 1948, p. 49. Quoted from *Izvori* VI, 626, N. Radosević.

iii Soulis, George Christos, *The Serbs and Byzantium during the Reign of Tsar Stephen Dušan 1331 to 1355, and his Successors*, Washington, 1984, p. 85.

iv Moon, Paul, 'A History of Medieval Serbia', Auckland, 1988, p. 16.

v Mileušnić, Slobodan, 'The Monastery of Krka', Belgrade, 1994, p. 11. Quoted Bishop Simeon Končarević.

vi Ibid., p. 12.

vii Ibid.

viii Ibid., p. 21.

ix Silber, Laura and Little, Allan, *The Death of Yugoslavia*, London, 1995, p. 224.

x Walker, Tom, 'Serbs threaten to defend Karadzic from Nato Swoop', *The Times*, 18 August 1997.

xi Powers, Gerard F., 'Religion, Conflict and Prospects for Peace in Bosnia, Croatia and Yugoslavia', in *Religion in Europe*, Vol. XVI, 5 October 1996, translation of 1995 interview with Karadžić in *Sveti Gora* magazine.

xii Anzulović, Branimir, *Heavenly Serbia: from Myth to Genocide*, New York, 1999, p. 17. Quoted from Patriarch Gavrilo, *Memoari Patrijarha Srpskog Gavrila*, 1990, p. 270.

xiii Silber, L. and Little, A., *op.cit.*, p. 205.

xiv Judah, Tim, *The Serbs: History, Myth and the Destruction of Yugoslavia*, Yale, 1997, p. 34. Quoted from *Marko the Prince: Serbo-Croat Heroic Songs*, Anne Pennington and Peter Levi, 1984, p. 17.

xv Anzulović, B., *op.cit.*, p. 31.

xvi Ibid., p. 13.

xvii Mihaljčić, Rade, *The Battle of Kosovo in History and Popular Tradition*, Belgrade, 1989, p. 61.

xviii Kindersley, Anne, *The Mountains of Serbia: Travels Through*

Inland Yugoslavia, London, 1976, p. 214. Quoted from *The Complete Letters of Lady Mary Wortley Montagu*, ed. Robert Halsband, 1965, I. 310.

xix Banac, Ivo, *The National Question in Yugoslavia: Origins, History, Politics*, Cornell, 1984, p. 143. From *Uspomene na politicke ljude I dogadjaje*, Ivan Mestrovic, 1961, p. 84.

xx Tachaios, A. E. N. (ed.), *Mount Athos and the EU*, Thessaloniki, 1993, p. 103.

xxi Truman, Ivan *The Serbian Orthodox Church in Kosovo*, from *Sobornost*, 1985, 1, vol. 7, 1.

xxii Silber, L. and Little, A., *op.cit.*, p. 72.

xxiii Durham, Mary E., *Through the Lands of the Serb*, London, 1904, pp. 307–8.

xxiv Kaplan, Robert D., *Balkan Ghosts*, New York, 1993, p. 33.

xxv Runciman, Steven, *Byzantine Civilisation*, London, 1933, p. 284.

xxvi Kindersley, A., *op.cit.*, quoted from Abbot Caplak.

xxvii Durham, M. E., *op.cit.*, p. 317.

xxviii Malcolm, Noel, *Kosovo: A Short History*, London, 1998, p. 38.

xxix I. M., *Vacation Tourists*, London, 1861, p. 380.

xxx Anzulović, B., *op.cit.*, p. 54.

xxxi Banac, I., *op.cit.*, p. 60.

Macedonia

i *Dr Browne's Travels through Hungary, Thessaly, Macedonia, etc.* London, 1673, p. 775.

ii Brailsford, H. N., *Macedonia: Its Races and their Future*, London, 1906, p. xi.

iii Levecque, J., *Coutumes Chrétiennes de Macedoine*, Salonika, 1918.

iv Carnegie Endowment, *The Other Balkan Wars*, Washington, 1993, p. 73.

v Acts 16:9,10.

vi Obolensky, Dimitri, *Byzantium and the Slavs*, St Vladimir's Seminary Press, 1994, p. 245. Quoted from *Vita Constantini*, XIV, 10.

vii Internet http://www.geocities.com/~makedonija/samuil.html, from *Makedonski Icelenuchki Almanac*, 1995, *Matitsa na Icelenitsite od Makedonija*, Skopje, 1995, p. 36.

viii Clogg, Richard (ed.), *The Movement for Greek Independence 1770–1821*, London, 1976. Quoted from Daniil Mikhali Adami, 1802.

ix Danforth, Loring M., *The Macedonian Conflict*, Princeton, 1995, p. 62.

x Carnegie Endowment, *op.cit.*, p. 95.

xi Abbott, G. F. (ed.), *Greece in Evolution*, London, 1909, p. 58.

xii Ilievski, Done, *The Macedonian Orthodox Church*, Skopje, 1973, p. 93.

xiii Ibid., p. 96.

xiv Brailsford, H. N., *op.cit.*, pp. 59–61.

xv Ibid., p. 65.

xvi Constantinople Patriarchate (ed.), *Official Documents concerning the Deplorable Condition of Affairs in Macedonia*, Constantinople, 1906, p. 21.

xvii Brailsford, H. N., *op.cit.*, pp. 192–4

xviii Ibid., p. 195.

xix Obolensky, Dimitri, *The Byzantine Inheritance of Eastern Europe*, Oxford, 1982, 'Cult of St Demetrius of Thessaloniki in the History of Byzantine-Slav Relations', p. 13.

xx Ibid., p. 16.

xxi Choukas, Michael, *Black Angels of Athos*, London, 1935, p.292. Quoted from Kornaros, Themistocles, 'The Holy Mountain: The Saints Unmasked', Athens, 1933, pp. 6–8.

xxii Ibid.

xxiii Brewster, Ralph, *The 6000 Beards of Athos*, London, 1935, p. 38.

xxiv Ibid.

xxv Choukas, M., *op.cit.*, p. 296.

xxvi Ibid., p. 61.

xxvii The Christian Activist, *Mt. Athos: An Introduction*, Graham Speake, March, 1996.

xxviii Loch, Sydney, *Athos: The Holy Mountain*, London, 1957, p. 101.

xxix Athens news agency bulletin, no. 1202, 3 June 1997.

xxx Smith, Helena, 'Gamble of the Macedonia Gambit', *Guardian*, 31 January 1992.

xxxi The sequence of these events was outlined in a lecture given by Charles Stewart at King's College, London, 2 March 1998.

NOTES

GREECE

i Ware, Kallistos, 'Patmos and its Monastery', *Eastern Churches Review*, 1967, I, 3. Quoted from F. Miklosich and Müller, *Acta et diplomata graeca medii aevi*, vol. iv, Vienna, 1890, p. 56.

ii Papadopoulos S. A., *Monastery of St John the Theologian*, Patmos, 1993, p. 8.

iii Oecomenos, Lysimaque, *La Vie Réligieuse dans l'Empire Byzantine au temps des Comnenes et des Anges*, 1918, pp. 148–9.

iv Levi, Peter, *The Hill of Kronos*, London, 1981.

v Papadopoulos, S. A., *op.cit.*, pp. 16–17.

vi Hill, Aaron, *A Full and Just Account of the Present State of the Ottoman Empire*, London, 1709, p. 215.

vii Revelation 1:9.

viii Clogg, Richard (ed.), *The Movement for Greek Independence 1770–1821*, London, 1976, p. 93.

xix Fermor, Patrick Leigh, *Roumeli: Travels in Northern Greece*, London, 1966, pp. 107–13.

x Walsh, Robert, *A Residence at Constantinople, during a period including the commencement, progress and termination of the Greek and Turkish revolutions*, London, 1836, p. 180.

xi Ibid., p. 179.

xii Clogg, Richard (ed.), *The Struggle for Greek Independence*, London, 1973. Quoted from *Kapodistrias and the Philiki Etairia (1814–1821)*, C. M. Woodhouse, p. 123.

xiii Bangerater, Kathryn Jean, *Three Hellenes in the Struggle for Greek Independence*, PhD thesis, University of California, 1982, p. 122.

xiv Economides, Irene, *The Two Faces of Greece: A Civilisation of 7,000 years*, Athens, 1990, p. 110.

xv Linner, Stuve (ed.), *W. H. Humphreys First Journal of the Greek War of Independence, July 1821–February 1822*, p. 76.

xvi Frazee, Charles, *The Orthodox Church and Independent Greece*, London, 1969, p. 40.

xvii Ibid., p. 30.

xviii Ibid., p. 34.

xix Clogg, Richard, *op.cit.*, p. 182.

xx Woodhouse, C. M., *Capodistrias: The Founder of Greek Independence*, Oxford, 1973, p. 393. Quoted from letter of Capodistrias to Jean-Gabriel Eyuard, Geneva.

432

xxi Clogg, Richard (ed.), *The Struggle for Greek Independence*, London, 1973, p. 239. Essay by Douglas Dakin.

xxii Ibid., p. 336. Quoted from letter to under-secretary for the colonies, Sir Robert Horton, *Correspondence* I, p. 265.

xxiii Frazee, C., *op.cit.*, p. 75. Quoted from letter of I. Capodistrias to C. Mustoxidis, 6 November 1827.

xxiv Par un Grec, *Renseignements sur la Grece et sur l'Administration du Comte Capodistrias*, 1833, p. 35.

xxv Woodhouse, C. M., *op.cit.*, p. 389. Quoted from *Apomnimonevmata* II, pp. 10–11.

xxvi Lialiatsis, Panos, *Nauplion, Touristic Guide*, Athens, 1972, p. 53.

xxvii Phillips, Walter Alison, *The War of Greek Independence, 1821–1833*, London, 1897, p. 369.

xxviii Serb Newspaper *Intervju*. Interview with Milorad Pavić, 13 December 1991, p. 8.

xxix Russian newspaper, *Nezavisimaya Gazeta*, Oleg Rumyantsev, 29 April 1993, p. 5.

ROMANIA

i Xenopol, A. D., *Histoire des Roumains*, Paris, 1896, vol. 1, p. 130.

ii Florescu, Radu R., and McNally, Raymond T., *Dracula: Prince of Many Faces*, Boston, 1989, p. 197.

iii Ibid., p. 198.

iv Wilkinson, William, *An Account of the Principalities of Wallachia and Moldavia with various political observations relating to them*, London, 1820, p. 71.

v Deletant, Dennis, *Ceauşescu and the Securitate: Coercion and Dissent in Romania, 1965–1989*, London, 1995, p. 233.

vi Iorga Nicolae, *History of Romania*, London, 1925, p. 205.

vii Ibid., p. 229.

viii Hitchens, Keith, 'Religion and the Romanian National Consciousness in 18th-century Transylvania', in *Slavonic and East European Review*, April 1979, 57, 2, p. 226.

ix Aubry, Michel, *St Paisius Velichkovky*, Lausanne, 1992, p. 98.

x Featherstone, J. M. E. (tr.), *The Life of Paisij Velyckovs'kyj*, Harvard, 1989, p. 9.

xi Aubry, M., *op.cit.*, p. 111.

xii Ibid., p. 66.

xiii Ibid. p. 94.

xiv Featherstone, J. M. E. (tr.), *op.cit.*, p. 136.

xv Chetverikov, S., *Starets Paisii Velichkovskii*, Massachusetts, 1980, p. 283–322.

xvi Featherstone J. M. E., *op.cit.*, p. 149.

xvii *Independent*, Obituary, December 1998.

RUSSIA

i Tarkovsky, Andrei, *The Diaries: Time Within Time*, Calcutta, 1989, p. 333.

ii Mullet, Margaret, and Kirby, Anthony (eds), *The Theotokos Evergetis and 11th-century Monasticism*, Belfast, 1994, p. 58. Quoted from Muriel Heppell, *The Early History of the Kievan Monastery of Caves*.

iii Maclean, Fitzroy, *Holy Russia*, London, 1978, p. 56.

iv Kampfer, Frank, *The Image of Russian Christianity in the West and the Concept of Holy Russia*, 1992, p. 198. Essay in *The Christianization of Ancient Russia: A millennium 988–1988*, Yves Hamant (ed.).

v Fedotov, G., *The Russian Religious Mind*, New York, 1946, p. 42.

vi Tolstoy, Graf M. B., *The History of the Russian Church*, Moscow, 1896, p. 41.

vii Zernov, Nicolas, *The Russians and their Church*, St Vladimir's Seminary Press, 1978, third edition, p. 10. Quoted from Vladimir Monomakh, 'A Charge to my Children'.

viii Meyendorff, John, *Byzantium and the Rise of Russia*, St Vladimir's Seminary Press, 1989, p. 292, Quoted from letter of Patriarch Cyprian to St Sergius, 3 June 1378.

ix Klyuchevsky, B. O., *Khozyaistvennaya Deyaltelnost Solovetskovo Monastiriya Belomorskom Krai*, 1958, p. 3.

x Tolstoy, Graf M. B., *op.cit.*, p. 414.

xi Bobrick, Benson, *Fearful Majesty*, New York, 1977, p. 187–8. Quoted from a letter to Prince Andrei Kurbsky.

xii Ibid.

xiii Apsler, Alfred, *Ivan the Terrible*, Folkestone, 1971, p. 166.

xiv Tolstoy, Graf M. B., *op.cit.*, p. 415.

xv Ibid. p. 415–6.

xvi Ibid.

xvii Graham, Stephen, *With the Russian Pilgrims to Jerusalem*, London, 1916, p. 61.

xviii Hosking, Geoffrey, *Russia: People and Empire 1552–1917*, London, 1997, p. 244.

xix Danchenko, Vladimir Nemirovich, *Solovki*, St Petersburg, 1905, p. 18.

xx Dostoyevsky, Fyodor, *The Brothers Karamazov*, Vintage, 1992, p. 256–257.

xxi Appeal of the Solovetski Startsi, given to Tsar Aleksei Mikhailovich in the city of Moscow, 1657 (Lenin Library, Moscow).

xxii Solzhenitsyn, Alexander, *Gulag Archipelago*, Harvill, 1985, p. 186.

xxiii Likhachev, Dmitri, *Vospominaniya*, Moscow, 1995, p. 198.

xxiv Zernov, *op.cit.*, p. 60.

xxv Moynahan, Brian, *Rasputin: The Saint Who Sinned*, London, 1998, p. 74.

xxvi Steinberg, Mark D. and Khrustalev, Vladimir M., *The Fall of the Romanovs*, Yale, 1995, p. 58.

xxvii King, Greg, *The Last Empress: the Life and Times of Alexandra Feodorovna, Tsarina of Russia*, New York, 1994, p. 95. Quoted from Alexander Mossolov, *At the Court of the Last Tsar*, 1935, p. 10–11.

xxviii Steinberg, M. D., and Khrustalev, V. M., *op.cit.* Quoted from the diary of Archpriest Afanasy Beliaev, dean of the Fyodorovsky cathedral, Tsarskoe Selo, 2–31 March 1917.

xxix *Russky Poryadok*, I, 1998.

xxx *Moskovsky Komsomolets* 14 July 1998.

xxxi I Corinthians, 3:18.

xxxii Ibid., 4:10.

xxxiii Thompson, Ewa M., *Understanding Russia: The Holy Fool in Russian Culture*, Lanham, 1987, p. 197.

xxxiv Milner-Gulland, *The Russians*, Oxford, 1997, p. 177 Quoted from Giles Fletcher.

xxxv Hosking, G., *op.cit.*, p. 241.

xxxvi Bolshakoff, Sergius, *Russian Mystics*, London, 1977, p. 181.

xxxvii Dostoyevsky, F., *op.cit.*, p. 297–308.

xxxviii Chetverikov, Father Sergius, *Elder Ambrose of Optina*, St Tikhon's Press, 1997, p. 141.

xxxix Zernov, Nicholas, *Three Russian Prophets*, London, 1944, p. 106.

    xl Wilson, A. N. *Tolstoy*, London, 1988, p. 292.

   xli Rasputin, Maria, *My Father*, London, 1934, p. 46.

  xlii Ibid., p. 47.

 xliii Ibid.

 xliv Ibid,. p. 157.

  xlv Ibid., p. 134.

 xlvi Ibid., p. 61.

xlvii Ibid., p. 100.

xlviii *Verkhoturskaya Starina*, 1998, issue 8–9, p. 7.

 xlix Moynahan, B., *op.cit.*, p. 183. Quoted from *St Petersburg Gazette*, 13 October 1917.

   l Thubron, Colin, *Journey into Cyprus*, Penguin, 1975, p. 217.

CYPRUS

   i Alastos, Doros, *Cyprus Guerrilla: Grivas, Makarios and the British*, London, 1960, p. 6.

  ii Courcas, N. and Riley-Smith, J. (eds), *Cyprus and the Crusades*, 1995, p. 78.

 iii Mayes, Stanley, *Cyprus and Makarios*, London, 1960, p. 33 Quoted from *Observer*, 17 October 1954.

 iv Mayes, Stanley, *Makarios: A Biography*, London, 1981, p. 88.

  v Le Geyt, P. S., *Makarios in Exile*, Nicosia, 1961, p. 102.

 vi Vanezis, P. N., *Makarios: Life and Leadership*, London, 1979, p. 120.

 vii Faulds, Andrew M. P. (ed.), *Excerpta Cypria for Today: A Source book on the Cyprus Problem*, Nicosia-Istanbul, 1988, p. 62.

viii Mayes, S., *op.cit.*, p. 238.

 ix Smith, Helena, 1997 newspaper interview with Giorgios Hadji-costas, head of the Motorcyclists' Association. The Archbishop personally telephoned the association to offer £10,000.

  x *Cyprus Mail*, 17 August 1996.

 xi Hackett J., *A History of the Orthodox Church of Cyprus*, Oxford, 1901, p. 336.

 xii Ibid., p. 153.

xiii Thubron, Colin, *Journey into Cyprus*, London, 1975, p. 123.

xiv Grishin, Alexander, *A Pilgrim's Account of Cyprus: Bars'kyj's*

Travels in Cyprus, Greece and Cyprus Research Centre, New York, 1996, p. 30.

xv Grishin, *op.cit.*, p. 76.

xvi Thubron, *op.cit.*, p. 116.

xvii Grishin *op.cit.*, p. 84.

xviii Ibid., p. 86.

xix Ibid., p. 89.

xx Thubron, *op.cit.*, p. 122.

xxi Defence and Foreign Affairs Department of the Turkish Republic of Northern Cyprus, *The Cultural Heritage of Northern Cyprus: Its Protection and Preservation*, Nicosia, 1996, p. 8.

xxii Letter 4 July 1999, from Bishop Artemije at Gračanica to H. E. Sergio De Mello UNMIK, Pristina, and General M. Jackson, KFOR HQ, Pristina.

ISTANBUL

i Goodwin, Jason *Lords of the Horizons: A History of the Ottoman Empire*, London, 1999, p. 9.

ii Oman C. W. C., *The Story of the Nations: the Byzantine Empire*, London, 1892 p. 109.

iii Dalrymple, William, *From the Holy Mountain*, London, 1997 p. 32.

iv Henry, Patrick, 'Schism looms with Byzantine Church', *Moscow Times*, 27 February 1996.

v Runciman, Steven, *The Great Church in Captivity*, Cambridge, 1968, p. 3.

vi Huntington, Samuel P., *The Clash of Civilisations and the Remaking of the World Order*, 1996, p. 321.

BIBLIOGRAPHY

GENERAL

Applebaum, Anne, *Between East and West*, London, Macmillan, 1994

Beeson, Trevor, *Discretion and Valour: Religious Conditions in Russia and Eastern Europe*, London, Fontana, 1974

Bideleux, Robert and Jeffries, Ian, *A History of Eastern Europe: Crisis and Change*, London, Routledge, 1998

Davies, Norman, *Europe: A History*, Oxford, OUP, 1996

Dimitrova, Ekaterina, *The Gospels of Tsar Ivan Alexander*, London, British Library, 1994

Fletcher, Richard, *The Conversion of Europe: from paganism to Christianity 371–1386 AD*, London, HarperCollins, 1997

Forbes, Nevill and Toynbee, Arnold J, *The Balkans: A History of Bulgaria, Serbia, Greece, Romania, Turkey*, Oxford, Clarendon Press, 1915

France, Peter, *Hermits: The Insights of Solitude*, London, Pimlico, 1996

Fortescue, Adrian, *The Orthodox Eastern Church*, London, Catholic Truth Society, 1911

French, R. M., *The Eastern Orthodox Church*, London, Hutchinson's University Library, 1951

Hobsbawm, E. J., *Nations and Nationalism since 1780*, Cambridge, CUP, 1990

Huntington, Samuel P., *The Clash of Civilisations and the Remaking of World Order*, New York, Simon and Schuster, 1996

Jelavich, Barbara, *History of the Balkans: Eighteenth and Nineteenth Centuries*, Cambridge, CUP, 1983

Kaplan, Robert D., *Balkan Ghosts*, New York, St Martin's Press, 1993

438

Knowles, David, *Christian Monasticism*, London, Weidenfeld & Nicolson, 1969

Lawrence, Sir John, *The Hammer and the Cross*, London, Ariel Books, 1986

Lendvai, Paul, *Eagles in Cobwebs: Nationalism and Communism in the Balkans*, London, Macdonald, 1970

Levi, Peter, *The Frontiers of Paradise: A Study of Monks and Monasteries*, London, Collins Harvill, 1987

Lossky, Vladimir, *The Mystical Theology of the Eastern Church*, London, James Clarke and Co., 1957

Mantzarides, Georgios I., *Time and Man*, South Canaan, Penn., St Tikhon's Seminary Press, 1996

Nafpaktos, Bishop Hierotheos of, *Orthodox Psychotherapy*, Levadia, Birth of the Theotokos Monastery, 1994

Olivier, Clement, *Conversations with the Ecumenical Patriarch Bartholomew I*, New York, St Vladimir's Seminary Press, 1997

Poulton, Hugh, *The Balkans: Minorities and States in Conflict*, London, Minority Rights Publications, 1991

Schmemann, Alexander, *The Historical Road of Eastern Orthodoxy*, London, Harvill Press, 1963

Sherrard, Philip, *The Greek East and Latin West: A Study in the Christian Tradition*, Limni, Evia, Denise Harvey, 1959

Stanley, Arthur Penrhyn, *Lectures on the History of the Eastern Church*, London, John Murray, 1883

Ware, Timothy, *The Orthodox Church* (new edition), London, Penguin, 1997

Zernov, Nicolas, *Eastern Christendom: A Study of the Origin and Development of Eastern Orthodox Christianity*, London, Weidenfeld & Nicolson, 1963

Byzantium

Alexander, Paul J., *Religion and Political History and Thought in the Byzantine Empire*, London, Variorum, 1978

Beaton, Roderick and Rouèche, Charlotte (eds.), *The Making of Byzantine History*, Aldershot, Variorum 1993

Billings, Malcolm, *The Cross and the Crescent*, London, BBC Publications, 1987

Boojamra, John Lawrence, *Church Reform in the Late Byzantine Empire,* Thessaloniki, Patriarchikon Hidryma Paterikon Meleton, 1982

Botsis, Peter A., 'What is Orthodoxy?', Athens

Byron, Robert, *The Byzantine Achievement,* London, G. Routledge & Sons, 1929

Curzon, Robert, *Visits to Monasteries in the Levant,* London, Arthur Barker, 1955

Dalrymple, William, *From the Holy Mountain,* London, HarperCollins, 1998

Davis, R. H. C., *A History of Medieval Europe: from Constantine to St Louis,* London, Longmans, 1957

Economides, Irene, *The Two Faces of Greece: A Civilisation of 7,000 years,* Athens, 1990

Freely, John, *Istanbul: The Imperial City,* London, Penguin, 1996

Gibbon, Edward, *The Decline and Fall of the Roman Empire* Vol. 6, London, J. M. Dent & Sons Ltd., 1910

Golitzyn, Hieromonk Alexander, *The Living Witness of the Holy Mountain: Contemporary Voices from Mount Athos,* South Canaan, Penn., St Tikhon's Seminary Press, 1996

Goodwin, Jason, *Lords of the Horizons: A History of the Ottoman Empire,* London, Vintage, 1999

Hackel, Sergei (ed.), *The Byzantine Saint: University of Birmingham 1981, 14th Spring Symposium of Byzantine Studies,* Oxford Fellowship of St Alban and St Sergius, 1981

Herrin, Judith, *The Formation of Christendom,* Oxford, Basil Blackwell, 1987

Hussey, J. M., *The Orthodox Church in the Byzantine Empire,* Oxford, OUP, 1986

Iorga, Nicolae, *Byzance après le Byzance,* Bucharest, Institut Roman de Byzantinologie, 1935

Jones, A. H. M., *Constantine and the Conversion of Europe,* London, Pelican, 1969

Levi, Peter, *The Hill of Kronos,* London, Collins, 1980

Liddell, Robert, *Byzantium and Istanbul,* London, Johnathan Cape, 1956

Mansel, Philip, *Constantinople: The World's Desire,* London, John Murray, 1995

Mayer, Hans Eberhard, *The Crusades,* Oxford, OUP, 1988

Melville-Jones, J. R. (tr.), *The Siege of Constantinople: Seven Contemporary Accounts,* Amsterdam, Adolf M. Hakkert, 1972

Meyendorff, John, *The Byzantine Legacy in the Orthodox Church,* New York, St Vladimir's Seminary Press, 1982

——*Byzantine Hesychasm: Historical, Theological and Social Problems,* London, 1974

Nicol, Donald M., *The Immortal Emperor: The Life and Legend of Constantine Palaiologus, Last Emperor of the Romans,* Cambridge, CUP, 1969

Norwich, John J., *A History of Byzantium,* 3 Vols, London, Penguin, 1995

Obolensky, Dimitri, *The Byzantine Commonwealth: Eastern Europe 500–1453,* New York, St Vladimir's Press, 1982

——*Byzantium and the Slavs,* New York, St Vladimir's Press, 1994

——*The Byzantine Inheritance of Eastern Europe,* London, Variorum Reprints, 1982

Oecomenos, Lysimaque, *La Vie Religieuse dans L'Empire Byzantine au temps des Comnènes et des Anges,* 1918

Oman, C. W. C., *The Story of the Nations: The Byzantine Empire,* London, T. Fisher Unwin, 1982

Ostrogorsky, George, *History of the Byzantine State,* Oxford, Basil Blackwell, 1968

Phillips, Fr. Andrew, 'Orthodox Christianity and the Old English Church', Greenprint and Design, 1996

Psellus, *Byzantine Rulers,* London, Penguin, 1966

Runciman, Steven, *Byzantine Civilisation,* London, Methuen, 1975

——*The Eastern Schism: A Study of the Papacy and Eastern churches during the 11th and 12th centuries,* Oxford, Clarendon Press, 1955

——*The Fall of Constantinople 1453,* Cambridge, CUP, 1965

——*The Great Church in Captivity,* Cambridge, CUP, 1968

Rycaut, Sir Paul, *The Present State of the Greek and Armenian Churches 1678,* London, 1679

Sherrard, Philip and Editors of Time-Life Books, *Byzantium,* Nederland, Time-Life Books, 1966

Smart, Ninian, *The Phenomenon of Christianity,* London, Collins, 1979

Tachaios, A. E. N. (ed.), *Mount Athos and the European Community,* Thessaloniki, Institute for Balkan Studies, 1993

Talbot-Rice, David, *Art of the Byzantine Era,* London, Thames & Hudson, 1963

Ware, Kallistos, *Act out of Stillness: the Influence of Hesychasm on Byzantine and Slav Civilisation,* Toronto, Hellenic Canadian

Association of Constantinople and Thessalonikean Society of Metro Toronto, 1995

Ware, Timothy, *Eustratios Argenti: A Study of the Greek Church under Turkish Rule*, Oxford, Clarendon Press, 1964

Winkler, Gabriele, *The Jesus Prayer in Eastern Spirituality*, Minneapolis, Light and Life Publishing Company, 1986

SERBS

Alexander, Stella, *Church and State in Yugoslavia since 1945*, Cambridge, CUP, 1979

Anzulović, Branimir, *Heavenly Serbia: From Myth to Genocide*, London, Hurst & Co., 1999

Banac, Ivo, *The National Question in Yugoslavia: Origins, History, Politics*, Ithica, Cornell University Press, 1984

Baynes, Norman H., and Moss, H. St L. B. (eds.), *Byzantium: an Introduction to East Roman Civilization*, Oxford, Clarendon Press, 1948

Bogdanović, D., Djurić, V. J. and Medaković, D., *Hilandar: On the Holy Mountain*, Belgrade, Jugoslavenska Revija, 1978

Durham, Mary Edith, *High Albania*, London, Edward Arnold, 1909

Through the Lands of the Serb, London, Edward Arnold, 1904

French, R. M., *Serbian Church Life*, London, SPCK, 1942

Glenny, Misha, *The Fall of Yugoslavia*, London, Penguin, 1992

Judah, Tim, *The Serbs: History, Myth and the Destruction of Yugoslavia*, New Haven, Yale University Press, 1997

Kindersley, Anne, *The Mountains of Serbia: Travels though Inland Yugoslavia*, London, John Murray, 1977

Malcolm, Noel, *Bosnia: A Short History*, London, Macmillan, 1994

Kosovo: A Short History, London, Macmillan, 1998

Mihaljčić, Rade, *The Battle of Kosovo: In History and Popular Tradition*, Belgrade, Beogradski Izdavačko-Grafički Zavod, 1989

Mileušnić, Slobodan, 'The Monastery of Krka', Belgrade, 1994

Moon, Paul, 'A History of Medieval Serbia', Auckland, 1988

Popović, Archimandrite Justin, *Orthodox Life and Faith in Christ*, Belmont, Mass., Institute for Byzantine and Modern Greek Studies, 1994

Reed, John, *War In Eastern Europe: Travels through the Balkans in 1915*, London, Orion Books, 1994

Samardzić, Radovan (ed.), 'The Serbs in European Civilization', Belgrade, 1993

Sells, Michael A., *The Bridge Betrayed: Religion and Genocide in Bosnia*, Berkeley, University of California Press, 1996

Silber, Laura and Little, Allan, *The Death of Yugoslavia*, London, Penguin, 1995

Soulis, George Christos, *The Serbs and Byzantium during the Reign of Tsar Stephen Dusan 1331–1355 and his Successors*, Washington DC, Dumbarton Oaks Library and Collection, 1984

Sudetic, Chuck, *Blood and Vengeance: One Family's Story of the War in Bosnia*, New York, W. W. Norton & Co. Inc., 1998

Todorovich, Slavko, *The Hilandarians*, New York, Columbia University Press, 1989

Tsernianski, Miloš, *Migrations*, London, Collins Harvill, 1994

Velimirovich, Bishop Nikolai and Popovic, Archimandrite Justin, *The Mystery and Meaning of Kosovo*, Illinois, The Free Serbian Orthodox Diocese of America and Canada, 1989

West, Rebecca, *Black Lamb and Grey Falcon*, London, Penguin, 1968

MACEDONIA

Abbott, G. F. (ed.), *Greece in Evolution*, London, Fisher Unwin, 1909

Balabanov, Kosta, *Ohrid: Cultural, historical and natural region in the catalogue of World Heritage*, Skopje, Skopje Misla, 1987

Brewster, Ralph H., *The 6000 Beards of Athos*, London, L. & V. Woolf, 1935

Browne, Dr Edward, *Dr Browne's Travels through Hungary, Thessaly, Macedonia etc*, London, 1673

Brailsford, H. N., *Macedonia: its Races and their Future*, London, Methuen & Co., 1906

Bulgarian Academy of Sciences, *Macedonia: Documents and Material*, Sofia, 1979

Byron, Robert, *The Station, Athos: Treasures and Men*, London, Duckworth, 1933

Carnegie Endowment for International Peace, *The Other Balkan Wars*, 1913

Choukas, Michael, *Black Angels of Athos*, London, Constable & Co., 1935

Constantinople Patriarchate (ed.), *Official documents Concerning the Deplorable Condition of Affairs in Macedonia*, Constantinople, 1906

Crampton, R. J., *A Short History of Bulgaria*, Cambridge, CUP, 1987

Danforth, Loring M., *The Macedonian Conflict*, Princeton, Princeton University Press, 1995

Dawkins, R. M., *The Monks of Athos*, London, George Allen & Unwin, 1936

Hasluck, F. W., *Athos and its Monasteries*, London, Keegan Paul & Co., 1924

Ilievski, Done, *The Macedonian Orthodox Church*, Skopje, Macedonian Review Editions, 1973

Institute for Balkan Studies, *Macedonia Past and Present*, Thessaloniki, 1992

Karakasidou, Anastasia N., *Fields of Wheat, Hills of Blood: Passages to Nationhood in Greek Macedonia 1870–1990*, Chicago, University of Chicago Press, 1997

Levecque, J., *Coutumes Chretiennes de Macedoine*, Salonica, Methuen & Co., 1918

Loch, Sydney, *Athos: The Holy Mountain*, London, Lutterworth Press, 1957

Mackridge, Peter and Yannakakis, Eleni (eds.), *Ourselves and Others: The Development of a Greek Macedonian Cultural Identity since 1912*, Oxford, Berg, 1997

Macdermott, Mercia, *Freedom or Death*, London, Journeyman Press, 1978

Poulton, Hugh, *Who are the Macedonians?*, London, Hurst & Co., 1995

Shea, John, *Macedonia and Greece: The Struggle to Define the New Balkan Nation*, Jefferson, NC, McFarland, 1997

GREECE

Benjamin, S. G. W., *The Turk and the Greek*, New York, Hurd & Houghton, 1867

Clogg, Richard, *A Concise History of Greece*, Cambridge, CUP, 1992

——(ed.) *The Struggle for Greek Independence*, London, Macmillan, 1973

——*The Movement for Greek Independence 1770–1821*, London, Macmillan, 1976

——*Greece in the 1980s*, London, Macmillan and University of London, 1983

——*Balkan Society in the Age of Greek Independence*, London, Macmillan and University of London, 1981

Durrell, Lawrence, *The Greek Islands*, London, Faber & Faber, 1978

Fleming, D. C., *John Capodistrias and the Conference of London 1828–1831*, Thessaloniki, Institute for Balkan Studies, 1970

Frazee, Charles A., *The Orthodox Church and Independent Greece*, London, CUP, 1969

Geil, William Edgar, *The Isle that is called Patmos*, Philadelphia, A. J. Rowland, 1896

Hill, Aaron, *A Full and Just Account of the present State of the Ottoman Empire*, London, 1709

Institute of Balkan Studies, *Hellenism and the First Greek War of Liberation 1821–1830*, Thessaloniki, 1976

Kizilos, Katherine, *The Olive Grove: Travels in Greece*, Melbourne, Lonely Planet Publications, 1997

Lear, Edward, *Journals of a Landscape Painter in Greece and Albania*, London, William Kimber, 1851

Leigh Fermor, Patrick, *Roumeli: Travels in Northern Greece*, London, Penguin, 1966

Lialiatsis, Panos, *Nauplion: Touristic Guide*, Athens, 1972

Mazower, Mark, *Inside Hitler's Greece*, New Haven, Yale University Press, 1993

Mustokidis, *Renseignements sur la Grèce et sur l'Administration du Comte Capodistrias*, Paris, 1933

Papadopoulos, S. A., *Monastery of St John the Theologian*, Patmos, 1993

Pettifer, James, *The Greeks*, London, Penguin, 1993

Phillips, Walter Alison, *The War of Greek Independence 1821–1833*, London, Smith, Elder & Co., 1897

Runciman, Steven, *Mistra*, London, Thames & Hudson, 1980

Sherrard, Philip (ed.), *The Pursuit of Greece*, London, John Murray, 1964

Storace, Patricia, *Dinner with Persephone*, London, Granta, 1996

Toynbee, Arnold, *The Greeks and their Heritages*, Oxford, OUP, 1981

Walsh, Robert, *A Residence at Constantinople during a period including the commencement, progress and termination of the Greek and Turkish revolutions*, London, 1836

Woodhouse, C. M., *Modern Greece: A Short History*, London, Faber & Faber, 1968

——*Capodistria: The Founder of Greek Independence*, London, OUP, 1973

445

——*The Greek War Of Independence*, London, Hutchinson's University Library, 1952

Yannaras, Christos, *The Freedom of Morality*, New York, St Vladimir's Seminary Press, 1984

Zakythinos, Dionysios, *The Making of Modern Greece*, Oxford, Blackwell, 1976

ROMANIA

Almond, Mark, *The Rise and Fall of Nicolae and Elena Ceaușescu*, London, Chapmans, 1992

Aubry, Michel, *St Paisius Velichkovsky*, Lausanne, L'Age de l'Homme, 1992

Castellan, Georges, *Histoire de la Roumanie*, Paris, Presses Universitaires de France, 1984

Chetverikov, Sergei, *Starets Paisii Velichkovskii*, Belmont Mass., Harvard, 1980

Deletant, Dennis, *Ceaușescu and the Securitate: Coercion and Dissent in Romania 1965–1989*, London, Hurst & Co., 1995

——*Some Aspects of the Byzantine Tradition in the Romanian Principalities*, Slavonic and East European Review Vol. 59, 1981, 1–14

Diaconescu, Mihai, *Romania: Biserici și Monastiri Ortodoxe*, Bucharest, 1998

Featherstone, J. M. E. (tr.), *The Life of St Paisij Velyckovs'kyj*, Belmont Mass., Harvard, 1989

Florescu, Radu R. and McNally, Raymond T., *Dracula: Prince of Many Faces*, Boston, Little, Brown & Co., 1989

——*The Uniate Church: Catalyst of Romanian National Consciousness*, Slavonic and East European Review Vol. 45, 1967

Hale, Julian, *Ceaușescu's Romania: A Political Documentary*, London, Harrap, 1971

Hitchins, Keith, *Religion and the Romanian National Consciousness in 18th-century Transylvania*, Slavonic and East European Review, Vol. 57, 1979

——*Orthodoxy and Nationality: Andrei Saguna and the Romanians of Transylvania 1846–1873*, Harvard, 1977

——*The Romanians: 1774–1866*, Oxford, Clarendon Press, 1996

Ioanid, Radu, *The Sword of the Archangel: Fascist Ideology in Romania,* New York, Columbia, 1990

Iorga, Nicolae, *History of Roumania,* London, T. Fisher Unwin, 1925

Kligman, Gail, *The Wedding of the Dead: Ritual, Poetics and Popular Culture in Transylvania,* Berkeley, University of California Press, 1988

Loughborough, Margaret R., *Romanian Pilgrimage,* London, SPCK, 1939

Lupaş, Ioan, *Istoria Bisericeasca a Romanilor Ardeleni,* Cluj-Napoca, Editura Dacia, 1995

Pakula, Hannah, *Queen of Roumania: The Life of Princess Marie, granddaughter of Queen Victoria,* London, Eland, 1989

Plamadeala, Dr Antonie, *Romanian Orthodox Church,* Bucharest, The Bible and Orthodox Mission Publishing House, 1987

Seton-Watson, R. W., *A History of the Roumanians,* Cambridge, CUP, 1934

Staniloae, Dumitru, *Uniatismul din Transilvania: Incercare de desmembrare a Poporului Roman,* Bucharest, 1973

Wilkinson, William, *An Account of the Principalities of Wallachia and Moldavia with various political observations relating to them,* London, 1820

Xenopol, A. D., *Histoire des Roumains,* Paris, 1896

RUSSIA

Albarigo, Giuseppe and Beozzo, Oscar, *The Holy Russian Church and Western Christianity,* London, SCM Press, 1996

Anisimov, Evgenii, *The Reforms of Peter the Great: Progress through Coercion in Russia,* New York, M. E. Sharpe, 1993

Apsler, Alfred, *Ivan the Terrible,* Folkestone, Bailey Bros. & Swinfen, 1971

Berdyaev, Nicholas, *The Russian Revolution,* London, Sheed & Ward, 1931

Berlin, Isaiah, *Russian Thinkers,* London, Penguin, 1978

Bobrick, Benson, *East of the Sun: The Conquest and Settlement of Siberia,* London, Heinemann, 1992

——*A Fearful Majesty: The Life and Reign of Ivan the Terrible,* New York, Putnam, 1987

Boddy, Aleksandr A., *With Russian Pilgrims*, London, Wells Gardner & Co., 1893

Bolshakoff, Sergius, *Russian Mystics*, London, Kalamazoo Cistercian Publications, 1977

Bruce, Lincoln W., *The Conquest of a Continent: Siberia and the Russians*, New York, 1994

——*The Romanovs: Autocrats of all the Russias*, New York, Doubleday, 1986

Bushkovich, Paul, *Religion and Society in Russia: the 16th and 17th centuries*, Oxford, OUP, 1992

Carrère d'Encausse, Hélène, *The Russian Syndrome: One Thousand Years of Political Murder*, New York, Holmes & Meier, 1992

Chetverikov, Fr. Sergius, *Elder Ambrose of Optina Pustyn*, Platina, Calif., Herman of Alaska Brotherhood, 1997

Clark, Bruce, *An Empire's New Clothes*, London, Vintage, 1995

Crummey, Robert, *The Formation of Muscovy 1304–1613*, London, Longman, 1987

Custine, Marquis de, *Letters from Russia*, London, Penguin, 1991

Davchenko, Vladimir Nemirovich, *Solovki*, St Petersburg, 1905

Davis, Nathaniel, *A Long Walk to Church: A Contemporary History of Russian Orthodoxy*, Boulder Col., Westview Press, 1995

Dostoyevsky, Fyodor *The Brothers Karamazov* London, Vintage, 1990 *The House of the Dead*, London, Penguin, 1985

Ellis, Jane, *The Russian Orthodox Church: Triumphalism and Defensiveness*, London, Macmillan with St Antony's College Oxford, 1996

——*The Russian Orthodox Church: A Contemporary History*, London, Croom Helm, 1986

Fedotov, G. P., *The Russian Religious Mind*, New York, Harper & Row, 1946

——*A Treasury of Russian Spirituality*, London, Sheed & Ward, 1950

Figes, Orlando, *A People's Tragedy*, London, Pimlico, 1996

French, R. M., *The Way of a Pilgrim*, London, SPCK, 1965

Graham, Stephen, *With the Russian Pilgrims to Jerusalem*, London, Macmillan, 1916

Hamel, J. von, *England and Russia*, London, 1854

Hosking, Geoffrey, *Russia: People and Empire 1552–1917*, London, HarperCollins, 1997

Howe, Sonia, *A Thousand Years of Russian History*, London, Williams & Morgate, 1915

Iswolsky, Helene, *Christ in Russia: The History, Tradition and Life of the Russian Church,* London, The Bruce Publishing Company, 1960

Johnston Pouncy, Carolyn, *The Domostroi: Rules for Russian Households in the time of Ivan the Terrible,* Ithica, Cornell University Press, 1994

King, Greg, *The Last Empress: the Life and Times of Alexandra Feodorovna, Tsarina of Russia,* London, Aurum Press, 1995

Klyuchevsky, B. O., *Khozyaistvennaya Deyatelnost Solovetskovo Monastiriya Belomorskom krai,* 1958

Lieven, Dominic, *Nicholas II: Emperor of all the Russias,* London, Pimlico, 1993

Likhachev, Dmitri, *Vospominaniya,* Moscow, 1995

Maclean, Fitzroy, *Holy Russia,* London, Weidenfeld & Nicolson, 1978

Massie, Robert K., *Nicholas and Alexandra,* London, Victor Gollancz, 1967

Meyendorff, John, *Byzantium and the Rise of Russia,* Crestwood, NY, St Vladimir's Seminary Press, 1989

Milner-Gulland, Robin, *The Russians,* Oxford, Blackwell, 1997

Moynahan, Brian, *Rasputin: The Saint who Sinned,* London, Aurum Press, 1998

Mullet, Margaret and Kirby, Anthony, *The Theotokos Evergetis and 11th-century Monasticism,* Belfast, Queen's University Press, 1994

Peskov, Vasily, *Lost in the Taiga: One Russian Family's Fifty-year Struggle for Survival and Religious Freedom in the Siberian Wilderness,* New York, Doubleday, 1994

Pipes, Richard, *Russia under the Old Regime,* London, Penguin, 1974

Radzinsky, Edvard, *The Last Tsar,* London, Doubleday, 1992

Rasputin, Maria, *My Father,* London, Cassell & Co., 1934

Remnick, David, *Lenin's Tomb,* London, Penguin, 1993

Solzhenitsyn, Alexander, *Gulag Archipelago* (Abridged), London, Collins Harvill, 1986

Steinberg, Mark D. and Khrustalev, Vladimir M., *The Fall of the Romanovs,* Yale, 1995

Tarkovsky, Andrei, *Tarkovsky: The Diaries 1970–1986,* Calcutta, Seagull Books Private Ltd., 1991

Thompson, Ewa, *Understanding Russia: The Holy Fool in Russian Culture,* Lanham, MD, University Press of America, 1987

Tolstoy, Leo, *A Confession and Other Writings,* London, Penguin, 1987

Tolstoy, Graf M. B., *The History of the Russian Church,* Moscow, 1896

Wilson, Francesca, *Muscovy: Russia through Foreign Eyes 1553–1900*, London, Allen & Unwin, 1970

Wilson, A. N., *Tolstoy*, London, Hamish Hamilton, 1988

Yeltsin, Boris, *Against the Grain*, London, Jonathan Cape, 1990

Zernov, Nicolas, *The Russians and their Church*, Crestwood, NY, St Vladimir's Seminary Press, 1994

CYPRUS

Alastos, Doros, *Cyprus Guerilla: Grivas, Makarios and the British*, London, Heinemann, 1960

Courcas, N. and Riley-Smith J. (eds.), *Cyprus and the Crusades*, 1995

Faulds, Andrew, (ed.), *Excerpta Cypria for Today: A Source book on the Cyprus Problem*, Nicosia-Istanbul, 1988

Foley, Charles, *Island in Revolt*, London, Longmans, 1962

Grishin, Alexander, *A Pilgrim's Account of Cyprus: Bars'kyj's Travels in Cyprus*, New York, Greece and Cyprus Research Centre, 1996

Hackett, J., *A History of the Orthodox Church of Cyprus*, London, Methuen & Co., 1901

Hill, Sir George, *A History of Cyprus*, 4 Vols, Cambridge, CUP, 1940

Hitchens, Christopher, *Hostage to History: Cyprus from the Ottomans to Kissinger*, London, Verso, 1997

Le Geyt, P. S., *Makarios in Exile*, Nicosia, Anagennisis Press, 1961

Mayes, Stanley, *Cyprus and Makarios*, London, Putnam, 1960

——*Makarios: A Biography*, London, Macmillan, 1981

Thubron, Colin, *Journey into Cyprus*, London, Penguin, 1975

Vanezis, Dr P. N., *Makarios: Life and Leadership*, London, Abelard Schuman, 1979

——*Makarios: Pragmatism and Idealism*, London, Abelard Schuman, 1974

INDEX

Adam of Usk, 32
Afanasy Beliaev, Archpriest, 291
Afxentiou, Grigory, 377
Aghia Lavra monastery, 180–82
Agnes, Sister, 191–2, 193, 300–301
Alba Iulia, 218, 219, 222
Albania, border, 128–9
Albanian Muslims, 77–9, 87, 109, 349,
    404–5
Alexander I, Tsar of Russia, 176, 177–8
Alexander III, Tsar of Russia, 289
Alexander Svirsky, Saint, 264, 288
Alexander the Great, 108–9, 118, 136,
    146, 309
Alexandra, Tsarina, 93, 289, 313, 335–7,
    341
Alexei, Tsarevich, 334–5, 341
Alexius, Emperor, 24–5
Alexy II, Patriarch: authority, 271, 343n,
    395, 406; Chrysanthos enquiry, 382;
    KGB informer, 305; relationship with
    Constantinople, 406; relationship
    with mayor, 295; Romanov funeral,
    301, 305, 306, 342; Trinity Sergeyev
    monastery, 306, 314, 342; visits to
    Solovetsky, 283
Ambrose (starets), 315–16
America, see United States
Amfilohije, Archbishop, 95–101, 133
Andrew, Saint, 313
Andronicus II, Emperor, 29, 291
Ann, Saint, 236–7
Antioch, 17
Antonij (monk), 259
Antony IV, Patriarch, 30
Apostolos Andhreas monastery, 396

Ariko (mukhtaris of Kambos), 364–70
Aristotle, 18, 33
Arkan (Željko Ražnatović), 55–7, 96
Arsenije III, Patriarch of Serbia, 73
Artemije, Bishop, 92n, 133
Atatürk, Kemal, 187
Atenogoras, Patriarch of Constantinople,
    133
Athanasios, Bishop of Limassol, 375
Athanasius, Patriarch, 29
Athanasius, Saint, 11
Athens, 191–9
Athos, Mount: ban on women, 3–6, 375;
    Cypriot monks, 343; Emperor's crack
    down, 31; first monastery, 12; Greek
    war of independence, 182;
    Hesychasm, 29, 284; influence, 375;
    Latin sack of, 28; modernity, 140–42,
    191; mystic tradition 35–9;
    nationality of monks, 42–3, 141–4;
    Ottoman rule, 22; Paissy's stay,
    239–40; pilgrims, 360; relics, 70;
    Russian presence, 143–4, 259; Sava's
    journey, 111; Schengen debate,
    144–5, 191; Serbian monastery, 42,
    51, 60, 86, 239–40; sexuality, 140;
    Treasures Exhibition, 39, 139, 145
Augustine of Hippo, Saint, 21
Austria, 216–17
Ayia Moni monastery, 372–3, 383
Avraam, Abbot, 329–32, 339, 343n

Balkan War, First (1912), 130, 146, 313
Balkan War, Second (1912–13), 122, 130,
    146
Ball, George, 353

Barlaam, 38

Bartholomaios, Ecumenical Partriarch of
    Constantinople: authority, 405–6;
    Heybeliada visits, 408–10; interview
    with, 407–8; Macedonian policy,
    118; relationship with Russia, 406;
    replies to questions, 407–8, 411–12;
    Romanian concerns, 216; view of
    Phyletism, 405, 411

Bartolomeo, Bishop of Cluj, 248

Basil, Grand Prince of Moscow, 30

Basil the Bulgar-Slayer, Emperor, 108

Basil the Wolf, Prince of Moldavia, 213

Becket, Thomas, 232, 270

Bedreddin, 402

Belarus, 7, 12

Belomorsk, White Sea, 287–8

Benedict, Archimandrite, 54–5, 56–9, 64

Berengaria, Queen of England, 347

Bijeljina, Bosnian Serb Republic, 55–66,
    381

Bistriţa monastery, Moldavia, 233–8,
    244–50, 313

Blair, Tony, 100

Blaj, Romania, 222–3, 227–8; Archbishop
    of, 227–8

Bogdan (Serb journalist): candle for, 356;
    encounter with Bishop Vasilije, 65;
    in Café Byzantium, 59, 61; in Greece,
    139; in Kosovo, 69, 79, 81–2, 91–2;
    in Macedonia (FYROM), 110, 112,
    118–19, 125, 128; in Montenegro,
    94, 98–9; in Serbia, 70, 76–7; in
    Thessaloniki, 139; return to Belgrade,
    66; spiritual father, 322

Boris, Saint, 259

Bosnian Muslims, 404

Bosphorus, 10, 22, 401

Brailsford, H.N., 130–31, 135–6

Brewster, Ralph, 140

Brezhnev, Leonid, 298

Bucharest, 221, 228–9, 373

Bukow, General, 216, 226

Bulgaria: anti-Islamic feeling, 8; EU
    relations, 7; Exarchate Church, 121,
    135, 146; Hesychasm, 263; monks, 12

Bulgars, 111, 122

Byron, George Gordon, Lord, 159, 181

Byron, Robert, 144

Byzantine Church: beliefs, 18–19;

influence, 29–30; Ottoman rule, 120;
    Schism (1054), 7, 17, 20–21; see also
    Schism; Russia, 259–61; Serbian
    independence, 52

Byzantium, 8–9, 10; see also
    Constantinople

Café Byzantium, 59–61, 381

Capodistrias, Count Ioannis, 178–9,
    184–90, 197

Carmen (in Romania), 221–2, 243

Catherine the Great, Empress of Russia,
    175, 257, 260

Ceauşescu, Nicolae, 203–4, 210, 220–21,
    232

Ceauşescu, Nicu, 232

Çem (in Istanbul), 401–2

Cenobitic Rule, 140, 158, 170, 240

Charlemagne, Emperor, 19, 195

Chechnya, war, 327, 404

Choniates, Nicetas, 26

Christodoulos, Archbishop, 199, 349

Christodoulos, Saint: life, 154–6, 241;
    Patmos monastery, 155–6, 158, 161,
    167–8, 173–4

Chrysanthos, Bishop of Limassol, 375, 382

Chrysorrhoyiatissa monastery, 371–2

Chrysostomos, Archbishop of Cyprus:
    appearance, 356; interview with, 383,
    391–3; political stance, 355, 359;
    status, 392, 395; successor, 375; view
    of miraculous icon, 361, 370

Chud, battle of Lake (1242), 262

Churchill, Winston, 192

Ciachir, Dan, 229–36, 243

Clement, Saint, 259

Cleopa, Archimandrite, 237, 238–43, 259,
    270, 359

Clinton, Bill, 98, 100, 379, 391

Cluj, Romania, 221–2

Communism: appeal, 90, 186; collapse,
    141–2, 271, 292, 404; in Greece,
    186–7; in Romania, 206, 235; in
    Russia, 197, 289–90, 291–2, 297; in
    Yugoslavia, 90

Constantin Brancoveanu, Prince of
    Wallachia, 214–15

Constantine I, Emperor, 9–13, 127, 164,
    213, 234

Constantine XI, Emperor, 39

Constantine II, King of Greece, 166
Constantinople: Byzantine recapture
    (1261), 28; churches, 16; decline,
    29–30; Ecumenical Patriarchate, 13,
    22, 110, 403–4, 405–7; English
    settlers, 17; fall (1453), 39–41, 156,
    267; foundation, 10; Haghia Sophia,
    16, 20, 26, 29, 39–40, 258, 402–3;
    Hippodrome, 14–15, 16, 27, 403;
    Latin rule, 28; monasteries, 10–11;
    Orthodox Christendom, 7; religion,
    14–15; Russian ambassadors, 16–17,
    258; sack (1204), 17, 23, 25–7, 101,
    205, 209, 262, 306, 348; wealth, 10;
    see also Istanbul
Cornea, Doina, 220, 221
Creed, 19, 30, 216, 223
Croatia: independence, 101; Krka
    monastery, 47–55
Crusade, First, 17
Crusade, Fourth, 23–7; collapse of
    Byzantine Empire, 52; effects, 27,
    205–6, 217, 262, 348–9, 413; name
    of Byzantium, 172–3, 195; Patmos,
    156; sack of Constantinople, 17, 23,
    25–7, 101, 205, 209, 262, 306, 348
Crusade, Third, 347
Curzon, Robert, 38
Cyprian, Patriarch, 263
Cyprus: British control, 342–3, 351–2,
    413; history, 347–55; Kykko
    monastery, 359–70, 371, 381, 383–7;
    Limassol, 378–83; monks, 12, 343;
    Nicosia, 347–59; northern, 123, 187;
    Orthodox Church, 349, 381–2, 395;
    partition, 8, 354–5; Russian presence,
    379–83; Troodos montains, 371–8;
    Turkish Republic of Northern
    Cyprus, 393–7
Cyril, Saint, 113–14, 121, 124, 212, 258
Cyrillic script, 113

Damaskinos, Archbishop, 192
Damaskinos, Father, 229–31, 233
Daniel, Metropolitan of Moldavia,
    247–50, 351
Danilo III, Patriarch of Serbia, 72
Danilovsky monastery, 304–6
Dečani monastery, 86–92, 111, 169, 234;
    refugees, 397

de Geyt, Captain, 352
Demetrius, Saint, 138
Diana, Princess, 83
Dimitri, Saint, 138
Dimos (in Nicosia), 357–9
Dionysius of Xanthe, Saint, 123
Dmitri Dudko, Father, 301–3, 305
Dorotheos, Father, 409–10, 413
Dositej, Archbishop of Ohrid and
    Macedonia, 125
Dostoyevsky, Fyodor, 275, 298, 315, 316
Dracula, 213
Dragomirna monastery, 240–41
Dumitru, Father, 372–3, 383
Durham, Edith, 80, 89, 92
Dušan, Tsar of Serbia: coronation, 127;
    death, 52; empire, 50–54, 69, 70, 76,
    146; excommunication, 50; family,
    51, 72, 87, 91

Eagleburger, Lawrence, 68
Elisabeth (on Patmos), 166, 171–2
Elizabeth I, Queen of England, 267
Emilian Poenaru, Father, 229–33
emperors, Byzantine, 13–14
EOKA, 350–52, 359–60, 362–3, 372, 377
Estonian Orthodox Churches, 406
European Union (EU): Greek
    membership, 4, 6, 122–3, 249;
    membership, 7, 249; Mount Athos,
    4n, 6, 141; Schengen Agreement,
    144–5, 168, 191, 193; Turkish
    membership, 405n

Fabri, Felix, 366
Famagusta, Cyprus, 394
Feri (in Romania), 209
Fermor, Patrick Leigh, 174–5
Ferrara, papal palace, 32
Finland, Orthodox Church, 407
First World War, 101
Florence, Council of (1438), 32–4, 196,
    217, 267
fools, holy, 311–13, 376
Former Yugoslav Republic of Macedonia
    (FYROM): border, 109n, 134–5;
    capital, 105; churches, 327–8;
    creation, 106–7; EU relations, 7;
    history, 105–9; monks, 12; Orthodox

Church, 109–11, 116, 125, 308, 405; Veljuša monastery, 129–34
Franz Ferdinand, Archduke, 67
Fyodor, Tsar of Russia, 324

Gavriil, Father, 386, 388
Gavriil, Patriarch, 61
Gennadius, Patriarch, 34–5, 40, 42, 120
Genscher, Hans Dietrich, 101
George Palamas, 51
Georgia, former Soviet Republic, 384–5
Georgy Mikhailovich, 341–2
Germanos, Bishop of Kastoria, 135–7
Germanos, Archbishop of Patras, 177, 180–81, 350
Gibbon, Edward, 26
Giorgios Metallinos, Father, 195–7, 199, 286–7
Gleb, Saint, 259
Gligorov, Kiro, 111
Goran (Serb journalist): encounter with Bishop Vasilije, 65; in Café Byzantium, 59–62, 381; in Kosovo, 69, 82, 91–3; in Montenegro, 97–8; in Serbia, 70, 77, 190; on Mount Athos, 191; return to Belgrade, 66
Gorbachev, Mikhail, 292, 331
Gračanica: church, 78, 84–6, 92n, 234, 327, 360, 413; Prince Lazar, 78–9; refugees, 397
Greece: border, 134–5; Church, 116, 147–8, 175, 182, 189–90, 193, 297, 394; citizenship, 42; civil war (1945–9), 146; Cyprus, 350–55, 404; earthquakes, 405n; EU membership, 4, 6, 8, 123, 144–5; flag, 137, 391; independence, 159, 180; Katastroph, 187, 404; Macedonia policy, 108–9, 118–19, 147–8; monks, 12; nationalism, 33, 54, 121–3, 193–4; Peloponnese, 180–90; terrorist manifesto, 193–4; War of Independence, 180–84, 215, 405
Greek language, 12, 121–2
Gregorios V, Patriarch of Constantinople, 181–2, 350, 405
Gregory, Metropolitan of Kiev, 37
Gregory, X, Pope, 30–31
Gregory of Nyssa, 14
Gregory Palamas, 38

Grisha (in Verkhoturye), 332
Grivas, Giorgios, 362–3
Guy de Lusignan, 347
Gytha, sister of King Harold of England, 261

Harold, King of England, 261
Helena, mother of Constantine, 127, 234
Henry II, King of England, 232, 270
Henry IV, King of England, 31–2
Henry VIII, King of England, 206, 267
Heraklitos, King of Georgia, 384
hermits, 414
Hesychasm: in Cyprus, 390–91; in Russia, 263–4, 283–4; influence, 37–9, 42, 139–40, 197; Jesus Prayer, 36, 239, 240, 271, 315, 322, 330, 376; model Hesychast, 239; Moldavian monks, 231; Patriarch's view, 411; Philokalia, 39; political outlook, 35, 37, 51–2; spiritual exercises, 35–7, 169; startsy, 314–17
Heybeliada (Halki) island, 404, 408
Hilandar monastery, 51, 60, 78, 86, 142, 239–40
Hill, Aaron, 158
Hitler, Adolf, 296, 297, 349, 379
Humor monastery, 246
Hungarians, 207–10, 224–5
Huntington, Samuel, 196, 249, 415

icons: Bistriţa, 234–5, 236–7; miraculous, 88, 155–6, 234–5, 236–7, 361–2, 370, 372; Mother of God (in Cyprus), 360–62, 370; Mount Athos, 39; painting, 193; Patmos, 155; Troodhitissa, 373–4; veneration, 170, 268
Idiorrhythmic Rule, 140, 158, 170
Igor, Father, 285–6, 305
Ilarion, Father, 305–6
Ilija, Father, 47–50, 53–4
Innocent III, Pope, 24, 27
Ioan, Father: finances, 211, 330; interview with, 210–11, 216–18, 239; on women, 302; pilgrims to, 205; vision, 221
Iorga, Nicolae, 224
Iosif, Archimandrite, 271–5, 276, 281, 305, 308

Isaias, Father, 384–91
Isidore, Metropolitan of Kiev, 34
Islam, 8, 34–5, 64, 258, 405
Istanbul, 401–15; *see also* Constantinople
Ivan IV (the Terrible), Tsar of Russia: death, 267–8; murder of Philip, 257, 269–70; paranoia, 266, 290; relationship with holy fools, 312–13; relationship with Philip, 265–6, 268–9, 272; religious policies, 266–7, 270, 281, 310; support for Solovetsky island, 264; veneration of Prince Lazar, 72–3
Izetbegović, Alija, 56, 101

Jelena, sister of Dušan, 50
Jerusalem: holy places, 99, 153; Latin kingdom, 347–8; Rasputin's pilgrimage, 335; relics, 16; Russian pilgrims, 360, sack by Romans, 11; souvenirs, 99, 235, 242, 370
Jews: Communism, 289–90, 299–300; connection with 666, 300–301; converts, 331; death of Tsar, 289–90, 303, 331; homelessness, 258; portrayed as enemies, 289; Rasputin's attitude, 338; Russian anti-semitism, 289–90, 296, 299–300, 303, 308; Tsar's attitude to, 282, 338
Joachim the Magnificent, Patriarch of Constantinople, 143
John (assistant to Patriarch), 409
John Climacus, Saint, 35
John Paleologus, Emperor, 32
John Paul II, Pope, 100–101, 116, 228, 250, 373
John the Theologian, Saint, 164–7, 211, 335
Jovandol monastery, Montenegro, 93–101, 244
Justin Popović, Archimandrite, 71–2
Justinian, Emperor, 16, 51

Kambos, Cyprus, 364–70
Kaplan, Robert D., 81
Karadjordje Petrović, King of Serbia, 177
Karadžić, Radovan, 57, 96, 101, 123
Karamanlis, Konstantinos, 198
Kastoria, 134–6, 376
Kem, Russian, 285–6, 291

Kiev, 258–9
Kievan Rus, 257–62
Kiprian, Abbot, 234–7, 238, 247–8, 339, 413
Kirillos, Father, 362–3, 367, 372
Kliment, Saint, 114, 124, 125
Knights Templar, 347
Kofos, Evangelos, 146–8
Kolokotronis, Theodore, 188
Korais, Adamantios, 183
Kornaros, Themistocles, 140
Kosma (holy fool), 325, 329
Kosovo: churches and monasteries, 78, 93n; Dečani, 86–92; Gračanica, 84–6; Hesychasm, 263; Milošević's policy, 78; Muslim population, 77–9, 404; Nato campaign, 92n, 109n, 199n, 331–2, 348–9, 357, 378–9, 380–81, 389, 397; Nato protectorate, 397; Peć, 78–82; Priština, 82–4; Serb crimes, 404–5, Serb patriarchate, 77–8, 79–81; status of region, 79
Kosovo, battle of: anniversary celebrations, 78; end of Serbian empire, 52, 69, 76; religious response to, 78, 100; role of Prince Lazar, 70–72, 74–5
Kosovo Liberation Army, 79
Krajina Republic, 48, 49, 54, 89
Kritikos, John, 160–63, 175
Krka monastery, Croatia, 47–55, 56–7, 58–9, 74, 396
Krstan, Father, 67–9
Kulikovo, battle (1380), 263
Kykko monastery, 359–70, 371, 372–3, 376, 381, 383–7
Kyriakos (in Kambos), 367

Latin language, 217
Lausanne, treaty of (1923), 42, 404
Lazar, Prince, 70–77, 79, 190
Lena (in Moscow), 296, 306–9, 314, 317–21, 323, 342
Lenin, Vladimir Ilich, 197, 272, 286, 300
Leonid (*starets*), 315
Likhachev, Dmitri, 279–80, 314
Limassol, 378–83
Lloyd George, David, 404
Loch, Sydney, 144
Lodeinoye Polye, 288–9
Louka (in Kambos), 367, 369, 370

Lucian Mureşan, Archbishop, 227
Luitprand of Cremona, 19
Luke, Saint, 360–61
Lusignan kings of Cyprus, 347, 365, 394
Luther, Martin, 206
Luzhkov, Yuri, 295, 327, 382
Lyon, Union of (1274), 31
Lyuba (at Solovetsky), 274–6, 284

Macarius (starets), 315
Macedonia, Former Yugoslav Republic of,
    see Former Yugoslav Republic
Macedonia, Greater, 117, 118–19, 137
Macedonia, province of Greece, 108–9,
    118–19, 134–49
Machiavelli, Niccolo, 267
Makarije, Patriarch of Serbia, 80
Makarios III, Archbishop of Cyprus,
    350–55, 357–9, 362–3, 371–2,
    377–8
Makarios the Egyptian, Saint, 100
Makarius (starets), 333–4
Makhairas monastery, 375–7, 391
Makrigiannis, General, 188
Maksim the Greek (monk), 273
Manuel Palaeologus, Emperor, 31–2, 236
Margaret (on Patmos), 170–71
Maria Theresa, Empress, 216, 226
Marie, Queen of Romania, 238
Mark Eugenicus, Metropolitan of Ephesus,
    34, 35
Marx, Karl, 206, 270–71
Mary I, Queen of England, 267
Mary, Virgin, 4, 15–16, 223, 333, 360–61
Maurer, Gheorghe, 189
Mavromichalis (outlaw chieftain), 188
Mehmet II, Sultan, 40, 120
Mehmet Sokolović, Second Vizier, 80
Methodius, Saint, 113–14, 121, 124, 212,
    258
Michael Palaeologus, Emperor, 28, 30–31
Micu-Klein, Ion-Innocentie, 224–8, 250
Mihail, Archbishop of Ohrid and
    Macedonia, 112–17, 119, 124, 129,
    133, 391–2
Mihailis Voutomedes, Duke of Cyprus,
    360–61
Mikhail Romanov, Tsar of Russia, 270
Milica, wife of Lazar, 72
Milorad, Father, 82–4, 86

Milošević, Slobodan: Kosovo policy, 82–3,
    84, 92n, 357; Mount Athos visit,
    142; relationship with Church, 68,
    75, 96, 137; relationship with
    Karadžić, 58; role, 57, 142; Serb
    nationalism, 81, 190
Milutin, King of Serbia, 85–6, 87
Mistra, 191–2
Mitya (holy fool), 313
Mladen (in Athens), 194–5
Moldavia: Bistriţa monastery, 233–8,
    244–50, 313; EU relations, 7;
    Hesychasm, 284; history, 120–21,
    195, 212–15; monks, 12; Sihastria
    monastery, 237, 238–43; Suceava
    monastery, 372
Moldova, 250
Moldoviţa monastery, 246
Mongols, 260–62, 263
monks: Byzantine empire, 10–11; Greek,
    139; influence, 11, 86; Macedonian
    (FYROM), 129; Moldavian, 231;
    monastic revival, 411; Mount Athos,
    3 6, 139–40; numbers, 129, 139;
    Serbian, 65
Montagu, Lady Mary Wortley, 73
Montenegro, 7, 93–101
Moravia, 113–14
Moscow: capital of Russia, 262, 298;
    cathedral, 295, 327; court, 265; Lenin
    Museum, 296; neo-Nazis, 296–7, 299;
    patriarchate, 287–8; third Rome, 260,
    342
Mossolov, Alexander, 290
Muslim-Croat Federation, 66–9

Nafplio, 184–90, 290
Napoleon Bonaparte, 176, 349
Nato: Bosnian involvement, 66; Cypriot
    attitude to, 366–7, 378–9; eastward
    advance, 274; Greek membership, 8,
    123, 249, 355; Kosovo campaign,
    92n, 109n, 199n, 331–2, 348–9, 357,
    378–9, 380, 388–9, 397; Kosovo
    protectorate, 397; membership, 7,
    249–50, 355; Serb attitude to, 59,
    366–7; Turkish membership, 355
Naum, Bishop of Strumica, 129–34, 169,
    308, 351, 388, 413
Naum, Saint, 114, 124, 128–9

Navarino, battle of (1827), 183
Neamţ monastery, 241
Nemanja dynasty, 72
Nestor (monk), 259
Netanyahu, Benjamin, 391
Nevsky, Prince Alexander, 262, 292
Nicholas III, Pope, 31
Nicholas I, Tsar of Russia, 178
Nicholas II, Tsar of Russia:
    abdication, 280, 291; Christ
    comparison, 289; court, 93; death,
    289, 300, 301; funeral, 286, 301, 305,
    306–7; portrait, 318; Rasputin's
    influence, 313, 334–6, 338, 340–41;
    rule, 290–91; Russian reverence for,
    291; view of intellectuals and Jews,
    282
Nicolae Lupea, Father, 223–4
Nicosia, 347–50, 390–91, 413
Nikčević family, 97, 99, 244
Nikephoros Phokas, Emperor, 12
Niki (wife of Ariko), 368, 370
Nikiforos, Abbot of Kykko: interview with,
    386–7; metochion issue, 384; political
    stance, 361–2, 389; Romanian
    contacts, 372–3; social engineering,
    367; view of miraculous icon,
    360–61, 370
Nikodim, Archimandrite, 53
Nikola, King of Montenegro, 93
Nikolai, Father, 292–4, 312, 413
Nikolai (holy fool), 312–13
Nikolayevna, Raisa, 338–40
Nikolayevsky monastery, Siberia, 326–43
Nikon, Bishop, 343n
Nikon, Patriarch, 277–8, 340
Nikos (theology student), 166
Nikon, Patriarch, 270
Nino, Saint, 384
Nixon, Richard M., 353
nuns: Greek, 191–2; Macedonian
    (FYROM), 129, 134; Peć, 80–81;
    Ravanica monastery, 69–70, 75–77;
    Romanian, 192–3, 214–15, 238;
    Serbian, 64–5, 69–70, 134; Veljuša
    monastery, 134

Ohrid: churches, 125–9, 376, 413; Lake,
    114, 123–9; patriarchate, 120, 121,
    212; university, 114, 123–4

Old Believers, 272, 277–8, 288, 340
Oleg (schoolteacher), 282–4, 294
Optina Pustyn monastery, 314–23
Otto I, Emperor, 19
Otto III, Emperor, 20
Otto I, King of Greece, 189
Ottoman Empire: capture of
    Constantinople (1453), 39–40;
    Cyprus, 343, 364–5, 394–5; decline,
    105–6; fall, 403–4; Kosovo battle
    (1389), 71–2; Mount Athos policy,
    4–5, 21–2; Patmos, 156–7;
    relationship with Church, 21–2,
    135–6, 156–7, 181–2; position,
    72–4, 76; Wallachia and Moldavia,
    212–13

Paisius, Saint, 169
Paissy Velichkovsky, Saint, 231, 239–41,
    314, 371
Palèologue, Maurice, 336, 343
Pankratios, Father, 144
Pantanassa convent, 191
Panteleimon, Saint, 376
Panteleimon monastery, 143–4
Papandreou, Andreas, 148, 198
Papandreou, Mimi, 148
Papaphlessas, Archimandrite, 181
Paraschiva, Saint, 232
Parthenios, Abbot of Makhairas, 376
Patmos: churches, 160, 328, 413; Easter
    celebrations, 153–4, 193; monastery,
    153–9, 161, 167–73; Ottoman rule,
    156–7; pilgrimage to, 211, 335;
    population, 158, 161–4; St John on,
    164–5, 335; school, 158–9; Xanthos'
    grave, 160, 175
Paul, Saint, 311, 360, 395
Pavić, Milorad, 194
Pavle, Patriarch, 54, 96
Pavlos, Father, 169–70, 413
Peć, 77–82, 397; patriarchate, 120, 121
Petar Karadjordjević, King of Serbia, 74
Petar Petrović-Njegoš II, Montenegrin
    prince-bishop, 95–6
Peter, Saint, 19
Peter II (the Great), Tsar of Russia:
    capital, 298; religious policies, 257,
    260, 270, 281, 307–8; survival, 310
Petre, Archbishop of Moldova, 250

Petru Rareş, Prince, 236
Phanariots, 178–80, 183, 215, 385, 403–4
Philiki Etairia, 176–80, 181, 184–5
Philip, Abbot of Solovetsky, 263, 265–6,
    268–72, 276–7, 281, 312, 340
Philokalia, The, 39, 237, 315
Philotheos of Pskov, Father, 260, 342
Phyletism: Greek independence, 159;
    heresy, 121, 405–6, 411–12;
    Hesychasm and, 39, 42, 411; history,
    121; influence, 42; Macedonia
    (FYROM), 117; Patriarch's view,
    405–6, 411; rise, 22; Serbia, 50
Plato, 18, 33
Plethon, Gemisthus, 33
popes, 19, 30–31
Priština, 82–4
Prizren, 78
Protestants, 65–6, 90, 274
Pskov, Russia, 290, 292, 312
Pyanikh, Yuri, 381

Rasputin, Grigory: career, 332–3; death,
    337; Easter celebrations, 356; family,
    336; holy fool, 313; influence, 291;
    pilgrimages, 143, 326, 333–4, 335;
    political views, 338; relationship with
    Tsar, 93, 291, 313, 334–5, 338, 341;
    Verkhoturye connection, 326, 327,
    341
Ravanica monastery, Serbia, 69–77
Reagan, Ronald, 292
Reformation, 21, 28, 205–6, 244, 267
relics, 9, 16, 26, 173, 258
Renaissance, 21, 28
Revelation, Book of, 164–6, 191, 246
Richard I (the Lionheart), King of
    England, 347, 396
Romaioi: beliefs, 12, 14–15, 18, 29, 414;
    descendants, 404; fall of
    Constantinople (1453), 41;
    Hesychast attitude, 37–8; history 12,
    172–3, 195, 403; Ottoman rule, 120;
    sack of Constantinople (1204), 27
Romania: Ceauşescu regime, 203–4;
    Church, 211, 215–16, 308; church
    property, 8; churches, 328; EU
    relations, 7; history, 120–21, 211–12;
    Monastery of the Birth of the Mother
    of God, 203–18, 228, 361; monks,

12, 215–16, 231; painted monasteries,
    245–7, 365, 413; religion, 193;
    revolution (1989), 220; rising,
    (1821), 179–80; Transylvania,
    218–28; Uniate Church, 217,
    219–28, 240–41, 373
Roman Catholic Church: borders, 7;
    church property, 8; Creed, 19, 30,
    216, 223; Croatia recognition, 101; in
    Cyprus, 365–6; in Transylvania, 373;
    missionaries, 276; papacy, 18–19;
    relationship with Orthodox Church,
    49, 90, 240, 315–16, 347–8; *see also*
    Crusade (Fourth); Florence (Council
    of); Schism
Roman Empire, 7, 9
Rome: invasions, 10; papacy, 18–19
Runciman, Sir Steven, 18, 85, 412
Russia: anti-Semitism, 8, 289, 296, 297,
    300, 303, 304–5, 331; Danilovsky
    monastery, 304–6; envoys to
    Constantinople, 16–17, 258; EU
    relations, 7; Greek nationalism,
    175–6; Hesychasm, 263–4, 284;
    imperial, 22; intelligentsia, 282–3;
    monks, 12, 143–4, 259; nationalism,
    8, 297; pilgrimage, 275, 292, 319,
    360; pillars of state ideology, 273–4,
    289, 297, 303; prison camps, 278–9;
    revolution, 186; Solovetsky
    monastery, 255–7, 265–87; Vikings,
    16, 138
Russian language, 270

St Varnavas monastery, Cyprus, 295
saints, 6, 18, 35, 60–61, 311
Salisbury, Lord, 342
Samuil, Tsar, 108, 113, 120, 124
Sarajevo, 66–9
Sarandi (on Patmos), 162–4
Sava, Father: border crossing problems,
    111, 115, 137; e-mails, 93n, 111, 134,
    397; interview with, 86–92, 131, 388,
    413; Kosovo crisis, 92n; on
    Communism, 89–90, 186; work-
    space, 318
Sava, Saint, 52, 55, 78, 111
Savvaty (monk), 264
Schengen Agreement, 144–5, 168, 191,
    193, 297, 299

Schism (1054), 20; borders, 7, 380–81; Christodoulos cult, 156; effects, 205–6, 373, 411, 414–15; history, 20, 195–6, 258; importance of, 17–18, 23

Second World War, 101, 192, 297

semantron, 91–2

Serapheim, Archbishop, 197–9

Serbia: Church, 52–3, 68, 106, 110, 125; Constantine's origins, 9; relations, 7; Great Migration, 73; medieval kingdom, 50–52, 70–72, 76, 86; monks, 12, 42; Ravanica monastery, 69–77

Sergei, Father, 287–8

Sergei (at Solovetsky), 274–5

Sergei (at Verkhoturye), 326–30, 332–3, 338–9, 342, 343, 343n, 367

Sergeyev Posad monastery, 263, 281, 306–7, 314, 342, 384, 396, 413

Sergius of Radonezh, Saint, 263–4, 277, 306–7, 310, 396.

Shishkina-Berrezovskaya, 337

Siberia: exports, 324–5; Rasputin, 332–3, 338; Verkhoturye, 324–33, 339–43

Sihastria monastery, 237, 238–43

Simeon, Saint, 325–6, 329, 335, 341

Simonida, Byzantine princess, 85–6

Sixtus IV, Pope, 238

Skopje, 105, 110–19

Slavonic language: Byzantine suppression of, 120; Romanian texts, 212; translation from Greek, 113, 241, 258, 263, 314; translation into Russian, 270

Slavophile movement, 282–3

Slavs, 29, 122

Snagov Island, Wallachia, 228–33

Snežana (in Gračanica), 86

Solovetsky monastery: interview with Archimandrite Iosif, 271–5; landscape and climate, 255–7, 274–6, 360; Old Believers, 277–8; pilgrims, 255, 281–2, 315; prison camp, 278–81; under Ivan the Terrible, 265–70

Solzhenitsyn, Alexander, 278–9

Spasovski, Ljupčo, 112, 115–17, 119

Stalin, Joseph: prison camps, 300, 302–3; religious policies, 219, 295, 301; view of intellectuals and Jews, 282

Stefan Dečanski, King of Serbia, 87

Stefan Nemanja, King of Serbia, 86

Stephen the Great, Prince of Moldavia, 237–8

Stoker, Bram, 213

Sucevița monastery, 246–7

Svyatoslav, Prince of Rus, 259

Symeon, Father (on Mount Athos), 37, 141

Symeon, Father (on Patmos), 168–71, 193

Symeon the Young, Saint, 11, 35

symphonia: Church of Rome, 21; Constantinople Patriarchate, 13, 22, 40–41; ideal, 414; Ottoman rule, 120; restoration, 199; Russian policy, 266–7, 295, 340

Tadej, Father, 237, 322

Tarantino, Quentin, 326–7, 329

Targu Mureș, 204, 209–10, 221, 228

Tarkovsky, Andrei, 255–6

Tassos (on Patmos), 166, 172–3

Tatiana, Mother, 246

Templars *see* Knights Templar

Teoctișt, Patriarch of Romania, 218, 219–21, 248, 250

Teutonic knights, 262, 349

Theodora, Empress, 13

Theodosius (monk), 259

Theofan, Father, 334

Theophylactus, Archbishop, 124

Thessaloniki, 111–12, 137–49, 193, 408; St Dimitri's Orthodox Cathedral, 137–8, 193

Thubron, Colin, 371, 372, 373–4, 376, 387, 396

Tikhon, Abbot of Verkhoturye, 326, 329, 336, 338–43, 351, 395

Tikhon, Archimandrite, 297–301, 305

Tito (Josip Broz), 59, 68, 90, 125

Tökes, László, 220, 221

Tolstoy, Leo, 295, 298, 315, 316–17

Transylvania: Alba Iulia, 218–19; Blaj, 222–3, 226–7; Cluj, 221–2; history, 211–18; Monastery of the Birth of the Mother of God, 213–18, 228, 361; Targu Mureș, 204–5, 209–10, 221, 228; Uniate Church, 217, 219–20, 224–8, 373

Trinity Sergeyev monastery, 263, 306–14, 396

Troodhitissa monastery, 373, 391
Troodos Mountains, 371–8, 413
Tsarkoye Selo, 289, 291, 335
Tudjman, Franjo, 101
Turgenev, Ivan, 282, 298
Turkey, 354–5, 403–5; earthquakes, 405n; EU membership, 405n; NATO membership, 355
Turkish Republic of Northern Cyprus, 393–7
Tuzla, 62–3

Ukraine: church property, 8; EU relations, 7; independence, 306; monks, 12; Uniate Church, 217, 219–20, 305–6
Uniate Church: abolition, 219; Blaj cathedral, 222–3, 227–8; Blaj seminary, 222–3, 227; creation, 217, 413; history, 217, 224–7; opposition to Ceauşescu regime, 220–21; reappearance, 219; relationship with Orthodox Church, 217, 220–22, 224–7, 240, 305, 373; Stalin's policy, 219
United States of America: Cyprus policy, 353; dollar bill, 300; Kosovo campaign, 348–9, 357, 389; miracles, 88; relationship with Greek nationalism, 193–4; religion, 374; world domination, 58, 81
Uralmash, 330

Vanya (artist): in Pskov, 292–5; in Solovetsky, 255–6, 271, 276, 281–2; in Verkhoturye, 330, 332, 338–9; journey to Kem, 284–6; newspaper reading, 336–7; travels in Russia, 287, 295, 324
Varnavas, Saint, 395
Vartzya, Georgia, 385–6

Vasilije Kačavenda, Bishop of Tuzla and Zvornik, 62–6, 69, 70, 78, 392
Vasily, Father, 317, 318–23, 413
Vasily Barsky, Father, 371–2, 373, 374, 376
Vasily the Blessed, Saint, 312
Veljuša monastery, 129–34, 360
Venice, 24, 27, 156–7
Verkhoturye, 323–6, 328–43, 360, 413
Villehardouin, Geoffrey de, 24–5
Viorel (in Romania), 203–5, 207, 209–11, 221, 228, 243
Vissarion (Serb monk), 226
Vlad the Impaler, Prince of Wallachia, 213–14, 228–30, 267
Vladika prince-bishops, 95–6
Vladimir, Prince of Kievan Rus, 258–9, 261, 262
Vladimir, Prince of Monomakh, 261
Voragine, Jacobus de, 237
Voroneţ monastery, 246
Vsevolod, Father, 304–5

Wallachia: history, 120–21, 195, 212–15; Snagov Island, 228–33
Walsh, Robert, 182
Ware, Kallistos, 141
White Sea, 255, 264, 413

Xanthos, Emmanuel, 159–60, 175–9

Yeats, W.B., 15
Yeltsin, Boris, 274, 280, 292, 301, 305, 342
Ypsilantis, Alexandros, 178–80, 215
Yugoslavia, former: collapse, 48, 59–60, 141–2; Serb policies, 8; wars, 412

Zara, sack, 24
Zoe (Byzantine princess), 20
Zographou monastery, 31
Zosima (monk), 264